**COMPOSITION, R
AND DISCIPLINAL**

# COMPOSITION, RHETORIC, AND DISCIPLINARITY

*Edited by*
**RITA MALENCZYK,
SUSAN MILLER-COCHRAN,
ELIZABETH WARDLE,
AND KATHLEEN BLAKE YANCEY**

UTAH STATE UNIVERSITY PRESS
*Logan*

© 2018 by University Press of Colorado

Published by Utah State University Press
An imprint of University Press of Colorado
245 Century Circle, Suite 202
Louisville, Colorado 80027

All rights reserved
Printed in the United States of America

The University Press of Colorado is a proud member of the Association of University Presses.

∞ This paper meets the requirements of the ANSI/NISO Z39.48-1992 (Permanence of Paper)

The University Press of Colorado is a cooperative publishing enterprise supported, in part, by Adams State University, Colorado State University, Fort Lewis College, Metropolitan State University of Denver, Regis University, University of Colorado, University of Northern Colorado, Utah State University, and Western State Colorado University.

ISBN: 978-1-60732-694-6 (pbk)
ISBN: 978-1-60732-695-3 (ebook)
DOI: https://doi.org/10.7330/9781607326953

Library of Congress Cataloging-in-Publication Data

Names: Malenczyk, Rita, 1959– editor. | Miller-Cochran, Susan K., editor. | Wardle, Elizabeth (Elizabeth Ann), editor. | Yancey, Kathleen Blake, 1950– editor.
Title: Composition, rhetoric, and disciplinarity / edited by Rita Malenczyk, Susan Miller-Cochran, Elizabeth Wardle, Kathleen Blake Yancey.
Description: Logan : Utah State University Press, [2018] | Includes bibliographical references and index.
Identifiers: LCCN 2017025370| ISBN 9781607326946 (pbk.) | ISBN 9781607326953 (ebook)
Subjects: LCSH: English language—Rhetoric—Study and teaching (Higher) | Composition (Language arts)—Study and teaching (Higher) | Universities and colleges—Curricula. | Academic writing—Study and teaching.
Classification: LCC PE1404 .C62557 2018 | DDC 808/.0420711—dc23
LC record available at https://lccn.loc.gov/2017025370

Cover photograph © Nkosi Shanga

# CONTENTS

*Editors' Introduction: Why This Book and Why Now?*
Rita Malenczyk, Susan Miller-Cochran, Elizabeth Wardle, and Kathleen Blake Yancey   3

### SECTION 1: WHERE HAVE WE BEEN, WHERE ARE WE NOW, AND WHY ARE WE HERE?

1  Mapping the Turn to Disciplinarity: A Historical Analysis of Composition's Trajectory and Its Current Moment
   *Kathleen Blake Yancey*   15

2  My Disciplinary History: A Personal Account
   *Barry Maid*   36

3  Acknowledging Disciplinary Contributions: On the Importance of Community College Scholarship to Rhetoric and Composition
   *Rochelle Rodrigo and Susan Miller-Cochran*   53

4  Learning from Bruffee: Collaboration, Students, and the Making of Knowledge in Writing Administration
   *Rita Malenczyk, Neal Lerner, and Elizabeth H. Boquet*   70

### SECTION 2: COMING TO TERMS: WHAT ARE WE TALKING ABOUT?

5  Classification and Its Discontents: Making Peace with Blurred Boundaries, Open Categories, and Diffuse Disciplines
   *Gwendolynne Reid and Carolyn R. Miller*   87

6  Understanding the Nature of Disciplinarity in Terms of Composition's Values
   *Elizabeth Wardle and Doug Downs*   111

7  Discipline and Profession: Can the Field of Rhetoric and Writing Be Both?
   *Kristine Hansen*   134

**SECTION 3: COMING TO TERMS: WHAT ARE THE COMPLICATIONS AND TENSIONS?**

8  Embracing the Virtue in Our Disciplinarity
   *Jennifer Helene Maher*     161

9  Disciplinarity and First-Year Composition: Shifting to a New Paradigm
   *Liane Robertson and Kara Taczak*     185

10 Writing, English, and a Translingual Model for Composition
   *Christiane Donahue*     206

11 Shared Landscapes, Contested Borders: Locating Disciplinarity in an MA Program Revision
   *Whitney Douglas, Heidi Estrem, Kelly Myers, and Dawn Shepherd*     225

**SECTION 4: WHERE ARE WE GOING AND HOW DO WE GET THERE?**

12 The Major in ~~Composition~~ Writing and Rhetoric: Tracking Changes in the Evolving Discipline
   *Sandra Jamieson*     243

13 Rhetoric and Composition Studies and Latinxs' Largest Group: Mexican Americans
   *Jaime Armin Mejía*     267

14 Redefining Disciplinarity in the Current Context of Higher Education
   *Doug Hesse*     287

15 Looking Outward: Disciplinarity and Dialogue in Landscapes of Practice
   *Linda Adler-Kassner*     303

Editors' Conclusion: Where Are We Going and How Do We Get There?
   *Rita Malenczyk, Susan Miller-Cochran, Elizabeth Wardle, and Kathleen Blake Yancey*     331

*Contributors*     343
*Index*     348

# COMPOSITION, RHETORIC, AND DISCIPLINARITY

# EDITORS' INTRODUCTION
*Why This Book and Why Now?*

Rita Malenczyk, Susan Miller-Cochran,
Elizabeth Wardle, and Kathleen Blake Yancey

This collection of essays responds to several exigences, among them a set of continuing tensions characterizing Rhetoric and Composition; a set of disagreements about whether or not we are, or should be, a discipline; and a nascent sense that at this particular moment in our history, Rhetoric and Composition is on the cusp of disciplinarity. After exploring this set of exigences, we turn to a rationale for this volume, in terms of why we should consider the disciplinary nature and quality of Rhetoric and Composition as well as the implications of identifying ourselves as a discipline, especially if we understand a discipline not as a site of consensus, but rather, in Ken Hyland's terms, as a context for debate and deliberation. And finally, given this context, we introduce the chapters of *Composition, Rhetoric, and Disciplinarity*.

## EXIGENCES

One of the first exigences to which this volume responds is our ambivalence, if not conflict, about the nature of who we are: are we a field, a discipline, or some hybrid—an interdiscipline or multidiscipline? Opinions on our status, of course, vary (see, e.g., Bartholomae 1989; Adler-Kassner and Wardle 2015). Identifying ourselves as a field seems preferable to some, in part because a field is understood to be both less hierarchical and more fluid than a discipline. Likewise, some in Rhetoric and Composition resist the idea of disciplinarity because such a status carries with it a sense of being fixed and hegemonic, often more interested in pursuing its own expertise than in teaching students, developing programs, or serving other purposes aligned with the origins of the field, at least as they were identified in 1949, one of the several dates vying for contention. And even assuming one understands Rhetoric and

DOI: 10.7330/9781607326953.c000

Composition as a discipline, what kind of discipline is being invoked? As several chapters here attest—among them, Carolyn R. Miller and Gwendolynne Reid's, and Kristine Hansen's—disciplines vary, which raises a question about what kind of discipline we might want to be, both foci—how we might *be* a discipline and what *kind* of discipline we might want to be—locating this volume.

A related issue is how we name ourselves: are we Composition and Rhetoric, are we Rhetoric and Composition, are we Composition Studies or Writing Studies, are we, as a recent journal title announced, *Literacy in Composition Studies*—or something else? Ample evidence suggests that we continue to struggle with what we should call ourselves. In 2004, for instance, a double special issue of *Enculturation*—with its theme of "Rhetoric/Composition: Intersections/Impasses/Differends"—highlighted how the historical linking of Rhetoric and Composition is both beneficial and vexed. More recently, we seem to be shifting to calling ourselves Writing Studies, as explained in the introduction to *Keywords in Writing Studies* (Heilker and Vandenberg 2015). In some ways a second edition of *Keywords in Composition Studies* (Heilker and Vandenberg 1996), at least in spirit, *Keywords in Writing Studies* is also a new edited collection. Arguing that the ubiquity of digital technologies and the field's recent attention to public and civic writing, among other causes, have widened our gaze beyond the (composition) classroom, editors Paul Heilker and Peter Vandenberg point to Writing Studies as a more accurate description of the field. Similarly, in this volume, Sandra Jamieson, analyzing the relationship of the major to disciplinarity, observes that "writing" is a far more common term than "composition" in titles of the major, which provides another reason to adopt Writing Studies as our name. And of course, as a descriptor, Writing Studies, with the addition of the word "studies" completing it—such that it parallels other fields of intellectual inquiry, including literary studies, cultural studies, and so on—underscores the idea that writing itself is *both* a practice and an object of study (Adler-Kassner and Wardle 2015). At the same time, it's worth noting that multiple names still coexist, as the chapters here demonstrate.[1]

Two other exigences inform *Composition, Rhetoric, and Disciplinarity*: concerns about unintended consequences of our disposition toward service; and loyalties toward English, which some identify as our historical home.[2] Historically, there has been ambivalence about the pervasive service role of Composition (Colomb 2010); many in the field, such as Doug Hesse in this volume, see service as a worthy contribution, while others worry that our service responsibilities can overwhelm or even subsume research and scholarship. In such cases and looking very *unlike* other disciplines, we can appear to have less legitimacy. Related to this concern is what we might call loyalty or allegiance to our collective historical home, the English department, which certainly saw us, with our initial exclusive attention to first-year composition, as a service endeavor. In this context, declaring ourselves a discipline means breaking with our past. Moreover, such loyalty is often personal as well as institutional: as Barry Maid in this volume observes, most of the early generations of teacher-scholars in Rhetoric and Composition were educated in English—and continued to find a home there. And even today, most of our classes, programs, and tenure still reside in English. Not surprisingly, then, there is something of a reluctance, at least on the part of some, to leave what has been a kind of nesting ground. Even for those who might want to assert more independence, English continues to function as a shadow discipline, reminding us of our historical commitment to service and our struggles for parity, if not equity.[3] How all this history might be newly understood were we to designate ourselves as a discipline is another question that this volume, both explicitly and implicitly, addresses.

## HISTORICAL LEGACY, FUTURE VISIONS, AND CURRENT SCHOLARSHIP

Another way of thinking about our relationship to disciplinarity is located in time: past, future, and current. Rhetoric and Composition, in several accounts (e.g., Berlin 1987; Harris 2012), sees teaching as the center of our identity, not only in the past, but currently. Bruce Horner (2015), for instance, conceptualizes Rhetoric and Composition as a teaching enterprise, one especially interested in the labor of composition. In his view, we are best advised to eschew claims to expertise and disciplinarity, a point with which John Trimbur (2011) agrees. For both, a commitment to what Trimbur calls solidarity is preferable to one located in expertise. It's also worth noting that even the more theoretically oriented scholarly organizations within Rhetoric and Composition, such as the Rhetoric Society of America, feature pedagogical sessions at conferences in a way very unlike conferences other disciplines sponsor, which likewise speaks to the central role of pedagogy in the field. Others, such as Sid Dobrin (2011), advise us to abandon the subject—that is, the student—as center of the field so that we might organize it around theory and focus on writing, which would enable us to take on a very different kind of disciplinary cast. And still others, notably Charles Bazerman, have argued that seeking to advance our pedagogy and curricular efforts in the absence of knowing more about writing itself, which he understands as the historical pattern, is unwise; in this view, research and pedagogy are equal parts of the same field, each supporting and extending the other. In an interview, Bazerman explains precisely why pedagogy, even if it were at the field's center, needs research.

> [We need] to take our research much more seriously. We view ourselves as practitioners. Even assuming we knew what writing was and kind of—let me find the right way to say this, it's not flowing so easily—but . . . there is this thing we kind of know what it is and we'll just teach people how to do it. Some people have a hard time getting it but not that we have a really—we also assume that to some degree we all know what it is to write. And that we have the sense of what the full competence is, whereas at the same time everyone still feels insecure about their writing. But we don't have the courage to go and find out what's the full extent and variety of writing, how complex it is. We are very much at the surface of understanding what writing is, so we have a responsibility to investigate it deeply. (qtd. in Craig et al. 2016, 294–95)

And not least, as Yancey argues in the next chapter, some members of the field—especially those participating in projects oriented toward threshold concepts and transfer of writing knowledge and practice—seem to understand the current moment as a disciplinary turn, even if heretofore it hasn't been articulated as such. In the fullness of this temporal context, then, the question that we might consider is whether we are a teaching subject, as Harris puts it, and therefore apparently a teaching (non) discipline, as some scholars seem to suggest, or whether, like Bazerman, we can imagine a Rhetoric and Composition discipline that continues its historical commitment to pedagogy without sacrificing equal (and some might say necessary) attention to other areas of activity such as research and theory. Put another way, are pedagogy, research, and theory mutually exclusive? If not, how might thinking of ourselves as a discipline forward a more fully imagined Rhetoric and Composition?

**IMPORTANCE AND IMPLICATIONS OF DISCIPLINARITY**

As editors, we've had the pleasure of talking to many about the issue of Rhetoric and Composition's disciplinarity. In those discussions, we heard about the issue from yet another angle: the perception of others regarding the rigor and respectability of the field. Although many, if not most, in Rhetoric and Composition would reject the label of remediation for students (see, for instance, Mike Rose 2012), some believe that our concern for our students, especially those most in need, "taints" us; in this view, we seem to be just like our students, that is, without appropriate scholarly rigor. The remedy for this situation, it was suggested, might be an embrace of disciplinarity, especially at the institutional level, allowing us to work with all students more effectively, precisely because as a disciplinary unit, we would control curriculum and budgets in ways we often now do not. Moreover, given the increasing rise of the major and a reinvigorated MA, the timing for such an embrace would be fortuitous. Put somewhat differently, the very perception of respectability could assist us in moving from positions of responsibility to positions with both responsibility and authority. And put more generally, the maxim here is that each construct we identify to describe us—from general education program reporting to student services to fully developed disciplinary department—brings with it implications and opportunities for our students as well as for us.

The positive implications of such a disciplinary identification are considerable. Although the disadvantages of claiming disciplinarity have enjoyed considerable discussion, we have not experienced a similarly robust or sustained discussion about the benefits of so claiming. Here we identify four.

- First, were we to claim disciplinarity, we would have the opportunity to shape the discipline, one paralleling the opportunity that the founders of Rhetoric and Composition enjoyed. We are today a pedagogically focused field in large part because of these founders' energy, values, and scholarship; this history influences who and what we are. Our parallel opportunity would be to consider what kind of discipline we would like to be and then shape it.
- Second, we would have the opportunity to be intentional in our actions. Currently, when we do good, it is almost against the odds; we don't have the benefit of disciplinarity as we plan and act, and we don't have it as a kind of continuing benefit when we succeed. In the context of disciplinarity, we could generate a kind of intentionality that contributes to a future.
- Third, we'd align our pedagogical interest in writing-as-epistemology with a disciplinary exercise of it. One of the tenets of disciplinarity is that disciplines make knowledge; a second is that writing provides the mechanism through which knowledge is made. It's thus something of an exquisite irony that the one field of inquiry whose focus is writing itself does not fully identify as a discipline. Put as a positive, defining our own disciplinarity is congruent with our intellectual activity.
- Fourth, given our research into writing, our theories of writing, and our pedagogical practices in support of writing, it is irresponsible *not* to claim the identity of a discipline. With such a claim, we can speak more authoritatively on writing matters and widen our research efforts to include writing beyond the classroom as we continue our commitment to students.

Among many, there seems to be an assumption that to claim the identity of a discipline, we would need to be in agreement on all these matters—on the balance between pedagogy, research, and service; on the center of the field; on all the values we hold. That isn't our view. Instead, we find ourselves aligned with Ken Hyland, who understands disciplinarity as a kind of cultural context supporting participants' opportunities to debate and to deliberate. As he says,

> Most disciplines are characterized by several competing perspectives and embody often bitterly contested beliefs and values . . . Communities are frequently pluralities of practices and beliefs which accommodate disagreement and allow subgroups and individuals to innovate within the margins of its practices in ways that do not weaken its ability to engage in common actions. Seeing disciplines as cultures helps to account for what and how issues can be discussed and for the understandings which are the basis for cooperative action and knowledge-creation. It is not important that everyone agrees but members should be able to engage with each others' ideas and analyses in agreed ways. Disciplines are the contexts in which disagreement can be deliberated. (Hyland 2004, 11)

The chapters within show us something of what such a disciplinarity, our disciplinarity—in terms of deliberations and common actions—could look like.

### CONTENT AND STRUCTURE

The four sections that organize this book reflect both our contributors' interests and our sense of the current major issues: the intellectual and embodied history that led us to this point; the question of how disciplinarity is, and might be, understood; the curricular, conceptual, and other sites of tension inherent in thinking of ourselves as a discipline; and the implications of disciplinarity for the future of our students and our work.

The first two chapters in Section 1, "Where Have We Been, Where Are We Now, and Why Are We Here?" address Rhetoric and Composition's disciplinarity through both intellectual and experiential lenses. The first chapter, Kathleen Blake Yancey's, traces the history of how various scholars have named or marked important moments in the development of the field, the "turns" that have characterized what we might call paradigm shifts in research and pedagogy. Yancey proposes that we are now making a *disciplinary* turn and asks what that might mean for the field. Barry Maid's chapter, something of a companion piece, takes a memoir-like approach to the changes in the field since the late 1970s and early 1980s, when a generation of teacher-scholars—many trained in literature PhD programs yet interested in writing and the teaching of writing—attended writing conferences, heard speakers declare the existence of a new field, and willingly embraced the opportunity to direct writing programs and centers, some of which (as in Maid's case) led to departments separate from English. Maid's chapter also addresses, implicitly, the importance of material conditions and local exigences for creating and sustaining programs and majors. Rochelle Rodrigo and Susan Miller-Cochran's chapter takes up the question of materiality and exigence in more detail but with a different focus: if nearly half of all US undergraduates take their first-year writing course at a community college, and if that number will soon increase, why do the contributions of community college faculty to the field remain underacknowledged? How might the field look different if we were to include those contributions more fully? To close this section, Rita Malenczyk, Neal Lerner, and Elizabeth H. Boquet recover the origins of what's come to be known as writing (program and center) administration. Recalling the beginnings of that work and scholarship—at least as we think of it today—in the 1970s, the authors call for a continued engagement with students as co-creators of the field, not just as learners within it.

If Section 1 narrates a range of disciplinary histories, then Section 2, "Coming to Terms: What Are We Talking About?," addresses the sticking points in those histories, in particular the definition of disciplinarity and how that might affect our perception of what it means to be a discipline. If we worry about disciplines as hierarchical and hegemonic, how might we conceive of disciplinarity in a way consonant with what Rhetoric and Composition has historically valued: openness and fluidity? Gwendolynne Reid and Carolyn Miller's chapter takes up that question by troubling traditional conceptions of disciplinarity. Arguing that categories, taxonomic codes, and other closed systems fail to "represent our best thinking about disciplinarity," they offer other (existing) conceptions of disciplines as inherently dynamic and active, depending on their participants—who interact with other disciplines as well—to continually invent and reinvent them. Elizabeth Wardle and Doug Downs reinforce this point in their chapter, calling attention to how Rhetoric and Composition has already achieved a disciplinarity that includes attention to the values of "inclusion, access, . . . difference, [and] interaction, localism, valuing diverse voices, and textual production." Claiming that disciplinarity, they suggest, would only strengthen those values. Coming to disciplinarity from another angle, Kristine Hansen introduces the term "profession" to underscore the role of teaching, labor, and students in any disciplinary formation and especially in ours. Failure to claim a disciplinary expertise many of us already have, she argues, is damaging to our first-year composition students as well as to the (increasingly) contingent labor force employed to teach them. She proposes another model, that of the professional/paraprofessional, to address this issue in ethically and pedagogically sound ways.

Section 3, "Coming to Terms: What Are the Complications and Tensions?," builds on the previous section by exploring particular sites of tension within the field. Jennifer Helene Maher's chapter employs Aristotle's conception of virtue to justify and embrace disciplinarity, again juxtaposing that concept with perhaps better-known ideas of disciplines as exclusive clubs, and suggests through a local narrative how an acknowledgment of expertise might benefit both us and our students—particularly where course content is concerned. The issue of content is explored more fully in the next chapter: where Maher's chapter focuses primarily on English department politics, Liane Robertson and Kara Taczak take up the vexed issue of the universal first-year composition requirement and the content of composition. Given what we now know about the role of content in supporting student writing development, they ask, how do we square the reality of writing teacher preparation, especially given the prevalence of contingent labor, with what are emerging as best practices in the field? To complicate matters further, Christiane Donahue explains the current move toward a translingual approach to teaching writing, shows how that approach differs from earlier orientations toward second-language writing, and speculates on how it might inform and influence the discipline. In the last chapter of this section, Whitney Douglas, Heidi Estrem, Kelly Myers, and Dawn Shepherd describe the process of a curricular revision on one campus, demonstrating how threshold concepts can anchor a program while providing room for colleagues with varying theoretical and pedagogical backgrounds to contribute their expertise in their own ways.

Section 4, "Where Are We Going and How Do We Get There?," speculates on what the future might look like for Rhetoric and Composition should it continue to move in a disciplinary direction. Sandra Jamieson charts the landscape of the Writing and Rhetoric major and how the major, which varies among institutions yet has certain commonalities, might ground the discipline while demonstrating its capacity for multivocality. Jaime Armin Mejía traces the history of Mexican Americans within the field, arguing that a truly rich discipline needs to be more inclusive intellectually and pedagogically than it has to this point been. Doug Hesse's chapter suggests that any disciplinary status we achieve within the changing university won't mirror the way disciplines looked twenty or even ten years ago—yet we can, he suggests, engage institutional exigencies so as to emphasize our strengths. Linda Adler-Kassner closes the section by broadening the significance of disciplinarity to the larger US educational landscape, offering "landscapes of practice" and "knowledgeability" as ways to engage larger publics by looking outward—as her title indicates. We then conclude, pulling the disparate threads of this book together and showing ways we might imagine the future of the discipline.

We ended the book on an "outward" note on purpose. As we've already suggested, collegial encounters at the Conference on College Composition and Communication (CCCC), online, and elsewhere sparked thought-provoking conversations that, in the end, raised more questions than any one edited collection can address. We know that conversation will continue, that this book is only a part of it. We also received more fine proposals for chapters than we were able to accept, and reading and responding to those—as well as the chapters that came to comprise the collection—showed us how vital and energetic the discipline—whether called Rhetoric and Composition, Writing Studies, or something else—will always be. We hope you'll learn as much from reading this book as we've learned from assembling it.

### Notes

1. Throughout the book, chapter authors refer to the discipline in a range of ways: as Rhetoric and Composition, as Writing Studies, as Writing and Rhetoric. We felt these differences in nomenclature reflected the current state of the discipline, and so didn't attempt to regularize the way that the discipline is referred to in the book.
2. Several sites compete for the founding of the field, among them English education. See, for example, Patricia Stock's (2011) edited collection *Composition's Roots in English Education*.
3. Interdisciplinary efforts are important as well, but they do assume a set of disciplines.

### References

Adler-Kassner, Linda, and Elizabeth Wardle. 2015. *Naming What We Know: Threshold Concepts of Writing Studies*. Logan: Utah State University Press.
Bartholomae, David. 1989. "Freshman English, Composition, and CCCC." *College Composition and Communication* 40 (1): 38–51. https://doi.org/10.2307/358179.
Berlin, James. 1987. *Rhetoric and Reality: Writing Instruction in American Colleges, 1900–1985. Studies in Writing and Rhetoric*. Carbondale: Southern Illinois University Press.
Colomb, Gregory G. 2010. "Franchising the Future." *College Composition and Communication* 62 (1): 11–30.
Craig, Jacob, Matt Davis, Christine Martorana, Josh Mehler, Kendra Mitchell, Tony Ricks, Bret Zawilski, and Kathleen Blake Yancey. 2016. "Against the Rhetoric and Composition Grain: A Microhistorical View." In *Microhistories of Composition*, ed. Bruce McComiskey, 284–306. Logan: Utah State University Press.

Dobrin, Sidney I. 2011. *Postcomposition*. Carbondale: Southern Illinois University Press.
Harris, Joseph. 2012. *A Teaching Subject: Composition since 1966*. New ed. Logan: Utah State University Press.
Heilker, Paul, and Peter Vandenberg, eds. 1996. *Keywords in Composition Studies*. Portsmouth, NH: Heinemann.
Heilker, Paul, and Peter Vandenberg, eds. 2015. *Keywords in Writing Studies*. Logan: Utah State University Press. https://doi.org/10.7330/9780874219746.
Horner, Bruce. 2015. "Rewriting Composition: Moving beyond a Discourse of Need." *College English* 77 (5): 450–79.
Hyland, Ken. 2004. *Disciplinary Discourses: Social Interactions in Academic Writing*. Ann Arbor: University of Michigan Press. https://doi.org/10.3998/mpub.6719.
Rose, Mike. 2012. *Back to School*. New York: New Press.
Stock, Patricia Lambert, ed. 2011. *Composition's Roots in English Education*. Portsmouth: Heinemann.
Trimbur, John. 2011. *Solidarity or Service: Composition and the Problem of Expertise*. Portsmouth: Heinemann.

# SECTION 1

*Where Have We Been, Where Are We Now, and Why Are We Here?*

# 1
## MAPPING THE TURN TO DISCIPLINARITY
*A Historical Analysis of Composition's Trajectory and Its Current Moment*

Kathleen Blake Yancey

> *We have made ourselves a new discipline. . . .*
> —Robert J. Connors

One way of thinking about both the history of Rhetoric and its current moment, especially in the context of disciplinarity, is provided through the metaphor of turns. The oft-cited social turn (Trimbur 1994) marks a shift from a more individually located composing to a sociocultural model, while other turns—the public (Farmer 2013); the queer (Alexander and Wallace 2009); the archival (Yancey 2004); and the global (*Composition Studies*)—continue to compete for attention. Of course, the expression the "x turn" is often employed simply as a quick reference, as a way of indicating that a new practice or theoretical orientation is gaining ground. Other times, however, the expression is used to articulate a shift of the Trimburian kind, that is, of a historical demarcation of the field. Paul Lynch (2014), for instance, has recently theorized what he understands as a(nother) new turn, that of the apocalyptic:

> Composition now faces a somewhat paradoxical turn, one in which the ground . . . may be solid but is also corrupted. I am speaking of an apocalyptic turn, in which the end of the world looms ever larger in our disciplinary and pedagogical imagination. Ours is of course not the first generation to worry about the world's end . . . . But the field does seem to be thinking more and more about what composition ought to do in the face of serious dangers to human flourishing. A growing list of authors—including Derek Owens, Kurt Spellmeyer, Lynn Worsham, and others—share a basic perspective: economic disruption, endless violence, and, perhaps most important, environmental collapse should force us to reexamine what it means to work in the field of composition, and this reexamination should go to the very heart of what *composition* means. (458)

Lynch's move here, much like John Trimbur's before him, is to stake a claim on the grounds of synthesis: in this logic, given the work of certain leading scholars all raising similar concerns, we can identify a turn, a shift to something new that provides a provocative and different trajectory than had been anticipated. The intent of a proposal like Lynch's, like Trimbur's before him, is in part to raise (and answer) important questions occupying the center of the field, ones that can help us move forward—and in equal part to write the history of the field as it develops.

John Trimbur's (1994) articulation of the social turn was expressed in a review essay for *College Composition and Communication*, "Taking the Social Turn: Teaching Writing Post-Process," where he contextualized and reviewed three books relative to the field's history and, more particularly, to the particular historical moment of the review. If we have experienced a social turn, he asks, what precisely is it, and what does it tell us about the field and its theories and practices? As Trimbur's example illustrates, establishing that we are in the midst of a turn, or have experienced a turn, is no small achievement: weaving the work of others into a coherent account that both looks back and looks forward, the writer is able to characterize previous scholarship, theories, and practices, and motivate new work in line with the turn just defined. Put succinctly, the rhetoric of such a turn can change both the forward movement of the field as well as our perception of its progression.

My aim in this chapter is to do likewise: working in a manner somewhat similar to Trimbur's, I trace here what I see as the field's turn to disciplinarity, not, however, based principally on what has already occurred, but rather on what *is* occurring in the current moment. Of course, what's happening in the current moment of the field is considerable—from continued interest in pedagogy to a resurgence of research into questions of continuing interest to the field (e.g., how students compose) and the development of new research activity (e.g., drawing from archives, analyzing big data). It's also worth noting my own usage here in referring to us as a field.[1] By most accounts we are a field at least; in terms of categorization, it's easier to call ourselves a field precisely because field-ness requires a lower threshold than a discipline does. We might pursue a field of interest without the methodology of a discipline, for example, and of course the two terms are also related, as Kristine Hansen suggests (this volume), to the idea of a profession. My focus here is on the more contentious issue of disciplinarity, my argument that we are making a disciplinary turn, shifting from field to disciplinarity, as four recurring themes collectively demonstrate. Here, then, after providing a brief account of the field's recent history, I more fully analyze the rhetoric of the social turn as a context for our current disciplinary turn; demonstrate that without our being very aware of it, we have begun to see the field as a discipline; and identify four trends in particular influencing this movement toward a recognition and embrace of disciplinarity: (1) a renewed research agenda, including continuing research into and theory about transfer of writing knowledge and practice; (2) the development of projects consolidating what the field has established as knowledge; (3) the continuing development of the major in Rhetoric and Composition; and (4) the changing location of Writing Studies within institutional structures. Based on this analysis, I conclude with several questions intended, first, to guide the reading of this volume speaking to Rhetoric and Composition's disciplinarity and, second, to frame the field's way forward.

## A(NOTHER) HISTORY OF RHETORIC AND COMPOSITION AND THE SIGNIFICANCE OF A TURN

A very simple narrative of the discipline can be divided into five episodes.[2] A first episode: In the middle of the twentieth century in the United States, teachers of composition, in the midst of teaching a group of students new to the academy, banded together to share knowledge about how to teach writing. Their subject matter was language, their role teaching, their practice enhanced by borrowings from linguistics, itself a discipline eager to be applied. In the second episode of this narrative, Composition focused on another subject matter, the composing process, which provided a focus both for researchers attempting to develop models of composing and for teachers helping students develop as writers. Process, in other words, became the new content, studied by teachers who were also scholars, and the dual identity of teacher-scholar became something of an idealized model for the community's members. In the third episode of this narrative, the field took what has become a trope for it, a turn, in this case a turn to cultural theory influenced by revolutionaries such as Paulo Freire, by Marxist critics such as Terry Eagleton, and by streetwise literacy researchers such as Alan Luke. In this episode, theory displaced research while underscoring the field's commitment to students and making the field look more like its literary cousins. In the fourth episode, the field, still influenced by all the activities in the previous episodes, returned to teaching as its subject matter, particularly in light of seemingly intractable labor problems plaguing the field and haunting the field's ethos. This turn, or return, to teaching offered several benefits. One: with teaching as subject matter, the field's members could teach what they wanted to teach as long as writing was included; in this moment, the content of the class was the prerogative of the teacher. Two: with teaching as a subject matter, the members of the community could continue a commitment to a field-ness, rather than to disciplinarity, speaking to our ethos; a field seems open, welcoming, and democratic, available especially to all members of the community, a discipline, closed, exclusive, and hierarchical, substituting its own content for the student who has consistently provided the center of the field and supplied its raison d'être. In the current moment, the fifth episode, Rhetoric and Composition seems to be making a disciplinary turn.

Before considering the context for a disciplinary turn, however, it's worth pausing to consider the role that any turn can play in the field. During the third episode described above, John Trimbur coined the phrase "social turn" as a way of describing the contributions of three books he was reviewing, all of which distinguished the early composing process theory from the postprocess composing theory "represent[ing] literacy as an ideological arena and composing as a cultural activity":

> What is significant about these books—and to my mind indicative of the current moment in rhetoric and composition studies—is that they make their arguments not so much in terms of students' reading and writing processes but rather in terms of the cultural politics of literacy. In this regard, taken together, the three books [Patricia Bizzell's (1992) *Academic Discourse and Critical Consciousness,* C. H. Knoblauch and Lil Brannon's *Critical Teaching and the Idea of Literacy,* and Kurt Spellmeyer's *Common Ground: Dialogue, Understanding, and the Teaching of Composition*] can be read as statements that both reflect and (especially in Bizzell's case) enact what has come to be called the "social turn" of the 1980s, a post-process, post-cognitivist theory and pedagogy that represent literacy as an ideological arena and composing as a cultural activity by which writers position and reposition themselves in relation to their own and others' subjectivities, discourses, practices, and institutions. (Trimbur 1994,109)

Here, Trimbur marks the divide between early models of composing more focused on the individual and the later, more situated models sensitive especially to ideological pressures, a move not unlike that made by Maxine Hairston (1982), in "Winds of Change," as she divides the earlier current-traditional models of teaching writing from newer models enacting then-current composing process ones. For our purposes, the key difference in these two characterizations of a shift, apart from their views of composing (a difference that is considerable), is that Trimbur *names* the shift as the social turn, uses it as part of his title for the review essay, and then continually refers to it throughout the essay, a process that allows him to define it and consider its consequence.[3] In his review essay, we thus learn not only about the three books under review, but also, and more important, about how they collectively articulate the divide between prior and new composing theory and how, in addressing the "disillusion" generated by the earlier "process paradigm," they as part of the social turn can provide a remedy addressing those ills.

> In fact, one might say that these books result from a crisis within the process paradigm and a growing disillusion with its limits and pressures. When process pedagogy emerged on the scene in the late 1960s and early 1970s, process teachers and theorists sought to free themselves from the formalism of current-traditional rhetoric and return the text to the student composer. But the distinction between product and process, which initially seemed so clarifying, not only proved conceptually inadequate to what writers do when they are writing, it also made writing instruction appear to be easier than it is. (109)

In addition, as Trimbur continues defining the social turn in the context of the review, we learn about the role that belief and intention play in the turn. In developing a theory of writing that is social, Bizzell's hope, as Trimbur explains, is that students would learn to work comfortably within "the academic world view without abandoning home perspectives or becoming deracinated (22–23)" (117).

> This hope, embodied in the first nine articles collected in *Academic Discourse and Critical Consciousness,* instituted, as it were, a charter of belief for the social turn I have alluded to. The perspective that emerged, which represents discourse communities not as static and hermetically sealed entities tied together by formal linguistic conventions but as dynamic ones with permeable textual and social boundaries, has inspired scholars in writing across the curriculum and the rhetoric of inquiry and also has exerted a useful pressure on the process movement—both on cognitivists who have begun to redescribe their object of inquiry in socio-cognitive terms, and on expressivists who are paying more attention to the voice in academic discourse instead of just writing it off as impersonal and jargon-laden. (117)

The social turn, in this version of history-in-the-making, thus not only marks a shift, but also acts as a corrective to previous theory. As important, invoking Patricia Bizzell as a leading participant in the social turn, Trimbur points to "a charter of belief," which is a kind of ideological commitment shared by those professing this theory.

Had the social turn remained merely the title of Trimbur's review essay, or a formation specific to him alone, it would be an interesting concept, but only one among many vying for significance. But the social turn as rhetorical construct captured simply and elegantly a shift that had already occurred—and it is now seen as something of a watershed moment in the field, in part because of Trimbur's able synopsis of changes underway, but also in part because of the way in which other scholars have also invoked the social turn, employing it as an historical signpost, as a schema for new theory, and as grounds for critique. Beth Daniell (1999), for instance, cites the social turn as a warrant for her own work in literacy:

> In 1986 Lester Faigley analyzed three competing theories of the writing process: the expressive, the cognitive, and the social. Although calling for a synthesis, Faigley was clearly endorsing the social view. He identified four strands of research which contributed to the social perspective he was advocating: post-structuralist theories of language, sociology of science, ethnographies of literacy and language, and Marxism. Two of these four, ethnography and Marxism, contributed texts about literacy that were instrumental in helping composition studies make what has been called the social turn (Trimbur, Taking; Bizzell, Academic 202). Indeed the move in composition studies away from the individualistic and cognitive perspectives of the seventies and early eighties toward the social theories and political consciousness that prevail today was encouraged, pushed along, impelled by competing narratives of literacy. These days, literacy, the term and concept, connects composition, with its emphasis on students and classrooms, to the social, political, economic, historical, and cultural. (393)

Likewise, in introducing the 2003 special issue of the *Journal of Second Language Writing* addressing postprocess, Dwight Atkinson (2003, 3) sets the tone of the issue by invoking the social turn—"I first encountered the term 'post-process' in John Trimbur's 1994 review essay, 'Taking the Social Turn: Teaching Writing Post-Process'"—before calling on Trimbur's definition of the social turn as a tool to scaffold his own analysis of the current moment in L2 writing: "In this introduction to the special issue, I attempt to lay out a coherent if still-heuristic notion of 'post-process.' I do so by first investigating four components of Trimbur's definition of 'post-process': the social; the post-cognitivist; literacy as an ideological arena; and composition as a cultural activity" (Atkinson 2003, 4). And not least, Richard Fulkerson (2005), some eleven years after Trimbur's review essay, employs the social turn as object of critique in his 2005 "Composition at the Turn of the Twenty-First Century": "Specifically, I shall argue that the 'social turn' in composition, the importation of cultural studies from the social sciences and literary theory, has made a writing teacher's role deeply problematic. I will argue that expressivism, despite numerous poundings by the cannons of postmodernism and resulting eulogies, is, in fact, quietly expanding its region of command. Finally, I'll argue that the rhetorical approach has now divided itself in three" (655).

The social turn, in other words, is now a recognizable moment in the field: it helps organize the field, provides exigence for new scholarship, and enables a kind of interrogation of practice and theory.

## SOUNDING NOTES OF DISCIPLINARITY

My own sense is that we are in the midst of a new turn, a disciplinary turn that will influence the field as much as, if not more than, the social turn. I'm not sure how I would date the beginnings of this current turn—as members of the field, we can't seem to forge agreement on when the modern iteration of the field itself began, as Kristine Hansen notes, (this volume), with 1949 and 1963 vying among others for the honor—but for at least twenty years now scholars have been talking about our (potential) disciplinarity and what that might mean. Robert Connors, for instance, both in his talk for the inaugural Watson Conference in 1996 and in the 1999 publication that followed, *History, Reflection, and Narrative: The Professionalization in Composition 1963–1983*, identified the conference itself as a sign of our nascent disciplinarity:

> The 1996 Watson Conference at Louisville was in some ways the outward and visible sign of who we have become. The reality of what we have been making is all around us at every Conference on College Composition and Communication, but the Watson Conference was the first meeting I know of that was specifically meant to look at the meanings of our making. What *does* it mean, what *will* it mean, for us to be a recognizable discipline, as opposed to a group of marginalized enthusiasts coming together for support and sympathy that we were 35 years ago? (Connors 1999, 3–4)

Connors here declares us a discipline in the making; moreover, he is sufficiently confident in his assessment of our disciplinarity that he outlines two possible paths our discipline might take. One, more aligned with our origin stories of students and service, "embrac[es] teaching and service as indispensible parts of the world of . . . research, and put[s] scholarly research in the service of action in colleges and universities"; a second, more aligned with literature, "mak[es] theoretical sophistication, specialized expertise, and sheer scholarly output the prime criteria of success in the field" (Connors 1999, 19).[4]

Charles Bazerman (2002), writing not a decade later in "The Case for Writing Studies as a Major Discipline," also argues for disciplinarity, but on very different grounds than Connors. Where Connors saw a maturing of the field and a clear choice between allegiances—on the one hand, to the values of the founding of Rhetoric and Composition, or on the other hand, to more prestigious, scholarly conventions and values—Bazerman sees what we have *not* accomplished and have not yet attempted—"put[ting] together the large, important, and multi-dimensional story of writing" (n.p.).[5] He then assigns us this overarching task, under which are included many others, including caring for students.

> Of all disciplines, composition is best positioned to begin to put together the large, important, and multi-dimensional story of writing. We are the only profession that sees writing as its center. The university, moreover—as central to contemporary society's knowledge, ambitions and professions; as the heir to many of the literate movements of history; and as an international meeting place of global projects—is as good a standpoint as any from which to view writing at this juncture in history. Yet we as a field must be willing to lift up our eyes to this larger charge. It is time for us to rise above the accidents of disciplinary history that have kept our truly significant subject only minimally visible and have blinded us to the enormity of the material we have taken to instruct our students in. It is time to recognize that writing provides some of the fundamental mechanisms that make our world work—and to assert that writing needs to be taken seriously along with the other major matters of inquiry supported by institutional structures. (n.p.)

Bazerman's argument, then, is that the discipline should take as its focus writing itself, not just ways of teaching writing.[6]

Other scholars sound other notes indicating that they too are considering our disciplinarity and what that might mean for us, often doing so less confidently than Bazerman or Connors, often finding themselves somewhat surprised by both inquiry and its potential consequences. John Trimbur (2000), reflecting on his teaching of the visual in "A Theory of Visual Design," identifies what he calls "problems" that challenge the way we think about the content of our teaching and, implicitly, the nature of the field. As he observes, the "larger problem" driving his reflection is "namely where and how visual literacy, visual communication, visual culture—whatever you want to call it—fits into writing instruction and rhetorical education" (106). In other words, our writing instruction has historically excluded content other than writing, but given what Trimbur is teaching—the idea that "visual communication constitutes part of the available means of persuasion"; that "writing itself is a form of visible language"; and that "visual design, such as page layout, typography, and text/graphic integration, is fundamental to composing"—he makes three observations: (1) that he is teaching the *what* as much as the how; (2) that these topics haven't been included under the writing umbrella; and (3) that "visual literacy, visual communication, visual culture—whatever you want to call it" brings with it its own content. In response to this reflection, Trimbur expresses two reservations, one located in questions of expertise, a second located in how we define writing and what the curriculum should look like:

> My main reservation in pressing this observation is the simple fact that students learn outside the curriculum as well as in it, and certainly a number

of undergraduates with little or no coursework in writing and rhetoric have done very well in Theory of Visual Design . . . On the other hand, the challenge of courses such as Theory of Visual Design is to explain why courses that don't take their primary aim as that of teaching writing—that instead want to *study* literacy, rhetorical theory, visual design, and a range of specialized topics we're just starting to imagine—have an equal claim to space in the writing curriculum.

Interestingly, Trimbur's backdoor question about the *study of,* rather than the practice of (writing and writing-related topics)—prompted by his review of a writing class involving the visual, leading to questions about the rationale for an undergraduate "*study* of literacy, rhetorical theory, and visual design"—provides the very warrant for Bazerman's vision of the field's disciplinarity. Put more generally, for some time various scholars have been thinking about our disciplinarity, coming to the question of Rhetoric and Composition's disciplinarity through diverse paths: historical, philosophical, and pedagogical. As important, what we see here is the context for a disciplinary turn.

## THE DISCIPLINARY TURN: FOUR CONTRIBUTORS
### Resurgence in Research

Four trends constitute the disciplinary turn: (1) a resurgence of interest in research, with a focus on the transfer of writing knowledge and practice; (2) a consolidation of what the field knows, especially as it's informing the threshold concepts project; (3) the rise of the major in Rhetoric and Composition; and (4) the positioning of Rhetoric and Composition in the academy, both locally and globally. Although each of these four trends is described and analyzed below, they work together epistemologically, defining Rhetoric and Composition as a mature knowledge-making discipline. In terms of the disciplinary turn, they are constitutive.

In the twenty-first century, Rhetoric and Composition has refocused energies on research interacting with and leading to theory, as we can date from several events: Rich Haswell's call for a return to the research orientation of the field; Chris Anson's repeat of that call; the creation of the biennial institutes hosted by the Rhetoric Society of America; the Elon Institute on Critical Transitions and Transfer; the Summer (Research) Seminar at Dartmouth; CompPile; the Research EX project; the CCCC Research Initiative; and the considerable research addressing transfer of practice and knowledge in writing—to name some but not all research activity occurring with the commencement of a new century.

Impatient with what he perceived as a dearth of empirical research in the field, for instance, Rich Haswell (2005) authored "NCTE/CCCC's Recent War on Scholarship," which argued that the field should return to empirical research, especially scholarship engaging in what he called RAD research—replicable, aggregable, and data supported—which would allow us to create a *body* of scholarship on any number of important topics. In 2008, Chris Anson echoed this call, but with specific application to writing programs, in "The Intelligent Design of Writing Programs: Reliance on Belief or a Future of Evidence," a cautionary tale about largely right-wing critiques of writing programs and the need for data to refute them (Anson 2008). In 2005, the Rhetoric Society of America initiated their biennial seminars, the first a single seminar at Kent State University, the seminars in 2015 numbering seven, with another twenty-three workshops offered as well. And at about the same time, the Dartmouth Summer Seminar was founded, its purpose to provide a sustained period for emerging and established scholars to design research projects and consult experts.

But 2004 marks the beginning of another activity, this one involving sustained *funding* for research: it's in 2004 that the Conference on College Composition and Communication established the "CCCC Research Initiative—What We Know, What We Need to Know," an effort which is no longer an initiative, but rather a continuing program.[7] Originally funded as a pilot, the CCCC Research Initiative "focused on supporting new meta-analytical research by providing funding and an opportunity for researchers from all participating institutions to gather to share ideas and receive advice." Since the beginning of the initiative, however, the effort has widened in scope, with some fifty-four projects being funded overall, fifteen of them in 2015, resulting in at least one large grant (a Spencer), numerous articles, and at least two books, one of which, *Writing across Contexts: Transfer, Composition, and Sites of Writing*, won the CCCC Research Impact Award and the Best Book Award from the Council of Writing Program Administrators. Interestingly, of the fifty-four funded projects, about 20 percent of them, or eleven, have focused on transfer of writing knowledge and practice: no other category is as large.

Most (but not all) of the transfer research, that sponsored by CCCC and other scholarship being conducted independently, is focused on first-year composition (FYC), which is not surprising given the field's commitment to FYC. That's where our work with students and our curricula begin, and that's where we have, at least in some ways, the most opportunity to consider what a writing curriculum might be and how it can support students as they enter college, as they complete FYC, and as they take up other writing tasks across campus. The research to date—which has also been supported by another research initiative, the Elon University 2011–13 Research Seminar on Critical Transitions: Writing and the Question of Transfer; by the Elon University Conference on Writing and the Question of Transfer; and by a special issue of *Composition Forum* focused on transfer—points to the role that content, a disciplinary issue, plays in the development of student writing, a point that Liane Robertson and Kara Taczak take up more fully in this volume. More specifically, the larger question being pursued is whether FYC content should be Writing Studies content, or whether it can be another content, especially as is so often the case, themed content; the content of any college course is, of course, a disciplinary issue. The content-informed curricular approaches employed in the transfer effort vary, as we might expect given that they operate independently of each other—from the Downs and Wardle Writing about Writing (WAW) curriculum and variants of the WAW approach to the Teaching for Transfer (TFT) approach and the digital multimodal approach used at Columbia College Chicago[8]—but they all share a commitment to placing Writing Studies at the center of FYC. Moreover, many of these curricular projects are engaged in research inquiring into the efficacy of the curriculum. Taken together, the research thus far suggests that even when other curricular elements such as reflection are put into place, curricula with a themed approach—that is, without a Writing Studies approach—do not support students' transfer (Hayes 2015; Taczak and Robertson 2016).[9] As important, research is demonstrating—and at very different kinds of institutions—the value of a Writing Studies FYC curriculum: not only that compared to other curricula, a Writing Studies curriculum is more efficacious in supporting transfer, but also that there are explanations about how and why such transfer is supported (Yancey, Robertson, and Taczak 2014; Taczak and Robertson 2016). In sum, one element of our disciplinary turn is renewed activity in research, especially research addressing the role of Writing Studies–related FYC curricula.

*Consolidating What We Know*

A second trend is a new interest in consolidating what we know—or more accurately put, it seems that we are at the point where we have learned enough that we can take stock, that we can identify *and* articulate the knowledge that is at the center of the discipline. Such consolidation has taken both internal and external forms.

Internally, two examples demonstrate current consolidation. First, the special issue on the future of Rhetoric and Composition published by *College Composition and Communication* in 2010 was by design a consolidation, an opportunity to look backward to look forward, to bring together scholars charting where we might go.[10] Reading across the contributions to that issue as editor, I remarked that there seemed to be an emerging agreement on disciplinarity without much exploration on what form it might take: "We have a history contextualizing the field without (over)determining our future or prescribing what we might or should do: we have a shared past; we have options. Likewise, there is a sense that this moment in the discipline—or is it field?—is propitious, weighty with opportunity, almost, in Malcolm Gladwell's formation, at a tipping point. But opportunity for what?" (Yancey 2010, 7).

Not long after this, Linda Adler-Kassner and Elizabeth Wardle, seeing the need for both consolidation and articulation of that consolidation, developed a project that by design would begin to gather and express what we as a discipline know. In leading this project, the Threshold Concepts project, Adler-Kassner and Wardle invited many members of the field to participate in a modified crowdsourcing activity aimed at identifying threshold concepts defining the discipline.

> We'll start with the numbers. 45 people invited; 29 participants who submitted two or more entries. 51 suggestions of what contributors considered to be threshold concepts after reading the introduction to *Overcoming Barriers to Student Understanding* by J.F. Meyer and Ray Land . . . In response to those 51 suggestions of initial threshold concepts, 139 comments in threaded discussions about the concepts. From those, a distillation: one meta-concept, *writing is a subject of study and an activity*, and five overarching concepts with somewhere between three and nine constituent elements—a total of 35 threshold concepts that the group engaged in this discussion have identified as "what we know"—from research in writing studies and aligned fields (i.e., linguistics, learning theory, and psychology). (Adler-Kassner and Wardle 2015, 4)

What this inclusive, dynamic process produced is equally important— a book, *Naming What We Know*, describing the process of identification of threshold concepts (TCs) thoroughly and providing demonstrations of how TCs can be helpful in any number of settings (e.g., faculty development, graduate education)—and, of course, sharing the threshold concepts themselves and their definitions. This project, in sum, creates the terms for debate, both about disciplinarity, seen through the lens of "epistemological participation in communities of practice," and about this particular set of TCs:

We use the lens of threshold concepts—concepts critical for epistemological participation in communities of practice—to raise this query. Our use of "communities of practice" draws on the work of Jean Lave and Etienne Wenger, who explain that these communities are physical or imagined locations (communities) that are bound together (and delineated from other communities) by shared rituals, practices, and commitments. To participate in any such community, novices must learn to recognize the threshold concepts of the community; if they are to be successful within that community, they must also come to "see through and see with" . . . those concepts so that they become a naturalized part of the lenses through which learners interpret. (Adler-Kassner and Wardle 2015, 5)

Disciplinarity isn't, however, merely a matter of scholars' agreement; external audiences exercise influence as well. Speaking to that dimension of disciplinarity, Louise Wetherbee Phelps and John M. Ackerman have reported on the Visibility Project, whose data-driven aim is to gain national recognition for Rhetoric and Composition by collecting and representing the data showing who we are and what we do according to a template employed by the US federal government (Phelps and Ackerman 2010). To do so, they focused "on the ways that fields of instruction and research are identified, coded, and represented statistically and descriptively for the purposes of data collection, reports, records, comparison, analysis, and assessment of higher education" (184), though such collection and representation is, as the authors note, also rhetorical. This kind of project, dedicated to establishing that Rhetoric and Composition is a discipline as the US government defines disciplines, consolidates who we are and what we do as it translates both into external terms.

### The Major in Rhetoric and Composition

Yet another factor contributing to Rhetoric and Composition's disciplinary turn is the major in Rhetoric and Composition; one critical effect of the major is to make Rhetoric and Composition look like other disciplines with majors. Put another way, with a major, we become more disciplinary.

The interest in having a major isn't entirely new; in 1975, for example, George Tade, Gary Tate, and Jim Corder outlined their own thinking about it in "For Sale, Lease, or Rent: A Curriculum for an Undergraduate Program in Rhetoric" (Tade et al. 1975). But their interest in it was never pursued. As the twentieth century turned into the twenty-first, however, there developed a set of interacting interests all contributing to the major being offered in many institutions: renewed attention to advanced composition (as represented, for example, in the edited collection *Coming of*

*Age*); a concerted effort to compile information about the majors that were developing in nearly every state; the founding of *Young Scholars in Writing*, a journal publishing the work of undergraduates; and the publication of considerable scholarship on the major, including in two dissertations (at least), in *College Composition and Communication*, in a special issue of *Composition Studies*, and in two edited collections.

The edited collection *Coming of Age*, published in 2000 in print with an accompanying CD, demonstrated not only what an advanced composition course might look like, but also what an advanced *curriculum* in Writing Studies might look like. In that sense, it forecast our interest in the major just as it commented on our own status as a field, as Alice Gillam (2001) observed in her review of the text: "The formation of an undergraduate writing curriculum seems a natural next step in our discipline's 'coming of age' in that it reflects the range of theoretical and practical work that has long made up our own notion of composition studies" (102). Not four years later, I called for a new major in my CCCC Chair's Address—"In other words, it is past time that we fill the glaringly empty spot between first year composition and graduate education with a composition major" (308)—and outlined some of what I hoped we might design into the major:

> These . . . approaches: all oriented to the circulation of texts, to genre, to media, and to ways that writing gets made, both individually and culturally. As important, all three of these approaches, in their analysis of textual relationships and contexts, in their theories and examples of how writing works, and in their situating the student as a maker of knowledge, map the content for new composition. And if you are saying, but I can't do all this in first year composition, I'm going to reply, "Exactly. First year composition is a place to begin; carrying this forward is the work of the major in composition and rhetoric." (444)

During that year, 2004, the CCCC Executive Committee established a CCCC Committee on the Major in Rhetoric and Composition, originally charged simply to gather information, later responsible for implementing four charges: documenting the variety of majors; identifying a common set of outcomes for the major; identifying courses and curricula that could be adapted to other majors; and track[ing] the employment of students graduating with these majors. That there is a variety of majors is made evident by the abundant research documenting them—in the special issue of *Composition Studies* dedicated to the major, for example, and in Giberson and Moriarty's (2010) *What We Are Becoming* and Giberson et al.'s (2015) *Writing Majors: Eighteen Program Profiles* as well as by scholarship of critique. Likewise, a CCCC SIG established in

2008 focused on the major in Rhetoric and Composition has become its own organization, the Association for Rhetoric and Writing Studies Undergraduate Programs hosting its first conference in October 2016. It's also worth noting that junior faculty are beginning to call for changes in graduate curricula that would help prepare them for this new professional responsibility given that the issues raised by the major differ considerably from those associated with our historical spheres of influence, FYC and graduate programming. In fact, at a 2015 CCCC session on the major, Elizabeth Wardle called for us to think collectively about the kinds of issues, especially the related issues of staffing and expertise, that will vex our best efforts contributing to the major if we don't plan judiciously; likewise, a CCCC workshop on this issue paying special attention to concerns about the need for and ways of credentialing faculty who teach in the major has been conducted.

*Our Place in the Academy*

The place of any field of inquiry isn't stable—home economics once offered a professional way forward for women—but the place of Rhetoric and Composition, without a strong research tradition, without a clear articulation of what we know, and without a major, has felt particularly vulnerable, especially unstable.[11] Nor have members of the field, especially as members of programs, found their expertise acknowledged, perhaps often and especially on their own campuses. With the 2002 publication of *Field of Dreams*, a balanced portrait of independent writing programs and the future they might point us toward, however, we had the first concerted expression of what an institutional future of our own might look like. In reviewing this volume, Sue McLeod speaks to the issues that together constitute the disciplinary turn, as we have seen, and that thus begin to raise for us the new set of issues such a turn invokes. McLeod (2006) begins her review with Larry Burton's afterword:

> Pointing to the relative youth of many of these new departments, he counsels us to remember that we are still in the experimental stage in developing freestanding writing programs or departments. Certainly labor issues, resources, and leadership are the key issues when thinking about separation. When these are satisfactorily addressed, "members of independent departments of writing will have discovered a new mentality—a refreshing mentality—out of which they conduct their professional lives" (300). To this sentiment, I would add one more issue: the development of a departmental major. Some independent writing departments remain service units, offering general education courses and perhaps also graduate courses in the teaching of writing. Such units are anomalous in the

university, and often find themselves at the bottom of the list when an influx of resources becomes possible. Yancey's chair's address was (and continues to be) a call to action. Independent writing programs may develop, but they will achieve equal footing with other disciplinary units in the university only when they offer a major. I share the optimism suggested by the title of this book: *if we build it, they will come.* (McLeod 2006, 110)

Our place in the academy, of course, is twofold. On the one hand, it's very local, but on the other, there are patterns across the local, as McLeod (2006) suggests: generally, being identified as a service unit only makes the unit more vulnerable, less able to exert influence over the unit's fate. How offering a major might change such vulnerability is still under discussion; how offering a major inside a Writing Studies department is even more under discussion—as programs such as those at Syracuse and DePaul can attest.

## CONCLUSION: CONTEXTUALIZING TENSIONS

As we might expect, the context for the disciplinary turn includes tensions, especially tensions related to the field's affection for interdisciplinarity; to our commitment to pedagogy; and to an impulse to direct all our research—and energy—toward teaching, often defined in terms of social justice. These tensions are not insignificant: many of them are historical and closely bound to our historical identity. At the same time, as we see in the work of several scholars, it is possible to honor past commitments and to explore new opportunities, as Charles Bazerman suggests. Thinking about the relationship of disciplinarity to interdisciplinarity, Bazerman (2001) finds a way to include them both:

> The complexity of writing studies poses puzzles to the field that we need to address as we establish ourselves as a discipline. If we choose the path to disciplinarity of narrowing the acceptable data, method, or theory, we are in danger of misunderstanding or even distorting the processes, practices, and products of writing. Rather I argue on the basis of my experience that we should choose a path that finds discipline in our questions and goals, allowing us to draw on the resources of many disciplines. While this multi-dimensional task is hard, through reflective understanding of our goals, questions, and methods, we can still maintain a coherent disciplinary discussion, while maintaining respect for the complexity of writing, its impact on individuals and societies, the creativity of individuals, and the challenges of teaching and learning to write. (8)

The commitment to pedagogy, which speaks to our historical identity, may be more difficult to address, as might a preference for research aligning with this commitment, which, stated differently, would have the effect of elevating the pedagogical imperative to a universalizing role. The conflict here is ably summarized by Rich Haswell (2015, n.p.), who begins a post on the topic, on the WPA-L listserv, by quoting Holly Hassel's interest in privileging research helping us teach FYC better: "Holly writes, 'My main point is that I see a big gap between what would help people who work in teaching-intensive jobs where they teach primarily in the lower-division, and the amount of disciplinary work taking place in those settings and being published in major journals.'"

Haswell's response is keyed to how we understand our field, which for him seems synonymous with disciplinarity:

> What is our field? Is it ONLY teaching how to write in academic and professional genres so students can do well in their post-secondary studies and then do well in their careers after college? If our field is ONLY that, then our field will always be treated as lesser than other professional fields. The people working in it basically will always be treated as subaltern. Because we will be projecting writing as secondary to more important endeavors. And that fits the way most people outside our field still view writing. They see writing is a means toward something more important. The news is written for the sake of the news. The hydrogeological report is written for the sake of safety in oil exploration. Writing experts are like auto mechanics. They belong to a trade, not a field of professional studies.
> ... But what if our field is seen as not about learning to write but about writing? What if writing studies were seen as bigger than learning to be a writer? Our field is the universe of written discourse in all its human dimensions. The activities of writing—the acts and products—are not secondary but primary. The language of the news is a legitimate part of the news, part of the "content" to the news. The language of the hydrogeological report is a constituent part of the report... This view does not exclude composition or WPA work from the field, nor does it demote them. It just makes the teaching of writing part of a field larger than itself—a legitimate part that should command its own respect, but a part none the less. (n.p.)

Of course, a turn doesn't dissipate tensions: it tends, rather, to bring them into focus. Moreover, this turn to disciplinarity, committed to the capaciousness of the discipline, builds on several interrelated efforts— on our rejuvenated research efforts, especially those focused on transfer of writing knowledge and practice, on the consolidation of our knowledge both inside and outside the field, on the major in Rhetoric and Composition, and on our position in the academy. Such a turn, as the social turn illustrates, can organize the field and can set the agenda for forward progress.

Given this context, the question we need to address as we continue to navigate the disciplinary turn is similarly and yet simply complex: now that we qualify as a discipline, what *kind* of discipline would we like to be?

## Notes

1. Given the scope of the question, how Rhetoric and Composition has thought of itself—as a field or as a discipline—is clearly a project for another time. It's worth noting, however, that (1) compared to other disciplines, our history and our commitments, especially to teaching, are unusual, thus making it unlikely that anyone, including faculty identifying with Rhetoric and Composition, would understand us as a discipline, especially in our early history; (2) Rhetoric and Composition's porous nature and our affection for interdisciplinary work functions not only to allow people from other disciplines into the field (an important consideration, as Wardle and Downs suggest: this volume), but also to invite them in, and such invitations seem at odds with disciplinarity as it is ordinarily construed; and (3) given its dearth of structure and boundaries, field-ness seems to carry with it an ideology congruent with the field's values (as I suggest later in the chapter). Another term that is useful here is "subdiscipline." It's difficult to see how one could have subdisciplines without a discipline to locate them, and Rhetoric and Composition seems to include many, from writing centers and writing assessment to computers and composition to medical rhetoric. As one former graduate student pointed out to me, the discipline has grown sufficiently large and complex that many newer members of Rhetoric and Composition come to it through the subdisciplines.

2. The field can be dated from the late nineteenth century at Harvard; in 1949 with the founding of the Conference for College Composition and Communication; in 1963 with the publication of the Braddock et al. (1963), *Research in Written Composition*. For fuller accounts, see James A. Berlin (1987), Robert Connors (1997), and Maureen Daley Goggin (2000), among others.

3. It's also worth noting that this theory of the social turn is developed not in an independent scholarly article, but in a review essay of other work, the point that even a genre that is often considered not quite first-rate can significantly influence the field.

4. It's a good question as to the kind of role that Connors might have played in our disciplinary turn had he lived. This chapter addressing disciplinarity stemming from the Watson Conference was one of his last publications; another was his afterward for *The Coming of Age* collection addressing advanced writing classes in the context of an upper-level undergraduate curriculum, where he argued for a new major in writing: "The advanced writing curriculum, for which this book is a prospectus and menu, is a much more thoroughgoing and radical idea. It proposes and provides a program for an entirely new conception of undergraduate literacy education, one based on the centrality of writing rather than literature. This conception will be, in fact, the alternative English major for the twenty-first century" (Connors 2000, 147).

5. In this sense, Bazerman also anticipates the threshold concept (TC) that writing is both a practice and an object of study, and it's no surprise that he is one of the contributors to the Adler-Kassner and Wardle volume. See also the role of TCs in the disciplinary turn later in the chapter.

6. In responding to Anne Gere's CCCC Chair's Address, Susan Miller (1994) also gestures to a different idea of the field in her suggestion that we consider a "different history of writing and different ways of connecting 'quality' to 'class": "But her [Gere's] elegant proof that Composition is and has been many forms of self- and group sponsored, culturally productive writing places the field in a different aspect toward its current self-declared agendas, particularly the one that isolates 'teaching' with almost breathless self-righteousness about innovative institutional curricula whose cultural results remain unspecified. Consequently, I'd like to

focus on her argument that the field's 'culture of professionalism' needs rethinking in light of a different history of writing and different ways of connecting 'quality' to 'class'" (102).
7. The CCCC Research Initiative has been funded continuously with the exception of one year, 2007.
8. A curricular approach oriented to WAW has been taken up by many and with various alterations and change of foci, as Downs and Wardle (2012) explain. In their taxonomy provided in the Ritter and Matsuda *Exploring Composition Studies* volume, those developing WAW curricula share a fundamental goal: "a desire to create a *transferable* and *empowering* focus on *understanding writing as a subject of study*" (2012: 131). At the same time, Downs and Wardle identify variations in WAW curricula keyed to four factors: (a) the particular angle or perspective a course takes—what subjects it prioritizes and how student research is focused (if the course includes research); (b) the end of student learning that is emphasized—a primary focus on personal growth versus a primary focus on contribution to the field; (c) types and numbers of readings; and (d) types and numbers of writing assignments (139). In addition, Downs and Wardle report on three approaches to WAW currently in development. The first focuses on literacy and discourse, on how writing and language demonstrate community membership. The second focuses on Writing Studies itself—the existence of the discipline qua discipline, with its knowledge and expertise on writing, emphasizing rhetorical strategies and its resultant strategies for writing. The third focuses on the nature of writing and writers' practices. . . . Other approaches, like the one at UCF, try to cover all of this ground by teaching "units" with particular declarative knowledge that must be covered (139–40).
9. Two studies have pursued this question. Carol Hayes reported at AAC&U on a multi-institutional approach employing themed courses and reflection, finding that while the students' work improved over the term, they did not transfer: at the same time, it's not clear what the reflective curriculum included. Robertson and Taczak have reported on a study of themed curriculum with a systematic approach to reflection similar to the one designed into the TFT curriculum, but, again, the students were unable to transfer.
10. Another effort was the *College Composition and Communication* creation of twenty key concepts, each of which was explained in a poster page published in the journal; their creation was also a community effort, as I explained in an editor's introduction to the February 2010 issue:

> A good question, of course, is, "What are the key concepts we need to explain?" For some, an obvious choice might be process; for others, genre; for others, digital technology or media; and for still others audience(s); discourse community; rhetorical knowledge or awareness; reflection; and/or revision—although these hardly exhaust the possibilities. Framing the question differently, we might ask, "If we had only twenty terms to distribute over the next five years, what terms would we choose, how would we sequence them during this time, and according to what logic?" And a concluding good question is how each concept might be defined and illustrated, and what helpful resources we might identify. To help answer these questions, I asked eleven of our colleagues for help, and they have developed a preliminary list of terms and expressions. You'll see the first of these here, at the back of the issue: *rhetorical situation*. And for their good work, I'm grateful to Jonathan Alexander, Amy Devitt, Heidi Estrem, Catherine Hobbs, Sue Hum, Irwin Weiser, Paul Kei Matsuda, Joyce Middleton, Cindy Selfe, Kip Strasma, and Howard Tinberg. (409)
>
> Other like projects have taken a more conventional approach, with editors inviting leading scholars to make more encyclopedic contributions: see, for example,

both editions (the original and the second) of *Keywords in Composition Studies* (1996) and *Keywords in Writing Studies* (2015).
11. See Ryan Skinnell's (2016) recent *Conceding Composition* for a fuller account of such vulnerability.

## References

Adler-Kassner, Linda, and Elizabeth Wardle. 2015. *Naming What We Know: Threshold Concepts of Writing Studies.* Logan: Utah State University Press.

Alexander, Jonathan, and David Wallace. 2009. "The Queer Turn in Composition Studies: Reviewing and Assessing an Emerging Scholarship." *College Composition and Communication* 61 (1): 300–20.

Anson, Chris. 2008. "The Intelligent Design of Writing Programs: Reliance on Belief or a Future of Evidence." *WPA: Writing Program Administration* 32 (1): 11–36.

Atkinson, Dwight. 2003. "L2 Writing in the Post-Process Era: Introduction." *Journal of Second Language Writing* 12 (1): 3–15. https://doi.org/10.1016/S1060-3743(02)00 123-6.

Bazerman, Charles. 2001. "The Disciplined Interdisciplinarity of Writing Studies." *Research in the Teaching of English* 46 (1): 8–21.

Bazerman, Charles. 2002. "The Case for Writing Studies as a Major Discipline." In *The Intellectual Work of Composition*, ed. Gary Olson, 32–38. Carbondale: Southern Illinois UP.

Berlin, James A. 1987. *Rhetoric and Reality: Writing Instruction in American Colleges, 1900–1985.* Carbondale: Southern Illinois University Press.

Bizzell, Patricia. 1992. *Academic Discourse and Critical Consciousness.* Pittsburgh: University of Pittsburgh Press.

Braddock, Richard, Richard Lloyd-Jones, and Lowell Schor. 1963. *Research in Written Composition.* Champaign, IL: National Council of Teachers of English.

Connors, Robert J. 1997. *Composition-Rhetoric: Backgrounds, Theory, and Pedagogy.* Pittsburgh: University Pittsburgh Press. https://doi.org/10.2307/j.ctt5hjt92.

Connors, Robert J. 1999. "Composition History and Disciplinarity." In *History, Reflection, and Narrative: The Professionalization of Composition 1963–1983*, ed. Mary Rosner, Beth Boehm, and Debra Journet, 3–22. Greenwich, CT: Ablex.

Connors, Robert J. 2000. "Afterword: 'Advanced Composition' and Advanced Writing." In *Coming of Age: The Advanced Writing Curriculum*, ed. Linda K. Shamoon, Rebecca Moore Howard, Sandra Jamieson, and Robert A. Schwegler, 143–50. Portsmouth, NH: Heinemann Boynton/Cook.

Daniell, Beth. 1999. "Narratives of Literacy: Connecting Composition to Culture." *College Composition and Communication* 50 (3): 393–410. https://doi.org/10.2307/358858.

Downs, Doug, and Elizabeth Wardle. 2012. "Reimagining the Nature of FYC Trends in Writing-about-Writing Pedagogies." In *Exploring Composition Studies: Sites, Issues, Perspectives*, ed. Kelly Ritter and Paul Kei Matsuda, 123–44. Logan: Utah State University Press.

Farmer, Frank. 2013. *After the Public Turn: Composition, Counterpublics, and the Citizen Bricoleur.* Logan: Utah State University Press.

Fulkerson, Richard. 2005. "Composition at the Turn of the Twenty-First Century." *College Composition and Communication* 56 (4): 654–87.

Giberson, Greg A., and Thomas A. Moriarty, eds. 2010. *What We Are Becoming: Developments in Undergraduate Writing Majors.* Logan: Utah State University Press. https://doi.org/10.2307/j.ctt4cgppw.

Giberson, Greg A., Jim Nugent, and Lori Ostergaard, eds. 2015. *Writing Majors: Eighteen Program Profiles.* Logan: Utah State University Press.

Gillam, Alice. 2001. "From Advanced Composition Courses to Advanced Writing Curriculum: The Difference between Lightning Bugs and Lightning." *WPA: Writing Program Administration* 24 (3): 99–102.

Goggin, Maureen Daly. 2000. *Authoring a Discipline: Scholarly Journals and the Post–World War II Emergence of Rhetoric and Composition*. Mahwah, NJ: Lawrence Erlbaum.

Hairston, Maxine. 1982. "The Winds of Change: Thomas Kuhn and the Revolution in the Teaching of Writing." *College Composition and Communication* 33 (1): 76–88. https://doi.org/10.2307/357846.

Haswell, Richard. 2005. "NCTE/CCCC's Recent War on Scholarship." *Written Communication* 22 (2): 198–223. https://doi.org/10.1177/0741088305275367.

Haswell, Richard. 2015. *"Re: Writing Pedagogy / 'The Essay' (Was Banks' Talk and Essay Writing)." WPA-L@ASU. EDU.*

Hayes, Carol. 2015. "New Research on the Transfer of Writing Knowledge and Practice and Its Implications for High-Impact Writing-Intensive Courses across the University." Association of American Colleges and Universities Conference.

Lynch, Paul. 2014. "Composition's New Thing: Bruno Latour and the Apocalyptic Turn." *College English* 74 (5): 458–75.

McLeod, Sue. 2006. "Review." *WPA: Writing Program Administration* 29 (3): 107–10.

Miller, Susan. 1994. "Things Inanimate May Move: A Different History of Writing and Class." *College Composition and Communication* 45 (1): 102–107. https://doi.org/10.2307/358591.

Phelps, Louise Wetherbee, and John M. Ackerman. 2010. "Making the Case for Disciplinarity in Rhetoric, Composition, and Writing Studies: The Visibility Project." *College Composition and Communication* 62 (1): 180–215.

Skinnell, Ryan. 2016. *Conceding Composition*. Logan: Utah State University Press.

Taczak, Kara, and Liane Robertson. 2016. "Reiterative Reflection in the 21st Century Writing Classroom: An Integrated Approach to Teaching for Transfer." In *A Rhetoric of Reflection*, ed. Kathleen Blake Yancey, 42–63. Logan: Utah State University Press. https://doi.org/10.7330/9781607325161.c003.

Tade, George, Gary Tate, and Jim Corder. 1975. "For Sale, Lease, or Rent: A Curriculum for an Undergraduate Program in Rhetoric." *College Composition and Communication* 26 (1): 20–24. https://doi.org/10.2307/356794.

Trimbur, John. 1994. "Taking the Social Turn: Teaching Writing Post-Process." *College Composition and Communication* 45 (1): 108–18. https://doi.org/10.2307/358592.

Trimbur, John. 2000. "Theory of Visual Design." In *Coming of Age: The Advanced Writing Curriculum*, ed. Linda K. Shamoon, Rebecca Moore Howard, Sandra Jamieson, and Robert A. Schwegler, 106–14. Portsmouth, NH: Heinemann Boynton/Cook.

Yancey, Kathleen Blake. 2004. "Made Not Only in Words: Composition for a New Key." *College Composition and Communication* 56 (2): 297–328. https://doi.org/10.2307/4140651.

Yancey, Kathleen Blake. 2010. "From the Editor: Designing the Future." *College Composition and Communication* 62 (1): 5–10.

Yancey, Kathleen Blake, Liane Robertson, and Kara Taczak. 2014. *Writing across Contexts: Transfer, Composition, and Sites of Writing*. Logan: Utah State University Press.

# 2
# MY DISCIPLINARY HISTORY
## A Personal Account

Barry Maid

Those of us who have spent the last part of the twentieth century and the first part of the twenty-first century teaching and studying writing have experienced careers characterized, pretty continuously, by discussion of the legitimacy of our endeavor. Like those of so many of our generation, my career has also been marked by the constant debates and discussions about the both the definition and the place of Writing Studies.[1] While countless numbers of these debates have taken place in our own academic units and universities, the discussion also seems to be an endless part of a much larger national conversation. I expect many of us may sometimes feel almost Forrest Gump–like as we live through various defining moments in our profession and careers.

In this chapter and drawing on my career, I relate three vignettes where my own professional story intersected with significant events in Writing Studies. The three moments, some of which I played a role in and others where I was only an observer, included

- Lee Odell's Keynote Address to the inaugural meeting of the SUNY Council on Writing in 1980
- Maxine Hairston's "Breaking Our Bonds" address at CCCC in 1985 and the creation of the Department of Rhetoric and Writing at the University of Arkansas at Little Rock (UALR) in 1993, and finally
- the creation of the independent Technical Communication program at Arizona State University (ASU) in 2000 and its eventual absorption into an amorphous humanities unit as a result of "austerity" in 2009.

To provide some context for these events, especially the early ones, I provide a brief timeline of what was happening in Writing Studies in those early years; while the list may appear idiosyncratic, it also indicates that several momentous events were taking place inside of a single decade.

1974 Creation of the Bay Area (later National) Writing Project
1976 Peter Elbow publishes *Writing without Teachers*
1976 *Writing Lab Newsletter* begins publication
1977 Mina Shaughnessy publishes *Errors and Expectations*
1977 Charles Cooper and Lee Odell publish *Evaluating Writing: Describing, Measuring, Judging*
1978 Council of Writing Program Administrators (CWPA) founded
1978 Charles Cooper and Lee Odell publish *Research on Composing: Points of Departure*
1983 National (later International) Writing Centers Association founded

## MOMENT ONE, 1980: IN WHICH A NEWCOMER HEARS LEE ODELL DECLARE THAT COMPOSITION IS A DISCIPLINE

In the fall of 1979, during my first few months of working in a staff position as a "Writing Skills Specialist" for the Special Services Project at the State University of New York (SUNY)–Plattsburgh, I attended what proved to be the organizational meeting of the first incarnation of the SUNY Council on Writing. Those of us attending decreed ourselves a steering committee and decided, among other things, to hold a systemwide conference in the spring of 1980. I enthusiastically and naively agreed to be program chair for the conference, and we named it "Composition: A Discipline." Prior to being the organizer of this conference, I didn't think about the importance of disciplinarity. When someone suggested the theme of the conference, I thought it was a good idea, though I'm not really sure why, perhaps because my own experience with Writing Studies was limited. As a graduate student in the English Department at the University of Massachusetts–Amherst, I had been exposed to teaching writing as a teaching assistant (TA) in the university's Rhetoric Program. Although engaged in writing a dissertation in literary studies, I was fortunate to be doing so at the same time that Charles Moran, C. Kay Smith, and Walker Gibson were doing National Endowment for the Humanities (NEH) summer institutes for high school teachers on teaching writing. Moran knew that through my teaching I had developed an interest in the teaching of writing, and he kept giving me copies of the reading lists he and his colleagues had developed for the institutes. That was my introduction to what I later came to understand was a field and led to my obtaining the job at SUNY-Plattsburgh. I only remember four of the books on the list: *Errors and Expectations*; *Writing without Teachers*; and the two Cooper and Odell volumes, *Evaluating Writing* and *Research on Composing*. All four had an impact on me, but when faced with the task of finding a keynote speaker to talk about Composition being a discipline, the obvious choice at that time was Lee Odell, especially since he was teaching at SUNY-Albany. I had never met Odell: in the late 1970s, he was already a star in Writing Studies, and I was barely a beginner. Still, I wrote Odell a letter inviting him to speak. He graciously accepted and gave a keynote address that set me thinking about questions that would engage my entire career.

The initial conference held on May 3, 1980, was targeted toward faculty teaching in the SUNY system and attracted sixty-seven attendees, fairly evenly split between faculty from two-year and four-year campuses, only one of whom was not affiliated with SUNY. In addition to Odell's address, there were breakout sections focusing on multiple topics:

- A SUNY-wide organization to promote Composition
- activities to promote effective teaching in Composition
- SUNY-wide testing for placement, minimum competence, and so on
- entrance, exit, and placement standards
- writing across the curriculum
- coordination of research, experimentation, and communication
- a SUNY journal for Composition
- remedial/developmental courses and credit.

Odell titled his keynote "Composition as a Discipline: What We Know and What We Need to Know." He began his talk with the idea of Composition as a discipline: "The theme of our meeting today is that composition is in fact a discipline: that we have some reasonably well-founded insights into the processes and structures of writing; that we have procedures for testing these insights and formulating new ones; that we know enough about our field to agree upon what we still need to know" (Odell 1980, 11).

However, we should also note that Odell's next sentence after this passage reads, "One must be cautious about pronouncing this theme too confidently. It's too easy for a group of like-minded people to agree with one another, especially when that agreement signifies their own importance" (11). In fact anticipating his audience's predilection, Odell says:

> So my purpose is not to discredit, to refute completely. My purpose here is to lead up to this assumption: Every bit of theory, every bit of pedagogy, every bit of practical advice must be carefully tested against the actual practice of writers. If we want to claim we have a discipline, we must be willing to test all our assumptions. And we must be willing to modify or discard those assumptions that are not borne out by the practice of writers. Otherwise, we run the risk of making sweeping pronouncements that

are only partially true or even misleading, to students who need all the good, valid advice they can get. (13–14)

Odell divides the rest of his talk into three sections: "The Process of Composition," "Audience and Purpose," and "Evaluation." In all three sections, he starts by using the textbooks of the 1960s as a baseline to show how Writing Studies had progressed by 1980. In the first section he mentions the work of Janet Emig, Richard Young, Donald Murray, and Peter Elbow as helping us better understand the importance of process. In the second section he calls those 1960s "a-rhetorical," and then goes on to cite the work of Walker Gibson, James Moffett, and James Kinneavy as helping us return to Aristotle and rhetoric. Finally, in the last section, after mentioning that the 1960s were not very helpful with regard to evaluation, he reiterates the substance of the 1977 collection, *Evaluating Writing*, which he coedited with Charles Cooper.

That SUNY conference and Odell's talk were a watershed for me. Perhaps that conference had more impact on me than others as a result of my role in the conference, which involved my chairing it and meeting and interacting with Lee Odell, one of my academic heroes. Coordinating the conference also helped to establish my credentials as a "compositionist." Odell also started me thinking about what it meant to be a discipline: if Odell were right, and I saw no reason to doubt him, anyone looking at our field and what we do would naturally come to the same conclusion. Obviously, my assumption from thirty-five years ago was wrong, given that we're still having the discussion. Put another way, there is clearly more to the issue than what I still see as Odell's well-reasoned and commonsense approach.

That first SUNY conference had a real impact on me, though I sometimes wonder if it was only on me. I've since asked Odell if he has further memories beyond giving the talk, and he doesn't. It was a long time ago. In looking at the list of attendees of that conference, it's jarring to note how few would be recognizable to the members of today's Writing Studies community.[2] Still, aside from the topic of the conference and the keynote, I would call that SUNY conference ordinary; it was simply a group of people who were committed to teaching and studying writing gathering to talk about their shared interests. It is an ordinary thing for people in an academic discipline to do just that.

Still, maybe there was something in the air in New York State in 1980. In October of that year, a little farther north from the Albany SUNY conference, Skidmore College sponsored a conference called The Writer's Mind, and some of the presentations were published in the 1983 NCTE collection *The Writer's Mind*, edited by conference organizers Janice

Hays, Phyllis Roth, Jon Ramsey, and Robert D. Foulke (Hays et al. 1983). I also attended the Skidmore conference; however, I needed to wait till 1985 for another conference event to exert a significant impact on me.

## MOMENT 2, 1985: IN WHICH I DISCOVER THAT MAXINE HAIRSTON IS WISE AND RIGHT

In 1980 I was convinced that Writing Studies would naturally evolve into being another discipline comfortably housed in college English departments. In 1981, based on that belief, I happily accepted the position of assistant professor of English at the University of Arkansas at Little Rock (UALR). I was their first Composition hire; I was the first faculty hire who was to teach writing exclusively, which was made clear to me when I was hired; and it was hinted by the search committee and department chair that I was to help them develop an MA in the teaching of writing. Upon arriving in Little Rock, I discovered that I also would be codirecting a new writing center with Sally Crisp, as well as assisting the writing program administrator (WPA), John Stratton, in supervising part-time faculty who taught first-year composition.[3] At the time, this all felt very good, and it would be easy to spin it as idyllic.

It's also helpful to understand what position Writing Studies held in Little Rock in 1981. First-Year Writing (FYW) produced the most student semester credit hours (SSCH) in the department. There were more sections of the three FYW courses—Composition Fundamentals (a basic writing class that in 1981 still could be taken for college credit), Composition I and Composition II—than in the rest of the English curriculum. All faculty taught FYW as at least half of their four course load, some of them grudgingly. The 1981 UALR English faculty wanted FYW to deliver good writing instruction—though they might not have known what that looked like. Like most academics, they wanted their students to be good writers, and they also saw teaching writing as part of their job as English faculty. In hiring me, they fantasized I would save them all from the Composition burden, which I did, though not in a way any of us imagined in 1981.

Although most of the faculty preferred not to teach writing, some of my colleagues were seriously invested in teaching FYW. Three of them had published FYW textbooks (of a current-traditional flavor) with major textbook houses. Two more were finishing up a trade publication on grammar and usage. Several more believed in teaching FYW because it was a kind of "badge of honor." None of them had any training in teaching writing beyond what they might have picked up as TAs when they were in graduate school, and that was also current-traditional.

My first year at UALR I taught two sections of FYW each semester; I also split time in a new writing center with Sally Crisp. In that first year, we were the only ones doing tutoring. (It wasn't until several years later, when I was WPA and Crisp was the full-time director of the writing center, that we developed a means to train and pay peer tutors.) The other quarter of my time during that first year was spent working with John Stratton, a Shakespearean serving as WPA, to supervise the twenty-something part-time instructors teaching FYW, which included my visiting the part-timers' classes. This was the first time classroom visitation had been done at UALR, and most of the instructors were terrified of me, the young, new Composition expert who was to pass judgment on their teaching. I've come to realize that the group of part-timers we had at UALR in 1981 was typical, but I didn't realize it then. Up to that point my only experience with part-time faculty occurred when I was one while finishing my PhD, when the other part-timers were my fellow grad students. In contrast, the part-timers at UALR were a group of people who found themselves in Little Rock but differed in their circumstances. Some had MAs in English and were looking for full-time work, some were stay-at-home moms who wanted to get out of the house, some were high school English teachers who wanted some extra work, and some were technical writers who liked maintaining a connection to the university. Likewise, the range of abilities in those instructors was wide: some were good writing teachers because they had good instincts and paid attention to their students as writers, but the most knowledgeable, in terms of writing pedagogy, tended to be the high school teachers who kept up with NCTE publications.

In the fall of 1982, after only one year, I became WPA. Between 1982 and 1984, we were able to develop the MA in Technical and Expository Writing and get it approved by the state boards. We also were able to write some grants that led to what was called "Quality Writing" money from the state, funds we used to support a National Writing Project site and some conference travel. We also hired full-time tenure track faculty—five by 1985. The writing programs at UALR seemed to be moving in a very positive direction.

As a result of the new travel funding, I traveled in 1985 to Minneapolis to my first CCCC. There I listened to Maxine Hairston present the Chair's Address, "Breaking Our Bonds and Reaffirming Our Connections." I have written elsewhere of that experience, summing up my response as: "I was too young, too naïve in my own profession, and too profoundly untenured to understand the accuracy of her perceptions and the depth of her wisdom" (Maid 2006, 104).

What do Hairston's views as exemplified in "Breaking Our Bonds" add to our conversation about disciplinarity? Hairston's Chair's Address was a public plea to get Writing Studies out of English Departments—at the least "psychologically," if not physically and administratively. Later published in *CCC*, it has become legendary, and at the time, it was even more revolutionary. While it was one thing for us to assert that Writing Studies was its own discipline, to argue that it should be removed in any way from English departments was new—to me, at least. It also felt a bit scary. Almost all of us in Writing Studies at the time were products of English departments, which provided a comfortable and secure home that Hairston was advising us to leave. Hairston's reasons, however, are not those based on arguments of traditional definitions of academic disciplinarity, but rather on disciplinary and institutional power structures. Hairston (1985) calls on us to "break our bonds—not necessarily physically, although in some cases that may be a good idea—but emotionally and intellectually. I think that as rhetoricians and writing teachers we will come of age and become autonomous professionals with a discipline of our own only if we can make a psychological break with the literary critics who today dominate the profession of English studies" (273).

I went back to Little Rock after listening to but not fully comprehending Hairston, and two years later I was tenured and elected chair of the English Department. If I were thinking about Hairston's words at that time, I assumed they didn't apply to my department. But others understood what I didn't. At the CCCC in Atlanta in 1987 after it became known that I was to become chair of English at UALR, I was approached by Elizabeth Cowan Neeld, who took both of my hands, looked me straight in the eye, and said, "You will be the only writing person who chairs an English Department. Remember what that can mean." From her role as Director of English Programs for MLA in the 1970s, she understood what it meant to have a writing person chair an English department. I learned the hard way.

My writing colleagues and I were able to do good things within the English department—hiring tenure-track writing faculty, developing the MA, taking over the chairship. We accomplished a lot, but, as I've written elsewhere (Maid 2001, 2006), the Writing Studies faculty at UALR ultimately hit a wall built by English Department faculty and their culture. In this way, UALR is representative, not only of many college English departments in the early 1980s, but also of many current English departments (see Rhoades, Gunter, and Carroll 2016). After six years of being chair of English, of consistently defending the notion of a big tent English Department, everything fell apart. I stepped back and wrote to the provost that we needed to be separate.[4] After much deliberation and many memos from faculty and administrators, the Provost decided to create the Department of Rhetoric and Writing.

Many academics don't think much about institutional organization. Their focus tends to be more on how they work within their discipline; I know I used to think that way. The creation of the Department of Rhetoric and Writing at UALR made me change my perspective.

After writing moved outside of English and started on its own, something changed. Like many people who run writing programs, I had previously experienced considerable contact with colleagues and administrators across the university and had always been treated well, and with respect. But after our separation from English, my whole unit seemed to attain a new degree of respect around the campus. Many of the non-tenure-track instructors, for example, were now fully accepted in Rhetoric and Writing and also accepted by others across the university.[5] I finally realized that location doesn't only matter in real estate; it clearly matters in university organizational charts.

Most narratives about the creation of independent writing units focus on the situation leading up to the start of the new unit. They are full of joy and hope. Less has been said about what happens the "morning after." One of the most significant changes in the new department was opening up teaching opportunities for the full-time instructors. In English they had been restricted to teaching FYW because that's what they had been hired to do. Once the new unit was created, it took along with it an already established MA degree in Technical and Expository Writing and a BA degree in Professional and Technical Writing, so there were new staffing needs. In English, only people with PhDs were allowed to teach upper-level classes. As a result some literature PhDs, most with no expertise in writing, were teaching in a writing major and graduate program. Some of the non-tenure-track instructors, by training and experience, were clearly qualified to teach some of the upper-level undergraduate courses. That happened quickly and without any dissent from the tenured writing faculty. I expect while there was a curricular need, the general agreement occurred because the new unit shared a belief common in Writing Studies: our primary responsibility, for all of us, was to teach writing. With the enthusiasm that came with independence, it made little difference whether it was a first-year or a senior class. In retrospect, though I may be viewing this time as a kind of idyllic past, it resulted from a fortunate local condition. The creation of the non-tenure-track lines several years before the split and the tensions leading up to the split led to a kind of professional solidarity among all the writing faculty.

The second most significant change in the new Rhetoric and Writing Department was the graduate program, an MA in Technical and Expository Writing. I'm convinced one of the primary reasons the provost moved to create the new department was that the stewardship of the graduate program in the English department was weak. Before the split, even though there was no graduate program in literature at UALR, the graduate coordinator position was elected by the faculty and held by a specialist in modern poetry. He tried to be conscientious, but he didn't know the field, which clearly concerned both the dean and the provost. Once the new unit was formed, a writing person coordinated the graduate program. Before the split, the graduate program, while attracting some good students, was small, but its most troublesome problem was that students would finish their coursework yet not complete their final project and get the degree. (In retrospect, this seems to have been a combination of a graduate coordinator who didn't really understand the program, and students who were receiving no guidance when faced with a task they had never encountered before.) That changed when Chuck Anderson became graduate coordinator. Anderson did many good things as graduate coordinator, but the most significant change he made, one that significantly increased the degree-completion rate, was to take the six hours of final project (thesis, applied project, or internship) and turn them into two courses, one a three-hour course preparing students to write the project, and a second three-hour segment to be supervised by the student's committee chair. Looking back, it's hard to imagine why in English we assigned students a major writing task they had no experience with without giving them some kind of guidance. Giving guidance is just good writing pedagogy.

Departmentally, we succeeded. UALR had an annual award for what they called the Department of Excellence. The Department of Rhetoric and Writing was one of the first departments to receive the award in the late 1990s. It accomplished that in fewer than seven years of existence.

My Little Rock experience taught me much about the relationship of disciplinarity to academic organization. Most significant was that if a faculty is going to be most productive, including reaching across disciplines for collaboration, they must have a clear sense of security in their own disciplinary home. That security is impossible when their primary need is to consistently prove their own legitimacy to the other members of their home unit.

## MOMENT 3, 2009: IN WHICH I LEARN THAT THINGS DON'T ALWAYS GO AS PLANNED

I took the lessons I learned in Little Rock to Arizona, when in 2000 I was hired by Arizona State to start the first technical communication program in Arizona. During my negotiations with David Schwalm (who was vice provost and dean, and a Writing Studies scholar), I was happy to learn that he agreed with me that the unit must stand on its own—outside of English. Initially we would start as a separate program and then move toward department status. After just a year or two, we were operating as a department would, including having our own budget. The only reason we were not a full-fledged department is that we were missing the requisite number of full-time faculty, which Schwalm had pegged at five. By the fall of 2008, we had reached four, were growing our major, were talking about a graduate program, and had strong working relationships with colleagues in other disciplines—especially those areas where we offered service courses.

Initially, we offered a service course for the engineering technology programs on the Polytechnic (originally East) Campus. When a small general engineering program began on campus, we worked with them as well. I had also worked with the head of the business program on our campus to create a business communication class as a required service class, which was also accepted in the College of Business on the Tempe campus. We had recently revised our business communication curriculum by working closely with the business faculty and some of their external stakeholders (D'Angelo and White 2009). In addition, we were talking with the Nutrition Department about possible courses, and I was also having some preliminary discussions with an associate dean of engineering in Tempe.

In the spring of 2009 everything changed. A new provost reorganized all of ASU, and we became part of a unit called Interdisciplinary Humanities and Communication. In that shift, we lost our identity, and most of the collaborations stopped. For the most part, no one at ASU even knows we exist anymore outside of our own college, which essentially serves as a home for general studies courses for two campuses and for generic undergraduate degrees (e.g., Bachelor of General Studies, Bachelor of Interdisciplinary Studies, and the like). Except for a productive collaboration with one of ASU's nursing programs, most of that time has felt like "wheel-spinning." Just before the reorganization, my colleague Barbara D'Angelo and I had started to work with ASU's RN-to-BSN program to create an applied writing course for their program, which required an interesting balance between academic writing and workplace writing. More recently, after the hire of a new program head,

Eva Brumberger, ASU finally approved an MS in Technical Communication. (The program was originally scheduled to be approved the day the reorganization was announced in 2009.) Most hopeful for the program, even though it still seems to be institutionally invisible, is that in the first year of the graduate degree, we already have thirty-five students. As the faculty begin to prepare to work with students on finishing their projects, we're seeing signs of greater collaborations among the technical communication faculty. It will be interesting to see what the dynamic of our program with relation to rest of Interdisciplinary Humanities and Communications becomes as we continue to grow both in number of students and faculty.

### LESSONS I'VE LEARNED: TURN OUTWARD AND LOCATION MATTERS

I've learned two very important lessons from these experiences: (1) that we must turn our attention outward, and (2) that our location matters.

*Lesson 1: Turn Outward*

My lesson from helping to create the Department of Rhetoric and Writing at UALR and the Technical Communication program at ASU, though admittedly anecdotal, is that doing all the right academic things is necessary but not sufficient if we want to succeed and flourish. We must, as Hairston states, be professional—research, write, publish; that is, do all those things that are expected of academics. However, until we are on our own—not just with our own budget that may or not be controlled by a department chair but with budgetary control equivalent to all other academic units, with complete control over our own curriculum, and control over our own hiring and promotion and tenure practices—we will never be seen as equals within the academy. Hairston suggests that if we can break the psychological bonds, we might be able to stay within an English department. I think once those bonds have been broken, it's impossible to stay. Others may see it differently, but from my perspective, it's similar to adult children attaining maturity and moving out. While those children sometimes return, the relationship is different and often very strained. Once attaining disciplinary maturity, it's best to move out of the old department. As long as we stay inside of English—even when the relationship appears good—we will never be seen as a real discipline by those outside the field. As my own experiences demonstrate, how others see us matters.

I am committed to the idea that we as members of the field (teachers, students, researchers, scholars) must actively help our external audiences understand us, and I am not alone. In their 2010 *CCC* article, "Making the Case for Disciplinarity in Rhetoric, Composition, and Writing Studies: The Visibility Project," Louise Wetherbee Phelps and John M. Ackerman tell the story of how the very aptly named Visibility Project, an effort of the Consortium of Doctoral Programs in Rhetoric and Composition, managed to get the National Research Council (NRC) to have Rhetoric and Composition / Writing Studies recognized as an "emerging discipline" in their taxonomy of research disciplines. In addition, they ensured that Rhetoric and Composition / Writing Studies was assigned a code in the federal Classification of Instructional Programs (CIP) (Phelps and Ackerman 2010). For a discipline to be recognized by the NRC means that researchers in that discipline have access to certain kind of federal research funds, and CIP codes are the way that institutions report graduates and are often reflected in funding models.

Most academics below the dean level don't get the opportunity to see and understand how institutions really work and especially interact with state and federal bureaucracies and regional accrediting agencies. Although I have served as a unit head in two institutions, my experience with the "bigger picture" took place because I served as chair of the Chair's Council for two years at UALR. That position gave me a seat in the Chancellor's Cabinet, which was comprised of the provost, the deans, all the vice-chancellors, the president of the faculty senate, and me in my role as chair of the chair's group. I learned an incredible amount about how higher education in America works in those two years. Having that knowledge, I am especially impressed and thankful for the work of the Visibility Project. I understand how difficult their task was, not only to accomplish but to even begin to undertake.

For most academics, doing the right kind of academic work is what's important in defining a discipline, a sentiment with an internal focus. Too often, as academics we find ourselves talking to ourselves. When Odell gave his 1980 keynote, he was speaking to an internal audience. Likewise, when Janice Lauer (1984) writes "Composition Studies: Dappled Discipline," she is "preaching to the choir." At some level, this is natural: we have an affinity for others who do what we do; we attend conferences and present on our research and listen to presentations by others who do what we do. However, if we are to be generally accepted as a discipline, like other disciplines, we need to do more than talk to ourselves. If my widely shared experiences and the work of the Visibility Project tell us anything, it is that we need to be conscious of how we are viewed by others. In fact, we need to follow up on the work of the Visibility Project by helping our multiple external audiences understand who we are and what we do and that we are, indeed, a legitimate and widely accepted academic discipline, a point echoed in Linda Adler-Kassner's chapter in this collection.

*Lesson 2: Location Matters*

I understand that institutional organizations may vary and that, especially at small liberal arts colleges (SLACs) and community colleges, departments as we know them at larger four-year institutions may not exist. Still, since I have argued that how others view us is crucial to our existence as a discipline, where we are located on our institution's organizational chart, and sometimes in relation to other recognized disciplines, is crucial. That said, the only sensible place for Writing Studies to be is in a department or school of Writing Studies. The head of the unit, be it a head, chair, or director, must report to a dean—or in some cases, if the unit is a school, to the provost.

Aside from the greater visibility that comes with being a department or school, there are at least three characteristics of academic units that are crucial for the unit to be successful in practicing its discipline and successfully delivering degree programs:

1. The unit must have budgetary control, insofar as all other academic units have budgetary control.
2. The unit must have curricular control.
3. The unit must have control over hires and tenure and promotion.

Without budgetary, curricular, hiring, and promotion and tenure control, units are incapable of consistently developing and delivering degree programs, and ultimately, they must offer degrees. Just being an independent service unit is not enough. While delivering those services is important, only degree-offering units will be seen as peers by the rest of the university. When writing programs are embedded in other units, appropriate allocation of resources, curriculum development, hiring, and promotion and tenure are necessarily contingent on those from outside the discipline. Based on my own experience as chair of a big-tent English department, I suggest that there is no greater indicator of divergent disciplinary values than in deciding those large issues. Colleagues who may agree on many things and have good personal relationships can vehemently disagree on issues of curriculum, hiring, and promotion and tenure when their individual disciplinary perspectives collide.

Indeed, in thinking back over my time as chair of English at UALR, the most bitter conflicts (aside from those that were merely personality based) were those that seemed to occur at annual review time. In retrospect, I can say that the conflicts occurred because the two disciplines, Writing Studies and English, valued different kinds of professional work. English valued traditional academic work that, when published, targeted a highly specific academic audience. Writing Studies valued multiple kinds of applied research, which was often published for a larger professional public than a small group of like-minded academics. Neither is right or wrong. They are merely different. While having a writing person or a "friend of the writing program" as chair might make things more palatable, no program is sustainable when its success is based on the accident of who is elected or appointed to lead the department.

Over the last thirty-five years, we have proven to ourselves that we are a full-fledged academic discipline. The chapter by Gwendolynne Reid and Carolyn R. Miller in this collection, for example, helps to define what academic audiences mean by disciplinarity and where Writing Studies fits. Likewise, Elizabeth Wardle and Doug Downs' chapter gives the academic perspective on disciplinarity, but also, as part of their definition, calls for us to attend to how the discipline is viewed by others—especially outside of the academy. We now are more likely to understand that to be truly accepted as a discipline it is necessary to have others understand us in that role and understand who we are and what we do. The single most powerful way to accomplish that is for us to be housed in independent units of Writing Studies.

## SO WHERE DO WE STAND?

When first thinking about why we are having the same discussion I was first introduced to thirty-five years ago, I was disheartened. My initial reaction was that during my entire career not much had changed. Then, in looking more closely at the state of our discipline, I can see that much has changed—and for the better. Among ourselves there is no question that we are a solid, respectable academic discipline. While the Department of Writing Studies at the University of Minnesota dates from 1909, in the last two decades, we have seen the number of independent writing departments continue to increase significantly. Now we simply need to continue down the path that will better explain to those outside of our field who we are and what we do.

# APPENDIX: ATTENDEES AT THE FIRST SUNY COUNCIL ON WRITING CONFERENCE

| Participant | Academic Institution |
|---|---|
| Inez Alfors | SUC Oswego |
| Suzanne Allen | SUNY Binghamton |
| Frank Anastasio | Corning CC |
| Gabriel J. Barra | SUNY Ag and Tech, Canton |
| Eleanor Bartholomae | SUNY Stony Brook |
| Libby Bay | Rockland CC |
| Sidney R. Bender | Genesee CC |
| Myra Berman | SUNY Stony Brook |
| David S. Betts | SUC Oneonta |
| Edwin Blech | Nassau CC |
| Jeri Brown | SUC Plattsburgh |
| Joseph Cambridge | Tompkins Cortland CC |
| Paul W. Cannon | SUC Oneonta |
| Gladyss W. Church | SUC Brockport |
| Mark Coleman | SUC Potsdam |
| Aniko Constantine | SUNY Ag and Tech, Alfred |
| Pat Coward | SUC Oswego |
| Antonia Dempster | Genesee CC |
| Louise M. DiCerbo | SUNY Ag and Tech, Cobbleskill |
| John Dwyer | SUNY Buffalo |
| Sandra Engel | Mohawk Valley CC |
| Janet Foresman | Clinton CC |
| Eugene K. Garber | SUNY Albany |
| Steve Hauptman | SUNY Stony Brook |
| Warren Herendeen | Mercy College |
| David W. Hill | SUC Oswego |
| Kate Hymes | SUC New Paltz |
| Joseph Inners | Suffolk County CC |
| Nancy Ives | SUC Geneseo |
| Scott Johnson | Suffolk County CC |

*My Disciplinary History* 51

| Participant | Academic Institution |
|---|---|
| Walter Johnston | SUNY Utica, Potter Sch. |
| Joseph Keefe | Ulster County CC |
| Eva Kerr | SUNY College of Tech, Utica |
| Bernice W. Kliman | Nassau CC |
| Kenneth MacKenzie | SUNY Administration |
| Frederick Madeo | Sullivan County CC |
| Barry Maid | SUC Plattsburgh |
| Robert Markes | Ulster County CC |
| Kathleen Martin | SUNY Ag and Tech, Delhi |
| Donald Masterson | SUC Oswego |
| Glenn A. Mayer | SUC Oneonta |
| Neil McAdorey | SUNY Ag and Tech, Farmingdale |
| Robert Moore | SUC Oswego |
| Thomas J. Morrissey | SUC Plattsburgh |
| Lee Odell | SUNY Albany |
| Raymond Osborne | Herkimer County CC |
| Donald G. Parker | Orange County CC |
| Elizabeth Pasti | SUC Plattsburgh |
| Barbara K. Rhodes | SUC Geneseo |
| Richard J. Ring | Adirondack CC |
| Carol Roper | Dutchess CC |
| Joseph K. Schwartz | Ulster County CC |
| Janet Selby | SUC Cortland |
| Patricia Silber | SUNY Stony Brook |
| Annelise Smith | SUNY Ag and Tech, Cobbleskill |
| R. E. Thorstensen | SUNY Albany |
| David Tobin | Niagara County CC |
| Elizabeth Tricomi | SUNY Binghamton |
| Tony Tyler | SUC Potsdam |
| Sara Varhus | SUC Oswego |
| Sindy Weiner | Adirondack CC |
| Mary Wiecha | SUC Oswego |
| Diana R. Wienbroer | Nassau CC |
| Don Wills | Mohawk Valley CC |
| Thomas J. Windt | SUNY Ag and Tech, Canton |
| Aline Wolff | SUC Purchase |
| Dale G. Yerpe | Jamestown CC |

*Note: SUC is for State University College*

## Notes

1. In this chapter I will refer to our field, our discipline, as Writing Studies. It may not be ideal, but it does describe who we are and what we study. It also is a term that is readily understandable to non-academics. I know more and more people are beginning to use Writing Studies both in their scholarly and casual conversation on our field. We are also seeing some academic units use the term "Writing Studies" in their name. My own reliance on the term is the result of much thought about what both describes us and makes sense.
2. The list of attendees and their institutions is in the Appendix.
3. I think it's important to notice how different the hiring world was in 1981. I accepted a tenure-track job, signed the hire letter, and moved to Little Rock. It was only after I actually arrived in town in August a few weeks before the school year began that my duties were given to me. Today, all of that would have been part of the initial negotiations.
4. For those interested in more specifics about what led to the creation of the Department of Rhetoric and Writing at UALR, I suggest they look at my chapter, "Creating Two Departments of Writing: One Past and One Future" (Maid 2002) in *A Field of Dreams*. My papers from that time are available at the National Archives of Composition and Rhetoric and the University of Rhode Island.
5. I have chronicled how the English Department hired full-time non-tenure-track instructors and how they were fully integrated into departmental life in Rhetoric and Writing in "Non-Tenure Track Instructors at UALR: Breaking Rules, Splitting Departments" (Maid 2001).

## References

D'Angelo, B. J., and O. White. 2009. "Learning from Our Stakeholders: Using Research to Redesign a Business Writing Course." Association for Business Communication Annual Convention, Lake Tahoe, NV.

Hairston, Maxine. 1985. "Breaking Our Bonds and Reaffirming Our Connections." *College Composition and Communication* 36 (3): 272–82.

Hays, J. N., P. A. Roth, J. R. Ramsey, and R. D. Foulke. 1983. *The Writer's Mind: Writing as a Mode of Thinking*. Urbana, IL: NCTE.

Lauer, J. M. 1984. "Composition Studies: Dappled Discipline." *Rhetoric Review* 3 (1): 20–29. https://doi.org/10.1080/07350198409359074.

Maid, B. M. 2001. "Non-Tenure Track Instructors at UALR: Breaking Rules, Splitting Departments." In *Moving a Mountain: Transforming the Role of Contingent Faculty in Composition Studies and Higher Education*, ed. E. E. Schell and P. L. Stock, 76–90. Urbana, IL: NCTE.

Maid, B. M. 2002. "Creating Two Departments of Writing: One Past and One Future." In *Field of Dreams*, ed. P. O'Neil, A. Crow, and L. Burton, 130–52. Logan: Utah State University Press.

Maid, B. M. 2006. "This Corner . . ." In *Composition and/or Literature*, ed. L. S. Bergmann and E. M. Baker, 93–108. Urbana, IL: NCTE.

Odell, L. 1980. "Keynote: Composition as a Discipline: What We Know and What We Need to Know." In *Composition: A Discipline* (conference program), 11–32. Albany, NY: SUNY Committee on Composition.

Phelps, L. W., and J. M. Ackerman. 2010. "Making the Case for Disciplinarity in Rhetoric, Composition, and Writing Studies: The Visibility Project." *College Composition and Communication* 62 (1): 180–215.

Rhoades, G., K. Gunter, and B. Carroll. 2016. "Support of Contingent Faculty: Lessons from an Ongoing Struggle for Writing Program Independence." In *Minefield of Dreams: Promises and Perils of Independent Writing Programs*, ed. J. Everett and C. Hanganu-Bresch, 133–48. Fort Collins, CO: WAC Clearinghouse.

# 3
# ACKNOWLEDGING DISCIPLINARY CONTRIBUTIONS
On the Importance of Community College Scholarship to Rhetoric and Composition

Rochelle Rodrigo and Susan Miller-Cochran

Mina Shaughnessy, Lynn Troyka, Howard Tinberg, Nell Ann Pickett, Diana Hacker. These are just a few of the community college faculty members and scholars who have made indelible impressions on Rhetoric and Composition, and they are widely acknowledged for their critical contributions to the discipline.[1] Three served as chairs of the Conference on College Composition and Communication (CCCC). They have written foundational studies and pedagogical resources about writing, and they are just a few of the many Rhetoric and Composition scholars who do immensely important work in the discipline and whose primary academic affiliation is with a community college.[2] As we discuss in this chapter, the scope of the influence of community college scholars in Rhetoric and Composition is vast, yet their work is not always recognized and valued either by their institutions or by the discipline. Our goal in this chapter is twofold: to acknowledge and highlight the quality of community college scholarship in Rhetoric and Composition, and to challenge how Rhetoric and Composition has historically defined "scholarship," which tends to exclude important scholarly work from many faculty in a variety of positions, institutions, and locations.

## WHAT IS (A) COMMUNITY COLLEGE SCHOLAR/SHIP?
First, we want to clarify how we are defining the boundaries of community college scholarship. When we discuss "community college faculty" or community colleges as sites of study, the possibilities are much more complex than they might initially seem, and the situation is much more fluid than these categories suggest. When identifying community college scholarship, we could include scholarship by teachers currently

DOI: 10.7330/9781607326953.c003

at community colleges, teachers who have been at community colleges but are now somewhere else, teachers who teach simultaneously at community colleges and other types of institutions, and scholars who study community colleges but might have never taught at one. As teachers and scholars, we are examples of that fluidity ourselves. While we both began our full-time teaching careers at community colleges, we have both also taught at two different four-year research universities. Yet, during our time at research universities, we both often taught as adjunct faculty at community colleges. One of us is currently teaching as an adjunct at a community college. As we refined our definition of community college scholarship, we found ourselves asking: should *this* chapter "count" as community college scholarship? Why? Because of the topic? Because of our prior experience? Since one of us is currently teaching one online course at a community college? Or does it not count as community college scholarship because we are not primarily teaching in or affiliated with a community college context? Other scholarship about and involving community colleges also falls into a complicated, liminal space. How, for example, should we categorize Mike Rose's 2012 book *Back to School: Why Everyone Deserves a Second Chance at Education*, which profiles the stories of students in an urban community college setting?

We argue that Rhetoric and Composition benefits from being more inclusive of all of these perspectives: scholarship written by community college faculty, scholarship that focuses on community colleges as sites of study, and scholarship that involves a combination of or variation of those perspectives. Without all of these kinds of scholarship, the discipline would be lessened because the community college context presents unique, complex, important opportunities for understanding and studying writing. Rhetoric and Composition must pay attention to these sites of teaching and learning for many reasons, including the number and diverse range of students who take writing courses at community colleges; Barry Alford (2001) highlights that 50 percent of first-year college students and over 40 percent of undergraduates take their foundational writing classes at community colleges (vii).

Drawing on a range of perspectives about/from/within community colleges can help accomplish the recentering that Holly Hassel and Joanne Baird Giordano called for when they urged that Rhetoric and Composition embrace "a scholarly reimagination that repositions two-year college teaching at the center of our disciplinary discourse about college composition" (Hassel and Giordano 2013, 118). In addition, Hassel and Giordano argue for "greater participation of two-year college faculty and contingent instructors in writing studies knowledge making"

(118) and support for "more research conducted at two-year colleges, research that can then inform the graduate training of instructors who will likely spend their teaching careers at such institutions" (134). We argue that to accomplish both of these goals, scholars at a variety of institutions and with a range of experience must focus their attention on community college perspectives and sites of study. Yet, we also argue that community college faculty and students should be involved in that research,[3] and Rhetoric and Composition scholars must guard against the colonization of community colleges as sites of study.

In addition to arguing that the perspectives of community college faculty members and their students are of great importance to Rhetoric and Composition, we also argue in this chapter that we must not assume that the experiences of all community college faculty and students are similar or that community college contexts are in any way homogenous. Karen Powers-Stubbs and Jeff Sommers highlight the range of community college faculty experiences, even for faculty teaching on the same campus or within the same system (Powers-Stubbs and Sommers 2001). In addition to the range of experiences of community college faculty members and the institutional contexts in which they work, the student population on community college campuses is shifting and increasingly diverse. Christopher Mullin (2012) explains these changing demographics in a report for the American Association of Community Colleges:

> Between 1993 and 2009, the student body—as defined by the distribution, not the number, of students—on community college campuses shifted. For instance, students under the age of 18 are increasingly enrolling in community colleges. While the student body is becoming increasingly younger, the characteristics of younger students are not homogenous across all sectors of higher education. Community college students have a greater proportion of students with various risk factors when compared to all of higher education. These colleges also provide access to nearly half of all minority undergraduate students and more than 40% of undergraduate students living in poverty. (4)

The range of students served by community colleges, and the ways that population of students changes over time, means that writing research needs to focus on community college contexts with persistent, ongoing attention. Indeed, this range of experiences and contexts is why it is of the utmost importance to engage with a multiplicity of voices in Rhetoric and Composition scholarship (including those, of course, beyond community college contexts).

We agree with Holly Hassel and Joanne Baird Giordano that "our profession must support more research conducted at two-year colleges, research that can then inform the graduate training of instructors who will likely spend their teaching careers at such institutions" (Hassel and Giordano 2013,134). However, we also argue that a great deal of work is already available; it is not, however, promoted and included in critical locations such as graduate courses and popular anthologies of scholarship in Rhetoric and Composition.

## ONGOING CONTRIBUTIONS TO THE DISCIPLINE

Community college scholars are and have been engaging in extensive inquiry and knowledge-making in the discipline, and there is more activity going on than the larger discipline often acknowledges. Mark Reynolds (2005) highlights what some of the most important contributions are from community college scholars of Rhetoric and Composition, explaining that it is their "teaching expertise" (8) from which we might learn the most. While we do not in any way argue that Rhetoric and Composition is only a "teaching subject" (Harris 1997), these contributions certainly make a difference in the discipline's research about and understanding of writing and teaching writing, as we outline later in this section. Reynolds (2005) lists several kinds of knowledge-making that community college faculty frequently engage in: explorations of teaching expertise, media and technology in teaching and learning, research about the development of writing centers, cross-disciplinary interaction and scholarship, and research on working with nontraditional students.[4]

Yet community college faculty contribute to the discipline in multiple ways, not just through dialogue about teaching or by engaging in what Stephen M. North (1987) terms "practitioner lore." In a position statement titled *Research and Scholarship in the Two-Year College*, the Two-Year College English Association (TYCA) identifies and provides examples of several categories of research in Rhetoric and Composition to which community college faculty actively contribute: data-driven research about writing, literary/biographical research, historical research, research about the profession, research about teaching with digital media, general pedagogical research, research about assessment, and creative work (Two-Year College English Association 2010). The TYCA statement draws on each of Ernest Boyer's (1990) four categories of scholarship (discovery, integration, application, and teaching and learning), demonstrating that community college faculty are engaged at all levels. The reference list at the end of the statement provides recent examples of over four dozen publications by community college faculty in Rhetoric and Composition in these areas.

Patrick Sullivan and Howard Tinberg's edited collection titled *What Is "College-Level" Writing?* offers a prominent example of how the unique position of community college faculty can enrich disciplinary dialogue about writing instruction (Sullivan and Tinberg 2006). Their collection, while certainly not focusing exclusively on community college contexts, includes those contexts and voices as a central part of the scholarly conversation about defining "college-level writing." Indeed, because teaching comprises the primary focus of their professional positions, community college scholars contribute significantly to the ongoing dialogue about how to teach and learn effectively in writing classes.

Many scholars currently or formerly in community colleges use their unique institutional locations to situate the main topic and contribution of their scholarship, yet their work is also relevant to teachers and administrators in contexts beyond community colleges[5]. For example, while many scholars in contexts outside of community colleges also teach and produce scholarship on basic and/or developmental writing, this has been a prominent research interest for many community college scholars in the last forty years since Mina Shaughnessy (1977) first published *Errors and Expectations*.[6] One of the current editors of the *Journal of Basic Writing*, Hope Parisi, is a community college faculty member. Similarly, several community college faculty have contributed to the growing amount of scholarship on digital course design and instructional technologies.[7] Jody Millward's (2008) study provides an overview of how writing technologies are being used by community college faculty through primary data collected as part of the TYCA Research Initiative. As community college faculty, we wrote about online course design (Miller-Cochran and Rodrigo 2006) and coedited a collection about usability from a rhetorical perspective (Miller-Cochran and Rodrigo 2009).

Community colleges have a long history of working with diverse student populations, stemming from their history as open admissions institutions. As part of a special issue marking the fiftieth anniversary of *CCC*, Cynthia Lewiecki-Wilson and Jeff Sommers argue that Rhetoric and Composition faculty should see open admissions composition teaching as an intellectually productive and transformative site of disciplinary practice (Lewiecki-Wilson and Sommers 1999).[8] Community college scholars also work with a great deal of language diversity in their classes, and they address that diversity in productive ways in their scholarship. Yu Ren Dong (1999) argues for teachers to understand ESL students' writing experiences in their native language. One of us (Miller-Cochran 2012), wrote about the possibilities of teaching cross-cultural composition for making language diversity part of the community college writing curriculum. And acknowledging important pedagogical connections between language diversity and basic writing, Deborah M. Sánchez and Eric J. Paulson argue for teachers to use Critical Language Awareness in basic writing classes (Sánchez and Paulson 2008).[9]

Community college scholars not only produce scholarship about teaching and learning, especially in the community college setting, but they also produce meta-scholarship about community college scholars' disciplinary contributions and future needs. For example, in 2013, Holly Hassel extended work by Kip Strasma and Paul Resnick in 1999 that identified six areas of needed research in the community college setting: diversity, technology, identity, literacy, methodology, and pedagogy (Strasma and Resnick 1999, 343). She called for more work from community college scholars in two of Strasma and Resnick's original areas, literacy and methodology, and she added new areas of need in community college scholarship: writing center studies, preparation of future faculty for work in two-year colleges, program development, and faculty development and working conditions (Hassel 2013).

As Hassel notes in her discussion, while more research is needed, many scholars writing in and about community colleges have contributed a great deal to Rhetoric and Composition's developing knowledge about labor issues and professional identity.[10] Jeffrey Andelora's four-article series (Andelora 2007a, 2007b, 2008a, 2008b) on the development of the community college English professional organization, TYCA, is not only a history important for new community college faculty, but also a critical history of the discipline of Rhetoric and Composition.

This rich scholarly tradition highlights the range of contributions community college scholars have made to Rhetoric and Composition, yet we are only scratching the surface. The argument can be made in all of these cases that the scholarly work emerging from the community college environment is not only relevant, but potentially crucial, for Rhetoric and Composition scholars, faculty, and administrators in all institutional contexts. Given the amount of writing instruction happening at community colleges and the diversity of those contexts and experiences, these perspectives are an essential part of our disciplinary dialogue.

## RETHINKING HOW SCHOLARSHIP IS ACKNOWLEDGED

As recently as 2013, Holly Hassel and Joanne Giordano conclude an argument about realigning the discipline better with community college context by calling for Rhetoric and Composition to support community college scholarship. In spite of the important work that community college scholars do in the discipline, perspectives and work from community colleges are not always recognized for the contributions they make to the development of Rhetoric and Composition. For example, the work of community college scholars is conspicuously absent from several representative "core" disciplinary texts that are often used to introduce graduate students to the study of Rhetoric and Composition. We found that 1 of 42 (2.4%) readings in the third edition of *Cross-Talk in Comp Theory* (Villanueva and Arola 2011), 1 of 101 (< 1%) readings in *The Norton Book of Composition Theory* (Miller 2009), and none of the chapters in *Exploring Composition Studies: Sites, Issues and Perspectives* (Ritter and Matsuda 2012) are authored by community college scholars. It also seems telling that the two chapters included in these three volumes, one each in Villanueva and Arola (2011) and Miller (2009), were both written by the same scholar (Mina Shaughnessy). While Shaughnessy's work certainly transformed the discipline's understanding of basic writers, open admissions, and teaching writing, both selections are nearly forty years old (originally published in 1976 and 1977, respectively), and much has happened in the decades since as the demographics of community college student populations have continued to shift (Mullin 2012).

Journals focusing on the work, perspectives, and locations of community college teaching and research are often overlooked in discussions of the history and development of Rhetoric and Composition. One of the premier journals focusing on community college English is *Teaching English in the Two-Year College* (*TETYC*), a publication of the National Council of Teachers of English (NCTE). Maureen Daly Goggin's (2000) *Authoring a Discipline*, which analyzes key journals in the discipline as part of the historical construction of Rhetoric and Composition, does not include *TETYC* in its analysis, even though the journal began publishing in 1974. Goggin does, however, list *TETYC* as one of the journals founded in Rhetoric and Composition between 1950 and 1990 (36). *The Bedford Bibliography for Teachers of Writing*, seventh edition (Reynolds et al., 2012), while listing the scholarship of several community college faculty members, does not include the scholarship in *TETYC* as part of the foundational list of research in writing. Of the 862 publications anthologized in the bibliography, none is from *TETYC*.

An exception that appears to defy the rule is Patrick Sullivan and Howard Tinberg's edited collection *What Is "College-Level" Writing?* (Sullivan and Tinberg 2006). In addition to the introduction and opening chapter the editors write, the collection includes two more chapters by community college faculty: Michael Dubson's (2006) chapter on student ownership and James M. Gentile's (2006) chapter on an administrative perspective. Certainly the editors' subject positions as community college scholars make them aware of the need to include these perspectives in scholarly collections, but we argue that scholarship by community college faculty and about community college contexts should not be solely found in collections edited by community college faculty.

While it might be easy to focus on the cases of these texts, the essence of the problem is not with individual editors, authors, or texts—it is systemic. As new members of the discipline emerge, they are socialized—even disciplined—into what is considered important to the profession. John Weidman et al. (2001) outline four stages of socialization through which graduate students move: anticipatory, formal, informal, and personal. In the anticipatory stage students become "aware of the behavioral, attitudinal, and cognitive expectations"; however, since they are not part of the field yet, their sources are generally more public (even from the mass media) and are usually "generalized and stereotypical" (12). The three texts we described above are examples of what are often used in the formal stage of socialization in Rhetoric and Composition graduate programs. In both cases, anticipatory and formal, graduate students are unlikely at this point to have access to much scholarship by community college scholars.

The informal stage of socialization occurs through interactions with others where "students receive behavioral clues" and "observe acceptable behavior" (14), such as in a conference setting. The CCCC highlights presenters from the community college in the program, but it would be interesting to track how often those sessions are "featured" in the program and how well attended they are. The conference of the Council on Writing Program Administrators has a similar challenge. While the Two-Year College caucus has a featured strand in the program, the strand can also serve as a double-edged sword: at the same time that it highlights sessions in the program, it can also mark them as "other." If graduate students have not been socialized already to value community college contexts and scholarship, they might be unlikely to see those sessions as relevant to them. The personal, and last, stage of socialization occurs when the graduate student "internalizes" disciplinary identity (14). Of course, none of these stages is discrete, and the experiences in prior stages overlap and influence the ways graduate students are disciplined and discipline themselves.

Since this initial socialization takes place at universities, where graduate students are earning their advanced degrees, they internalize very specific ideas of what counts as scholarship. For example, students might be likely to internalize the idea that knowledge about teaching or knowledge gained from classroom experience is less important than (and categorically different from) "real" research. This distinction was made most famously by Stephen North's (1987) categorization of "Practitioner lore" as separate from "Scholarly contributions" and "Research contributions" (capitalization his). While North's characterizations and conclusions about knowledge-making in Composition have been analyzed and critiqued a great deal in the decades since publication (most recently and extensively in Massey and Gebhardt's 2011 collection), the privileging of certain kinds of knowledge-making persists. The result is that graduate students might be directly or indirectly steered away from writing or perhaps even citing publications focused on teaching such as those in the Praxis Wiki section of *Kairos*, the "Virtual Classroom" section of *Computers and Composition Online*, the Program Profiles section of *Composition Forum*, or even multimedia publications such as the 2002 CD-Rom *The OWL Construction and Maintenance Guide*, by James Inman and Clint Gardner (a community college scholar) (Inman and Gardner 2002). These publication venues are not necessarily focused on or by community college scholar/ship, but they are places where pedagogically focused scholarship is privileged and shared.

## RETHINKING ASSUMPTIONS ABOUT DISCIPLINARY PARTICIPATION

Notions of faculty disciplinary identity are complex, perhaps more today than ever before. Ann M. Penrose's (2012) article on professional identity in Writing Studies opens with an experienced, non-tenure-track faculty member describing his or her feelings of not being a member of the profession; Penrose questions that response when most other professionals in other fields would not have that problem (108). Hansen (this volume) complicates this discussion as well by exploring the connections between a discipline and a profession, and she calls for a paraprofessional category to bridge the gap. While we do not necessarily agree with Hansen's proposal, we argue that Rhetoric and Composition would do well to define our discipline to have inclusive paths of participation for teachers/scholars.

Instead of using the categories of teaching, research, and service as markers of professional identity, Penrose (2012) proposes using expertise, autonomy, and community participation as markers of professionalism. She states: "Composition experts are identified not by the possession of a finite body of knowledge but by a rhetorical understanding that motivates them to assess, apply, and adapt their knowledge and develop new expertise as needed to meet teaching challenges in varied contexts" (121).

At the institutional level, faculty roles at community colleges are most often defined as exclusively devoted to teaching and service, and "(f)aculty efforts that focus on research and publication, on the other hand, are likely to fall under the radar and receive little formal recognition" (Two-Year College English Association 2010, 3). As full-time faculty who teach anywhere from a four/four to a seven/seven load of primarily Composition courses and usually do not have promotion and tenure requirements that require scholarly activity, many community college professors are neither motivated nor rewarded for publishing in traditionally recognized scholarly venues.

Community college faculty certainly have professional expertise, however. In addition, they often have a great deal of autonomy, and they are most likely participating in professional communities (sometimes in interdisciplinary groups that focus on issues such as developmental education and/or educational technology rather in more traditionally defined disciplinary organizations). And thus far, we (and Penrose) have primarily been focusing on full-time faculty members; how can we also open our model to be inclusive of the experience, knowledge, and contributions of faculty members who teach classes on a short-term contractual basis, sometimes at multiple institutions, sometimes part-time, and sometimes in more than one type of institution at a time? Consider the expertise such a teacher has in comparing different student populations and/or discussing labor issues. How might a high school English teacher who teaches in multiple environments, including nights at the local community college and/or dual-enrollment courses, contribute to contemporary discussion on transfer and threshold concepts, for example? Even if a community college scholar is *only* sharing experience in negotiating the expertise, autonomy, and community participation of working in (a) specific environment(s), the discipline should welcome the additional knowledge that helps us understand how to succeed, live, and work in a personally and professionally fulfilling manner.

## MORE READING, NOT MORE WRITING

But how do we accomplish the goals of being more inclusive of these perspectives and also recognizing the scholarship that is already being produced? Richard Gebhardt (1995) warns us away from the "Research versus Teaching" trap and argues that "once teaching, students, and the integration of research with theory so that both are more useful in teaching students are seen as appropriate *objects* of research, the range of appropriate *genres* of publication will begin to increase" (13).

Many community college scholars write book reviews of work produced by their colleagues at four-year institutions, potentially commenting upon the work from their often-overlooked professional perspective. Community college scholars also serve on, and sometimes lead, organizational committees that produce critical policy statements and professional guidelines. In other words, we should be both searching for the variety of scholarship introduced by Ernest Boyer (1990)—discovery, application, integration, and teaching—and also reading in different genres and from different outlets.

We can't just depend on larger institutional efforts, such as the cross-disciplinary and cross-institutional Preparing Future Faculty initiative from the late 1990s, to expand graduate student socialization efforts. As individual members of a discipline we need to systematically request, read, and use scholarship from a variety of different perspectives—including, but not limited to, community college scholars—so that we both begin to internalize and personalize our own self-disciplining process as well as model that to new members of the discipline. Not only might we read and use the scholarship by and about community college scholars listed above and/or published in *TETYC*, but we might also look in publication spaces that invite alternative formats and genres, as well as more practical topics, that might be more relevant to community college contexts, such *Kairos's* Kairos Wiki; *Composition Forum's* Program Profiles; *Computers and Composition Online's* Virtual Classroom; CompPile's WPA-CompPile Research Bibliographies; and spaces such as *MediaCommons, Writing Commons,* and *Writing Spaces.*

Rhetoric and Composition must retain space for the range of scholarship, scholarly identities, and important roles that community college faculty play in shaping the discipline. This is already a discipline that explicitly embraces scholarship from a multiplicity of voices and perspectives. The contributions of community college faculty are already present and influential in the discipline. Community college faculty are already occupying important positions and producing scholarship in the field. Our limited acknowledgment of that work stems from our history of privileging certain objects of study, types of scholarship, venues for publication, and disciplinary identities. Instead of calling for community college faculty to produce more scholarship, we might call upon our colleagues at large in Rhetoric and Composition to explicitly look for and engage with the already-existing scholarship by community college faculty. In numbers of publications and conference presentations, the contributions from community college faculty might not appear to be as prevalent as that of noncommunity college faculty, but if we complicate notions of professional identity and broaden the concept of what counts as scholarship, we see that community college faculty are very active and present in our disciplinary conversations—even more so than we might acknowledge. Their influence is palpable and essential.

*Notes*

1. In this chapter, we have chosen to refer to the discipline by the title "Rhetoric and Composition," although we realize that other terms, such as "Writing Studies," are also commonly used (Maid, this volume). Additionally, we acknowledge that disciplines are contested, constantly changing spaces (Miller and Reid, this volume). For the purposes of our argument, however, we are identifying the space of Rhetoric and Composition in similar ways to those argued for in Yancey (this volume) and Wardle and Downs (this volume).

2. We acknowledge that some two-year institutions do not always identify as community colleges, such as various technical colleges and art institutes. However, using "two-year" as the representative phrase is also problematic because it either emphasizes that these institutions *only* cover coursework for the first two years of a bachelor's degree, thereby privileging the four-year degree, or it emphasizes that these students should complete their work at one of these institutions within two years, which is often not the case for community college students. In this chapter we use "community college" to represent a variety of non-four-year (and beyond) colleges and universities while also acknowledging the diversity of communities working at and attending these institutions and the variety of disciplinary and professional fields, programs, and degrees offered.

3. Community college faculty and students can be involved in many ways in research about the community college context. Of course, they are often the primary researchers, and we highlight many examples of that work in this chapter. But qualitative research has long upheld the importance of having participants in a community contribute to the interpretation of data and results from a site of study through member checking (Lincoln and Guba 1985). In our discipline, Cynthia L. Selfe and Gail E. Hawisher have modeled how to go beyond member checking and have participants co-author qualitative research in Rhetoric and Composition (Selfe and Hawisher 2004).

4. There are many important issues relevant to community colleges that research in Rhetoric and Composition could address. Namely, labor and contingency issues are important considerations in discussions of research, knowledge-making, and working conditions at community colleges. While recent research from community college faculty has not focused on labor issues (with the notable exception of Sullivan 2015 about activism and identity), we hope that future research from community college faculty will bring increasing attention to their perspectives on issues of labor and contingency in the profession.

5. Just in the past five years of issues in *Teaching English in the Two-Year College (TETYC)*, community college scholars have written about self-assessment (Ihara 2014), transfer (Tinberg 2015) and threshold concepts (Blaauw-Hara 2014), service learning

(Maloy and Carroll 2014), visual rhetoric (Ernster 2014), writing across the curriculum (Berger 2015), using writing portfolios in the classroom (Parisi 2014), and community building and a liberal arts education (Almeda and Stotz-Ghosh 2013). In addition to these traditionally published scholarly articles, journals such as *TETYC* also publish a great deal of work from community college faculty related to teaching writing in pedagogically focused sections of the journal such as *TETYC*'s "What Works for Me." Peter Moe's (2013) longitudinal study of the "What Works for Me" articles demonstrated that all of the sixty-six pieces written by fifty-six authors "are grounded in rhetorics much larger than the bounds of the classroom" (375).

6. Recent publications by community college scholars related to basic/developmental writing include those by Bill Marsh (2015), Cheryl Hogue Smith and Maya Jiménez (Smith and Jiménez 2014), Patrick Sullivan (2013), Leigh Jonaitis (2012), and Smith (2012).

7. Community college scholars have studied topics common in writing research through the lens of digital technologies such as multimodal composition (Bickmore and Christiansen 2010), grammar applications (Quint Gray and Trillin 1977; Thomas and Austin 2005), writing centers (Gardner 2012), basic writing (Jonaitis 2012; Klages and Clark 2009), and working with ESL students (Nakamura 2011). Additionally, community college faculty study specific technologies in relation to the teaching and learning of writing such as email (Courant Rife 2007), *Wikipedia* (Kuhne and Creel 2012), blogs (Gallagher 2010; Zhao 2012), and games (Bisz 2012).

8. Libby Bay (1999) conducted an empirical study of returning adult students at a community college to help instructors understand their motivations, difficulties, and satisfactions. On the other end of the age continuum, Miles McCrimmon (2010) explored the contested space of dual enrollment and the race to have students complete college credits as early as possible.

9. Eric J. Paulson, like us, spent a significant time working in a community college setting prior to working at a four-year institution. Paulson usually includes reference to this significant time in his biographic entries as we also do, since that experience shaped the lens through which we understand writing pedagogy.

10. Jeffrey Klausman (2010, 2013)—along with Carolyn Calhoon-Dillahunt, in a keynote address at the 2010 Council of Writing Program Administrators (CWPA) Summer Conference and the later *WPA: Writing Program Administration* publication (Calhoon-Dillahunt 2011)—explicitly writes about doing the work of a writing program administrator within the community college setting. Their discussion of working with rapidly decreasing resources and growing numbers of contingent faculty members is relevant and useful to all WPAs, however. Expanding on that conversation, Christie Toth (2014) argues for the need to support adjunct faculty professionalization through engagement with disciplinary organizations, and her article with Brett Griffiths and Kathryn Thirolf (2013) in *CCC* teases out the distinctions of professional identities of community college faculty (Toth, Griffiths, and Thirolf 2013).

## References

Alford, Barry. 2001. "Introduction." In *The Politics of Writing in the 2 Year College*, ed. Barry Alford and Keith Kroll, v–viii. Portsmouth, NH: Boynton/Cook Publishers.

Almeda, Cheryl, and Julie Stotz-Ghosh. 2013. "Emphasizing 'Community' in the Community College Experience: The Value of a Liberal Arts Education." *Teaching English in the Two-Year College* 41 (2): 164–76.

Andelora, Jeffrey. 2007a. "The Professionalization of Two-Year College English Faculty: 1950–1990." *Teaching English in the Two-Year College* 35 (1): 6–19.

Andelora, Jeffrey. 2007b. "TYCA and the Struggle for a National Voice: 1991–1993." *Teaching English in the Two-Year College* 35 (2): 133–48.

Andelora, Jeffrey. 2008a. "TYCA and the Struggle for a National Voice: 1994–1997." *Teaching English in the Two-Year College* 35 (3): 252–65.

Andelora, Jeffrey. 2008b. "Forging a National Identity: TYCA and the Two-Year College Teacher-Scholar." *Teaching English in the Two-Year College* 35 (4): 350–62.

Bay, Libby. 1999. "Twists, Turns, and Returns: Returning Adult Students." *Teaching English in the Two-Year College* 26 (3): 305–12.

Berger, Michael. 2015. "Developing a Writing across the Curriculum Program for a Two-Year Nursing College." *Teaching English in the Two-Year College* 42 (4): 400–9.

Bickmore, Lisa, and Ron Christiansen. 2010. "'Who Will Be the Inventors? Why Not Us?' Multimodal Compositions in the Two-Year College Classroom." *Teaching English in the Two-Year College* 37 (3): 230–42.

Bisz, Joe. 2012. "Composition Games for the Classroom." *Computers and Composition Online*. https://www.bgsu.edu/departments/english/cconline/index.htm.

Blaauw-Hara, Mark. 2014. "Transfer Theory, Threshold Concepts, and First-Year Composition: Connecting Writing Courses to the Rest of the College." *Teaching English in the Two-Year College* 41 (4): 354–65.

Boyer, Ernest. 1990. *Scholarship Reconsidered: Priorities of the Professoriate.* New York: Carnegie Foundation for the Advancement of Teaching.

Calhoon-Dillahunt, Carolyn. 2011. "Writing Programs without Administrators: Frameworks for Successful Writing Programs in the Two-Year College." *WPA: Writing Program Administration* 35 (1): 118–34.

Courant Rife, Martine. 2007. "The Professional E-Mail Assignment, or, whatsyername@howyadoin.com." *Teaching English in the Two-Year College* 34 (3): 264–70.

Dong, Yu Ren. 1999. "The Need to Understand ESL Students' Native Language Writing Experiences." *Teaching English in the Two-Year College* 26 (3): 277–85.

Dubson, Michael. 2006. "'Whose Paper Is This, Anyway?' Why Most Students Don't Embrace the Writing They Do for Their Writing Classes." In *What Is "College-Level" Writing?* ed. Patrick Sullivan and Howard Tinberg, 92–109. Urbana, IL: National Council of Teachers of English.

Ernster, Thomas. 2014. "A Case for Visual Rhetoric in Two-Year College Composition." *Teaching English in the Two-Year College* 41 (4): 384–93.

Gallagher, Jamey. 2010. "'As Ya'll Know': Blog as Bridge." *Teaching English in the Two-Year College* 37 (3): 286–94.

Gardner, Clint. 2012. "Rhetorical Media and the Twenty First Century Open-Access Writing Center: Predictions, Predilections, and Realities." *Computers and Composition Online*. https://www.bgsu.edu/departments/english/cconline/index.htm.

Gebhardt, Richard C. 1995. "Avoiding the 'Research versus Teaching' Trap: Expanding the Criteria for Evaluating Scholarship." In *The Politics and Processes of Scholarship*, ed. Joseph M. Moxley and Lagretta T. Lenker, 9–17. Westport, CT: Greenwood Press.

Gentile, James M. 2006. "College-Level Writing: A Departmental Perspective." In *What Is "College-Level" Writing?* ed. Patrick Sullivan and Howard Tinberg, 311–29. Urbana, IL: National Council of Teachers of English.

Harris, Joseph. 1997. *A Teaching Subject: Composition Since 1966.* Upper Saddle River, NJ: Prentice Hall.

Hassel, Holly. 2013. "Research Gaps in Teaching English in the Two-Year College." *Teaching English in the Two-Year College* 40 (4): 343–63.

Hassel, Holly, and Joanne Baird Giordano. 2013. "Occupy Writing Studies: Rethinking College Composition for the Needs of the Teaching Majority." *College Composition and Communication* 65 (1): 117–39.

Ihara, Rachel. 2014. "Student Perspectives on Self-Assessment: Insights and Implications." *Teaching English in the Two-Year College* 41 (3): 223–38.

Inman, James A., and Clint Gardner. 2002. *The OWL Construction and Maintenance Guide*. CD-Rom. New York: Routledge.

Jonaitis, Leigh A. 2012. "Troubling Discourse: Basic Writing and Computer-Mediated Technologies." *Journal of Basic Writing* 31 (1): 36–58.

Klages, Marisa A., and Elizabeth J. Clark. 2009. "New Worlds of Errors and Expectations: Basic Writers and Digital Assumptions." *Journal of Basic Writing* 28 (1): 32–49.

Klausman, Jeffrey. 2010. "Not Just a Matter of Fairness: Adjunct Faculty and Writing Programs in Two-Year Colleges." *Teaching English in the Two-Year College* 37 (4): 363–71.

Klausman, Jeffrey. 2013. "Toward a Definition of a Writing Program at a Two-Year College: You Say You Want a Revolution?" *Teaching English in the Two-Year College* 40 (3): 257–73.

Kuhne, Michael, and Gill Creel. 2012. "Wikipedia, 'the People Formerly Known as the Audience,' and First-Year Writing." *Teaching English in the Two-Year College* 40 (2): 177–89.

Lewiecki-Wilson, Cynthia, and Jeff Sommers. 1999. "Professing at the Fault Lines: Composition at Open Admissions Institutions." *College Composition and Communication* 50 (3): 438–462. https://doi.org/10.2307/358860.

Lincoln, Yvonna S., and Egon G. Guba. 1985. *Naturalistic Inquiry*. Newbury Park, CA: Sage Publications.

Maloy, Jennifer, and Julia Carroll. 2014. "Critical Reflection on the Road to Understanding the Holocaust: A Unique Service-Learning Project at a Two-Year College." *Teaching English in the Two-Year College* 41 (4): 369–83.

Marsh, Bill. 2015. "Reading-Writing Integration in Developmental and First-Year Composition." *Teaching English in the Two-Year College* 43 (1): 58–70.

Massey, Lance, and Richard C. Gebhardt. 2011. *The Changing of Knowledge in Composition: Contemporary Perspectives*. Logan: Utah State University Press.

McCrimmon, Miles. 2010. "Contesting the Territoriality of 'Freshman English': The Political Ecology of Dual Enrollment." In *College Credit for Writing in High School: The "Taking Care of" Business*, ed. Kristine Hansen and Christine R. Farris, 208–26. Urbana, IL: National Council of Teachers of English.

Miller, Susan. 2009. *The Norton Book of Composition Theory*. New York: W. W. Norton & Company.

Miller-Cochran, Susan. 2012. "Beyond 'ESL Writing': Teaching Cross-Cultural Composition at a Community College." *Teaching English in the Two-Year College* 40 (1): 20–30.

Miller-Cochran, Susan K., and Rochelle Rodrigo. 2006. "Determining Effective Distance Learning Designs through Usability Testing." *Computers and Composition* 23 (1): 91–107. https://doi.org/10.1016/j.compcom.2005.12.002.

Miller-Cochran, Susan K., and Rochelle Rodrigo, eds. 2009. *Rhetorically Rethinking Usability: Theories, Practices, and Methodologies*. New York: Hampton Press.

Millward, Jody. 2008. "An Analysis of the National 'TYCA Research Initiative Survey Section III: Technology and Pedagogy' in Two-Year College English Programs." *Teaching English in the Two-Year College* 35 (4): 372–97.

Moe, Peter Wayne. 2013. "What Works for Me, and for that Matter, for Us." *Teaching English in the Two-Year College* 40 (4): 364–83.

Mullin, Christopher M. 2012. *Why Access Matters: The Community College Student Body (Policy Brief 2012–01PBL)*. Washington, DC: American Association of Community College; https://archive.org/details/ERIC_ED532204.

Nakamura, Sarah. 2011. "Making (and Not Making) Connections with Web 2.0 Technology in the ESL Composition Classroom." *Teaching English in the Two-Year College* 38 (4): 377–90.

North, Stephen M. 1987. *The Making of Knowledge in Composition: Portrait of an Emerging Field*. Portsmouth, NH: Heinemann.

Parisi, Hope. 2014. "Third-Party Address: A Dialogic Option in Portfolio Reflection for Basic Writers." *Teaching English in the Two-Year College* 42 (1): 7–26.

Penrose, Ann M. 2012. "Professional Identity in a Contingent-Labor Profession: Expertise, Autonomy, Community in Composition Teaching." *WPA: Writing Program Administration* 35 (2): 108–26.

Powers-Stubbs, Karen, and Jeff Sommers. 2001. "'Where We Are Is Who We Are': Location, Professional Identity, and the Two-Year College." In *The Politics of Writing in the Two-Year College*, ed. Barry Alford and Keith Kroll, 19–41. Portsmouth, NH: Boynton/Cook.

Quint Gray, Barbara, and Alice Trillin. 1977. "Animating Grammar: Principles for the Development of Video-Tape Materials." *Journal of Basic Writing* 1 (3): 77–91.

Reynolds, Mark. 2005. "Two-Year-College Teachers as Knowledge Makers." In *The Profession of English in the 2 Year College*, ed. Mark Reynolds and Sylvia Holladay-Hicks, 1–15. Portsmouth, NH: Boynton/Cook Publishers, Inc.

Reynolds, Nedra, Jay Dolmage, Patricia Bizzell, and Bruce Herzberg. 2012. *The Bedford Bibliography for Teachers of Writing*. 7th ed. Boston: Bedford/St. Martin's.

Ritter, Kelly, and Paul Kei Matsuda. 2012. *Exploring Composition Studies: Sites, Issues, and Perspectives*. Logan: Utah State University Press.

Rose, Mike. 2012. *Back to School: Why Everyone Deserves a Second Chance at Education*. New York: The New Press.

Sánchez, Deborah M., and Eric J. Paulson. 2008. "Critical Language Awareness and Learners in College Transitional English." *Teaching English in the Two-Year College* 36 (2): 164–76.

Selfe, Cynthia L., and Gail E. Hawisher. 2004. *Literate Lives in the Information Age: Narratives of Literacy from the United States*. Mahwah, NJ: Lawrence Erlbaum.

Shaughnessy, Mina. 1977. *Errors and Expectations: A Guide for Teachers of Basic Writing*. New York: Oxford UP.

Smith, Cheryl Hogue. 2012. "Interrogating Texts: From Deferent to Efferent and Aesthetic Reading Practices." *Journal of Basic Writing* 31 (1): 59–79.

Smith, Cheryl Hogue, and Maya Jiménez. 2014. "Razing the Bar: Developmental Students Shattering Expectations in a First-Year Learning Community." *Teaching English in the Two-Year College* 42 (1): 41–54.

Strasma, Kip, and Paul Resnick. 1999. "Future Research in Two-Year College English." *Teaching English in the Two-Year College* 27 (1): 106–14.

Sullivan, Patrick. 2013. "'Just-in-Time' Curriculum for the Basic Writing Classroom." *Teaching English in the Two-Year College* 41 (2): 118–34.

Sullivan, Patrick. 2015. "The Two-Year College Teacher-Scholar-Activist." *Teaching English in the Two-Year College* 42 (4): 327–50.

Sullivan, Patrick, and Howard Tinberg, eds. 2006. *What Is "College-Level" Writing?* Urbana, IL: National Council of Teachers of English.

Thomas, Katherine M., and Marlisa Austin. 2005. "Fun with Fundamentals: Games and Electronic Activities to Reinforce Grammar in the College Writing Classroom." *Teaching English in the Two-Year College* 33 (1): 62–69.

Tinberg, Howard. 2015. "Reconsidering Transfer Knowledge at the Community College: Challenges and Opportunities." *Teaching English in the Two-Year College* 43 (1): 7–31.

Toth, Christie. 2014. "Unmeasured Engagement: Two-Year College English Faculty and Disciplinary Professional Organizations." *Teaching English in the Two-Year College* 41 (4): 335–53.

Toth, Christina M., Brett M. Griffiths, and Kathryn Thirolf. 2013. "'Distinct and Significant': Professional Identities of Two-Year College English Faculty." *College Composition and Communication* 65 (1): 90–116.

Two-Year College English Association. 2010. *Research and Scholarship in the Two-Year College.* Urbana, IL: NCTE Position Statement.

Villanueva, Victor, and Kristin L. Arola. 2011. *Cross-Talk in Comp Theory.* 3rd ed. Urbana, IL: National Council of Teachers of English.

Weidman, John C., Darla J. Twale, and Elizabeth Leahy Stein. 2001. *Socialization of Graduate and Professional Students in Higher Education: A Perilous Passage? ASHE-ERIC Higher Education Research Report 28(3).* New York: John Wiley & Sons.

Zhao, Ruijie Fall. 2012. "Integrating Blogs into A Developmental Writing Class." *Computers and Composition Online.* https://www.bgsu.edu/departments/english/cconline/index.htm.

# 4
## LEARNING FROM BRUFFEE
### Collaboration, Students, and the Making of Knowledge in Writing Administration

Rita Malenczyk, Neal Lerner, and Elizabeth H. Boquet

In the first chapter of this volume, Kathleen Blake Yancey asks, "What *kind* of discipline would we like to be?" To imagine this future, the three of us, with experience in writing centers, writing across the curriculum, and writing program administration, wonder: What kind of discipline are we? While disciplinarity might have certain hallmarks—departmentalization, peer-reviewed journals, professional organizations, and conferences—for us, the very basis of Writing Studies as a knowledge-producing discipline rests upon the idea of students as knowledge makers, not merely knowledge consumers. We admit to being strongly influenced by our many collective years tutoring in, directing, and researching writing centers, sites in which students teaching and learning from other students is woven into the fabric. While such pedagogical practices might not rank as high in the disciplinary pecking order as the items in the list we offer above, we believe that such practices are fundamental acts of knowledge making, of the social construction of knowledge to which our field has long allied. And these practices are found not merely in writing centers, but in writing classes, in libraries, cafes, and off-campus sites where students co-construct knowledge about writing and disciplinary content. We have often gone where students have led us—in our teaching, in our research, in our writing centers, in our program development—and we have followed others in the field who have championed students as knowledge makers.

In this chapter, we look primarily at the ways one such figure, Kenneth Bruffee, guides us in placing and keeping student knowledge-making front and center in our current "disciplinary turn" (Yancey, this volume). In the history of Composition and Rhetoric, Bruffee is positioned as the founder of collaborative learning models that continue to underpin much of our current teaching practice, both in classrooms and elsewhere on our campuses. We believe that the history of Bruffee's and others' work at City University of New York (CUNY) in the 1970s reveals that without student knowledge-making, teachers and writing administrators could not have built the peer-led structures that have become central to our most essential principles and practices: that teaching and learning about writing are collaborative, are socially constructed. Further, Bruffee's story attests to the ongoing need to put student knowledge-making at the center of our efforts at discipline formation as we continue to co-create with our students the contexts and conditions for learning. In short, we see students as key members of Writing Studies as a discipline, a claim that few other disciplines might dare to make.

We also see keeping Bruffee's history in mind as particularly crucial at this historical moment when practically everyone (students, parents, legislators, even the president) is framing students as "consumers" of higher education, a position used to justify reorganizations and realignments purporting to respond to market demand. In this organizational climate, writing program administrators (WPAs) need to do more than simply recognize students' roles in knowledge making.[1] WPAs need to demonstrate that calls for student knowledge making in writing program and center administration are grounded not just in a recognition of articulated fiscal pressures but also in the fundamental responsibilities of institutions of higher education in a democratic society. We see student knowledge making and the exigencies leading to a demand for such knowledge as we study Bruffee's career; and we draw inspiration from Bruffee and his cohort when they were responding to student exigency in the era of Open Admissions. In this chapter, we offer a counternarrative to student-as-consumer, highlighting an important moment in our disciplinary history when students emerged as producers, not consumers, of the knowledge circulated through and about higher education.

\* \* \*

One of the first things we learn from Kenneth Bruffee's history is that his initial impulse to make knowledge about the teaching of writing came when he was a student himself, and emerged from his own struggles as a writer. In an extended interview conducted in 2004 by Harvey Kail for the Writing Centers Research Project (WCRP; Bruffee 2004), Bruffee characterizes his undergraduate self as someone who was "not good at writing" and who searched in vain for teachers who could help him improve. He was motivated by social class, an economic factor that—along with other economic factors—would continue to be an exigence for knowledge making throughout his career. A native of East Hartford, Connecticut, a working-class suburb of the state capital, Bruffee attended public schools and, in fall 1952, Wesleyan University, then (as now) an elite East Coast liberal arts college. When his roommate, a private high school graduate, got an A on a paper assignment for which Bruffee received a B, Bruffee describes going back to the professor and asking why:

> I went back to this guy and I said, "Can you please explain to me what is the difference between his paper and mine? I'd like to be able to [do] that. I don't have to do it overnight, but I'd like to know what it was that he did. The instructor didn't have the language to explain what he expected. The answer was simple. That my roommate met his expectations, but this teacher couldn't state his expectations in terms of saying something and explaining and developing it, you know, some kind of coherent writing. So I sat down with my roommate and I said look, you know this is very puzzling to me, what is the difference in our background that makes this? It turned out he went to a private school. And I have since talked to the head of the English department at one of the private schools in Brooklyn. And he said "Well, the difference between private school and public school is they teach you to write and they teach you to be nice. Otherwise there's really not much difference except money." (Bruffee 2004, 3)

A working-class kid among relatively wealthy students, Bruffee identified writing as an area in which he, unlike his private school counterparts, was ill prepared: "That was the difference between me and them" (Bruffee 2004, 3). Reflecting on his own transition to college, Bruffee says, "Nobody there—this is Wesleyan University, I want to say this loud and clear—nobody there could teach me . . . People were very nice to me, when it came to writing. But they didn't have a clue about teaching [writing]" (2).

Given that Composition and Rhetoric had not yet begun to emerge as a discipline in the 1950s, Bruffee's teachers "not having a clue" about how to teach writing is understandable. Yet his struggles to learn to write, and the fact that nobody at "this spiffy little Connecticut college," as he called Wesleyan, or anybody else seemed to be able to teach him something his more privileged friends had apparently already been taught, shaped his academic path: "I developed an interest in writing because I'd struggled with it myself more than anything else" (Bruffee 2004, 6). Even as an undergraduate, then, Bruffee had begun to formulate a research question, or questions, that would come to shape not only his own priorities but also those of future writing program and center administrators: How do we design programs, courses, and spaces that help students from a range of backgrounds learn to write? How do we "create a context for learning" (Bruffee 1978, 6) for the students in front of us? What knowledge do we need in order to do that? In short, the kind of knowledge making that Bruffee needed to develop for himself anticipates the needs of an emerging field.

Bruffee's questions didn't go away when he went to graduate school for an MA and, then, a PhD in literature. Instead, they grew stronger and more compelling as he took on responsibility for students other than himself. Not only was Bruffee unable to find anyone who could teach him to write in college; later, as a graduate teaching assistant, he was even unable to find anyone to teach him how to *teach* writing. In fact, the first knowledge he seems to have gained about teaching writing was the dawning awareness of how ineffective he was. After college, Bruffee received an MA at Northwestern, was drafted into the military, and found himself stationed in Albuquerque and teaching writing at the University of New Mexico with no training: "I was horrible. I was a terrible teacher. These poor people. I didn't have the foggiest notion of what I was doing" (Bruffee 2004, 5). By 1959, when he returned to Northwestern for his PhD, he "knew that [it was] possible to be really bad—which is a start" (Bruffee 2004, 5). Once back at Northwestern as a teaching assistant, however, he found no training program (or not what "you or I would think of as one"): "We had little meetings which some people attended and some people didn't attend." His frustration, even decades later, is palpable: "It's inexcusable when all the people you respect don't have a language to tell you a very simple thing . . . When I got my degree I still didn't really know what the hell I was doing" (5).

He would be faced with a critical need to figure that out, however, when his next job turned out to be at the City University of New York (CUNY). Newly degreed with a specialty in British Romantic literature, Bruffee was hired at Brooklyn College in 1966, where social exigencies— the Vietnam War to an extent, the Civil Rights Movement in particular— took center stage. At Brooklyn, Bruffee found himself in what Mayor John Lindsay referred to as "Berkeley East" (Schumach, qtd. in Hawkes 2008, 26), "the stage for student protests, boycotts, rallies, strikes, and police brutality" (Hawkes 2008, 25). Peter Hawkes, a participant in the 1980 Bruffee-led Brooklyn College Summer Institute in Training Peer Writing Tutors, draws a connection between the Vietnam protests and the Open Admissions pressure on campuses such as at Brooklyn College, noting that "most of those drafted to serve in Vietnam were blacks and Puerto Ricans who did not have college deferments because their grades were not high enough to be accepted into the CUNY system" (26).

Race, in fact, played a critical role in what would soon be the transformation of CUNY and in Bruffee's and others' knowledge making. The college had been an all-white system until 1965, when the "token desegregation" the system leaders had planned—an enrollment of 10 percent Black and 5 percent Puerto Rican students by 1975 (Trimbur 2016, 220)—was challenged by Black and Puerto Rican students' refusal to accept the limited gains the system had planned for them. In 1965, as John Trimbur recalls, CUNY started a program called Search for Excellence, Elevation, and Knowledge (SEEK) that by 1968 enrolled 1,500 Black and Puerto Rican students, yet those students "were treated as second-class citizens, even denied the right to vote in student government elections" (220). Trimbur describes the situation, and its result, in some detail:

> What CUNY policymakers did not foresee was how Black and Puerto Rican students at City College were energized by Third World politics and the rise of Black Power and a worldwide New Left. In spring 1969, the Black and Puerto Rican Student Community . . . at City College led demonstrations for an admissions policy that reflected the racial composition of New York City, creation of departments of Black and Puerto Rican studies, and other reforms. By early May, demonstrators had seized college buildings, radical and right-wing students were openly skirmishing on campus, and eventually the police occupied City College. On May 8, the Finley Student Center was firebombed, and ten smaller fires were set. Deputy Chancellor Seymour H. Hyman drew the inevitable conclusion: ". . .the only question in my mind was, how can we save City College? And the only answer was, hell, let everybody in" . . . On May 9, 1969, the CUNY Board of Higher Education declared it would institute open admissions the following fall. (221)

It was at that moment that Bruffee stepped in to serve as director of Brooklyn College's director of freshman English (Hawkes 2008, 27), facing the situation as he describes it in the WCRP interview: "[I was appointed] in April. In June, the university announced open enrollment. The chair hadn't the foggiest notion of what to do. I didn't either, obviously. Suddenly I was faced with 108 sections of Freshman English, some sixty or odd new adjunct people who themselves had little or no experience, except for a few who had some high school instruction teaching experience, but even then, given the nature of what was going on, they didn't know much, either. And we just muddled. We didn't really know what we were doing. That's the truth. We didn't know" (Bruffee 2004, 7; see also Heckathorn 2004, 215–16).

Bruffee and the teachers in his program, then, needed to figure out ways to bring this new population of students—by conventional definitions, poorly prepared for higher education, yet more than ready to fight for their right to attend college—into the community and discourses of academia. Creating a discipline was likely far from their intention—more immediate needs came first. But the knowledge making prompted by the new CUNY reality was as essential to disciplinary formation as was any planned research and scholarship, and it required collaboration not just with teachers and other administrators but with students. And students' rights and responsibilities as knowledge makers needed to be acknowledged.

As Trimbur makes clear, Bruffee was not the only CUNY faculty member who needed, and was forced to create, knowledge about how to teach the new population of students that demanded their attention. Mina Shaughnessy, who repurposed her New Critical background to read student texts seriously, is perhaps the most noteworthy example (Trimbur 2016, 221). Bruffee, however, initially turned not to theory but to collaboration in order to develop knowledge he and his colleagues might use in teaching. To begin, he conducted what Stephen A. North (1987) would call practitioner inquiry: he experimented in his classes, encouraged his teaching colleagues to do likewise, and listened to what they had to say. "My job . . . was to help these people learn how to teach these people. So I taught a remedial class . . . I taught one of those classes every semester, . . . and I sat in on other people's classes. I gave workshops of various aspects of this, parading my ignorance before my peers. They were telling me as much as I told them or more. And in the course of that, I developed in a kind of Xerox form a little text book" (Bruffee 2004, 7). This book, which would later become *A Short Course in Writing*—essentially a course in argumentation—came out of Bruffee's teaching and the lore he assembled by collaborating with other practitioners.

However, Bruffee's continuing struggles to provide effective teaching to the students who came to Brooklyn College as a result of Open Admissions pushed him beyond curriculum about effective argumentation and, eventually, beyond lore. It pushed him to turn to the students themselves, who were exerting social and (by extension) fiscal pressure on Brooklyn College, to deliver effective instruction. While Bruffee and his teaching colleagues worked toward a curriculum that they felt responded to students' needs, the students themselves were not quite convinced, particularly given the stark social, racial, and ethnic differences between themselves and the Brooklyn College writing teachers. As Bruffee described, "These were high school students, and not very well educated high school students from a vastly different class and ethnic background than the faculty, who were all, I mean, we were jacket and tie, right? MLA, right?" (Bruffee 2004, 8). Bruffee realized that just as he experienced as "a senior in college, this spiffy little Connecticut college didn't have the language to explain to me what you did" (8), the students at Brooklyn were finding the same class divide. As a result, the students "voted with their feet. They simply didn't show up. They weren't going. College for them was a very strange experience; professors even stranger" (8).

To tackle this new crisis—what we would today call a retention crisis—Bruffee and his CUNY colleagues first wrestled with to how to meet students where they were rather than to blame them for their shortcomings: "I had called up Mina Shaughnessy [at City College], Don McQuade [at Queens College], and Harvey Wiener [at LaGuardia Community College] and a couple other people, and we had begun crying on each other's shoulder. Meeting for coffee or beers or something and sharing questions" (Bruffee 2004, 11–12; see also Strickland 2011, 84; Heckathorn 2004, 215). The realization that CUNY faculty needed to co-construct with students their learning and teaching was accelerated once Bruffee adapted an instructional model he learned about from one of those students: When a teacher- and grad-student-staffed writing tutoring service faltered while a drop-in, peer-driven counseling service flourished, Bruffee reconfigured the staffing structure for writing tutoring, using undergraduate peers rather than teacher-types—an idea he got from a chance encounter with the undergraduate in charge. In the WCRP interview, Bruffee describes how he decided to develop a peer-staffed center:

> About that time I met a guy—this is all 60's stuff, very heavily laid in the 60s spirit . . . This guy was an undergraduate who was running a set of peer mentoring centers in the student center . . . And he had undergraduates advising other undergraduates on things like finances, difficulty with home . . . And we talked a lot, and there was something about this that began to muddle in my head you know. And finally I said to him—I visited his thing, and he showed me how it worked—he was very proud of it—as well he might. And I finally said to him or to myself "Gee, they can do all that." (Bruffee 2004, 9)

Figuring that "If they could do this [counseling], sure as hell they could teach somebody how to make a point and defend it," Bruffee and his chair immediately obtained funding from the "desperate" provost: "Whatever you say! Where do you want to put it? When do you want to do it?" (9). Bruffee then designed a tutor-training program based on *A Short Course in Writing*: "Bells, whistles, collaboration started. To teach these kids my first gesture was to make sure they knew how to write themselves. And to try to get them over a little bit of the sense that they're mounting the podium, becoming little teachers. Mainly the first thing I wanted to make sure is that they knew how to do it themselves, so I'm teaching them something. And we installed them, and they came in [droves]. We kept records and we would have a thousand kids a semester. And it was a big success, and so we got funded" (Bruffee 2004, 9).

And the rest, as they say, is history: the "Brooklyn Plan" became, and still is, a model for writing centers and writing programs around the country, as well as a significant international influence. To the extent that it shows the success of a model of students learning, teaching, and making knowledge collaboratively, of creating inclusive learning spaces in response to students' needs, it offers a disciplinary history rooted in student experience, in students as producers, not merely consumers.

\* \* \*

We have, of course, elided much from this history, notably the additional collaborative work, networking, and foraging (North's term) Bruffee did to provide scholarly underpinning and, ultimately, disciplinary status and credibility to the collaborative models and pedagogy he justifies in "Collaborative Learning and the Conversation of Mankind" (Bruffee 1984a), as well as in the essay nearly all new peer writing tutors read at the start of their work, "Peer Tutoring and the Conversation of Mankind" (Bruffee 1984b). Again, students were central to the making of this knowledge. At the same time as he established the Brooklyn College Writing Center, Bruffee experimented with the use of peer groups in his classes and found he had a lot to learn: why sometimes peer groups worked and other times they didn't; how to translate the knowledge he was gaining about small-group process theory to a classroom setting; how to embed not only successful peer-group practices but to develop the epistemology for the approaches (Hawkes 2008, 28–29). To fill in these gaps in his understanding, Bruffee also turned to more traditional sources of knowledge: he took courses about group work in the School of Social Work at Columbia University and met Alex Gitterman, a professor and dean at the school, who sat in on his tutor training and helped Bruffee understand its workings in social work terms (Bruffee 2004, 16). Later, wanting to learn more about "what's underneath the iceberg" of tutor-tutee interaction, Bruffee took a course in epistemology; read the work of Richard Rorty, Stanley Fish, Thomas Kuhn, and others; and came to understand knowledge as socially constructed (18). This led him to further conclusions about collaboration in education: "I'd settled myself on the notion that if writing is a social construct, then it must follow that education is a social process, and so that brought me back to collaboration in classrooms and in the writing center or learning center . . . That was what justified, in a sense, that kind of activity as I couldn't justify it before using the traditional notions of what knowledge is" (18). Or, as he put it while imagining a skeptical audience in "Peer Tutoring and the Conversation of Mankind": "[Peer tutoring] is of course exactly the blind leading the blind if we insist on the Cartesian model of knowledge: that to know is to 'see,' and that knowledge is information impressed upon the individual mind by some outside source. But if we accept the premise that knowledge is an artifact created by a community of knowledgeable peers and that learning is a social process not an individual one, then learning is not assimilating information and improving our mental eyesight. Learning is an activity in which people work collaboratively to create knowledge among themselves by socially justifying belief" (Bruffee 1984b, 11–12).

That knowledge is socially constructed is, then, a claim that has received a great deal of attention in Writing Studies since Bruffee first posited it. Said knowledge making started, as we see from Bruffee's history at CUNY, with like-minded colleagues getting together to see how they could support each other in their work; it led to acknowledging students as not just the subjects of that work, but as partners in it. In *The Social Life of Information,* John Seely Brown and Paul Duguid discuss office design and stress the importance of good design for what they call "incidental learning": "people often find what they need to know by virtue of where they sit and who they see rather than by direct communication" (Brown and Duguid 2002, 72). Although obviously not an office, CUNY provided Bruffee with many and varied opportunities for "incidental learning": not only did he create knowledge with the teachers who staffed his program and with his colleagues from other schools, but simply being on campus (and, we might add, having an open and creative mind) led him to one day meet the undergraduate who gave him the idea for a peer-staffed Writing Center in which students were authorized to create knowledge with other students.

History also tells us that networking through the Conference on College Composition and Communication (CCCC), the Modern Language Association (MLA), and elsewhere led writing program administrators, including Bruffee, to form an organization devoted to their concerns (Heckathorn 2004, 215–17); writing center administrators from across the country did much the same thing, forming an assembly at the National Council of Teachers of English (NCTE) and establishing a national organization, the National Writing Centers Association (NWCA) (now the International Writing Centers Association [IWCA]), from the many active regional affiliates (see Kinkead 1996; Simpson n.d.). Both organizations led to the disciplinary hallmarks we have now—departments, books, conferences, journals (Bruffee himself was the first editor of *WPA: Writing Program Administration* and a strong voice for the work of writing administration to be taken seriously by the academy). However, those of us who consider ourselves members of the field of writing administration shouldn't let those hallmarks overshadow our foundations. Looking back at the history we've narrated, we recognize students as active participants in creating the discipline we have been, and, most important, the discipline we aspire to be.

\* \* \*

As we write, undergraduate and graduate students also write, individually and collaboratively, independently and with the guidance of peers and mentors. Opportunities for publishing this work have increased, as students from a range of fields within Writing Studies submit their work to national venues such as *Young Scholars in Writing* and to local publications (see also Grobman and Kinkead 2010). On many campuses, students are responsible for the data gathering, composition, and production of documents central to writing program development. Writing center studies is at the forefront of these efforts to strengthen the role of students in our disciplinary conversations. The "Tutor's Column" in *Writing Lab Newsletter* (now *WLN*) stands as a fairly early example. Peer-reviewed journals specifically for student-conducted writing center research include *The Dangling Modifier* (http://sites.psu.edu/thedanglingmodifier/) and, most recently, *The Peer Review* (http://thepeerreview-iwca.org); in 2012, the editors of *Writing Center Journal* devoted an entire issue to undergraduate research, with all articles in the issue researched and written by student tutors (Fitzgerald and Ianetta 2012).[2] The journal has continued its commitment to showcasing undergraduate research, and the recently published *The Oxford Guide for Writing Tutors* (Fitzgerald and Ianetta 2015) stresses the role of tutors in disciplinary knowledge-making, also placing knowledge making itself as crucial in the development of tutoring practice. As Lauren Fitzgerald (2016) explains on the *WCJ* blog, with reference to the debate about how directive tutors should be in their work with writers, tutor researchers have "shifted the terms of the discussion, introducing new forms of evidence and subjectivities from which to make arguments about what matters in tutoring writing. Moreover, they've provided a blueprint for how other tutors can confront this and other exigencies, finding the gaps and questions and answering them with their own research."

On a less formal (often unpublished) level, too, WPAs outside of writing centers have acknowledged the role of student knowledge-making in program development and classroom pedagogy, with directed self-placement (Royer and Gilles 1998) and contract grading (Danielewicz and Elbow 2009; Inoue 2015) as cases in point. Directed self-placement asks students to turn inward, to answer—with help, hence the word "directed"—questions about their experiences and strengths as writers and apply those answers to course choice. Contract grading requires students to reflect upon their own abilities and commitment to their own learning, to understand that commitment and engagement are crucial to their education. WPA-researchers focused on transfer (e.g., Yancey et al. 2014) and assessment (e.g., Wardle and Roozen 2012) have also turned increasingly to the extracurricular literacies students bring to the classroom and how those literacies contribute to the development of writing ability. A cross-institutional study of what students describe as their most "meaningful writing projects" demonstrates that in addition to the "incomes" (Guerra 2008) that students bring to their learning, writing, when meaningful, is also an opportunity for students to construct future identities and aspirations and the role that writing will play in their lives after graduation (Eodice et al. 2016). These practices and scholarship acknowledge that students don't simply learn what we deliver to them via programmatic elements or classroom teaching; rather, students in our programs and classrooms co-create their knowledge with us, bringing prior knowledge to bear on their development of new knowledge.

We are presuming in this chapter that undergraduate research counts as research, that the modifier "undergraduate" does not negate its being "research." We know some readers might disagree. Among the three of us, this is a shared value and a central premise: disciplinarity in Writing Studies is indebted to and dependent on student knowledge-making in, through, and about writing. The Writing Studies tent should be a large one, and students as researchers (not only as subjects or objects) need to be in it. Students will not make every kind of disciplinary knowledge in the field, but they will make some of it, and they should be invited to make more, as much of it as possible. Here, Writing Studies is not alone, or even ahead of the curve, in encouraging student knowledge-making: the Council on Undergraduate Research, founded in 1978, is organized "in a divisional structure that includes arts and humanities, biology, chemistry, education, engineering, geosciences, health sciences, mathematics and computer science, physics and astronomy, [and] social sciences" (Council on Undergraduate Research 2016). Furthermore, national academic leadership organizations continue to call for undergraduates to take a more active role in their own education, through research at all levels and in all fields. The Association of American Colleges and Universities (AAC&U) and the National Survey of Student Engagement (NSSE), for example, emphasize that undergraduate research is a "high-impact practice" that contributes to student engagement as well as to retention (Kuh 2008; NSSE 2016). Students are, then, being encouraged to make knowledge in a range of ways, at national levels. As these organizations acknowledge, students who engage deeply in their own research to answer compelling and difficult questions are more likely to stay in school and succeed.

As might be expected, college and university presidents, provosts, and deans find these recommendations heartening, as they suggest, if not promise, a solution to what has become a major concern of many institutions of higher education: student retention and its impact on institutions' bottom line. Colleges and universities with high retention rates are less likely to have to close or merge departments, eliminate majors, lay off or fire faculty and staff, or—in the most dreaded scenario—close their doors entirely. Here we recall, again, Bruffee's history at CUNY, when his turn to students and student expertise helped retain students who were, for any number of reasons, at risk of leaving—and sound a cautionary note. While we embrace student knowledge-making and, certainly, its potential to help students stay in school, we encourage WPAs to remember the real reasons why they're doing what they do: the students themselves. Too often, as others (e.g., Powell 2013) have pointed out, retention efforts become focused on the good of the institutions themselves rather than on the good of the students, and can be instruments of surveillance (Malenczyk 2017) rather than education.

Writing Studies has long positioned itself as "student centered" and attentive to issues of power and authority. However, the history we've narrated shows students at the very center of the formation of Writing Studies, not just as recipients of knowledge created by faculty or administrators but as producers of knowledge that continues to guide how we structure our classrooms and programs. In other words, disciplinary markers such as doctoral programs, professional conferences, and peer-reviewed journals can serve to construe disciplinary status more narrowly than the history of our field would seem to suggest. Further, we are concerned that traditional notions of disciplinarity run the risk of creating regulatory structures of learning and teaching, rather than opportunities to co-construct that learning with our students. These risks seem particularly acute for nonmainstream and underprepared students for whom Bruffee's (1984b, 11) depiction of "the Cartesian model of knowledge: that to know is to 'see,' and that knowledge is information impressed upon the individual mind by some outside source" can too easily be found in textbook-driven curricula and standardized assessments. The work of teaching writing, as Bruffee found in his experiences as an undergraduate struggling for instruction and a new teacher/administrator struggling to reach his students, belies exclusionary approaches and aligns perfectly with calls for inclusive practices and pedagogies that are themselves coming from the highest reaches of higher education.

How to implement these practices and pedagogies? Whether in classrooms, in writing centers, in community literacy storefronts or in libraries and cafes, the teaching of writing often starts with the act of listening to students' stories. Where they've been, why they are there, what they bring, and who they want to be as writers are often the first acts of knowledge making in this teaching and learning situation. Bruffee knew this. In his 2007 keynote address at the National Conference on Peer Tutoring in Writing, he told the attendees just what this knowledge making looks like: "You are telling [tutees] that *writing is a personally engaging social activity*. You're saying that we never write alone. Writing opens doors into worlds of conversation with other writers, with readers, and with yourself. Writing is a form of civil exchange that thoughtful people engage in when they try to live reasonable lives with one another. Writing is way of caring about people, and sometimes it's a way of caring for people, too" (Bruffee 2008, 7–8).

In our present moment, these practices that characterize the mutual engagement between students and peer tutors and between students and their teachers are crucial to remember. It's the answer to "What kind of a discipline would we like to be?" Our answer to that question is a discipline that has students at its core, as key members, and learning, teaching, and research as mutually constitutive practices. We cannot necessarily predict what the next crisis will be—whether financial, political, or ideological—but we can remember Kenneth Bruffee and CUNY, and turn to students at those moments of crisis and trust what they have to tell us.

*Notes*

1. When we refer to WPAs in this chapter, we refer to writing center administrators as well; in other words, we're talking about "writing administration" in a more capacious sense than it's sometimes used.
2. Many of the tutors' columns in *Writing Lab Newsletter* are based in lore, rather than in directed research; as Melissa Ianetta has made clear, however, what now counts as undergraduate research has shifted as the Council on Undergraduate Research has established more rigorous guidelines that include "the identification of and acquisition of a disciplinary or interdisciplinary methodology" (CUR, qtd. in Ianetta 2016).

## References

Brown, John Seely, and Paul Duguid. 2002. *The Social Life of Information.* Cambridge, MA: Harvard Business Review Press.

Bruffee, Kenneth A. 1978. "Editorial." *WPA: Writing Program Administration* 1 (3): 6–12.

Bruffee, Kenneth A. 1984a. "Collaborative Learning and the 'Conversation of Mankind.'" *College English* 46 (7): 635–52. https://doi.org/10.2307/376924.

Bruffee, Kenneth A. 1984b. "Peer Tutoring and the Conversation of Mankind." In *Writing Centers: Theory and Administration*, ed. Gary A. Olson, 3–15. Urbana, IL: NCTE.

Bruffee, Kenneth A. 2004. *Interview by Harvey Kail. Interview transcript, Writing Centers Research Project.* Little Rock, AR: University of Arkansas at Little Rock.

Bruffee, Kenneth A. 2008. ""What Being a Peer Writing Tutor Can Do for You." Special issue." *Writing Center Journal* 28 (2): 5–10.

Council on Undergraduate Research. 2016. Accessed January 26, 2017. www.cur.org/about_cur/.

Danielewicz, Jane, and Peter Elbow. 2009. "A Unilateral Grading Contract to Improve Learning and Teaching." *College Composition and Communication* 61 (2): 244–68.3.

Eodice, Michele, Anne Ellen Geller, and Neal Lerner. 2016. *The Meaningful Writing Project: Learning, Teaching, and Writing in Higher Education.* Logan: Utah State University Press.

Fitzgerald, Lauren. 2016. "Tutors Respond to Tutors: Undergraduate Researchers Take on Nondirective Tutoring." *WCJ Blog Community*, April 8. http://www.writingcenterjournal.org/new-blog//tutors-respond-to-tutors-undergraduate-tutor-researchers-take-on-nondirective-tutoring.

Fitzgerald, Lauren, and Melissa Ianetta, eds. 2012. "'Peer Tutors and the Conversation of Writing Center Studies.' Special issue." *Writing Center Journal* 32 (1).

Fitzgerald, Lauren, and Melissa Ianetta. 2015. *The Oxford Guide for Writing Tutors: Practice and Research.* New York: Oxford University Press.

Grobman, Laurie, and Joyce Kinkead. 2010. *Undergraduate Research in English Studies.* Urbana: NCTE.

Guerra, Juan. 2008. "Cultivating Transcultural Citizenship: A Writing across Communities Model." *Language Arts* 85 (4): 296–304.

Hawkes, Peter. 2008. ""Vietnam Protests, Open Admissions, Peer Tutor Training, and the Brooklyn Institute: Tracing Kenneth Bruffee's Collaborative Learning." Special issue." *Writing Center Journal* 28 (2): 25–32.

Heckathorn, Amy. 2004. "Moving toward a Group Identity: WPA Professionalization from the 1940s to the 1970s." In *Historical Studies of Writing Program Administration: Individuals, Communities, and the Formation of a Discipline*, ed. Barbara L'Eplattenier and Lisa Mastrangelo, 191–220. W. Lafayette, IN: Parlor Press.

Ianetta, Melissa. 2016. "What Is Undergraduate Research?" *WCJ Blog Community*, April 17. http://www.writingcenterjournal.org/new-blog//what-is-undergraduate-research.

Inoue, Asao. 2015. *Antiracist Writing Assessment Ecologies: Teaching and Assessing Writing for a Socially Just Future.* Anderson, SC: Parlor Press, WAC Clearinghouse.

Kinkead, Joyce. 1996. "The National Writing Centers Association as Mooring: A Personal History of the First Decade." *Writing Center Journal* 16 (2): 131–43.

Kuh, George D. 2008. *High-Impact Educational Practices: What They Are, Who Has Access to Them, and Why They Matter.* Washington, DC: AAC&U.

North, Stephen A. 1987. *The Making of Knowledge in Composition.* Portsmouth, NH: Heinemann.

Malenczyk, Rita. 2017. "Retention ≠ Panopticon: What WPAs Should Bring to the Table in Discussions of Student Success." In *Retention, Persistence and Writing Programs*, ed. Todd Ruecker, Dawn Shepherd, Heidi Estrem, and Beth Brunk-Chavez, 21–37. Logan: Utah State University Press. https://doi.org/10.7330/9781607326021.c002.

NSSE. 2016. "Annual Results 2016." Accessed January 16, 2017. http://nsse.indiana.edu/html/annual_results.cfm.

Powell, Pegeen Reichert. 2013. *Retention and Resistance: Writing Instruction and Students Who Leave*. Logan: Utah State University Press.

Royer, Daniel J., and Roger Gilles. 1998. "Directed Self-Placement: An Attitude of Orientation." *College Composition and Communication* 50 (1): 54–70. https://doi.org/10.2307/358352.

Simpson, Jeanne. n.d. "Brief History of the N/IWCA." Accessed March 28, 2016. www.writingcenters.org/about/iwca-history.

Strickland, Donna. 2011. *The Managerial Unconscious in the History of Composition Studies. CCCC Studies in Writing and Rhetoric*. Carbondale: Southern Illinois University Press.

Trimbur, John. 2016. ""Translingualism and Close Reading." Special issue." *College English* 78 (3): 219–27.

Wardle, Elizabeth, and Kevin Roozen. 2012. "Addressing the Complexity of Writing Development: Toward an Ecological Model of Assessment." *Assessing Writing* 17 (2): 106–19. https://doi.org/10.1016/j.asw.2012.01.001.

Yancey, Kathleen Blake, Liane Robertson, and Kara Taczak. 2014. *Writing across Contexts: Transfer, Composition, and Sites of Writing*. Logan: Utah State University Press.

# SECTION 2

**Coming to Terms**

*What Are We Talking About?*

# 5
## CLASSIFICATION AND ITS DISCONTENTS
Making Peace with Blurred Boundaries, Open Categories, and Diffuse Disciplines

Gwendolynne Reid and Carolyn R. Miller

> *We are already pursuing research paths so disparate that many thoughtful people have feared that the discipline may fly apart like a dollar watch . . . It is for this reason, I submit, that part of the intellectual task of composition studies today is to understand and unify itself as a discipline.*
> —Robert J. Connors (1989)

The question of disciplinarity is by now a familiar stasis point for those who participate in conversations related to Rhetoric and Composition. For a variety of reasons, disciplinarity has often been cast as the ultimate goal in the field's coming-of-age narrative. Louise Wetherbee Phelps, for example, writing in 1986 of the field's quest "for a keener sense of identity as a discipline," described Composition as in its "adolescence" and engaged in "charting more accurately and rigorously the intellectual territory" that it "claims for its own" (Phelps 1986, 182). A recurring concern among those participating in this work has been a perceived lack of disciplinary unity on a variety of fronts—epistemology, methodology, literature, pedagogy, even our objects of inquiry; Maureen Goggin, for example, has noted that a "lack of consensus has led some in the field to deny Rhetoric and Composition the status of a discipline" (Goggin 1997, 336).

For those who need to represent the work of Composition, Rhetoric, and related enterprises in wider contexts, this apparent lack of disciplinary consensus can make their task quite challenging. Writing again more than twenty years later, for example, Phelps and John Ackerman explain the complexities of representing this universe to the bodies responsible

DOI: 10.7330/9781607326953.c005

for important taxonomic classifications for higher education. They determined that they would achieve success only by representing Rhetoric and Composition "as a collectivity, finding identity in our commonalities," rather than "as a set of contending micro-disciplines" (Phelps and Ackerman 2010, 189). In their report on what they called the "Visibility Project," Phelps and Ackerman describe the implications of being recognized as a discipline in these taxonomies, including influence over higher education planning and assessment at both national and state levels, access to funding for research and educational reform, and visas for faculty and students (186, 195).

Clearly, then, disciplinarity is an issue with stakes, and there are powerful expectations about what disciplinary recognition for Rhetoric and Composition could achieve, expectations related to both respect and resources. "The goal," in Joseph Harris's (2004) words, "of so many of us working in composition has been to gain the status of a discipline, to bring the sad women and men of the writing program out of the basement and into the upstairs offices and lounges of academic respectability" (357). As Deirdre McMahon and Ann Green point out, however, the increasingly widespread reliance on contingent faculty means that "the number of 'sad women in the basement' has multiplied" in recent decades (McMahon and Green 2008, 16), with this phenomenon not confined to writing programs. The ongoing sense of urgency behind calls for disciplinarity among those in Rhetoric and Composition, however, suggests that many still see the achievement of disciplinarity as the key to achieving equitable working conditions for that discipline's members, though how to define that discipline and what to call it remain points of debate. Because nomenclature has been so unsettled, underscoring the entire question about disciplinarity, we are reluctant to choose among the many options (Rhetoric and Composition, Composition and Rhetoric, Composition Studies, Writing Studies, etc.), and will instead use the terms offered by the voices we weave into our discussion. The one exception is our occasional focus on "Rhetoric," which tends to be the less examined term in these discussions, serving sometimes as an easy ally with Composition but sometimes pointing in quite different directions. Thus, we highlight Rhetoric to explore what might be missing from mainstream conversations about "Rhetoric-and-Composition" (we will use the hyphenated term as a default, when needed).

Of course, "discipline" itself is not always so clear-cut a term, and so we turn here to Stephen Toulmin's (1972) discussion of disciplines as "rational enterprises." Toulmin notes that it is not subject matter that distinguishes one discipline from another but rather "intellectual ideals" or "explanatory ambitions" (151). A discipline is not defined by the structure of the world but rather by the shared, collective desires of people to understand some aspects of the world. Disciplines, then, are sociohistorical phenomena, as well as intellectual enterprises; they are learned cultural categories. Thus, we suggest, discussions about disciplinary identity and status might be informed by a look at the approaches to categories and classification that have been useful in other fields of inquiry, such as genre studies. While many approaches to classification exist, two main approaches stand out as particularly relevant: (1) the closed or "container" approach derived from Plato and favored by biological taxonomists until Charles Darwin and (2) the open or "family resemblance" approach derived from Ludwig Wittgenstein and supported by research in cognitive psychology. The closed approach, based on essential features and preexisting categories, produces a hierarchical system of closed categories with specific criteria determining membership and clear boundaries between containers; the open approach is organized around socially perceived similarities based in multiple shared traits, with no rules defining membership and no single feature necessarily shared by all members. This latter approach leads to open categories without predetermined boundaries and, in the context of genre studies, has been favored recently as affording a more dynamic view of genres in their social context (Bazerman and Prior 2005; C. R. Miller 2015). Closed categories, in trying to hammer criteria and boundaries down, tend to give us static taxonomies that do not reflect cultural variation and historical change, and therefore tend to be more limited in the insight they offer about the functions and consequences of social categories such as disciplines. We suspect that the anxiety within Rhetoric-and-Composition about disciplinary status suffers from tensions between these two approaches to classification.

Putting category theory in conversation with discussions about disciplinarity, we specifically ask what an understanding of discipline as open, evolving, networked category might afford. Understanding disciplines as closed categories, for example, may lead to counterproductive debates over the criteria for inclusion and exclusion and may belie the diversity and dynamism of disciplinary work. Understanding disciplines as open categories, on the other hand, may allow for greater diversity in what disciplinary participation looks like and help us think about intellectual change and academic work more productively. As our question implies, we are not arguing for or against disciplinarity, but rather for an approach that conceptualizes disciplines as continually emergent intellectual categories of networked interests, goals, and practices. Rather than offering solutions to the multiple stakes often associated with disciplinarity or advocating for a particular institutional instantiation of the disciplinary system, our intention in this chapter is to provide the theoretical and historical perspective necessary to interrogate the schema of classification through which disciplinarity is understood and, perhaps, to adjust the expectations many in Rhetoric-and-Composition have for disciplinarity. Toward this end, we begin by putting category theory in conversation with disciplinarity, then applying this to the case of Rhetoric-and-Composition more specifically, before further complicating the picture with insights from the history of departmentalization.

## CLASSIFYING THE RHETORICAL AND LANGUAGE ARTS

In *Sorting Things Out*, Geoffrey C. Bowker and Susan Leigh Star suggest that classifications and categories are information infrastructures that underlie the social and moral order and exert material force, sometimes visibly, often invisibly (Bowker and Star 1999, 3). Bowker and Star's examples include the International Classification of Diseases developed in the nineteenth century but still influencing medical information systems today. Disciplines can be thought of as the information infrastructure of the academy, the classifications and categories that "sort out" both the domains of knowledge and the people and activities that produce, curate, and disseminate knowledge. While the cognitive and social processes involved are abstract, the signs of classification at work are often quite concrete. For example, one concrete space where disciplinary categories become manifest is in professional conference programs. Another such space is in higher education databases. To think through disciplines as cultural categories, we begin with several recent examples along these lines relevant to Rhetoric-and-Composition.

In 2014 the Modern Language Association (MLA) completed a massive effort to reorganize its equally massive annual conventions, from a dual structure of divisions and discussion groups to a system of forums organized under nine top-level categories that in effect serves as a taxonomy of intellectual interests within the organization. One of the new top-level categories is Rhetoric, Composition, and Writing Studies, which includes five subcategories: Creative Writing, History and Theory of Composition, History and Theory of Rhetoric, Literacy Studies, and Writing Pedagogies.[1] The revision, the first in forty years, involved much commentary from members and took three years.[2] The original proposal from the working group in charge of the process included only six top-level categories, with "Rhetoric, Composition, and Writing Studies" included as a subcategory under the top-level Language Studies, which included eleven other subcategories such as "Germanic Philology and Linguistics" and "Translation Studies."[3] Extensive commentary in MLA's online forum by those in the field(s) of Rhetoric-and-Composition, plus the late inclusion of David Bartholomae on the working group, as well as other lobbying, was successful in promoting Rhetoric-and-Composition to a major, visible component of the MLA's taxonomy. But the initial subordination suggests that the positioning of Rhetoric-and-Composition as a category within the language arts is both nonobvious and subject to deliberation. The entire exercise in fact suggests that the intellectual structure of the language arts does not reduce to a logical hierarchy of closed disciplinary categories, but can be better thought of as an open network of negotiated relationships: the scope and relations between research areas are historically contingent, with divisions more provisional than "real."

Phelps and Ackerman's experience with the Visibility Project is also instructive. Working with the Consortium of Doctoral Programs in Rhetoric and Composition, they pursued a specific route toward disciplinary identity and identification, focusing on powerful classification systems and taxonomies used to evaluate and measure the work of the academy: "The codes used for naming, describing, and organizing data about subject fields, instructional programs, research specializations, publications, and other academic facts both manifest and shape perceptions and conceptions of disciplines and disciplinarity. They determine what kind of information can flow into databases, what 'counts' and what can be counted, and how this information is analyzed and interpreted. Without appropriate codes, the informational correlates of disciplinary activity simply disappear into a black hole, diffused into this network of data where no search can find them" (Phelps and Ackerman 2010, 186).

Phelps and Ackerman succeeded in revising two such taxonomic codes to better represent Rhetoric-and-Composition: the classification of doctoral programs maintained by the National Research Council (NRC) and the Classification of Instructional Programs ("CIP" codes) used by the National Center for Education Statistics (Phelps and Ackerman 2010, 183).[4] Although the NRC taxonomy allows for the inclusion of "emerging fields" under strict criteria, and the CIP codes usually include an "other" placeholder, such codes, by their very nature, are discrete boxes into which research and instructional programs must be placed.

Thus, as a result of the work by Phelps and a Conference on College Composition and Communication (CCCC) Task Force, the NRC taxonomy now includes "Rhetoric and Composition" as an emerging field,[5] and under the new CIP taxonomy an instructional program may now be coded 23.1301, "Writing, General," or 23.1302, "Creative Writing," or 23.1303, "Professional, Technical, Business and Scientific Writing," or 23.1304, "Rhetoric and Composition," or 23.1399, "Rhetoric and Composition/Writing Studies/Other" but may not be placed in more than one of these boxes (Phelps and Ackerman 2010, 199).[6] However, if we search for "Rhetoric" alone, we find no fewer than eight curricular codes that include it in the description, including those noted above, under code 23, English Language and Literature/Letters, and two under code 09, Communication, Journalism, and Related Programs, in subcategories 09.0100, "Communication, General," and 09.0101, "Speech Communication and Rhetoric." The CIP thus reifies the division of Rhetoric into two houses, communication studies and English studies (see C. R. Miller et al. 2003). In sorting out the instructional programs that see their work as connected with ancient and contemporary rhetorical theory in this way, the CIP taxonomy reflects and perpetuates perception of these areas of rhetoric-related disciplinary activity as separate, with networked affiliations between them, in Phelps and Ackerman's (2010) words, "simply disappear[ing] into a black hole" (186). The challenges in defining and categorizing the intellectual work related to Composition, Rhetoric, and related enterprises in these two databases once more illustrate that there is no obvious or logical taxonomy of disciplines. These classifications, as technical systems, require a hierarchy and closed sets of categories, reinforcing a common view of how both disciplines and categories work.

The taxonomic problems that Rhetoric poses for the CIP are heightened for us in view of the movement represented by the Mt. Oread Manifesto, a call to reunite the rhetorical arts after their century of separation into departments of English and departments of communication (Keith and Mountford 2014). Believing that "the formal divisions between speaking and writing are untenable and indeed, in practice, are beginning to dissolve," especially with the integration of digital technologies into communicative and instructional practices, the signatories argue that these divisions "impoverish education for all students" and that we need an "integrated vision of rhetorical education" drawing on "the civic dimension of the rhetorical tradition [that] is plainly crucial to producing students with the communicative capabilities needed in this world" (1, 2). They propose that "rhetoricians should cross departmental and disciplinary lines and collaborate to design and implement an integrated curriculum in rhetorical education to replace separate introductory courses in communication (public speaking or presentation) and first-year written composition in order to develop citizen participants, not simply future employees or more literate students" (3). Doing so, they argue, will not only have many pedagogical benefits, but will also strengthen Rhetoric itself with respect to other disciplines and other instructional agendas within the academy. Similarly, Carolyn Miller, Victoria Gallagher, and Michael Carter argued in 2003 that boxing research and instruction in oral, written, and visual modes of rhetorical expression into English-based or communication-based categories might stultify the development of cross-disciplinary synergy that seems necessary in the age of new media (C. R. Miller et al. 2003).[7] The closed disciplinary boxes of taxonomies and traditional academic programs make certain pedagogical innovations difficult.

## DISCIPLINARITY AND CATEGORY THEORY

These classificatory conundrums may be inevitable in the statistical and information management efforts for which taxonomic codes are intended. But do such codes represent our best thinking about disciplinarity? We can gain some perspective on the workings of codes and taxonomies and, perhaps, rethink our expectations for disciplinarity, by exploring the psychology of categories, which has shed light both on the persistence of the closed, classical approach to categories and on the need for alternative approaches. We divide the world into categories, repeatable units, to which we refer when we use common nouns such as "table" or "chair," "horse" or "zebra," "department" or "discipline." A closed, logical approach to classification would enable us to place any instance unambiguously into one and only one category; ideally the hierarchical levels of the category system would show us degrees of similarity or relation between categories. And, indeed, as George Lakoff notes in his study of human categorization, "the idea that there is a single right taxonomy of natural things is remarkably persistent" (Lakoff 1987, 119). Yet, biologists have found that there are multiple ways to classify the phenomena of the organic world, none of them completely adequate. For example, there are three species of zebras, two of them closely related through shared ancestry, but the third more closely related to the horse than to either of the other two kinds of zebra. So there seems to be no "natural" or biological category that includes all zebras and nothing but zebras (119).[8] Arguments about biological classification are still seriously split between pheneticists, cladists, and traditionalists who prefer the Linnaean approach, and there seems to be no one "best" or "truest" biological taxonomy, in large part because of the complex dynamics of evolutionary change and also because of the different uses to which taxonomies are put (Benton 2000).

The study of human category formation has recently become an important subfield of cognitive psychology. According to Eleanor Rosch, who did some of the earliest landmark work in category theory, the "basic cuts in categorization are made at . . . discontinuities" between "information-rich bundles of perceptual and functional attributes" (Rosch 1978, 6). Thus, "the division of the world into categories is not arbitrary" (Rosch and Mervis 1975, 602) but rather is based on the principles of cognitive economy and perceived world structure, or experiential correlations. Categories both reflect and constitute the perceived structure not only of the social world but also of our goals and tasks (functions). Because perceptions and functions change over time with new conditions and new capabilities and may differ between social groups, category systems may not be stable or consistent. If perceived discontinuities are relatively stable, however, the categories may come to seem like "natural kinds" (rather than social kinds), with criterial features that discriminate, once and for all, the chair from the table, the zebra from the horse, the novel from the inaugural address, psychology from linguistics. But just as biologists have surrendered the concept of "species" as an unchanging essence to the continual flux posited by evolution, cognitive psychologists have demonstrated that our everyday categories are similarly difficult to square with a criterial, or logical, approach. Like species, our categories do not have clear boundaries; they change over time and across locations and groups, and they do not produce logical taxonomies based on consistent criteria (Lakoff 1987, 187–95): in other words, our categories are always social and not "natural."[9]

Conceptual categories, like biological species, are better understood through Wittgenstein's notion of family resemblances than through "natural kinds," essences, or logical criteria (Rosch 1978; Rosch and Mervis 1975). This means, first, that we don't need criteria in order to judge how well a specimen fits a category, and second, that specimens within a category do not necessarily all share any common feature but each shares at least one feature with another specimen. Within a family, for example, some members will have similar noses, perhaps many will have similar skin and hair coloring, and some will have similar body types. Some may share many features with many other members, and some may share only one feature with only a few others. But all, as a "population," share fewer features with members of other families, though families also change through the addition of new members (in the case of disciplines, as Toulmin reminds us, "members" can include concepts, goals, methods, people, etc.). A category, then, is a loose cluster with open boundaries, perhaps questionable instances on the margins, and some instances that seem fairly "central" or most representative of the concept. These central specimens are "prototypes" that are most easily identified. Rosch's research shows that specimens that function as prototypes are "those which bear the greatest family resemblance to other members of their own category and have the least overlap with other categories" (Rosch and Mervis 1975, 598–99). In keeping with the family metaphor, the category as a whole is better thought of as a dynamic network than as a logical system because of these varied and multiple affiliations and similarity relations.

The implications for our understanding of disciplines are several. First and not surprisingly, if we understand disciplines as a set of cognitive categories that are socially constructed and historically positioned, they will change over time, not only in their prototypical research projects and curricula but also in their relationships to other disciplines. For these reasons, of course, the NRC and NCES periodically revise their taxonomies, allowing for the inclusion of new or reconfigured disciplinary formations and for their repositioning within the higher-level coded categories.[10] Another implication is that fully systematic taxonomies may be impossible even at a given point in time, because the experiential correlations—the perceptual discontinuities and functions of the categories—differ among those who use the taxonomies: scholars, administrators, government officials, legislators, and so on. Thus, in the taxonomic system used by the CIP, Rhetoric can seem to belong naturally to both the communication discipline and to languages and literatures, as well as to have a minor place within linguistics (16.0102), which itself is classified within Foreign Languages and Literatures. But the consequences for Rhetoric itself are to divide its territory and thus to debilitate and obscure it. A different set of disciplinary categories, a different taxonomy, might unify Rhetoric but do violence to the conventional separation of the humanities and social sciences into distinct categories or to the historical affiliations between Composition programs and their traditional departmental companion, literary studies. The point is that classification systems, and the categories of which they are composed, are themselves rhetorical constructions, embedded in historical conditions, and serving, in the words of Kenneth Burke, as ways of both seeing and not-seeing (Burke [1935] 1965, 49).

## RHETORIC-AND-COMPOSITION AS OPEN, NETWORKED DISCIPLINE

What, then, are the implications for Rhetoric-and-Composition of understanding disciplines as open, networked, and continually emergent? For one, it casts doubt on concerns raised about disciplines as hegemonic, modernist structures of power. As Wardle and Downs point out in this volume, disciplinarity has been understood as necessarily "modernist, hegemonic, stultifying, limiting" and therefore potentially "even unethical." We argue that this criticism has less to do with disciplinarity as such and more to do with the schema for classification through which we understand disciplines. Joseph Harris, for example, describes disciplines as "conservative structures—both politically and intellectually" (Harris 2004, 358), a point also made by Thomas Kuhn in emphasizing the "central role" of a scientific tradition or "paradigm" that often seems to function as dogma (Kuhn 1977, 236). Invoking the common spatial metaphor of discipline as territory, Harris states, "The point of a discipline is to define turf, to limit what can be said, to regulate the work of its members" (Harris 2004, 358). When combined with hyperspecialization, he continues, "a single field of study divides and expands into an inchoate array of competing methods and interests—and you begin to form a picture of intellectual work that is at once constrained and incoherent" (358). The dual concerns Harris expresses reflect an understanding of disciplines as part of a closed system organized around criteria, an understanding for which diversity within categories entails chaos. Harris's concerns echo those of other compositionists,[11] notably Stephen North's assessment of Composition as "gradually pulling itself apart" and "fragmenting" (North 1987, 364).

One of the criteria commonly emphasized in disciplinary classification, in fact, is methodology, something North uses to organize the typology of compositionists he develops. North was concerned that what he saw as a lack of methodological integrity put the whole intellectual enterprise into jeopardy. For others, however, the diversity of methodologies routinely employed to study rhetoric and writing calls into question whether there was ever anything unified enough to "fragment" or put in jeopardy. If this intellectual enterprise routinely employs methods associated with both humanistic inquiry and with social science inquiry, can it be a discipline? Because the closed, classical approach to categories also makes it necessary to specify hierarchical relations, as in the multiple nested levels of the CIP, the humanities and the social sciences become broader disciplinary domains in a hierarchy that branches down, making it difficult to see how a coherent discipline could routinely employ methods originating from both.

This closed approach to disciplinary classification also leads to questions about whether "Rhetoric" and "Composition" are two subdisciplines, or, in combination, a single subdiscipline of English studies. Continuing this line of reasoning, would related fields such as Computers and Composition be *sub*-subdisciplines? And what about areas such as the rhetoric of science or the history of rhetoric that are claimed by both English and communication departments? A closed approach to categories makes it difficult to accept that these areas are often researched in the same institution by scholars in two different academic units, often with similar approaches, and may encourage us to find ways to eliminate this irregularity, potentially by "disciplining" members and their work.

If we shift our model to understand disciplines as open and networked, however, this sort of heterogeneity no longer poses a problem in need of reconciliation and "disciplining." This, in fact, is a point Charles Bazerman and Paul Prior have made recently in their work on literacy education. Invoking Bruno Latour's notion of "heterogeneous networks" and Wittgenstein's "family resemblance," they argue that we need to "move from a . . . notion of disciplines as unified social and/or cognitive spaces to a notion of disciplinarity as the ongoing, mediated constitution of a kind of social network" (Bazerman and Prior 2005, 152–53). Their preference for the notion of "disciplinarity" over "discipline" reflects an understanding of "participation" as more salient for understanding the dynamics of knowledge construction than essential criteria and static boundaries. That is, it's more important that an activity or an individual be understood as contributing to a disciplinary project than it is that the contribution measure up to some set of defining criteria. This is much the same point Prior made in his earlier study of graduate student disciplinary acculturation where he used "disciplinarity" as a term evoking process, activity, and "doing," in preference to the abstract concept of "discipline," which can seem to exist independently of human actors' continual constitution of it (Prior 1998, 26). Bazerman and Prior's work on the ongoing interconnections and intertextuality at play in the dynamic work of disciplinarity renders "mundane" the "interdiscursive blendings and blurrings" that are often termed interdisciplinary (Bazerman and Prior 2005, 154). In other words, rather than being the exception, hybridity and interdisciplinarity may be the norm, a condition that family resemblance can describe more satisfactorily than a logical hierarchy can. Rather than "Rhetoric-and-Composition" as a putatively unified entity, then, we can see the combination as a strategically networked alliance of interests and activities. This means, for example, that there may well be no single, central prototype research project or scholar, and few canonical knowledge claims. Rather, we find some scholars conducting textual analysis to understand the citational patterns of American Catholic bishops after sexual abuses have come to light (O'Keefe 2015), others exploring slave literacy instruction in the eighteenth century (Watson 2009), and yet others interrogating the affordances of digital delivery for Composition pedagogy and theory (Adsanatham et al. 2013).

Beyond the social and intellectual oppression a closed model of disciplinary categories can yield, a criterial schema for disciplinary categorization that inevitably results in "narrowing the acceptable data, method, or theory," also puts us, in Bazerman's words, "in danger of misunderstanding or even distorting the processes, practices, and products" of our objects of study (Bazerman 2011, 8). As Bazerman's own work illustrates nicely, combining methods and theory developed elsewhere can yield insights we might not otherwise come to. Yet a closed, criteria-based schema for categorizing our work can often prevent us from even exploring these possibilities, as we constrain our scholarly identities and participation to fit our understanding of disciplinary categories. The open model, in contrast, allows for participation in multiple disciplinary conversations and looks more like a network than a container or a hierarchical system of boxes. The network metaphor for knowledge construction and disciplines is not new. John Swales (1990), for example, uses the notion of "sociorhetorical network" to explain his view of disciplinary discourse communities (9). And in her examination of the rhetoric of interdisciplinarity, Julie Klein (2009) points out that the metaphors of both "network" and "rhizome" have been used to represent more dynamic, less hierarchical understandings of disciplinarity (269, 273). For those who participate in constituting Rhetoric-and-Composition, the network metaphor makes it clearer how, for example, one member, research project, or method (one node) might simultaneously participate in Rhetoric-and-Composition as disciplinary network and at the same time participate in another network such as distance education, feminism, or disability studies. Or, to look at it differently, we might find research contributions that form a network connecting ethnographic methods from anthropology, concepts both from classical rhetoric and from feminist theory, research sites from writing across the curriculum, and activities from computers and writing.

Bazerman and Prior theorize disciplinarity broadly, and their understanding of disciplines as multivocal and heterogeneous supports arguments for a pluralistic understanding of Rhetoric-and-Composition, arguments that have run parallel to the ongoing fears over

Rhetoric-and-Composition's fragmentation and disunity. Janice Lauer's "dappled discipline" comes to mind here. In her frequently cited article, Lauer (1984) points out that Composition (and it is worth noting that she focuses exclusively on Composition) has long understood and embraced "what a number of disciplines are just starting to admit—that many of their most important problems can be properly investigated only with multiple research methods" (26). In her words, Composition from very early on "saw the value of building on relevant work in other fields and of using methods of investigation refined elsewhere" (26). While admitting the potential disadvantages of operating as a "dappled" discipline, she clearly favored accepting its diversity at that time. Her remarks in an interview marking the thirtieth anniversary of that article reveal her continued optimism about the discipline's inclusivity and pluralism, though inflected with a consciousness of the combined "centripetal and centrifugal movement[s]" generated by developments since then (Vealey and Rivers 2014, 177). Her focus on Composition, however, suggests a schema in which Composition operates as a distinct disciplinary network, though it might also engage with rhetoric-as-network in conjunction with other disciplinary networks to address the research problems related to composing.

Lauer has not been alone in advocating that Rhetoric-and-Composition embrace an epistemologically and methodologically diverse disciplinary identity. Phelps (1986), for example, while seeking to outline the discipline's boundaries, notes its "marginal fluidity" and advocates for "'syntopical research,' which synthesizes and applies the work of other fields according to its own pragmatic principle" (191). Noting the potentially mythical quality of disciplinarity unity, Maureen Goggin (1997), surmises that "univocalism is not possible," in part because "disciplines are made up of individuals who are enmeshed in a complex web of institutions that both make possible a range of problems and activities . . . [and] limit other problems and activities in which they can engage" (338).

This pluralistic thread, of course, continues today, most obviously in conversations on multimodality and digital, networked composition, conversations that so clearly benefit from theories, methods, and insights developed in other disciplines such as design, communication, information science, computer science, and so on. Jonathan Alexander and Jacqueline Rhodes, in their recent work *On Multimodality*, ascribe disciplinary status to what they term "composition studies" and suggest that exploring the questions raised by modes and media beyond print-based alphabetic writing will require a pluralistic approach to disciplinary work (Alexander and Rhodes 2014). They point out that "trying to figure the 'field' as one thing, a monolithic entity, would be ludicrous" and advocate "diversity—of method, of inquiry, of practice, of pedagogy" (5). Their assessment of the intellectual affordances of a pluralistic approach, in fact, leads them to suggest we might "reimagin[e] composition as a multidiscipline that takes seriously the challenges of new media's many rhetorical affordances" (7). This need to find a new term like "multidiscipline" seems to us simply a need to name the lived experience of plurality inherent in all academic work and the "interdiscursive blendings and blurrings" that are often termed interdisciplinary, but which are, according to Bazerman and Prior (2005, 154), "mundane." Understanding the "discipline" of Rhetoric-and-Composition as a strategically networked alliance of interests and activities, then, means that maintaining the distinction between a discipline and a multidiscipline, between interdisciplinarity and multidisciplinarity,[12] becomes increasingly difficult and possibly pointless: because the boundaries of the category are blurred, the network is constantly adjusting to new goals, new conditions, new opportunities. Shifting our understanding of disciplinary categories away from the closed, hierarchical approach that results in the discrete, monolithic categories Alexander and Rhodes find so unproductive makes disciplinary status a provisional, rhetorically constructed condition.

As scholars and teachers in a number of areas increasingly find themselves confronting questions of definition and territory in the course of their work on language and communication in the contemporary digital context, using a network schema for disciplinarity has the added benefit of allowing scholars to move away from the issue of ownership of research. For the issue of ownership (or territory), in fact, has sometimes prevented collaboration where it would be most useful—a clear casualty of the closed approach to disciplinary categories. A networked understanding of disciplinarity might embolden more of us to participate in conversations relevant to Rhetoric-and-Composition but occurring in other networks, such as those in user experience design, educational research, media studies, and rhetorical criticism. At the institutional level, this understanding might also liberate us to experiment with departmental and programmatic arrangements, something we already see in doctoral programs such as Clemson's Rhetorics, Communication, and Information Design and North Carolina State University's Communication, Rhetoric, and Digital Media programs.[13] At the undergraduate level, multiliteracy centers such as Michigan Tech's and Iowa State University's ISUComm,[14] which focuses on what they call "WOVE"—written, oral, visual, and electronic communication across the curriculum—exemplify strategic networks that are consistent with an understanding of disciplines as open categories. These examples, however, call forth another element that figures prominently in discussions of disciplinarity and that merits separate examination: departments.

## DEPARTMENTALIZATION, PAST AND FUTURE

Disciplines are reified not only in administrative taxonomies but also in institutional structures, such as academic departments. Departmentalization is often taken as a marker of disciplinary status, but it is instructive—in considering the disciplinary status of Rhetoric, Composition, and related enterprises—to remember the institutional history of departments of English, as it suggests how different departments and disciplines are. William Riley Parker told this story in 1967,[15] and while his version is now fifty years old, it yields some insights that are still relevant.

First, Parker reminds us that departmentalization in the university is itself just over 100 years old now, becoming the norm only in the 1890s, when enrollments were increasing dramatically and intellectual specialization was becoming the expectation. Second, instruction in English (about the language or the literature) was not common until the very late nineteenth century, when the classical curriculum was increasingly replaced by a system of majors and electives; Parker reminds us that in 1857 Matthew Arnold "broke all traditions by lecturing in English instead of in Latin," that Harvard had no professor of English literature until 1876, that Oxford and Cambridge were the last universities in the English-speaking world to establish professorships in the field, and that it was the historical study of language as it developed in the latter half of the nineteenth century that undergirded the emergence of "English" as a discipline in both Britain and the United States. Third, Parker shows the historical contingency of locating the teaching of composition within the same units that taught English language and literature: although "there was . . . no compelling reason at the outset why the teaching of *composition* should have been entrusted to teachers of the English language and literature," Parker claims that it was this development that "quickly entrenched" English departments into institutional structures (Parker 1967, 347). Overall, he points out, English departments have been "aggressive" and possibly "acquisitive" (348), becoming the "catchall for the work of teachers of extremely diverse interests and training," such as rhetoric (including oratory and elocution as well as composition), journalism, drama and theater, writing for engineers, business writing, comparative literature, American literature, and other areas. "English," he concludes, "has never really defined itself as a discipline" (348). And in the context of this essay, we might conclude that the Department of English is not by any means a "natural kind."[16]

Parker maintained that the expedient origins and "greedy" development of departments of English made their "disintegration" inevitable (Parker 1967, 348), as many of its early subfields have spun off into their own academic units: linguistics, journalism, speech-communication, comparative literature, and so on. The recent movement of many composition programs into independent academic units may be just the latest example of the trend that Parker discerned. And though the question of departmentalization is not identical to the question of disciplinarity, they are related, and our approach to the latter is complicated by the former. Institutional structures constitute the practical conditions in which disciplines evolve, and departments themselves, as institutional categories, grow and change, evolve and decay, and sometimes go extinct, subject to local conditions such as institutional history and mission, the particularities of leadership and funding, the politics and economy of the region, and the like. Both disciplines and departments change over time, though they are subject to different forms of constraint and different impulses for change, both local and national. And if we take the long view, these mutually implicated yet different evolutionary processes yield results that are never logical, never completely satisfactory, and only, as Catherine Schryer said about genres, "stabilized-enough" and "stabilized-for-now" (Schryer 1993).

The trajectory of academic departmentalization has taken a new turn in the past decade, with many institutions establishing units such as centers and institutes that transcend department lines to promote collaboration in complex research and instructional areas; most of these units are in the natural and applied sciences, but closer to home this movement is perhaps best represented by the numerous centers for the digital humanities (e.g., the Maryland Institute for Technology in the Humanities and the Center for Digital Research in the Humanities at Nebraska).[17] Institutions have also begun to engage in hiring practices to support such efforts by superseding departmental priorities with a focus on multidisciplinary faculty "clusters." These new practices have the effect of weakening department boundaries and encouraging intellectual exchange and focused collaboration. The aim is to create institutional structures that better match or adapt to evolving intellectual interests and connections. The practices we describe below accelerate the trends we saw above in our brief history of English departments, challenging the bureaucratic inertia of institutions as well as our cognitive inertia about departments as seemingly logical and historically sanctioned categories.

This movement in higher education reflects an earlier one in corporate management and administration. As summarized in the 2013 *Handbook of Psychology*, "The latter part of the 20th, and the beginning of the 21st, centuries have witnessed a remarkable transformation of organizational structures worldwide . . . with one of its more compelling aspects being the shift from work organized around individual jobs to team-based work structures . . . as the core building blocks of organizations" (Kozlowski and Bell 2013, 412). These changes are attributed to "Increasing global competition, consolidation, and innovation" that require "more rapid, flexible, and adaptive responses" (412). This shift in organizational structuring has taken several forms and acquired several labels, including "the fractal organization" (Pasmore 1994), "the learning organization" (Sun 2003), and the "temporary organization" (Lundin and Söderholm 1995), but the rationale and practices are similar.

Cluster hiring is one way that academic institutions have found to implement this kind of flexible organizational structure, in response to the pressures for timely and focused problem-oriented teaching and collaborative research. As Laura Severin describes these pressures, "Students are demanding academic programs focused on real-world issues. Employers are asking for graduates who can work in teams across disciplinary specialties. And, despite budget cuts, governmental agencies, nonprofits, and businesses are looking to higher education to help them solve the 'big problems,' such as global climate change, food security, health care, political instability, and new-age literacy" (Severin 2013). Thus, the virtues of the temporary, fractal, learning organization are relevant to the academy, and the inertia of departmental structures and disciplinary traditions are viewed as increasingly disabling. Because interdisciplinarity characterizes much current work in research-intensive areas such as environmental sciences and materials engineering, many academic institutions are seeking ways to nurture cross-boundary relationships and paying less attention to departmental structures and traditional disciplinary boundaries. "Interdisciplinarity" remains a useful way to characterize deliberate attempts to put disciplinary networks into conversation with each other.

Pressures for restructuring the academy come in part from funding agencies. For example, the National Science Foundation issued a report in 2008 addressing how academic institutions and funding agencies can best support the crosscutting interdisciplinary research and graduate education understood to be essential for "cutting-edge science and technology" and "economic and societal growth and vitality" (Van Hartesveldt and Giordan 2008, 1). The report observes that "content and methods used in research are in constant flux both within and between disciplines, and researchers must frequently employ interdisciplinary approaches to respond to emerging research problems" (2) and notes that "supra-departmental structures such as centers and institutes can play an important role in supporting interdisciplinary research and education" (5). Universities are urged to "move away from rigid hierarchical structures to more dynamic and flexible structures in which faculty have some fluidity of movement between or across disciplinary homes" (5) and to "form research teams driven by basic or applied problem-oriented research challenges that serve to reduce the emphasis on whether a given research matter is disciplinary or interdisciplinary" (2). The report goes so far as to suggest that universities "consider separating the research/graduate teaching functions from the academic unit-driven undergraduate teaching mission" (3). We are not endorsing these recommendations, but it's useful to be aware of them as indicators of the broader institutional and economic climate in which our programs exist and must create their futures.

If indeed the academic department has outlived its usefulness, we should worry about the uncertainties that flexible and temporary structures will create for faculty, students, and academic programs, both during periods of transition and in the longer term. Replacing the modernist-Fordist-hierarchical approach to academic organization with a neoliberal market-driven approach may not serve instructional needs, even if it does advance certain kinds of research. But as we noted earlier, the academic department is a historical structure, one rooted in the demographic and economic transformations of just over 100 years ago, and we should recognize that it may not survive current trends in globalization, digital communication, and intellectual hybridization. But disciplines, as intellectual enterprises, can be stronger than departments. Rhetoric-and-composition as a network of inquiry and instruction has already demonstrated its independence of departmentalization with the recent movement of many programs outside departments of English, to independent units. The fact that some of these new units subsequently become departmentalized may say more about the prevailing political economy of the academy than about the need of intellectual and instructional practices for departmentalization. And while we don't advocate separating research and graduate education from undergraduate instruction, we do think it helpful to distinguish disciplinarity, as constituted primarily by research and inquiry, not only from departmentalization, as noted already, but also, as Joseph Harris (2004) does, from instructional programs. Although these layers are not independent of each other, they are distinguishable.

## CONCLUDING THOUGHTS

Toulmin's discussion of disciplines as rational enterprises takes as its central model what he calls "compact disciplines," based on well-established fields in the physical and biological sciences. He outlines five features they share: (1) there is a "specific and realistic set of agreed collective ideals," or explanatory ambitions; (2) these collective ideals govern the activities of those professionally committed to the discipline; (3) these activities produce "justificatory arguments" aimed at meeting the explanatory goals; (4) the arguments are employed within recognized professional forums; and (5) the collective ideals "determine the criteria of adequacy" for judging the arguments (Toulmin 1972, 379). Disciplines that fail to satisfy these conditions to one extent or another Toulmin calls "diffuse disciplines," and "would-be disciplines." It is surprising to learn, for example, that among the would-be disciplines, Toulmin counts psychology and sociology, because they have no "common set of disciplinary goals," and include a "diversity of approaches of a kind unparalleled in physics" (382). Rhetoric-and-composition is (or are?) certainly not a compact discipline, and much of the commentary with which we began suggests that the field fears being a would-be discipline. But our point here is that in some respects all disciplines can usefully be thought of as "diffuse." In the first place, a discipline, as a category of intellectual effort and achievement, is not a closed, definable territory, with completely known contents. And in the second place, disciplines have blurred and permeable borders and are networked with other diffusely defined disciplinary enterprises. If the disciplinary ambition for Rhetoric-and-Composition assumes compactness as the ideal, we believe this ambition is misdirected, both because such a model does not suit the ideals of Rhetoric-and-Composition specifically, and because, more generally, fields that are intellectually dynamic and productive, as well as highly valued within their institutions, are not well described as "compact."

With ongoing revisions in departmentalization at many institutions, frequent intellectual alliances with new media studies and other domains, continuing institutional emphasis on interdisciplinarity, and the dissemination of teaching and intellectual practices through "across-the-curriculum" programs, we suggest that Rhetoric-and-Composition can be usefully understood as a "diffuse discipline." And the situation of Rhetoric-and-Composition represents what may be the future of many disciplinary-institutional-professional constellations, with distributed intellectual authority, opportunistic networks, and multiple institutional instantiations. In many ways, Rhetoric and Composition, separately, do have different intellectual ambitions and explanatory goals, yet they frequently gain a lot from their alliance. Maybe that's as good as it gets: sometimes the hyphens are useful, but sometimes Rhetoric and Composition will go their separate ways.

Our argument here is that shifting the model of classification that we apply to disciplinarity, like shifting a terministic screen, changes the possibilities and constraints visible to us, giving us permission to be more inventive in our scholarship, pedagogy, and programs, while helping us avoid some of the oppressive aspects of "being disciplined." The weight of history and habit on disciplinarity is not negligible or unimportant, but realizing that the shape a disciplinary network takes has nothing essential or static about it gives us the freedom to more purposefully expand and reshape that network and our work in response to changing research needs and the changing communication landscape that has influenced so many research and teaching interests.

*Notes*

1. https://executivecouncil.mla.hcommons.org/list-of-mla-forums/ (accessed December 21, 2017).
2. https://executivecouncil.mla.hcommons.org/2014/05/14/an-introduction-to-the-new-forum-structure/ (accessed December 21, 2017).
3. https://groupsdiscussion.mla.hcommons.org/draft-proposal/ (accessed December 21, 2017); the section on "Rhetoric, Composition, and Writing Studies" in this original proposal had the third-highest number of comments in the online forum, suggesting the level of concern expressed.
4. An earlier effort by the consortium, under the leadership of Janice Lauer and Linda Ferreira-Buckley, obtained a code for "Rhetoric and Composition" in Dissertation Abstracts International in 1996 (Phelps and Ackerman 2010, 185).
5. http://sites.nationalacademies.org/PGA/Resdoc/PGA_044521 (last revised July 29, 2006).
6. https://nces.ed.gov/ipeds/cipcode/Default.aspx?y=55 (accessed December 21, 2017).
7. We should also acknowledge here the unsuccessful effort at integrating writing and speaking instruction known as the "communications movement" of the 1940s and 1950s, a movement whose only apparent lasting success was to give the fourth *C* to the Conference on College Composition and Communication (George and Trimbur 1999).
8. Lakoff takes this example from Stephen Jay Gould's 1981 essay "What, If Anything, Is a Zebra?" (Gould 1981).

9. The family resemblance model is similar to the "radial category" used by Wardle and Downs (this volume), both deriving from Lakoff (1987). Here, we use "family resemblance" as a general term to refer to Lakoff's argument for a cognitive-model theory of categories; "radial category" is a special kind of cognitive category in which there is a prototype and variations on it that cannot be predicted by rules but are conventional and have to be learned (Lakoff 1987, 83).
10. According to Phelps and Ackerman, however, such revisions occur under differing conditions, with the NRC having an open and transparent process and the NCES having a process that was "extraordinarily opaque, even secretive" (Phelps and Ackerman 2010, 196).
11. Here we follow Harris's and North's lead in our terminology.
12. Klein (2010) provides a "taxonomy" of interdisciplinarity, carefully distinguishing interdisciplinarity (which emphasizes integration), multidisciplinarity (which emphasizes juxtaposition), and transdisciplinarity (which emphasizes transcending and transforming). However, these detailed distinctions are less to our point than the fact that disciplines are not the closed, logical categories that such distinctions presuppose. Thus, it may be that any discipline is actually a multidiscipline. It is certainly the case that every discipline develops through hybridizing and integration of new concepts and methods. And in this respect, Rhetoric-and-Composition seems to be a model discipline.
13. See https://rcid.sites.clemson.edu/ and https://crdm.chass.ncsu.edu/ (accessed December 21, 2017).
14. https://www.engl.iastate.edu/isucomm/, accessed by December 21, 2017.
15. At the time, Parker was former secretary of the MLA and former editor of *PMLA*.
16. There have subsequently been several versions of the history of English studies as a discipline and English departments as an institutional unit (Graff 1987; T. Miller 2010; Ohmann 1976), all of which affirm Parker's account. In addition, there are works examining the history of the speech communication discipline and the communication department (Benson 1985; Cohen 1994; Keith 2007) and any number of studies exploring the relationships among Rhetoric, Composition, English, and communication (Halloran 1982, 1987; Keith 2000; Leff 2000; Mailloux 2006; T. Miller 2001; Murphy 2012). All of these are worth reading by those interested in the disciplinarity and disciplinary relations of Rhetoric and Composition.
17. See http://mith.umd.edu/ and https://cdrh.unl.edu/, accessed December 21, 2017.

## References

Adsanatham, Chanon, Bre Garrett, and Aurora Matzke. 2013. "Re-Inventing Digital Delivery for Multimodal Composing: A Theory and Heuristic for Composition Pedagogy." *Computers and Composition* 30 (4): 315–31. https://doi.org/10.1016/j.compcom.2013.10.004.

Alexander, Jonathan, and Jacqueline Rhodes. 2014. *On Multimodality: New Media in Composition Studies*. Urbana, IL: National Council of Teachers of English.

Bazerman, Charles. 2011. "The Disciplined Interdisciplinarity of Writing Studies." *Research in the Teaching of English* 46 (1): 8–21.

Bazerman, Charles, and Paul Prior. 2005. "Participating in Emergent Socioliterate Worlds: Genre, Disciplinarity, Interdisciplinarity." In *Multidisciplinary Perspectives on Literacy Research*, 2nd ed., ed. Richard Beach, Judith L. Green, Michael Kamil, and Timothy Shanahan, 133–78. Language and Social Processes. New York: Hampton Press.

Benson, Thomas W., ed. 1985. *Speech Communication in the 20th Century*. Carbondale: Southern Illinois University Press.
Benton, Michael J. 2000. "Stems, Nodes, Crown Clades, and Rank-Free Lists: Is Linnaeus Dead?" *Biological Reviews of the Cambridge Philosophical Society* 75 (4): 633–48. https://doi.org/10.1111/j.1469-185X.2000.tb00055.x.
Bowker, Geoffrey C., and Susan Leigh Star. 1999. *Sorting Things Out: Classification and Its Consequences*. Cambridge, MA: MIT Press.
Burke, Kenneth. [1935] 1965. *Permanence and Change: An Anatomy of Purpose*. Reprint ed. Indianapolis: Bobbs-Merrill.
Cohen, Herman. 1994. *The History of Speech Communication: The Emergence of a Discipline, 1914–1945*. Annandale, VA: Speech Communication Association.
Connors, Robert J. 1989. "Rhetorical History as a Component of Composition Studies." *Rhetoric Review* 7 (2): 230–40. https://doi.org/10.1080/07350198909388858.
George, Diana, and John Trimbur. 1999. "The 'Communication Battle,' or Whatever Happened to the 4th C?" *College Composition and Communication* 50 (4): 682–98. https://doi.org/10.2307/358487.
Goggin, Maureen Daly. 1997. "Composing a Discipline: The Role of Scholarly Journals in the Disciplinary Emergence of Rhetoric and Composition since 1950." *Rhetoric Review* 15 (2): 322–48. https://doi.org/10.1080/07350199709359222.
Gould, Stephen Jay. 1981. "What, If Anything, Is a Zebra?" *Natural History* 90 (7): 6–12.
Graff, Gerald. 1987. *Professing Literature: An Institutional History*. Chicago: University of Chicago Press.
Halloran, S. Michael. 1982. "Rhetoric in the American College Curriculum: The Decline of Public Discourse." *Pre/Text* 3 (3): 245–69.
Halloran, S. Michael. 1987. "Rhetoric and the English Department." *Rhetoric Society Quarterly* 17 (1): 3–10. https://doi.org/10.1080/02773948709390762.
Harris, Joseph. 2004. "Thinking Like a Program." *Pedagogy* 4 (3): 357–63. https://doi.org/10.1215/15314200-4-3-357.
Keith, William. 2000. "Rhetoric and Myth: A Response to Mailloux and Leff." *Rhetoric Society Quarterly* 30 (4): 95–106. https://doi.org/10.1080/02773940009391190.
Keith, William. 2007. *Democracy as Discussion: Civic Education and the American Forum Movement*. Lanham, MD: Lexington Books.
Keith, William, and Roxanne Mountford. 2014. "The Mt. Oread Manifesto on Rhetorical Education 2013." *Rhetoric Society Quarterly* 44 (1): 1–5. https://doi.org/10.1080/02773945.2014.874871.
Klein, Julie Thompson. 2009. "The Rhetoric of Interdisciplinarity: Boundary Work in the Construction of New Knowledge." In *The Sage Handbook of Rhetorical Studies*, ed. Andrea A. Lunsford, Kirt H. Wilson, and Rosa A. Eberly, 265–83. Los Angeles: Sage.
Klein, Julie Thompson. 2010. "A Taxonomy of Interdisciplinarity." In *The Oxford Handbook of Interdisciplinarity*, ed. Robert Frodeman, 15–30. New York: Oxford University Press.
Kozlowski, Steve W. J., and Bradford S. Bell. 2013. "Work Groups and Teams in Organizations." In *Industrial and Organizational Psychology*, 2nd ed., ed. N. W. Schmitt and S. Highhouse, 412–69. Hoboken, NJ: John Wiley and Sons.
Kuhn, Thomas S. 1977. *The Essential Tension: Selected Studies in Scientific Tradition and Change*. Chicago: University of Chicago Press.
Lakoff, George. 1987. *Women, Fire, and Dangerous Things: What Categories Reveal about the Human Mind*. Chicago: University of Chicago Press. https://doi.org/10.7208/chicago/9780226471013.001.0001.
Lauer, Janice M. 1984. "Composition Studies: Dappled Discipline." *Rhetoric Review* 3 (1): 20–29. https://doi.org/10.1080/07350198409359074.
Leff, Michael. 2000. "Rhetorical Disciplines and Rhetorical Disciplinarity: A Response to Mailloux." *Rhetoric Society Quarterly* 30 (4): 83–93. https://doi.org/10.1080/02773940009391189.

Lundin, Rolf A., and Anders Söderholm. 1995. "A Theory of the Temporary Organization." *Scandinavian Journal of Management* 11 (4): 437–55. https://doi.org/10.1016/0956-5221(95)00036-U.

Mailloux, Steven. 2006. *Disciplinary Identities: Rhetorical Paths of English, Speech, and Composition*. New York: Modern Language Association of America.

McMahon, Deirdre, and Ann Green. 2008. "Gender, Contingent Labor, and Writing Studies." *Academe* 94 (6): 16–19.

Miller, Carolyn R. 2015. "Genre Change and Evolution." In *Genre Studies around the Globe: Beyond the Three Traditions*, ed. N. Artemeva and A. Freedman, 154–85. Edmonton, AB: Inkshed Publications.

Miller, Carolyn R., Victoria Gallagher, and Michael Carter. 2003. "Integrated Approaches to Teaching Rhetoric: Unifying a Divided House." In *The Realms of Rhetoric: The Prospects for Rhetoric Education*, ed. J. Petraglia and D. Bahri, 209–28. Albany: State University of New York Press.

Miller, Thomas. 2001. "Disciplinary Identifications/Public Identities: A Response to Mailloux, Leff, and Keith." *Rhetoric Society Quarterly* 31 (3): 105–17. https://doi.org/10.1080/02773940109391209.

Miller, Thomas. 2010. *The Evolution of College English: Literacy Studies from the Puritans to the Postmoderns*, ed. D. Bartholomae and J. F. Carr. Pittsburgh Series in Composition, Literacy, and Culture. Pittsburgh, PA: University of Pittsburgh Press.

Murphy, James J., ed. 2012. *A Short History of Writing Instruction: From Ancient Greece to Contemporary America*. 3rd ed. New York: Routledge.

North, Stephen M. 1987. *The Making of Knowledge in Composition: Portrait of an Emerging Field*. Upper Montclair, NJ: Boynton/Cook.

Ohmann, Richard. 1976. *English in America: A Radical View of the Profession*. New York: Oxford University Press.

O'Keefe, Meaghan M. 2015. "Borrowed Authority: The American Catholic Bishops' Argument by Citation." *Written Communication* 32 (2): 150–73. https://doi.org/10.1177/0741088315574704.

Parker, William Riley. 1967. "Where Do English Departments Come From?" *College English* 28 (5): 339–51. https://doi.org/10.2307/374593.

Pasmore, William A. 1994. *Creating Strategic Change: Designing the Flexible, High-Performing Organization*. Hoboken, NJ: John Wiley and Sons.

Phelps, Louise Wetherbee. 1986. "The Domain of Composition." *Rhetoric Review* 4 (2): 182–95. https://doi.org/10.1080/07350198609359122.

Phelps, Louise Wetherbee, and John M. Ackerman. 2010. "Making the Case for Disciplinarity in Rhetoric, Composition, and Writing Studies: The Visibility Project." *College Composition and Communication* 62 (1): 180–215.

Prior, Paul. 1998. *Writing/Disciplinarity: A Sociohistoric Account of Literate Activity in the Academy. Rhetoric, Knowledge, and Society*. New York: Routledge.

Rosch, Eleanor. 1978. "Principles of Categorization." In *Cognition and Categorization*, 27–48. Hillsdale, NJ: Lawrence Erlbaum Associates.

Rosch, Eleanor, and Carolyn B. Mervis. 1975. "Family Resemblances: Studies in the Internal Structure of Categories." *Cognitive Psychology* 7 (4): 573–605. https://doi.org/10.1016/0010-0285(75)90024-9.

Schryer, Catherine F. 1993. "Records as Genre." *Written Communication* 10 (2): 200–234. https://doi.org/10.1177/0741088393010002003.

Severin, Laura. 2013. "Doing 'Cluster Hiring' Right." *Inside Higher Ed*, September 30. https://www.insidehighered.com/advice/2013/09/30/essay-how-colleges-can-engage-cluster-hiring.

Sun, He-Chuan. 2003. "Conceptual Clarifications for 'Organizational Learning,' 'Learning Organization' and 'A Learning Organization.'" *Human Resource Development International* 6 (2): 153–66. https://doi.org/10.1080/13678860110086465.

Swales, John. 1990. *Genre Analysis: English in Academic and Research Settings.* New York: Cambridge University Press.
Toulmin, Stephen. 1972. *Human Understanding: The Collective Use and Evolution of Concepts.* Princeton: Princeton University Press.
Van Hartesveltd, Carol, and Judith Giordan. 2008. *Impact of Transformative Interdisciplinary Research and Graduate Education on Academic Institutions.* National Science Foundation. http://www.nsf.gov/pubs/2009/nsf0933/igert_workshop08.pdf.
Vealey, Kyle P., and Nathaniel A. Rivers. 2014. "Dappled Discipline at Thirty: An Interview with Janice M. Lauer." *Rhetoric Review* 33 (2): 165–80. https://doi.org/10.1080/07350198.2014.884418.
Watson, Shevaun E. 2009. "'Good Will Come of This Evil': Enslaved Teachers and the Transatlantic Politics of Early Black Literacy." *College Composition and Communication* 61 (1): W66–89.

# 6
# UNDERSTANDING THE NATURE OF DISCIPLINARITY IN TERMS OF COMPOSITION'S VALUES

Elizabeth Wardle and Doug Downs

Composition Studies' path to disciplinary standing in the academy has been lengthened and complicated by the reticence of some of its practitioners to embrace the notion of disciplinarity and all that might entail.[1] Over a period of several decades, many of the field's leading lights expressed discomfort with disciplinarity, which they perceived as modernist, hegemonic, stultifying, limiting, and possibly even unethical. Yet, as this collection argues, disciplinarity offers institutional standing crucial to the development of a field of study and to the ability of its participants to make meaningful change in the areas they study. Mary Boland (2007) frames this question in terms of academic freedom itself: "Administrators and faculty typically presume that professors working in their fields are entitled to freedom in that work. This presumption has not yet been accorded to compositionists because our field has not been accurately recognized" (44).

In this chapter, we consider the source of our field's historical discomfort with disciplinarity in two key ways. First, we interrogate the nature of "disciplinarity" itself, and second, we consider how notions of disciplinarity conflict or align with some central values of Composition Studies. In these examinations, we suggest that disciplinarity, rather than being somehow inimical to the values that have shaped our field, is actually congruent with these values. In many cases, in fact, the nature of disciplinarity actively supports our work.

## DESCRIBING DISCIPLINARITY

In various dialogues and debates about Composition Studies' disciplinary standing, scholars have argued that it is a discipline, a postdiscipline, an antidiscipline, a metadiscipline, and/or an interdiscipline. At times, these terms have been used without accompanying definitions, or with assumed definitions that do not draw on available research regarding disciplinarity. Part of our work here is to attempt to define these terms and describe the nature of "disciplinarity," in the belief that clarifying terms can assist in coming to some agreement about what Composition Studies may be and what that might mean in material terms.

An academic discipline, by most conceptions, is a field or site of scholarly inquiry (often linked to a profession outside the academy) having a central object of study, set of questions, or activity that causes people with related projects to identify with the discipline. While disciplines were once understood as branches of the tree of knowledge, knowledge is significantly more entangled than that metaphor seems to permit. Instead, the notion of "field" can help us think about the nature of disciplines. A field, in the physics sense of the term, is a space defined or touched by a particular characteristic or force. For example, a magnetic field bounds an area of space where magnetic force is present. Similarly, a discipline is a field of inquiry defined by the characteristics of that inquiry. In this way, we understand "field" as Anne Ruggles Gere (1993) does, as the "complex of forces . . ., the [charged] space" in which Composition Studies can be reconceptualized and restructured (4).

Pierre Bourdieu also made extensive use of the term "field" as a social context in which habitus and circumstance interact to instantiate given behaviors, as recounted by Julie Klein (1996). For Pierre Bourdieu, Klein says, a field is a "market" in which one form of capital (economic, social, cultural, symbolic) can be converted to another. Bourdieu's field is, in Klein's terms, "a separate social universe with its own laws of functioning and specific relations of force" (5). So we can understand a discipline as a field in the sense of social force or power that establishes relationships inside the discipline and relationships among disciplines and professions. John Trimbur (1996) thinks of fields in this sense as "social formations which allow recognition and help determine who may speak, about what, and on whose behalf" (138). These formations take both ideological and material forms.

Susan Brown Carlton (1995), writing in *Rhetoric Review*, thus defines disciplines as having "a defined object of study, texts that theorize and historicize that object, methodologies that produce knowledge about that object, and the capacity to reproduce disciplinary practitioners" (79) and as being "distinct from other fields" (80). How do people actually recognize disciplines as distinct, given that disciplinary boundaries on a scholar-by-scholar basis are often less clear cut? We seem to recognize disciplines less by running down a checklist of questions, methods, projects, and canonical texts than by categorization based on prototypes, such as George Lakoff (1990) discusses in *Women, Fire, and Dangerous Things*. Drawing on other cognitive psychologists as well as Wittgenstein's notion of family resemblances, Lakoff develops the construct of "radial categories," whose members may not look much like each other but which all somehow resemble the prototype at the center of the category. "Bird" is a radial category because, as much as ducks do not look like ostriches, both look quite a bit like our mental prototype of a "bird": wings, feathers, beaks, laying eggs, two-legged, and flying. Bats, however, are rarely thought of as birds. While they fly (and ostriches don't), bats lack feathers, beaks, and egg-laying. In radial categories, membership is determined by closeness to or difference from the category prototype. People seem to treat academic disciplines as radial categories: for instance, cognitive linguistics, sociolinguistics, general linguistics, and applied linguistics don't look a great deal like each other, yet they all look like "linguistics" because they do what linguistics does and what other fields usually do not. The implication of disciplines as radial categories is that it is fairly easy to establish participation in a discipline but more difficult to map its boundaries. A sociolinguist may clearly be a linguist but also look a lot like a sociologist or an anthropologist.

Understanding disciplines as fields and radial categories, then, undermines the notion of a discipline as a rigid box. As fields, disciplines "inhabit" any space hospitable to their defining characteristics. As radial categories, disciplines have a prototypical core with which all of their members somehow identify, which means that a discipline's boundaries will tend to spread out to a ragged, idiosyncratic, imprecise and unstable circumference.

This imprecision has sometimes been taken as a *failure* of the notion of disciplines. But disciplinary theorists such as Klein (1996) and Andrew Abbott (2002) suggest that conceiving of disciplines as rigid and clear-cut in the first place is, in fact, the failure. Instead, disciplines should be understood as "fissured sites comprising multiple strata and influenced by other disciplines" (Klein 1996, 55). Such an understanding accounts for the fact that we can recognize cognitive linguistics as a kind of linguistics while recognizing that it could not exist apart from cognitive psychology, yet we don't confuse a cognitive linguist with a cognitive psychologist. Such examples of cross-disciplinary influence lead Klein to characterize disciplinary boundaries as "permeable membranes," concluding that "disciplines are not isolated units. Permeation is part of their character" (38).

This permeability also contradicts a perspective sometimes identified as *postdisciplinarity*, in which disciplinarity is critiqued as hostile to methodological variance, focused (in academic settings) on expert practitioners rather than students, and inimical to cross-disciplinary inquiry (Carlton 1995, 79). Of some disciplines, these criticisms are probably valid. But it seems important not to confuse the shortcomings of a *given discipline* with the nature of *disciplinarity itself*. There is no reason a discipline cannot adopt values of methodological variance, student-centeredness, and borrowing from and interacting with other disciplines—as Carlton argues that Composition Studies does. So there doesn't seem to be anything about postdisciplinarity that disciplinarity can't encompass if its practitioners wish it to.

Abbott (2002) argues that while disciplinary boundaries are defined by, among other things, agreed-upon methods and objects of study, they are not rigid, structuralist, closed enterprises. Rather, he argues, disciplines "do not . . . place many constraints on the kinds of knowledge possible within them" (211) and "are astonishingly diverse internally" (213). The kind of dynamism Abbott proposes does not fit critiques of disciplinarity as fixed and modernist. It is certainly true that in some disciplines (particularly some in the natural and life sciences), inquiry is constrained to particular focuses for which funding is available. It's also true that not every site within a discipline will allow unfettered inquiry in any direction a scholar wishes. A university that wishes to invest all its genetics research money in a cancer lab will probably "discipline" its researchers to do only the kind of research that lab can support. But returning again to the notion of radial categories, disciplines are not "contained" by their prototypes, which is what Abbott is driving at. Knowledge creation and inquiry work in fits and starts (we're thinking of Thomas Kuhn's 1962 S*tructure of Scientific Revolutions* here), but historically it has trended toward greater openness and diversity of inquiry, and disciplines *as wholes* have generally broadened rather than narrowed and opened rather than restricted or self-censored.

This dynamism plays on the canonizing nature of disciplines. In Abbott's (2002) view, disciplinary boundaries provide scholars "with a general conception of intellectual existence, a conception of the proper units of knowledge . . . and by preventing knowledge from becoming too abstract or overwhelming . . . They define what it is permissible not to know and thereby limit the body of books one must have read" (210). Evidence for dynamism in canonization exists in the creation of subdisciplines, which track the expansion of texts in a discipline. Knowledge in any discipline expands exponentially, resulting in greater specialization as any given practitioner can only be responsible for deep knowledge of a roughly fixed amount of material. Disciplines therefore specify not what one is *allowed* to read, but the bare minimum one *must* read for disciplinary participation. The subdiscipline of ethics does not say, "You may not be an ethicist if you read metaphysics." It says, "To be a credible ethicist, you need to have read *this* material but you need not have read *that* material." Then the ethicist is welcome to read all the metaphysics, epistemology, and psychology she can, in order to pursue work related to ethics and also to these other disciplines. The "disciplining" force of some shared set of "must-reads" seems necessary to the formation of a community of practice, but members of that community are certainly not limited to that list.

Given the nature of radial categories, disciplines are not actually characterized by hegemonic, impermeable boundaries and static areas of study, and neither are they immutable or stable *across time*. Over time, the prototypes that infuse a given radial category can shift with new knowledge, methods, and objects. The definition of linguistics, for example, has evolved from 1950 to today, first influenced by the Chomskyan revolution and since shaped by newer knowledge, interests, methods, and foci. This combination of stability and dynamism makes disciplines, as Catherine Schryer (1993) might say, only ever "stabilized for now"—much like genres. Disciplines have a dynamic stability that allows for a moveable past, present, and future.

One of the strongest sources of disciplinary instability or dynamism is *inter*disciplinarity, when multiple fields overlap the same area of inquiry. Disciplines can do this because they function more like fields than galaxies. Galaxies are distinct entities whose member stars, except in times of crisis (galactic collisions), do not interact with or even encounter other galaxies. But as fields, disciplines can and do overlap and interact. If, as Klein (1996) and Abbott (2002) each maintain, disciplines have relatively permeable boundaries, then we should see a great deal of such overlap and fuzziness—and we do. Several disciplines, for example, have specialized knowledge about how people become consumers. Business, marketing, management, economics, psychology, sociology, and other disciplines can all bring their own methods and values to bear on such a question, and sometimes they borrow theory, methods, and findings from other fields. Klein (1996) notes that interdisciplinarity is thus the effect created by an overlap of disciplinary boundaries themselves, characterizing these boundary effects as "productive tensions in a dynamic of supplement, complement, and critique" (4). It is awareness of existing disciplinary boundaries that lets scholars think in interdisciplinary ways;

disciplinary boundaries themselves provide for the boundary crossing that constitutes interdisciplinary fermentation (46–48).

Interdisciplines—often represented in the academy by "Centers for the Study of X" or similar structures—can quickly adopt the institutional trappings of disciplines themselves. Klein (1996) characterizes these trappings as "critical mass," which includes adequate faculty, infrastructure, economic and symbolic capital, autonomy in budget matters, undergraduate coursework and majors, control over degree requirements, and power to appoint and grant tenure. Critical mass necessitates all four of Bourdieu's forms of capital: economic, social, cultural, and symbolic (Klein 1996, 36); shortfalls of either economic or social capital can inhibit or undermine the buildup of critical mass.

## IS COMPOSITION STUDIES A DISCIPLINE?

Given these principles of the nature of disciplinarity, we want to stop to consider to what extent Composition Studies does or does not fit a disciplinary mold. Returning to Carlton's (1995) definition of a discipline and Klein's (1996) notion of disciplinary critical mass, we can ask whether Composition Studies is, in fact, the discipline that many of us claim it is. If a discipline, it ought to have a defined object of study, texts that theorize and historicize that object, methodologies that produce knowledge about that object, and the capacity to reproduce disciplinary practitioners. It should also have a name agreed on by its practitioners.

Because other chapters in this volume detail our disciplinary history, here we will only briefly note that whatever steps the field had made toward disciplinarity in the 1970s and 1980s, by the 1990s and early 2000s there appeared to be little coherence in pedagogy, object of study, or disciplinary project. By 2001, the situation was such that James Sledd (2001) accused compositionists of being "polysyllabists," and "composition studies" of being "whatever compositionists may study" (n.p.). As documented by Richard Haswell (2005) in his *Written Communication* article "NCTE/CCCC's Recent War on Scholarship," compositionists had come to agree less and less about objects of study and research methods—or even the use of research itself over the preceding two decades. This situation was, perhaps, related to the prevalence of critical theory during that time, which questioned the possibility of any center, denied the validity of empirical research, and dismissed the project of disciplinarity as hegemonic. The field seemed to lose any compass toward central objects of study, such as "how discourse works" (Olson 2002, 24), instead arguing endlessly over whether we should be about cultural studies or pedagogy or cognitivism or expressivism or resisting hegemony. As we argued over opposing conceptions, we overlooked ecumenical definitions of "Writing Studies" such as the one offered by Susan Miller (2002):

> The distinct focus . . . on writing itself as our object of study . . . Those who witnessed the response of literary critics to Mina Shaughnessy's explanations of Basic Writing can attest that it is *knowledge of how texts "got this way"* that justifiably defines our recognized expertise. That is, our own archive readily shows how the twentieth-century formation of composition as a discipline first depended on our knowing more about composing than others do. We find identity there, in *taking up what, who, to what ends, and, especially, how people have written and do write* . . . This is the greatest benefit of writing studies to all: the provision of well-formed, vividly engaging information about how and to what far-reaching ends people write and have written. (51–52; emphasis added).

Definitions like this still often go unnoticed as some corners of the field continue to question the underlying value of desiring any such coherence to begin with.

Still, though, the past ten years have seen much greater energy and movement in aspects of disciplinarity that seem essential to building critical mass (particularly as defined by Carlton [1995] and Klein [1996]):

- A nameable, consensually recognized central project;
- consensually established research methods conducted through collaborative division of labor;
- resulting "closed" questions whose answers can be shared with public audiences and students at all levels;
- coursework for beginning and advanced students;
- departments to organize and fund faculty positions, majors, related coursework, and graduate programs.

All of this leads to

- external (public) audiences that grant authority to members of the discipline and to disciplinary knowledge.

How, then, are we doing in terms of these aspects of disciplinary standing?

*Name and Project*

The field still goes by many names. The National Research Council, thanks to Louise Wetherbee Phelps's tireless efforts, knows us as Rhetoric and Composition (Phelps 2006). To some, we are Comp/Rhet rather than Rhet/Comp. To others, Writing Studies. So, we could be doing better in this regard. However, what we have now that we did not ten years ago is the fact that the NRC *does* know us by a name—and there have been similar advances in public awareness (see also Reid and Miller, and Maid, this volume).

Along with still needing a capacious, publicly meaningful name, we still need to be able to describe our field's interests, concerns, and projects more holistically, compactly, and agreeably than we are so far able to. What is this field *about?* There seems no broadly shared narrative yet to answer this question.

*Research Methods and Collaboration*

One source of tension in the field is the roots of our ways of knowing in both the humanities and the social sciences. That we span these ways of knowing is sensible, given the scope of what's involved with writing and the angles of vision available to examine it, from philosophy and rhetoric, to social theories and neurocognition. While we cannot say that factionalism has disappeared, it does seem possible to claim that collectively we are improving in implementing our preferred methods—and increasing our attention to their quality. Historiography and archival research in the field, for example, have reached highs not just exemplary in our field, but across the whole of the academy. Meanwhile, recognizing weakness in our social-science methods, the past ten years have seen the field bootstrap through various research institutes and initiatives, including the Dartmouth Institute for Writing and Rhetoric's Summer Institutes. The Conference on College Composition has seen an increasing emphasis not only on research-based panels, but also on grants for research initiatives (a program in its eleventh year as of 2015), its Advancement of Knowledge Award and Research Impact Award (both initiated in 2012), and a standing Research Committee.

*Closed Questions*

Even very recently, it would have been difficult to support a claim that Composition Studies possessed declarative knowledge agreeable to a large majority of practitioners. "Writing is a process" might have been the limit of our consensus. Even asking what our agreed-upon declarative knowledge was might have created real misgivings among a significant faction of the field, which was uncomfortable with the codification of emergent knowledge.

Recently, however, we seem to be experiencing more consensus regarding closed questions. First, improving research on learning transfer (e.g., Driscoll and Wells 2012; Rounsaville 2012; Wardle 2012; Yancey et al. 2014) has suggested the real value of declarative knowledge, particularly in the form of *threshold concepts* (Meyer and Land 2006). Linda Adler-Kassner and Elizabeth Wardle's (2015) collection on threshold concepts names thirty-seven threshold concepts—or underlying, assumed, agreed-upon knowledge critical for participation in a discipline—that its numerous contributors found to be agreed-upon questions for Composition Studies (Adler-Kassner and Wardle 2015). This suggests both that we have stable disciplinary knowledge to build upon and that there is value in doing so. Second, within Composition Studies, these threshold concepts have been developed through what Adler-Kassner and Wardle (2015) describe as "modified crowdsourcing" methods, named from the ground up and extrapolated from existing research, rather than imposed from the top down; this sort of methodology seems to increase comfort with the project of identifying this stable knowledge (these "closed questions") to begin with.

*Coursework, Majors, and Departments*

While our historical roots are in general education courses, the incorporation of rhetorical theory into composition instruction in the 1960s began edging us toward a disciplinary specialization and identity that continued with the well-known pedagogical movements of the 1970s, '80s, and '90s. Wide-scale implementations of writing-about-writing and other content-focused pedagogies over the past decade have made it possible to teach fully disciplinary curricula even in general-education writing courses.

Perhaps even more important for disciplinarity recognition is the explosion of writing majors in the last decade, both inside English departments and, increasingly, in freestanding writing departments. Research by Alice Myatt (forthcoming) suggests that independent writing majors and writing programs now number more than eighty across the country.

The diversity of majors and of the coursework in them showcases the increasing specialties and subspecialities in Composition Studies. For example, in the writing major within the freestanding Department of Writing and Rhetoric at the University of Central Florida, there is undergraduate coursework in rhetoric, literacy, digital rhetoric, professional communication, and advanced composition, among many others. Even at the undergraduate level, then, there are specialized courses that not all the Composition Studies faculty can teach. Rather than seeing this as a sign of fragmentation, we see this as a characteristic of a maturing discipline—one that has enough research and scenes of interest to have the diversity and subspecialities that all other disciplines have.

PhD programs have essentially reached full maturity over the past twenty years. Increasingly—if not typically—they, like writing majors, are housed in departments of their own—departments of Writing and Rhetoric and Communication and Digital Studies and New Media, independent of traditional departmental homes such as English.

Charles Bazerman wrote in 2002: "Inquiry into the skills, practices, objects, and consequences of reading and writing is the concern of only a few scholars fragmented across university disciplines; such inquiry has no serious home of its own" (Bazerman 2002, 32). While this may still be the case in many places, the increasing numbers of freestanding departments and majors lead us to think it is much less the case than it was fifteen years ago.

*External Credibility*

In his 2005 Conference on College Composition and Communication (CCCC) address, Doug Hesse asked, "Who owns writing?" That he even had to ask that question says a great deal about the nature of Composition Studies (Hesse 2005). Although we have been achieving increasing clarity about our shared projects and knowledge, and increasing external recognition, our external credibility and impact remain negligible. Few movements related to writing in the past decades' many educational re/deforms have been led or strongly influenced by writing researchers or experts. The National Council of Teachers of English (NCTE) opted out of participating in the Common Core State Standards writing process because it didn't trust that movement and the resulting testing schemes by the Partnership for Assessment of Readiness for College and Careers (PARCC) and the Smarter Balanced Assessment Consortium, instead choosing to create a parallel commentary by publishing with the Council of the Writing Program Administrators (CWPA) and the National Writing Project a "Framework for Success in Postsecondary Writing" (Council of Writing Program Administrators, National Council of Teachers of English, and National Writing Project 2011), whose impact is as yet unclear. We have seen greater success in resisting timed-essay standardized writing assessments such as those implemented in the SAT and ACT in the mid-2000s. And, experts in the field seem to have achieved serious public traction in the realm of resisting machine reading of student writing, such as Les Perelman's (2014) success in publicly calling these practices into question.

These limited successes do herald signs of positive growth. The last decade has seen leaders of our professional organizations talking about college writing instruction at the White House and on Capitol Hill, seated on public panels dedicated to advocacy for literacy and writing instruction, and in general becoming ever more media savvy and effective. It seems fair to believe that our influence on public awareness is increasing and will continue to do so. It seems unquestionable that we are becoming increasingly concerned about the *need* to do so.

Our examination of Composition Studies' current status suggests that the field has achieved limited, though growing, ability to act out of disciplinary knowledge in order to positively impact the lives of individual students, educational policy more broadly, and public policy related to matters of writing, language, and literacy. Although critics such as Lynn Worsham (2002) argue that a desire for institutional power should be resisted (102–3), we agree with Carlton (1995): a power play for cultural capital is only a problem "if one prefers for composition studies to be without a voice in the department meetings, administrative offices, and university committees where decisions about institutional resources and commitments are made" (81).

Although external forces and the ubiquitous nature of writing itself are partially to blame for our difficulties naming our shared enterprise and having an impact on national writing-related initiatives, another reason for our limited success continues to be internal misgivings about the nature of disciplinarity. Yet given what we have outlined about the nature of disciplinarity, it seems to us that Composition Studies is well positioned, through its own demonstrable values that clearly *are* shared across the field, to be a discipline par excellence, both in breadth and flexibility and in ethics. The remainder of our chapter examines these values in order to make this case.

## COMPOSITION STUDIES' VALUES AND THEIR RELATION TO THE NATURE OF DISCIPLINARITY

Some members of our field have been uncomfortable with disciplinarity because of the values on which our work has been built. However, we argue that embracing disciplinarity does not mean giving up the qualities that make our field unique; it means building on them. In the rest of this chapter, we outline some of these shared values in order to demonstrate how our field's values are actively consonant with disciplinarity.

Of the current discomforts with disciplinarity felt in some parts of the field, most might be described as what Klein (1996) calls critical or cultural studies objections. These objections stem from the belief that "opting in" by becoming a discipline reinscribes current unethical practices and forcibly privileges one view of what counts as knowledge. Take, for example, Trimbur's (1996) argument that disciplines enforce "normalizing of intellectual work, subjugation of counterknowledges, overemphasis on specialization, monopolies of expertise . . . monopoly and concentration . . . leading to internal differentiation—or a stratified class system" (135–36, 138). Similarly, Kristensen and Claycomb (2009) suppose that disciplinary writing "produced under the auspices of highly controlled and tightly guarded disciplines is subject to surveillance and restriction that governs what knowledge can be made, under what conditions it can be made, and how it is authorized" (2).

These objections assume that disciplinarity creates and perpetuates power imbalances, such as the exploitation of undervalued part-time instructors. Some critics fear that disciplinarity would worsen this system—or even be its source. Sledd (2001) notes that the disciplinizing of composition studies "neatly *paralleled* . . . the deepening exploitation of composition's most numerous teachers, the teaching assistants, part-timers, and other contingent workers" (sec. 2). Clyde Moneyhun (1994) goes further, arguing that the rise of Writing Studies doctoral programs and tenure lines actually *created* "a permanent underclass of overworked, underpaid 'adjuncts' with little control over the workplace, no job security, few benefits, no future" (Moneyhun qtd. in Carlton 1995, 83). There is a fear, then, that in achieving disciplinarity, Composition Studies would further entrench a system that "serves those already authorized to speak, to decide, to implement, or to erase" (Carlton 1995, 85). As Sledd (2001) puts it, disciplining Composition is "really about power, but limited power within the academic system as it existed (and exists)" (sec. 21).

As we've shown, though, such thinking is not entirely in keeping with current descriptions of disciplinarity, or with the field's own history. As Carlton (1995) points out, recent professionalization could not have created composition's underclass, as composition has been taught from its inception mostly by "teachers outside the power structure of the university" (84). Carlton argues that in fact it is professionalization that has allowed composition classes and programs to be "conducted by individuals who have a say in the university" (84). And, of course, we would argue that the notion of omnipotent, monolithic, static disciplines is undermined by evidence of dynamism: porous boundaries, changing centers, and cross-fertilization.

Nonetheless, these objections convey a number of implicit values and ideologies, exposing a number of our field's central values, values often explicitly grounding some of this skepticism toward disciplinarity. It seems worthwhile, then, to examine several long-standing values of the field—inclusion, access, difference, interaction, localism, valuing diverse voices, and textual production—in terms of what each means for our field as a potential discipline. Far from seeing these values as incompatible with disciplinarity, it seems to us that practitioners have *already invented our discipline with these values as grounding principles.*

*Inclusion and Access*

Our field's visceral distaste for exclusion may explain much resistance to centralized disciplinarity. Andrea Lunsford (1990) applauds our ethic of inclusion as a choice to "resist the temptation to make ourselves over in the image of traditional humanistic disciplines, defined by what we exclude, and instead have allowed for a different way to compose ourselves" (76). When practitioners argue about the value of disciplinarity, one of the first concerns is always who will no longer "belong" if we "lock in" a disciplinary identity; disciplinarity is immediately presumed to radically narrow who "counts." When we argued in a *CCC* article (Downs and Wardle 2007) that most composition instructors lack the field-specific expertise to be able to teach students the field's research, many readers heard us saying that only Composition Studies PhDs are qualified to teach writing. That was never a reading we had intended, but the widespread fear that we *had* served to forefront the field's value of inclusivity.

One of our field's most enduring ethics is that we are the people who foster belonging. Almost as long as some in the university have attempted to use writing—entrance exams, remedial coursework, proficiency exams—to disqualify and exclude, compositionists have worked to subvert those very instruments toward *access* and *inclusion*. As long as the university has defined students by what they cannot do, compositionists have defined students by what they *can* do—and dedicated their efforts to helping students do even more. This value has swelled our own ranks: we have always been a heterogenous field, taking all comers and defining "one of us" by participation rather than by certification. After all, the field was created by people with other degrees and from varied backgrounds who opted to *do this work,* as Adam Banks (2015) eloquently reminded in his 2015 CCCC Chair's Address. And our field continues to draw people in *after* they have studied and even published in other fields. We value participation and lived experience as a kind of expertise and are at the cutting edge of crowdsourcing our various expertises broadly in collaborative research. Different practitioners have varying levels of engagement with or knowledge of the field, but few compositionists would deny that anyone who wishes to be a part of this field can be a part of it.

Yet all inclusion has limits. Not everyone who teaches a composition class is or wants to be a member of our field. On some campuses every English faculty member must teach composition, but not every faculty member is a compositionist—and those who are not would often be the first to say they are not. Some might even deny there is a field to be a part of in the first place. Writing teachers, scholars, and—particularly—writing program administrators, have no trouble identifying noncompositionists teaching writing and labeling them as outsiders. Writing program administrators (WPAs) spend a great deal of time determining how to meet program goals when some teachers won't agree to teach to those goals because they are not and do not wish to be part of the enterprise of Composition Studies—perhaps they do not value student writing, or production over consumption, or see as a goal empowering students from all backgrounds, or necessarily believe there is anything to know *about* writing as a subject of study. This difficulty is exacerbated when we must consider who is qualified to teach specialized, upper-level courses in writing majors and in graduate programs.

As a field, then, we are *already* deciding who is in and who is out. Articulating our felt sense of this requires no more judgments than we already make. Rather, it requires explicitly acknowledging the disciplinary criteria already inherent in our existing judgments—stating what those judgments are, and what counts as expertise in various aspects of our disciplinary work.

Nothing in the nature of disciplinarity itself would force the field to abandon its ethic of inclusivity, its current practice of including those who wish to be included and wish to learn what the field has to offer. As enculturation theorists such as Jean Lave and Etienne Wenger remind us, there are multiple levels of belonging (Lave and Wenger 1991). Newcomers certainly belong and can engage in the practices of the discipline, but as their knowledge and participation increase, they can effect more change within those disciplines and outside them as recognized members of those disciplines. Even when we delineate who is in and who is out, being a member of a discipline is not a one-time, all-or-nothing endeavor. In addition, exclusion on ideological grounds is hardly unheard of in Composition Studies. We can think of the field's chilly reception of Maxine Hairston's questioning of its hard-left social turn, or Gary Olson's (2000) polemic against Wendy Bishop and "creative writing" ideologies. Behaving as if we are a discipline and having explicit discussions of what counts as expertise and how one gains it and demonstrates it might simply provide an open and honest forum for debates and judgments that are already being made.[2]

In recognition of the irony Jacques Derrida enjoyed so much—that to say "is" demands us simultaneously to say "is not"—the field seems to have largely avoided the former in hopes of avoiding the latter. Yet Derrida would be the first to remind us that avoiding "is not" is impossible; if we imagine we have avoided saying "is not," avoiding privileging and exclusion, we delude ourselves. Our field has already long been marking insiders and outsiders. Explicitly undertaking this endeavor—defining expertise, identifying practicing members—as a field would only change the way this marking is done and make more explicit our largely unspoken criteria for doing so. In the process we hope that we would also pursue myriad ways to make "insider-ness" more attainable. For example, enlarging efforts such as the Dartmouth Summer Institutes or the Ohio State Digital Media Conference, which enable people who may not have had graduate training in a particular area to gain experience, expertise—and access.

### Difference

In valuing inclusion, most practitioners in our field also value difference and thus are uncomfortable with the idea of privileging dominant points of view. To the extent that the field has accepted constructivism and antifoundationalism, it finds itself deeply suspicious of centering moves that establish privilege and marginalize difference. The field thus values inclusion in something, while also valuing the right not to define that something beyond desiring that it include diverse identities. From that angle, disciplinarity might seem to inevitably privilege a master narrative, impose "the" Truth.

The question is whether disciplinarity *must* level difference or privilege the dominant. Returning to our definitions of disciplines as radial categories, quite different constituents are organized around a prototypical core in which all recognize part of themselves. From this perspective, disciplines can handle difference very well *if* their members can agree on the disciplinary core or prototype. Disciplines don't necessarily suppress difference in membership; it is establishing the prototype that can be seen as privileging or centering

Then there is the nature of privileging or centering itself. The act of claiming, "There is no Truth" itself asserts a Truth. Privilege taken from one group doesn't disappear, it just goes to another group. Human experience and cognition suggest that we can only ever privilege something else, not privilege nothing. It seems either naive or disingenuous to resist a center on the grounds that privileging is itself fundamentally unethical or immoral. That argument is always-already an act of privileging, of suppressing difference. The question is not *whether* to privilege a center, but simply *which* center will be privileged. So it makes little sense to argue against disciplinarity in hopes of preventing privileging. Yes, affirming a disciplinary prototype will privilege some ideology—but so does refusing disciplinarity.

*Interaction*

To privilege access and difference is inevitably to also privilege interaction, so it's no coincidence that our field's modern roots lie in fostering interaction among students and between students and faculty to a degree never before seen in the academy. From Shaughnessy's (1979) insistence on recognizing even the most fractured student writing as communicative interaction with readers, to Ken Macrorie's denouncement of one-way lecture classes in 1970s *Uptaught*, to Peter Elbow's and Donald Graves' and Donald Murray's long-standing valuing of student writing produced in class and read aloud, the field's value for *interacting through writing* emerged powerfully (Macrorie 1970). Teachers such as Roger Garrison (1974) and Murray (1979) actually propounded all-conferencing pedagogies centrally based on one-on-one student/faculty interaction.

Since the 1980s, we have also come to understand a key implication of rhetorical theory as the field has largely come to accept constructivist principles of reading: meaning does not inhere in texts, but rather is instantiated by every individual reading of a text based on how a reader's particular background and experience allow her or him to interpret the blueprint any given text provides. Meaning is not transmitted; it is literally spun out of *interaction* with the text.

We can see the same value for interaction in best-practices philosophies and recommendations for WPAs, who long ago learned that fostering interaction among writing instructors is not simply a tool for propagating pedagogical training, but rather the very heart of our field: the open gathering of people over a shared project whose interaction will in fact invent new and stronger approaches to writing instruction than we had known before.

## Localism

Explicitly claiming and naming such core, prototypical values for the discipline could be more difficult because of one of those apparent values itself: localism. Situationality is perhaps *the* central tenet of rhetoric: recognizing that appropriate action and communication are contingent on location in time and space. Much of rhetorical theory has to do with gaining an understanding of the rhetor's situation (audience, kairos, context) and adapting to it. It is no surprise, then, that our theoretical, research, administrative, and teaching literatures comprise an echo chamber of injunctions to limit our claims to specific local contexts.

In research, for example, this expectation of situatedness manifested itself, particularly from the late 1980s to the late 1990s, as a suspicion of the validity of empirical research altogether, in part because of a belief that empiricism's call to generalizable knowledge was inimical to the *situated* knowledge to which most members of the field grant credence. Discomfort with unsituated research also leads to the field's current appreciation of ethnographic research, with its thick description of context. The same holds true of our professional statements, such as *Students' Right to Their Own Language* (National Council of Teachers of English 1974), the *WPA Outcomes Statement* (National Council of Writing Program Administrators 2014), and assessment and plagiarism statements. They are premised, implicitly and explicitly, on the preeminence of the situated local: what works *here* may not work *there*. Different groups and institutions have different needs. And the same holds pedagogically: the field has been slow to create any universal sense of best practices in teaching because different teachers have different strengths, and pedagogy and curriculum must meet local needs—as local as individual teachers in individual classrooms. This is why the *WPA Outcomes Statement* (National Council of Writing Program Administrators 2014) is about *outcomes*, not *pedagogy*: the most we could agree was on what, in general, students should learn. *How* they learn is a local problem.

It is possible to invent a discipline that makes the local and the situated a foundational value. Rhetoric has, for thousands of years, been an organized body of knowledge centered on the notion that universal principles can be supplely derived from local situations and applied in others. Our professional organizations' position statements successfully embrace the value of situatedness, while in fact imposing that value as a universal, with increasing public credibility. Furthermore, the past five years in particular *have* shown increasingly interest and willingness in articulating principles that define best practices in teaching as well as widely shared principles in writing instruction beyond local situations. In 2011, the CWPA's Network for Media Action proposed, and the CWPA Executive Board approved, a "message framework" on "Effective Teaching Practices in General Studies Writing Classes." The framework identifies noncontroversial, best-practices principles such as attending to process and teaching rhetorical principles. The NCTE, CWPA, and National Writers Association's (NWA's) "Framework for Success in Postsecondary Writing" similarly identifies "habits of mind," which are hoped to benefit students in any writing situation they might encounter—habits including curiosity, openness, creativity, and flexibility (Council of Writing Program Administrators, National Council of Teachers of English, and National Writing Project 2011). Clearly, we can distinguish between broad categories and principles with which writers must concern themselves, and the local "answers" to the questions they raise. These examples demonstrate that disciplinary coherence need not *of necessity* threaten our field's core value of localism.

As the need for such national statements suggests, however, localism does have limits. In work on teaching assistant (TA) preparation, Kathleen Blake Yancey (2002) used the term "tyranny of the local" to describe the point where localism breaks down. If taken too far, it presents the same problem as difference: to share nothing in common is, ultimately, to value nothing as relevant to more than the individual (situation), to say that our knowledge cannot be meaningful to multiple institutions or policy makers or students. The tyranny of the local is that, taken to extremes, the ethic of localism forces the wheel to be always reinvented in ways that we know writers actually *don't*. So a very radical localism might be theoretically demanded, but would rarely reflect lived writerly experience.

*Empowering Disenfranchised Voices*

Few concepts in Composition Studies have incited as much disagreement as the term, and notion of, "voice" in writing. (See Elbow 2007 for a sense of the breadth of this disagreement.) But the field has consistently rallied around one notion that shares etymology with this divisive concept of a "writer's voice": the principle that *all students have a right to speak and to be heard and listened to* and that our work lies in helping them achieve such voice. The field's roots are in finding ways to help empower disenfranchised voices of historically marginalized participants in higher education, both students and instructors, be they marginalized races, ethnicities, and genders, or at-risk students and students from nondominant discourses. One of our central goals is to help people "write back" when they feel written on, to use Malea Powell's words (Powell 2008, 118). This goal has formed a steady thread across our decades of work.

*Textual Production*

Since at least the late 1960s, Composition Studies has been most interested in, as Susan Miller (2002) says, "how texts got that way." Where does a given text come from—what are the material, social, cognitive, and embodied processes by which it actually comes into existence? What constrains it, what calls it into existence, what choices does a writer make, and who all *are* the "writers" of the text (Prior 2004)?

Such questions have consumed many branches of our field's research for several decades now. They have also consumed teachers in their reading of and feedback on student texts. While we do not have grounds to suggest that this should be the *main* project of Writing Studies, there seems plenty of activity around the question to justify posing it as *one of* the field's central projects—one of its prototypes, or a part of its prototype. It is without question a major shared project of the field (even apart from Miller's [2002] characteristically incisive commentary in favor of making it *the* project). Our question is, what are other such projects—how would we recognize and articulate them, and what mechanism does the field have for reaching consensus on the importance of a given project and centering resources on it?

## CONCLUSION

Even as we write this, we imagine some readers worrying that these judgments are meant to exclude what Banks calls "the funky," but we envision quite the opposite. While he rightly notes that respectability will not save us, we are suggesting that naming our criteria and living as a discipline are not about becoming "respectable," but about having the authority and freedom to honor what we value: varied kinds of textual production, inviting students from all backgrounds to the table, valuing many kinds of expertise. Naming and honoring our inclusive goals is, in fact, what will enable us to embody the "funky" discipline we want to be a part of—and one that has enough authority to share its values with others, rather than be held to the values other disciplines (and administrators and legislators and testing companies) create, to which we might not want to adhere.

Embracing disciplinarity, then, does not mean giving up the qualities that make our field unique; it means *building on* them. We can still answer the call Lunsford (1990) made more than twenty-five years ago in her CCCC Chair's Address, to compose ourselves as a postmodern discipline according to our own foundational values. Embracing disciplinarity empowers us to help empower others, to work from our values and principles in a way that can have greater impact than our historical institutional positions have allowed.

Further movement toward establishing disciplinarity for our field necessitates an accounting of our common projects, methods, and values—in answer to questions such as these:

- How should define ourselves to outside stakeholders?
- What concepts are central to our field?
- What research methods should practitioners be familiar with?
- What values are central to our field?
- What constitutes "expertise" to teach in our field?
- What name best conveys the answers to the preceding questions?

We are well along the path of this work, with initiatives over the past ten to fifteen years, including the CWPA's Network for Media Action, theorizing on threshold concepts in composition, collaborative research fostered by Haswell's (2005) notion of RAD (replicable, aggregable, data-driven) research, increased access to methodological training, research grant initiatives and research awards, and work that indeed focuses on values and fostering expertise.

We would argue that what will enable us to continue to create a strong discipline that has the ability to positively impact writers' lives is the growing recognition that we don't have to choose between disciplinarity and our long-standing core values. Our history of inclusion, access, respecting difference, facilitating interaction, emphasizing localism, valuing diverse voices, and empowering writers to engage in textual production are, in fact, what make our discipline what it is. Our work is to continue to consciously construct ourselves as a discipline *of* our values—and to find increasingly effective ways to share these values with other stakeholders who compose and who have power over how composing is taught, assessed, and understood.

*Notes*

1. We have chosen to use the term "Composition Studies" throughout in order to emphasize the totality of what people in this field study, which is not limited to strictly scribal "written" texts, but also composing more broadly and in more modalities.
2. The tension between democratic lay input and expert knowledge in a culture increasingly driven by specialization is a long-standing one, taken up by Kenneth

Burke (1950) as a main problem in *A Rhetoric of Motives* and later by Walter Fisher (1984) in his work on a "narrative paradigm" of human communication. What Composition Studies knows as "lore" (North 1987) is nonspecialist "expertise" growing democratically even when it's "wrong" or in disagreement with expert knowledge.

## References

Abbott, Andrew. 2002. "The Disciplines and the Future." In *The Future of the City of Intellect: The Changing American University*, ed. Steven Brint, 205–30. Stanford, CA: Stanford University Press.

Adler-Kassner, Linda, and Elizabeth Wardle, eds. 2015. *Naming What We Know: Threshold Concepts of Writing Studies*. Logan: Utah State University Press.

Banks, Adam. 2015. *Funk, Flight, and Freedom*. Tampa: CCCC Chair's Address.

Bazerman, Charles. 2002. "The Case for Writing Studies as a Major Discipline." In *Rhetoric and Composition as Intellectual Work*, ed. Gary Olson, 28–32. Carbondale: Southern Illinois University Press.

Boland, Mary R. 2007. "The Stakes of Not Staking Our Claim: Academic Freedom and the Subject of Composition." *College English* 70 (1): 32–51.

Burke, Kenneth. 1950. *A Rhetoric of Motives*. Upper Saddle River, NJ: Prentice-Hall.

Carlton, Susan Brown. 1995. "Composition as a Postdisciplinary Formation." *Rhetoric Review* 14 (1): 78–87. https://doi.org/10.1080/07350199509389053.

Council of Writing Program Administrators, National Council of Teachers of English, and National Writing Project. 2011. "Framework for Success in Postsecondary Writing." http://wpacouncil.org/files/framework-for-success-postsecondary-writing.pdf.

Downs, Douglas, and Elizabeth Wardle. 2007. "Teaching about Writing, Righting Misconceptions: (Re)Envisioning First-Year Composition as Introduction to Writing Studies." *College Composition and Communication* 58 (4): 552–84.

Driscoll, Dana Lynn, and Jennifer Wells. 2012. "Beyond Knowledge and Skills: Writing Transfer and the Role of Student Dispositions." *Composition Forum* 26. http://compositionforum.com/issue/26/beyond-knowledge-skills.php.

Elbow, Peter. 2007. "Voice in Writing Again." *College English* 70 (2): 168–88.

Fisher, Walter. 1984. "Narration as a Human Communication Paradigm: The Case of Public Moral Argument." *Communication Monographs* 51 (1): 1–22. https://doi.org/10.1080/03637758409390180.

Garrison, Roger. 1974. "One-to-One: Tutorial Instruction in Freshman Composition." *New Directions for Community Colleges* 1974 (5): 55–84. https://doi.org/10.1002/cc.36819740509.

Gere, Anne Ruggles. 1993. "Introduction." In *Into the Field: Sites of Composition Studies*, ed. Anne Ruggles Gere, 1–14. New York: MLA.

Haswell, Richard. 2005. "NCTE/CCCC's Recent War on Scholarship." *Written Communication* 22 (2): 198–223. https://doi.org/10.1177/0741088305275367.

Hesse, Douglas D. 2005. "2005 CCCC Chair's Address: Who Owns Writing?" *College Composition and Communication* 57 (2): 335–57.

Klein, Julie. 1996. *Crossing Boundaries: Knowledge, Disciplinarities, and Interdisciplinarities*. Charlottesville: University of Virginia Press.

Kuhn, Thomas. 1962. *The Structure of Scientific Revolutions*. Chicago: University of Chicago Press.

Kristensen, Randi Gray, and Ryan M. Claycomb. 2009. *Writing against the Curriculum: Anti-Disciplinarity in the Writing and Cultural Studies Classroom*. Lanham, MD: Lexington Books.

Lakoff, George. 1990. *Women, Fire, and Dangerous Things: What Categories Reveal about the Mind*. Chicago: University of Chicago Press.

Lave, Jean, and Etienne Wenger. 1991. *Situated Learning: Legitimate Peripheral Participation*. Cambridge: Cambridge University Press. https://doi.org/10.1017/CBO9780511 815355.

Lunsford, Andrea. 1990. "Composing Ourselves: Politics, Commitment, and the Teaching of Writing." *College Composition and Communication* 41 (1): 71–82. https://doi.org/10.2307/357884.

Macrorie, Ken. 1970. *Uptaught*. New York: Hayden.

Meyer, Jan H. F., and Ray Land. 2006. *Overcoming Barriers to Student Understanding*. London: Routledge.

Miller, Susan. 2002. "Writing Studies as a Mode of Inquiry." In *Rhetoric and Composition as Intellectual Work*, ed. Gary Olson, 41–54. Carbondale: Southern Illinois University Press.

Moneyhun, Clyde. 1994. "All Dressed Up and OTM: One ABD's View of the Profession." *Rhetoric Review* 12 (2): 406–12. https://doi.org/10.1080/07350199409389046.

Murray, Donald. 1979. "The Listening Eye: Reflections on the Writing Conference." *College English* 41 (1): 13–18. https://doi.org/10.2307/376356.

National Council of Teachers of English. 1974. "Resolution on the Students' Right to Their Own Language." *College Composition and Communication* 25 (special issue). NCTE.

National Council of Writing Program Administrators. 2014. "WPA Outcomes Statement for First-Year Composition." http://www.wpacouncil.org/positions/outcomes.html.

North, Stephen. 1987. *The Making of Knowledge in Composition: Portrait of an Emerging Field*. Upper Montclair, NJ: Boynton/Cook.

Olson, Gary. 2000. "The Death of Composition as an Intellectual Discipline." *Composition Studies* 28(2): 3–42. Reprinted in *Rhetoric and Composition as Intellectual Work*, ed. Gary Olson, 23–31. Carbondale: Southern Illinois University Press.

Olson, Gary, ed. 2002. *Rhetoric and Composition as Intellectual Work*. Carbondale: Southern Illinois University Press.

Perelman, Les. 2014. "Flunk the Robo-Graders." *Boston Globe*, April 30. http://www.bostonglobe.com/opinion/2014/04/30/standardized-test-robo-graders-flunk/xYxc4fJPzDr42wlK6HETpO/story.html.

Phelps, Louise Wetherbee. 2006. Personal Communication, February 6.

Powell, Malea. 2008. "Dreaming Charles Eastman: Cultural Memory, Autobiography, and Geography in Indigenous Rhetorical Histories." In *Beyond the Archives: Research as a Lived Process*, ed. Gesa Kirsch and Liz Rohan, 116–27. Carbondale: Southern Illinois University Press.

Prior, Paul. 2004. "Tracing Process: How Texts Come into Being." In *What Writing Does and How It Does It*, ed. Charles Bazerman and Paul Prior, 167–200. Mahwah, NJ: Lawrence Earlbaum.

Rounsaville, Angela. 2012. "Selecting Genres for Transfer: The Role of Uptake in Students' Antecedent Genre Knowledge." *Composition Forum* 26. http://compositionforum.com/issue/26/selecting-genres-uptake.php.

Schryer, Catherine. 1993. "Records as Genre." *Written Communication* 10 (2): 200–234. https://doi.org/10.1177/0741088393010002003.

Shaughnessy, Mina. 1979. *Errors and Expectations: A Guide for the Teacher of Basic Writing*. London: Oxford University Press.

Sledd, James. 2001. "Disciplinarity and Exploitation: Compositionists as Good Professionals." *Workplace: A Journal for Academic Labor* 4(1). http://ices.library.ubc.ca/index.php/workplace/article/view/184511.

Trimbur, John. 1996. "Writing Instruction and the Politics of Professionalization." In *Composition in the Twenty-First Century: Crisis and Change*, ed. Lynn Bloom, Donald

Daiker, and Edward White, 133–45. Carbondale: Southern Illinois University Press.

Wardle, Elizabeth. 2012. "Creative Repurposing for Expansive Learning: Considering 'Problem-Exploring' and 'Answer-Getting' Dispositions in Individuals and Fields." *Composition Forum* 26. http://compositionforum.com/issue/26/creative-repurposing.php.

Worsham, Lynn. 2002. "Coming to Terms: Theory, Writing, Politics." In *Rhetoric and Composition as Intellectual Work*, ed. Gary Olson, 101–14. Carbondale: Southern Illinois University Press.

Yancey, Kathleen Blake. 2002. "The Professionalization of TA Development Programs: A Heuristic for Curriculum Design." In *Preparing College Teachers of Writing: Histories, Theories, Programs, Practices*, ed. Betty P. Pytlik and Sarah Liggett, 63–74. New York: Oxford University Press.

Yancey, Kathleen Blake, Liane Robertson, and Kara Taczak. 2014. *Writing across Contexts: Transfer, Composition, and Sites of Writing*. Logan: Utah State University Press.

# 7
# DISCIPLINE AND PROFESSION
## Can the Field of Rhetoric and Writing Be Both?

Kristine Hansen

> *You can't teach what you don't know any more than you can come back from a place you haven't been.*
> —Will Rogers

Imagine that virtually all 4,000-plus postsecondary institutions in the United States required all entering students to take an introductory statistics course. This course—let's call it Stats 101—exists because of long-standing tradition and the near-universal belief that students will use statistics frequently in college and later in their careers. But in fewer than 100 of the 4,000 institutions can an undergraduate actually major in statistics; in fact, only a handful of these institutions even have a statistics department. As a result, the Stats 101 course is nearly always housed in the math department—but no one considers this strange because both statistics and math use numbers. Despite the paucity of statistics departments, there are people who hold PhDs in statistics, earned in one of about seventy-five PhD programs in statistics, many of them also in math departments, particularly in prominent research universities. Since so few statistics departments exist, nearly all statistics PhDs seek jobs in math departments, usually at universities, where it is acknowledged they have a "service" role to play keeping the large Stats 101 program staffed. At the community colleges, however, there are often no PhD holders in statistics, only in math. But because community colleges also offer Stats 101, generally all of the math teachers agree to teach it as part of their load, relying on whatever statistics training they got in graduate school or picked up from books or other sources.

Because there is little supply of people with bachelor's degrees in statistics to teach the tens of thousands of Stats 101 sections required across the country each year—and because it is acknowledged that sections

DOI: 10.7330/9781607326953.c007

must be small to give students individual attention and grade their frequent assignments—the few PhD holders in statistics often find themselves training thousands of graduate students who are studying math how to teach Stats 101. After all, the reasoning goes, students who studied math as undergraduates ought to do just fine teaching introductory statistics after a week or two of training just before fall semester—provided they have a common syllabus and textbook to use. Usually, these rookies are given an introductory course in the history and theory of statistics during their first semester of teaching. But many of them fail to appreciate this course because they are desperate instead for successful, preferably fun, learning activities to use in Stats 101 next Monday morning. In fact, many math graduate students teach Stats 101 because it's their main option to support themselves, not because they feel well qualified to teach it or find the job to their liking. About the time they get the hang of teaching stats, they finish their graduate studies and move on, to be replaced by more novice math graduates.

At universities, the Stats 101 Program Administrators (or SPAs, as they call themselves) are also often required to train and supervise adjunct instructors, especially where there are few or no math graduate students. At community colleges, there are seldom SPAs and of course no graduate students; but there are often plenty of adjuncts, usually with degrees in math, who are simply assigned to teach statistics, often with little pre- or in-service training or supervision. Still, wherever they are, statistics PhD holders firmly believe that every first-year student deserves a good course in statistics, so they work diligently to make a virtue of necessity. Where they can train and supervise teachers, they do. They sponsor journals and hold conferences where they share their theoretical, historical, and pedagogical knowledge. They work with a massive publishing industry supporting Stats 101 to create textbooks and electronic media for Stats 101 and for teacher training needs. Almost everyone supposes the system is working well, and only in the past fifteen to twenty years has anyone started to wonder why there are so few undergraduate courses in statistics or so few opportunities to major in it. After all, wouldn't it be better if future teachers of Stats 101 entered the classroom with a deep, broad, articulate understanding of the subject *before* they presume to teach it?

My readers will no doubt recognize that this imagined scenario is analogous to what is so often the case with writing courses, especially introductory writing courses, in perhaps thousands of postsecondary institutions across America.[1] High percentages of first-year writing courses are taught by graduate students and/or adjuncts with, *at best*, minimal preparation for their jobs—rarely with an undergraduate degree in Rhetoric and Writing Studies because, until recently, there have been no such degrees to be had. My claim that new teachers have minimal preparation "at best" may seem to some too strongly worded because writing programs have made great strides, particularly since 1970, in preparing teachers for the classroom. Betty Pytlik's (2002) historical survey of how graduate students were prepared to teach writing from 1850 to 1970 shows that training was practically nonexistent for the first ninety years and only spotty from about 1940 to 1970. In contrast, Steve Wilhoit's (2002) survey of developments in TA and adjunct training after 1970 shows the field can now boast of more widespread preparation that is conscientious and well planned.

My claim here must be interpreted in the larger context of the argument I make below about instilling disciplinary knowledge in and working to professionalize new members of the field. I assert that unless longer and deeper education in rhetoric and writing begins some years *prior* to the time one begins to teach, the preparation given to graduate students and adjuncts is likely to be superficial and too little, too late. In fact, E. Shelley Reid, Heidi Estrem, and Marcia Belcheir found that, even after careful training, key principles of composition pedagogy were unevenly and only shallowly integrated into TAs' views of teaching writing, regardless of whether the TAs were in their first, second, or third year of teaching (Reid et al. 2012). Reid et al. recommend that the education of TAs in writing pedagogy be extended into all the years that TAs work in writing programs. While that would help, I think such education should begin *before* people become TAs or adjuncts. Currently, TAs and adjuncts are often supervised by someone with a high degree of preparation in writing and rhetoric, usually a PhD with a full-time, tenure-track position. In other words, one person (sometimes two or more) with disciplinary expertise and professional status is expected to constantly make writing teachers out of dozens of people who have had little or no opportunity to study the discipline of Writing and Rhetoric prior to teaching. As I will argue in what follows, because these teachers have little disciplinary knowledge and have a low, often temporary, status at the institution, it would be inaccurate to use the term "professional" to describe them.

I propose to define and explore the relationships among the phenomena of disciplines, professions, and expertise. I argue that Rhetoric and Writing became a discipline without simultaneously becoming a fully developed profession where people who have appropriate credentials in the discipline can enter positions with job security, good pay, and adequate material conditions in which to ply their expertise. Through examining Conference on College Composition and Communication (CCCC) position statements about principles and standards for writing teachers, I evaluate what has been proposed but also what is still lacking to create a truly professionalized Rhetoric and Writing discipline. Then I propose three steps that could be taken at this point in the discipline's history to raise the professionalism of writing teachers: (1) developing more undergraduate majors, minors, concentrations, and certificates in Rhetoric and Writing; (2) experimenting with new kinds of curricular structures; and (3) conceptualizing and developing a paraprofessional category to set minimum standards for employing writing teachers. I realize my third proposal faces being swamped by the growing corporatization of universities and corresponding pressures to use the cheapest labor to achieve minimally satisfactory outcomes. But too much is at stake here not to make the effort. In today's world, where mass literacy is being redefined by the "rise of writing" (see Brandt 2015), students deserve the best writing teachers we can provide, teachers whose judgment is founded on deep disciplinary knowledge and whose professional status is unmistakable.

## WHAT ARE DISCIPLINES? DO WE HAVE ONE?

The reader will find in this book many answers to the questions posed above. I base my argument on the conceptualization of disciplines offered by Ellen Messer-Davidow, David R. Shumway, and David Sylvan (Messer-Davidow et al. 1993). They assert university disciplines are historical, social, and rhetorical formations, most having emerged in North America with the rise of the research university in the late nineteenth and early twentieth centuries. Disciplines have four characteristics, each of which I elaborate on with respect to what the National Research Council (2006) has called the "emerging field" of Rhetoric and Composition. While I believe our field has made remarkable and laudatory progress in the last fifty years, we have much work ahead in order to solidify our gains; still, I will use the word "discipline" to refer to what we know.

First, Messer-Davidow et al. (1993) state that disciplines "help produce our world" (vii) by specifying objects of study and relations among them, creating methods to make knowledge, and providing criteria to determine what constitutes knowledge. The formalized study of rhetoric and writing, which has accelerated since the 1960s and '70s, has identified numerous objects of study and relations among them, as anyone can see by leafing through the pages of our journals. Members of this discipline are now studying and writing about an almost mind-boggling proliferation of topics. We have developed sound peer review processes for establishing our knowledge base. However, I would argue—and have (see Hansen 2011)—that our discipline doesn't make full use of the range of research methods at our disposal and also that the body of knowledge we have developed has grown more by accretion rather than by conscious collective decisions about the directions we should take to produce a well-shaped body of knowledge with easily understood axioms and principles that produce well-attested pedagogical results. I believe we need more practical empirical knowledge, particularly for our pedagogies and for strategic planning to improve our chances to establish a respected profession.

Second, disciplines produce practitioners of all kinds, among them the "orthodox and heterodox, specialist and generalist, theoretical and experimental" (Messer-Davidow et al. 1993, vii). Even a cursory look at our journals and books shows that Writing and Rhetoric has practitioners of many kinds. Like any discipline, ours produces practitioners who perpetuate the discipline in the academy, people I will call academic practitioners. Unlike other disciplines, however, ours produces fewer certified practitioners who apply disciplinary knowledge outside the academy. By comparison, a relatively few law professors who practice in universities produce a great many lawyers who practice in various careers outside the university. So far, our discipline has focused mainly on producing more academic practitioners, mainly to work as graduate educators, seemingly with the aim of enlarging our numbers in postsecondary institutions and replacing us when we retire. We have an admirable subdiscipline of professional and technical communication that produces practitioners for other workplaces, but we could do more to strategize about how to produce practitioners of Rhetoric and Writing who do significant work outside the field of education. Obviously, there are many rhetoricians (who would likely not call themselves by that name) and writers who work outside the academy. But how many institutions can boast of an undergraduate curriculum aimed at producing people who will become the next generation of effective rhetoricians and writers in business, industry, the arts, the sciences, civic life, politics, government, and religion? We need more academic practitioners to take up this kind of work; having them will strengthen our discipline and our bid for status as a profession.

Third, disciplines produce "economies of value" by manufacturing discourse of all kinds (books, articles, proposals, reports, reviews, etc.), creating jobs, securing funding, and generating prestige for individuals, departments, and universities (Messer-Davidow et al. 1993, vii). By this criterion Rhetoric and Writing has a mixed record. We do manufacture discourse of all kinds that creates economic value for its producers in the form of promotions, salary raises, book royalties, research grants, consulting fees, and so on. Academic jobs for people in Rhetoric and Writing have been created and filled at an amazing rate over the last fifty years (with some recent slowing). Prestigious awards and honors have also come to individuals, with glory reflected on their departments and institutions. But compared to the number of people engaged in teaching writing, relatively few people gain much economic value from our discipline. As Peter Vandenberg has noted, the ability of PhD-holding scholars to produce disciplinary research rests on the work of a "vast majority of writing teachers" who do not research and write but "sustain the privilege of publishing professionals" by teaching heavy course loads of the many sections of writing required in higher education (Vandenberg 1998, 28–29). Also, our discipline is at the low end of the pecking order in the academy. For example, my university's home page features almost daily the achievements of professors in sciences, engineering, business, and sometimes the arts. But research by and honors for people in Rhetoric and Writing are almost never publicized. While economic rewards do accrue to those people, their achievements are not valued in the wider university or public context.

Fourth, disciplines produce "the idea of progress" by finding new objects to study, improving explanations of phenomena, acquiring more believers for their theories, and simply telling tales of progress (Messer-Davidow et al. 1993, viii). Here again, despite our inability to make headlines, we have successfully produced the idea of and told many tales of progress—at least among ourselves and perhaps among colleagues in the English departments where most of us work. We have acquired more disciples, mainly by attracting graduate students and producing new PhDs who write dissertations about cutting-edge topics. We haven't always improved explanations of phenomena, however, since we seem to have a penchant for the novel rather than for revisiting and replicating past research to refute or refine it—a main reason I believe our body of knowledge isn't as shapely, compact, and useful as it could be. Significant progress doesn't always come from working on the edge or trying to extend it, particularly if it what was behind that edge was never adequately researched in the first place.

In addition to these four characteristics of disciplines, Shumway and Messer-Davidow (1991) identify five important functions disciplines carry out: they sponsor disciplinary activities, promulgate disciplinary values, fund research, provide peer reviewers who evaluate disciplinary work, and publish journals of specialized research (208). Since about

1963, the year some scholars agree marked the birth of the discipline, practitioners have created several professional organizations that perform these functions. As a result, the discipline's work is widely felt, probably even at institutions where Rhetoric and Writing PhDs are rare, because changes in the knowledge base of the discipline have made themselves broadly (if not deeply) felt in the textbooks and classroom pedagogies now used in writing courses.

We are succeeding as a discipline by most measures. But Shumway and Messer-Davidow (1991) also write of a discipline's need to define and control its boundaries. The "boundary-work" of disciplines entails developing "explicit arguments to justify particular divisions of knowledge and the social strategies to prevail in them" (208). Boundary-work differentiates one discipline from another in "goals, methods, capabilities, and substantive expertise" (Gieryn 1983, qtd. in Shumway and Messer-Davidow 1991, 208). Boundary-work not only establishes and protects a discipline, but regulates it by determining what objects to study and how, then by certifying its masters. Young disciples learn about and acquire expertise through courses, then demonstrate learning through examinations that evaluate and rank students based on norms developed by older disciples (see Shumway and Messer-Davidow 1991, 208, 211–12). Once established in universities, a discipline establishes boundaries by determining its members, since it has—at least in principle—the power to hire, grant tenure to, and fire employees, as well as to admit students and to create and change curriculum. I will return to the idea of boundary-work below, but I note here that insufficient attention to our discipline's boundaries is a serious threat to its vitality as well as to our ability to establish and maintain a well-respected profession.

## WHAT ARE PROFESSIONS? DO WE HAVE ONE?

Professions are certainly related to disciplines, but the two concepts aren't the same. The sociological literature on professions is vast and far from unanimous in its definitions. Sifting through the discussions about professions from the 1920s through the 1990s, Graham Cheetham and Geoff Chivers settled on this definition of profession: "An occupation based upon specialized study, training, or experience, the purpose of which is to apply skilled service or advice to others, or to apply technical, managerial, or administrative services to, or within, organizations for a fee or salary" (Cheetham and Chivers 2005, 13). A profession rests on a cognitive base developed in its members by required education in a discipline. This education sometimes leads to formal licensing, as in medicine and law; if not, it at least leads to credentialing, such as a university degree in a particular discipline. Shumway and Messer-Davidow (1991) define credentialing as "cognitive exclusiveness" over a particular region of the academic world (207). In turn, licensing or credentialing is meant to lead to a paid position in which the professional works autonomously, subject to the oversight and control of colleagues organized in professional associations. A code of ethics is often associated with a profession, as are high standards of intellectual and practitioner excellence, defined by colleagues and policed by such formal and ad hoc reviews as seem necessary.

Magali Sarfatti Larson's (2013) analysis of the rise of professions in the age of industrial capitalism and Andrew Abbott's (1988) inferences from case studies of professions are instructive. Larson argues that professions were established so that "producers of special services could constitute and control a market for their expertise" (xvi; emphasis in original). Members of professions collectively asserted "special social status" and engaged in "a collective process of upward social mobility" (xvi) in order to "translate one order of scarce resources—special knowledge and skills—into another—social and economic rewards" (xvii). Larson argues that professions "depended on establishing structural links between relatively high levels of formal education and relatively desirable positions or rewards in the social division of labor" (xxiv; emphasis in original). To create these links, professions in effect established market shelters in order to regulate competition for professional positions, thus ensuring some prestige and an acceptable (if not always high) level of pay for members of the profession. So in Larson's view there is a reciprocal relationship between professions and disciplines. Professions are economic formations based on the knowledge formations of disciplines.

Professions operate in the marketplace, but education for professions does not. As Larson says, the education of professionals means the "'production of producers' whose education must be branded as superior in a competitive market." Nevertheless, the principles for justifying the superior education of professionals "reside outside the market" in a disinterested realm that seeks "the public's greater good above and beyond the 'cash nexus'" (xxv; emphasis in original). One enters a profession by mastering the knowledge and values of the discipline, then passing exams created and controlled by established members of the discipline to earn a license or credentials that signify readiness to enter the linked profession. To illustrate, our discipline produces professionals when it produces PhD and MA holders in Rhetoric and Writing.[2] But we produce relatively few of those, certainly not enough for all the teaching required in writing courses. And we cannot boast that we have given our many temporary teachers an education in how to teach writing that we can brand as superior in a competitive market. Yet this kind of branding would be necessary to admit them to the status of professional.

Abbott's (1988) analysis sheds additional light here, as he argues that professions are distinguished from crafts—which emphasize techniques per se—by the acquisition of abstract knowledge. Preparing for a profession involves learning an abstract system of knowledge, from which practical skills will grow as the professional learns to apply the abstract knowledge in specific instances. "Any occupation can obtain licensure (e.g., beauticians) or develop an ethics code (e.g., real estate)," Abbott explains. "But only a knowledge system governed by abstractions can redefine its problems and tasks, defend them from interlopers, and seize new problems" (8–9). Abbott argues that a professional's survival is guaranteed by the ability to understand abstract knowledge and then apply it in ways that revise the professional's skill according to each new case. Studying how professions such as medicine and law have succeeded or failed in developing and in relating to rivalrous would-be professions, Abbott shows that professions thrive when disciplinary experts establish well-demarcated boundaries for their expertise and best their rivals in winning public confidence (30).

Does the discipline of Rhetoric and Writing have a structurally linked profession based on abstract knowledge? Yes, but it's a small one. As David Smit (2004) has noted, our discipline has succeeded in professionalizing only "one small segment of the population concerned with the teaching of writing—the professoriate, those in tenure-track lines" (5). These professionals are concerned mainly with graduate education and/or with supervising temporary laborers, hired for a season and given minimal training to do their work. In the main, we do not professionalize our ranks, because the temporary workers experience nothing like full immersion in the discipline to develop abstract knowledge they can learn to apply in new situations. As a result, they enjoy none of the benefits of professionalization. As Richard Ohmann (2002) reminds us, a profession aims at "winning and sustaining privileged conditions of labor, at control over its content and procedures, regulation of the market for it, exclusion of the uncertified from practice, control over admission of new members, public respect for its authority, good pay, and so on" (215). These conditions are simply not met for the majority of those engaged in teaching writing.

In more damning terms, Marc Bousquet (2003) argues that the members of our discipline who *are* professional can only be called so because they have been willing either to become or to produce those who become lower-level managers in the "managed university," a manifestation of "academic capitalism." This ideology holds that universities should be centrally controlled by business-like executives and that the central values of higher education are accumulation, profitability, corporate alliances, and marketability. Rhetoric and writing professionals who accept jobs in the managed university are implicated, Bousquet contends, "in delivering cheap teaching, training a supervisory stratum, and producing a group of intellectuals theorizing and legitimizing this scene of managed labor" (17). Bousquet even charges that "managerialism" has become the "core subjectivity of the discipline of rhetoric and composition" (23). He believes our discipline will not become a peer among other disciplines until it sheds this identity and gets rid of WPAs altogether. His ideal would be a university without a WPA (32), where all teachers of writing are colleagues, not related to each other in a two-tiered system of a few professional managers and many casual laborers. In short, he would like to see a professional class of writing teachers at universities. So would I. But we diverge somewhat in proposed methods to achieve this goal. Bousquet argues that professional managers of writing programs must learn from their employees to "practice institutional critique" and learn the "arts of solidarity from labor" in order to "question the inevitability of the scene of managed labor" in postsecondary writing courses (31). While I concede that we who have tenure-track jobs do need to learn more about organizing labor and criticizing institutions, Bousquet neglects to mention that the laboring class of writing teachers usually don't have the disciplinary knowledge of the professional managerial class. I argue that before we get rid of WPAs, we need more teachers who understand our discipline thoroughly, teachers whom we can legitimately defend as thoroughly competent in the discipline. Only then can we claim they deserve to be paid and treated like professionals. Let me explain.

## OF EXPERTISE AND EXPERTS AND HOW TO CREATE THEM

The reason our discipline and our profession are so small and so precariously situated is that they didn't develop at the same time as did other academic disciplines, with their linked professions, in the late nineteenth and early twentieth centuries. That's when newly minted PhDs in philology, who could claim expertise, began to establish the study of literature as a discipline in the newly created English departments of the rising research universities. As the study of literature ascended, the study of rhetoric sank and dwindled, and a vast underclass of poorly paid and untrained writing teachers was created—long before there were "managed universities" (see Connors 1997). The underclass of writing teachers is still stubbornly with us, so the questions we must ask ourselves now are these: Is it possible to develop expertise rapidly and effectively in such large numbers of people as we currently have teaching writing without adequate disciplinary knowledge? And given the effects of today's political and economic climate on university budgets (particularly at public institutions), could it be more than a pipe dream to expand the borders of the profession to include more people with disciplinary expertise? What would be entailed if either or both of these questions were to be answered "yes"?

I avow at the outset that, despite the difficulties to be overcome, the answers can and should be affirmative. I agree with Cary Nelson (2008) that, when it comes to facing the managed university, "resistance is not futile." Many useful actions could be taken to change beliefs held by the public, by politicians, and by university administrators to help them understand why the higher purposes and functions of universities must be carried out by professional experts. Because Bousquet and others have already described the labor tactics that would be part of a strategy to resist and overturn the corporatization of the university, I will focus here on ways we might use to get our disciplinary horse ready to pull a more professional cart. Too often we have tried to put the cart before the horse. The first time we did so was with the 1986 Wyoming Resolution, an action that James McDonald and Eileen Schell say symbolized "the beginning of the discipline's serious attention to late twentieth century labor issues in writing instruction" (McDonald and Schell 2011, 360). The resolution itself was relatively short, calling for just three things: "professional standards and expectations for salary levels and working conditions" for postsecondary teachers of writing, a grievance procedure, and a procedure to censure noncompliant institutions (qtd. in McDonald and Schell 386–87). By 1989 a CCCC committee had acted on the Wyoming Resolution, creating the Statement of Principles and Standards for the Postsecondary Teaching of Writing. This 1989 document called for almost completely professionalizing the ranks of writing teachers by recommending that virtually all writing faculty should be in tenure-track positions with no more than 10 percent of classes taught by part-time faculty. It recommended using full-time non-tenure-line faculty only to fill nonrecurring instructional needs. Although this proposal seemed hopelessly ambitious at the time, it nevertheless made a bold and accurate assertion: writing teachers should be professionals, people with the disciplinary knowledge to perform the work properly. What it failed to do, however, was explain how the field could rapidly find or educate enough people with the requisite disciplinary knowledge for admission to our profession—assuming universities had been willing to meet this demand in 1989 or shortly thereafter.

Not only was there a lack of enough qualified people, there was considerable backlash to the 1989 Statement, particularly from part-time teachers who did not want full-time jobs and from full-time lecturers who had achieved reasonable salaries and working conditions in non-tenure-line positions and who did not want to assume the service and research expectations of tenure-line professors (McDonald and Schell 2011, 371–72). These teachers felt that the 1989 CCCC statement had departed from the intent of the Wyoming Resolution—which they thought was mainly to improve the working conditions of contingent faculty—and focused instead on how to increase the number and improve the professional status of tenure-line faculty in Rhetoric and Writing. In this, the critics were largely right. While the statement did delineate a few standards for employing graduate students and part-time faculty, its goal of having 90 percent of all writing courses taught by full-time, tenure-track teachers was meant to address the fact that, at that time, "more than half the English faculty in two-year colleges, and nearly one-third of the English faculty in four-year colleges and universities work[ing] on part-time and/or temporary contracts [were] almost universally . . . teachers of writing" (*CCCC Statement of Principles* 1989, 330). By 1989, our field was already a leading indicator of the managed university; moreover, employment practices used in writing programs were starting to spread. By 2007, "nearly 70 percent of all composition courses and roughly 40 percent of all lower-division literature courses [were] taught by faculty in contingent positions" (2007 ADE Ad Hoc Committee on Staffing, qtd. in Palmquist and Doe 2011, 354). By 2013, according to an AAUP report, "some 76 percent of college and university instructors in the U.S. [fell] into a contingent faculty category"—full-time but non-tenure track, part-time, or graduate student employees. The AAUP attributes higher use of contingent faculty in part to "an 18 percent decline in higher education appropriations between 2008 and 2013" at public institutions (Roach 2013). The lack of adequate public funding is a grave concern, to be sure, one I don't have space to address here, though I refer the reader to Cary Nelson's list of actions we could still try to improve the funding picture. Yet even if universities were flush with funding, it would take years to develop adequate expertise in enough teachers. We would have to, as it were, renovate our house while still living and working in it.

To approach this task, we must understand what expertise is. K. Anders Ericsson et al. (2007) claim that *"experts are always made, not born"* (1, emphasis in original) and report that at least a decade (or 10,000 hours) of frequent, deliberate practice under the direction of loving and wise yet demanding mentors is required to reach expert status. If we are talking about expertise in teaching writing, having all writing teachers reach the stage of expert (i.e., 10,000 hours of frequent, deliberate well-mentored practice in teaching) is likely beyond what our currently small profession can manage rapidly on a wide scale. But we might start by noting that expertise is developed in stages. Hubert and Stuart Dreyfus have postulated five stages of expertise: (1) novice, (2) advanced beginner, (3) competent performer, (4) proficient performer, and (5) virtuoso. Further, they claim there is a big leap between the first three and the last two stages (Dreyfus and Dreyfus 1986). The leap from stage 3 to 4 means abandoning rule-based thinking and replacing it with contextually based action founded in intuition, defined as an ability to make judgments without analytical deliberation because of internalized bodily, emotional, and intellectual experience (see Flyvbjerg 2001, 20–21). Even if we can reverse the direction of the managed university, I think we will be using graduate student and adjunct teachers in writing programs for some years to come. But we could begin *now* to explore collectively questions such as these: Do first-time teachers always have to start as the greenest of novices? Do we have to content ourselves with getting them only to the stage of advanced beginner before they leave? As I will explain below, I think we could work smarter to get more of these teachers to the competent performer stage before they enter a classroom as the sole teacher. Over a period of years, we may be able to accumulate in our ranks significant numbers of teachers who have reached the proficient performer and even virtuoso stage. What these stage-labels would mean with respect to teaching writing would have to be defined, but this is a task we should be willing and happy to take up. Clearly defined traits and abilities of teachers at the third, fourth, and fifth levels of expertise would let us better manage and expand the borders of our profession.

A good place to start strategizing how to get more teachers who are at advanced stages of expertise would be to examine the CCCC position statements on preparing and professionalizing writing teachers in order to determine whether they offer a comprehensive vision and workable strategies for establishing and/or upgrading the professionalism of rhetoric and writing teachers. The first *Position Statement on the Preparation and Professional Development of Writing Teachers*, written in 1982, was replaced in November 2015 by *Preparing Teachers of College Writing* (Conference on College Composition and Communication 2015). In some ways, the 1982 document was evidence that the emerging discipline of Rhetoric and Writing had not yet clearly defined its boundaries. It directed writing teachers to study not only the areas of inquiry that the new field was opening up, but also the disciplines of applied linguistics; second-language learning; language acquisition and development; sociolinguistics; psycholinguistics; cognitive and interpersonal psychology; history; and anthropology. It also told teachers to learn how professionals write in language arts, fine and performing arts, history, social and natural sciences—a tall order. In contrast, the 2015 *Preparing Teachers of College Writing* seems more focused. While it acknowledges that "the study of writing is multidisciplinary, building on the work of rhetoricians, compositionists, cognitive psychologists, linguists, librarians, educators, and anthropologists," it calls for teachers to have a "broad base of theoretical knowledge" in rhetoric, linguistics, pedagogy, research methods, and technology. It acknowledges the present stratified labor conditions in the field by listing required and recommended coursework, knowledge, experiences, and opportunities for (in this order) secondary teachers of dual credit courses, graduate teaching assistants, and new and continuing full-time writing faculty. It pragmatically also recommends what institutions and programs must do to enable each group of teachers to meet the specified requirements and recommendations.

For example, it would require graduate students to have "coursework in composition theory, research, and pedagogy; in rhetorical theory and research; in writing assessment, both formative and summative, and in working with diverse populations" (Conference on College Composition and Communication 2015). It would be helpful if the statement were clearer about how many courses, whether they are graduate or undergraduate courses, and when they are to be taken. Presumably, the coursework would have been completed prior to the time that students become graduate teaching assistants because the document would also require "*graduate* coursework in teaching with technology, including learning management systems, and experience with facilitating writing courses where students practice multimodal genres of textual production and refine their digital literacies" (Conference on College Composition and Communication 2015; emphasis added). This ambitious requirement is followed by the requirement of "intensive and comprehensive TA training that could include pre-semester training for an extended duration (1–3 weeks), a one- or two-semester long graduate composition theory course, and frequent workshops discussing aspects of composition pedagogy"—a specification that most readers will recognize as, up to now, pretty much the only requirement for graduate students to teach writing. The 2015 Statement also requires that graduate students have mentoring partnerships with experienced teachers of college writing, and it recommends that they participate in programmatic assessment, work in writing centers, and gain experience with curriculum development. If all of these requirements and recommendations were to be implemented for graduate students who teach writing courses, our field would be years ahead of where it presently is in developing expertise and a higher degree of professionalism in its youngest teachers.

When we consider the 2015 document on teacher preparation in tandem with another CCCC position statement, *Second Language Writing and Writers* (first written in 2001, revised in 2009, and reaffirmed in 2014; Conference on College Composition and Communication 2001), however, we realize we still have much further to go. The statement on second-language writing notes that postsecondary institutions across North America are seeing growing numbers of second-language writers, although few teachers are prepared to deal with their unique linguistic and cultural needs. It recommends that writing programs "take responsibility for the regular presence of second-language writers in writing classes" and develop appropriate instructional and administrative practices by giving teachers "preparation in second language writing theory, research, and instruction" through faculty workshops, conferences, or graduate courses. The statement twice recommends that graduate courses be required "when possible." Finally, the statement recommends that second-language concerns be studied not only in first-year writing programs but also "undergraduate and graduate technical, creative, and theoretical writing courses, writing centers, and Writing across the Curriculum programs" so that second-language perspectives are considered when "developing theories, designing studies, analyzing data, and discussing implications of studies of writing" (Conference on College Composition and Communication 2001).

These recommendations are perfectly reasonable, but the caveat "when possible" suggests the statement's authors have doubts about whether our discipline actually will start to demand some minimum coursework from would-be teachers. This raises the question: Why don't we begin to insist that this kind of coursework—and the coursework recommended in *Preparing Teachers of College Writing*—become possible? Rather than having future teachers merely read one or two articles about second language learners in one catch-all teacher preparation course, why don't we as a discipline and a profession insist that our future teachers take one or two courses on second-language writing theory, research, and instruction before they teach? Why don't we make these and other courses, such as the ones recommended in *Preparing Teachers of College Writing*, a condition of employment, part of the disciplinary knowledge a new teacher must bring to the job?

It is time to rethink what we expect teachers to know before they teach. In 2013, CCCC replaced the 1989 statement that attempted to implement the Wyoming Resolution with a new *Statement of Principles for the Postsecondary Teaching of Writing* (Conference on College Composition and Communication 2013). However, rather than focus on the status and working conditions of teachers, as its predecessor did, the 2013 statement focuses, first, on what sound writing instruction is and, second, on the enabling conditions that allow teachers to deliver it. Most intriguing about this document is that its description of the following eight characteristics of sound writing instruction also implies eight knowledge areas that teachers should command:

- "emphasizes the rhetorical nature of writing" suggests teachers know about the rhetorical tradition, the canons of rhetoric, and how to teach students to analyze and respond to new rhetorical situations;
- "considers the needs of real audiences" suggests teachers know what is involved in analyzing and addressing audiences;
- "recognizes writing as a social act" suggests teachers understand theories and practices of composing;
- "enables students to analyze and practice with a variety of genres" suggests that teachers know genre theory and have themselves read and produced many genres;
- "recognizes writing processes as iterative and complex" suggests teachers have used different writing processes and know how to analyze and teach them;
- "depends upon frequent, timely, and context-specific feedback from an experienced postsecondary instructor" suggests teachers understand formative and summative evaluation and can create and use grading criteria and rubrics;
- "emphasizes relationships between writing and technology" suggests teachers are comfortable with theories and practices of using electronic media to produce effective rhetoric and can teach students to do the same;
- "supports learning, engagement, and critical thinking in courses across the curriculum" suggests that teachers understand not only how thinking and writing vary by discipline but also how students can be helped to transfer writing abilities to other courses they are taking.

This list of eight knowledge areas teachers should understand in order to deliver state-of-the-art writing instruction could be set alongside the recommendations in *Preparing Teachers of College Writing* and *Second Language Writing and Writers* to identify where they overlap and where each contributes something unique. These statements could become the basis for an outline of what a college writing teacher should know. Together, these three CCCC position statements suggest how the discipline of Rhetoric and Writing Studies has matured. We have identified our disciplinary boundaries more narrowly and carefully, and we can now state more surely what we uniquely cultivate and offer in the academic terrain.

Even more suggestive of the maturity of our discipline is the assertion that the principles of the 2013 statement "presume that sound writing instruction is provided by *professionals with degree-based credentials in Writing Studies, Composition and Rhetoric, or related fields*, or [by people who] have been provided with and/or have sought out professional development in this area" (Conference on College Composition and Communication 2013; emphasis added). This statement, the first by CCCC to mention "degree-based credentials" in appropriate fields, acknowledges that sound writing instruction should be delivered by people with higher levels of disciplinary knowledge than we have hitherto demanded. Given the distance we have come from the CCCC statements of 1982 and 1989, the language about teacher credentials is most encouraging (Conference on College Composition and Communication 1982, 1989). But, if we are to renovate our house as we continue to live and work in it, how do we find ways to upgrade the credentials of the current labor force? I have three recommendations followed by a plea for urgency.

### HOW TO PROFESSIONALIZE WRITING TEACHERS WHO LACK DEGREES IN RHETORIC AND WRITING

My first recommendation is to establish more undergraduate majors, minors, emphases, concentrations, and certificates in Rhetoric and Writing. I began this chapter with a fictitious story about a nation in which statistics is taught only in math departments, mainly by graduate students, adjuncts, or teachers with degrees in math. But we all know that statistics is its own discipline, that undergraduates can major in it, and that statisticians are professionals in their own right. We also know that statistics departments would never allow their introductory courses to be taught by unqualified math graduate students. Similarly, our discipline must work to make it increasingly unlikely that people inside and outside the academy would imagine that English departments must always be the home of writing courses, courses taught of necessity only or mainly by teachers—graduate student, adjunct, or otherwise—whose baccalaureate and/or graduate degrees are in literature. As quickly as we can, we need to make it seem unthinkable that people would presume to become writing teachers without first having studied the discipline of Rhetoric and Writing at the undergraduate level and the graduate level. Over the next twenty or thirty years, the expectation should become routine that would-be writing teachers will apply for jobs with appropriate baccalaureate and/or graduate course work on their transcripts. A BA or MA degree in Rhetoric and Writing would not obviate the need for additional pre-service or in-service education for teachers, but it would supply the solid, deep foundation that currently isn't achieved by our quick methods of instilling pedagogical knowledge (see Reid et al. 2012). Granting more BA degrees in Rhetoric and Writing will require big changes. As of 2009 there were only sixty-two (the number could be higher now) postsecondary institutions offering curricula that led to some sort of certification in Rhetoric and Writing. Not all offered a major, but the sixty-two institutions combined offered more than seventy concentrations, emphases, or majors in writing (CCCC Committee on the Major in Rhetoric and Composition 2009). Many of these courses of study are offered not in English departments, but in autonomous departments having the words "writing," "rhetoric," "rhetoric and writing," "professional writing," "language" and/or "communication" as the most prominent terms in their various titles. We can point to these curricula and departments when speaking to university administrators and members of other disciplines—who may be ignorant of the fact—that there is such a thing as the formal, disciplined study of Writing and Rhetoric at the undergraduate level. That, in turn, should make it easier to argue that writing teachers can and should be educated in our discipline. As more institutions create at least a minor or concentration in Rhetoric and Writing, we can in turn expect that writing teachers should meet a certain standard of preparation when we hire them. If professionals in our discipline collectively work to establish hiring standards—a big part of what professions do—we can insist that would-be employees present themselves at hiring interviews with transcripts showing they have disciplinary knowledge of Rhetoric and Writing.

But what about teachers with degrees in other fields who are already teaching writing? We can take a cue from Michael Murphy, Director of College Writing at SUNY Oswego in central New York State. Murphy worked with the director of the writing program at nearby Onondaga

Community College, Malkiel Choseed, who wished that more of his teachers—both adjunct and tenure track—knew more about composition theory. Murphy developed a graduate course in composition theory that could be taken by writing teachers from both Onondaga and several other institutions within easy driving distance. A little-used provision of the state university system made it possible to offer the course at a heavily discounted tuition rate to teachers from as many as ten nearby institutions. The first three semesters he taught the course at night, Murphy encouraged the enrolled teachers from four campuses to do projects such as overhauling old courses or designing new units such as digital storytelling instead of writing traditional course papers. The state has since rescinded the tuition help, but Murphy and colleagues in his area are still exploring ways to offer a four-course certificate in Teaching First-Year Writing to teachers already employed at two- and four-year colleges in central New York. Their reasoning is that teachers who have terminal degrees in literature are eager for more graduate-level work to help them with their main teaching assignment in writing, and some faculty members with PhDs in Rhetoric and Writing are willing to teach local teachers because a certification program could transform the market for first-year writing teachers in that area. "How powerful would it be," Murphy asks, "in negotiations over salary and appointments if the expectation was not only that teaching first-year writing required some significant level of training but also that most teachers in the labor pool indeed had that training?" (Murphy 2017, 83).

My second recommendation is that we experiment more widely with new curricular content and course structures. Since 2007, Wardle and Downs have urged us to make the knowledge of our own discipline—its threshold concepts—the subject matter of introductory writing courses. These courses, usually called WAW courses because they are "writing about writing," not only initiate first-year students into some of the knowledge we have developed in the last fifty years, but they teach the teachers too. When Downs and Wardle (2007) first wrote about their experiments, it seemed unlikely that teachers with little or no disciplinary background could succeed in teaching WAW courses, but Wardle and Downs's (2013) update on their experience claims that it is possible "to invite willing faculty members [from other disciplines] to learn about writing studies research while bringing their own expertise to bear" as they teach WAW courses. Wardle and Downs further claim that this may be a way of "professionalizing large corps of instructors without rhet/comp backgrounds." While this claim remains to be widely tested, it is certainly an avenue worth exploring. Wardle (2013) claims that the WAW approach changed the culture of the writing program at University of Central Florida from its former focus on managerial concerns to a lively conversation on professional concerns. As teachers "read and enacted composition theory and research," they changed their classrooms and their professional positioning. As a result of the pilot program's success, Wardle was able to make the case that such teachers should no longer be contingent labor, and fifteen new full-time permanent positions with benefits were created at her institution.

In addition to curricula that focus on our discipline's knowledge for students and help professionalize more teachers, we should experiment with new ways of structuring and delivering courses that help students interested in Rhetoric and Writing to begin their disciplinary education and start on the path to becoming professionals while they are still undergraduates. An excellent model is offered by California State University–Chico, which has created a "jumbo" section of its first-year writing course (Jaxon and Fosen 2014). At the 2016 CCCC in Houston, Kim Jaxon and Tom Fox, professors who have taught the course, adamantly maintained it was created neither by institutional or budgetary pressures nor by enrollment bottlenecks or faculty shortages. The jumbo course is not a mere "scaling up" of a smaller course; rather, it is intentionally designed to capitalize on the advantages that come with "epic" projects (Jaxon, personal communication; see also Jaxon and Fox 2016). The jumbo section enrolls ninety students and is taught two hours a week by a tenure-track professor with credentials in Rhetoric and Writing. For every ten students, there is a peer mentor (usually an undergraduate) who attends the large lecture course and is also responsible for teaching his or her ten students two hours a week and doing all formative evaluation of those students' writing. (Summative evaluation is done of e-portfolios by the professor.) But the nine peer mentors are not merely TAs or graders. Before they can serve as peer mentors, they must take a course called "Theories and Practices of Tutoring Writing" and demonstrate curiosity and the ability to think about problems of practice. The mentors are considered co-teachers, and they spend two hours a week meeting with the professor to plan the course activities and reading and responding to student writing together. Jaxon states that "mentors often point to this work we do together as the best part of their own growth as professionals" (personal communication). Since 2009, Jaxon and others have worked with some 300 students who have served as mentors either in the jumbo course or in workshops attached to the regular sections; these students are now teachers of English and ESL in high schools and community colleges or have gone on to graduate study in Composition and Rhetoric and/or literacy programs. Their early initiation into the discipline contributes to a firm foundation for eventually earning professional credentials. It also helps create boundaries to our field's expertise.[3]

My third suggestion I must sketch in broad strokes because I think CWPA and/or CCCC committees would need to undertake the task of working out the details. I propose that we conceptualize a paraprofessional status in Rhetoric and Writing pedagogy. The professions of medicine and law have long made use of paraprofessionals, people who works beside (para) a professional but who don't have the same amount or kind of schooling that full professionals do. Licensed public school teachers are often assisted by paraprofessionals who don't do the more abstract work of designing curriculum, teaching classes, or creating assignments and tests. But they may grade homework and tests and tutor individual students. Recently, the American Library Association–Allied Professional Association proposed a certification program for library paraprofessionals in response to constant pressures from higher-level managers to hire more workers in libraries who do not have the MLS degree—heretofore the gold standard for professional librarians. In other words, library professionals were willing to allow a certain level of deprofessionalization among some library employees, but they still insisted on a certain level of disciplinary training and on defining what that training would be. As a profession, they defined seven elective competency sets, from which would-be paraprofessionals would choose three to master (see Litwin 2009). The difference between us and the librarians is that their paraprofessional category responds to attempts to partly deprofessionalize their work, while I recommend we attempt what has seldom been done in our field: to establish minimum disciplinary requirements for being allowed to perform the professional work of teaching. We might, for example, decide what a person at the "competent performer" stage of expertise should know and do, then make that the standard for being designated a paraprofessional. Perhaps not all paraprofessional requirements would be met by taking courses; some might be met through apprenticeship, observation, and supervised on-the-job training.

What would we gain by creating a paraprofessional status or by widely implementing the other suggestions I have sketched above? We would be asserting our status as a discipline and as a profession; we would be determining and protecting our profession's boundaries. Right now, our profession is like a house with dozens of holes in the walls. Many of us have to employ as teachers all the graduate students who show up each fall in the

English department, regardless of their academic background or interests in teaching. Many of us have to hunt up overworked, underpaid adjuncts at the last minute to teach the extra sections of writing classes added to meet enrollments. Because we haven't protected our profession's boundaries by insisting on qualified teachers with adequate disciplinary knowledge, the boundaries we should have set are now often out of our control. Our first-year course—which, let us not forget, has traditionally been the foundation on which the discipline rests—is increasingly being outsourced to high schools and in some cases is taught by high school teachers who know even less about our discipline than the adjuncts and graduate students whom we at least try to teach when they work on our campuses.[4] But we need to remember that this isn't just about us, our jobs, or perpetuating our place in the academy. It's about the students, whose literacy needs we understand much better than the public and campus colleagues usually give us credit for. It's about how much better prepared and rhetorically versatile students need to be to keep up with the pace of change in the work they will do in the Information Age. It's about enacting a vision and a version of college that used to be widely agreed on but has been lost as our society has acquiesced in reducing university education to amassing credit hours as quickly and cheaply and preferably as early in one's life as possible. It's about whether we will prepare students to take their place in a democracy as well-informed citizens who can express themselves articulately in the ongoing conversation about how to advance the public good. And it's about having a truly professional class of teachers whose judgment is grounded in deep, broad disciplinary knowledge before they undertake this important work.

*Notes*

1. I acknowledge that my analogy between math/statistics and English/writing exaggerates and distorts for rhetorical effect. As my readers know, not all postsecondary institutions operate writing programs in the way the analogy suggests. At some universities, all English faculty, even those on the tenure track with academic specialties other than Rhetoric and Writing, are expected to help teach writing courses, and there is an ongoing department conversation, in which everyone participates, about how best to do this. At other institutions, full-time non-tenure-track lecturers are hired for their abilities to teach writing on the assumption that they have already learned about teaching writing elsewhere. In two-year colleges—which generally use high percentages of part-time adjunct labor to teach writing courses—frequently no one is assigned to serve as a WPA, and there is generally no extensive pre-service or in-serving training of adjunct teachers of writing. But it's important to remember that many adjuncts and non-tenure-track teachers take jobs at community colleges or elsewhere after having studied at universities with graduate programs and WPA-supervised writing programs. Because of the way graduate

universities influence the rest of the postsecondary scene in writing, my focus in this chapter is heavily on how our field could develop deeper disciplinary knowledge in those who are likely to do their first teaching of writing in universities. I think the best hope of eventually creating a true profession for writing teachers is in instilling disciplinary knowledge about Rhetoric and Writing in students while they are undergraduates and beginning graduate students. For that reason, I do not focus heavily in this chapter on the teaching of writing in two-year colleges, small liberal arts colleges, or universities without graduate programs.

2. I acknowledge that there are undergraduate programs that lead to degrees, minors, certificates, and so forth in various manifestations of writing—professional, technical, journalism, creative writing, and the like. I think all of those would be valuable in helping to prepare students to become writing teachers. But my focus here is on teaching writing as a profession, and what it would take to make professional teachers rather than professional writers of some sort.

3. Jaxon and Fox reported at the 2016 CCCC in Houston that students pass the jumbo course at a rate of 98 percent (with "passing" defined as C- or better), a rate slightly higher than the pass rate of students enrolled in small sections. They also reported that students value the course because its "epic" nature—its large number of peers and mentors and the resources devoted to it—changes the ways they perceive themselves as writers. Although the size of the jumbo course admittedly goes against CWPA recommendations for small sections, Jaxon and Fox argue that the virality and contagious assumptions that come from large courses suggest we ought to revisit the accepted wisdom about writing class size. Joseph Harris is currently teaching large sections of 130 students with graduate TAs at the University of Delaware, and Harris also reported promising results at the 2016 CCCC.

4. The granting of credit for high school courses where we can't vouch for the disciplinary and professional abilities of the high school teacher is also a manifestation of the problem I describe in this chapter—something I have written about elsewhere (see Hansen 2010). Universities and community colleges often grant college credit for high school AP and dual credit courses, assuming these experiences perfectly substitute for the courses we have designed and are trying to have taught at colleges by teachers with some disciplinary knowledge. Collectively, we must more vigorously assert our disciplinary expertise and our authority as a profession with a unique and valuable service to perform in developing the literacy of students in late adolescence and early adulthood. We need to be involved in deciding who should teach our courses, what the curriculum should be, and what standards students should reach. NCTE's *First-Year Writing: What Good Does It Do?* rightly asserts that "the decision to exempt students [because of AP scores or dual credit courses] should be made on an individual basis and should be based on actual writing samples from the student that are read by instructors at the school they will attend" (National Council of Teachers of English 2013, 3). Such a stance claims professional authority by asserting the value of our disciplined judgment. We must be similarly assertive about all issues affecting our discipline and profession.

## References

Abbott, Andrew. 1988. *The System of Professions: An Essay on the Division of Expert Labor.* Chicago: University of Chicago Press.

Bousquet, Marc. 2003. "Composition as Management Science." In *Tenured Bosses and Disposable Teachers: Writing Instruction in the Managed University*, ed. Marc Bousquet, 11–35. Carbondale: Southern Illinois University Press.

Brandt, Deborah. 2015. *The Rise of Writing: Redefining Mass Literacy*. Cambridge: Cambridge UP. https://doi.org/10.1017/CBO9781316106372.
CCCC Committee on the Major in Rhetoric and Composition. 2009. *Writing Majors at a Glance*. http://www.ncte.org/cccc/gov/committees/majorrhetcomp.
Cheetham, Graham, and Geoff Chivers. 2005. *Professions, Competence and Informal Learning*. Northampton, MA: Edward Elgar.
Conference on College Composition and Communication. 1982. *Position Statement on the Preparation and Professional Development of Teachers of Writing*.
Conference on College Composition and Communication. 1989. "Statement of Principles and Standards for the Postsecondary Teaching of Writing." *CCC* 40 (3): 329–36.
Conference on College Composition and Communication. 2001. *Statement on Second Language Writing and Writers*. Revised 2009. http://cccc.ncte.org/cccc/resources/positions/secondlangwriting.
Conference on College Composition and Communication. 2013. *Statement of Principles for the Postsecondary Teaching of Writing*. http://cccc.ncte.org/cccc/resources/positions/postsecondarywriting.
Conference on College Composition and Communication. 2015. *Preparing Teachers of College Writing*. http://cccc.ncte.org/cccc/resources/positions/statementonprep.
Connors, Robert. 1997. *Composition-Rhetoric: Backgrounds, Theory, and Pedagogy*. Pittsburgh: University of Pittsburgh Press. https://doi.org/10.2307/j.ctt5hjt92.
Downs, Douglas, and Elizabeth Wardle. 2007. "Teaching about Writing, Righting Misconceptions: (Re)Envisioning 'First-Year Composition' as 'Introduction to Writing Studies.'" *CCC* 58 (4): 552–84.
Dreyfus, Hubert, and Stuart Dreyfus. 1986. *Mind over Machine: The Power of Human Intuition and Expertise in the Era of the Computer*. New York: The Free Press.
Ericsson, K. Anders, Michael J. Prietula, and Edward T. Cokely. 2007. "The Making of an Expert." *Harvard Business Review* (July–August): 1–7.
Flyvbjerg, Bent. 2001. *Making Social Science Matter: Why Social Inquiry Fails and How It Can Succeed Again*. Cambridge: Cambridge University Press. https://doi.org/10.1017/CBO9780511810503.
Hansen, Kristine. 2011. "Are We There Yet? The Making of a Discipline in Composition." In *The Changing of Knowledge in Composition: Perspectives on an Evolving Field*, ed. Richard Gebhardt and Lance Massey, 236–63. Logan: Utah State University Press.
Hansen, Kristine. 2010. "The Composition Marketplace: Shopping for Credit vs. Learning to Write." In *College Credit for Writing in High School: The "Taking-Care-of" Business*, ed. Kristine Hansen and Christine R. Farris, 1–39. Urbana, IL: NCTE.
Jaxon, Kim B., and Chris Fosen. 2014. "Sites for Epic Learning: Studio-Workshops in a 'Jumbo' Writing Course." Unpublished manuscript.
Jaxon, Kim B., and Tom Fox. 2016. "Epic Composition." *CCCC*, Houston, TX. http://kimjaxon.com/?s=epic+composition.
Larson, Magali Sarfatti. [1977] 2013. *The Rise of Professionalism: Monopolies of Competence and Sheltered Markets*. New Brunswick, NJ: Transaction Publishers.
Litwin, Rory. 2009. "The Library Paraprofessional Movement and the Deprofessionalization of Librarianship." *Progressive Librarian* 33 (Summer/Fall): 43–60.
McDonald, James C., and Eileen E. Schell. 2011. "The Spirit and Influence of the Wyoming Resolution: Looking Back to Look Forward." *College English* 73 (4): 360–78.
Messer-Davidow, Ellen, David R. Shumway, and David Sylvan, eds. 1993. *Knowledges: Historical and Critical Studies in Disciplinarity*. Charlottesville: University of Virginia Press.
Murphy, Michael. 2017. "Head to Head with edX? Toward a New Rhetoric for Academic Labor." In *Contingency, Exploitation, and Solidarity: Labor and Action in English Composition*, ed. Seth Kahn, Bill Lalicker, and Amy Lynch-Biniek, 71–89. Fort Collins, CO: WAC Clearinghouse.

National Council of Teachers of English. 2013. *First-Year Writing: What Good Does It Do?* http://www2.ncte.org.

National Research Council. 2006. "Taxonomy of Fields and their Sub-Fields." http://sites.nationalacademies.org/pga/resdoc/pga_044522.

Nelson, Cary. 2008. "Foreword: Resistance Is Not Futile." In *How the University Works: Higher Education and the Low-Wage Nation*, ed. Marc Bousquet, xiii–xviii. New York: New York University Press.

Ohmann, Richard. 2002. "Afterword." In *Disciplining English: Alternative Histories, Critical Perspectives*, ed. David Shumway and Craig Dionne, 213–19. Albany: SUNY Press.

Palmquist, Mike, and Sue Doe. 2011. "Contingent Faculty: Introduction." *College English* 73 (4): 353–55.

Pytlik, Betty. 2002. "How Graduate Students Were Prepared to Teach Writing—1850–1970." In *Preparing College Teachers of Writing: Histories, Theories, Programs, Practices*, ed. Betty Pytlik and Sarah M. Liggett, 3–16. New York: Oxford University Press.

Reid, E. Shelley, and Heidi Estrem with Marcia Belcheir. 2012. "The Effects of Writing Pedagogy Education on Graduate Teaching Assistants' Approaches to Teaching Composition." *Writing Program Administration* 36 (1): 32–73.

Roach, Ronald. 2013. "AAUP Faculty Salary Report Highlights Contingent Faculty, State Funding Concerns." *Diverse Issues in Higher Education* (April 7). http://diverseeducation.com/article/52422/.

Shumway, David R., and Ellen Messer-Davidow. 1991. "Disciplinarity: An Introduction." *Poetics Today* 12 (2): 201–25. https://doi.org/10.2307/1772850.

Smit, David W. 2004. *The End of Composition Studies*. Carbondale: Southern Illinois University Press.

Vandenberg, Peter. 1998. "Composing Composition Studies." In *Under Construction: Working at the Intersections of Composition Theory, Research, and Practice*, ed. Christine Farris and Chris M. Anson, 19–29. Logan: Utah State University Press. https://doi.org/10.2307/j.ctt46nrqf.5.

Wardle, Elizabeth. 2013. "Intractable Writing Program Problems, *Kairos*, and Writing about Writing: A Profile of Central Florida's First-Year Composition Program." *Composition Forum* 27 (Spring). http://compositionforum.com/issue/27/ucf/php.

Wardle, Elizabeth, and Doug Downs. 2013. "Reflecting Back and Looking Forward: Revisiting 'Teaching about Writing, Righting Misconceptions' Five Years On." *Composition Forum* 27 (Spring). http://compositionforum.com/issue/27/reflecting-back/php.

Wilhoit, Steve. 2002. "Recent Trends in TA Instruction: A Bibliographic Essay." In *Preparing College Teachers of Writing: Histories, Theories, Programs, Practices*, ed. Betty Pytlik and Sarah M. Liggett, 17–27. New York: Oxford University Press.

# SECTION 3

**Coming to Terms**

*What Are the Complications and Tensions?*

# 8
## EMBRACING THE VIRTUE IN OUR DISCIPLINARITY

Jennifer Helene Maher

There is virtue in Rhetoric and Composition's claim to be a discipline. But to make such an assertion is not without challenge, as disciplines have come to be associated more with vice than virtue. In Pierre Bourdieu's (1984) analysis of the social structure of French universities, we can see why. Writing of what had been considered long-standing virtues of academia and its disciplines, Bourdieu identifies the virtues of "autonomy, . . . the values of disinterestedness, magnanimity and indifference to the sanctions and demands of practice" (124). Until the student uprisings of the late 1960s, academics often experienced such a degree of entitlement, autonomy, and pride that they seldom, if ever, had to justify their work. In fact, the need for such justification was unfathomable: "Conscious that he is expressing the ultimate values, which it would be better not to have to publish, of a community of belief—'objectivity', 'good taste', 'clarity', 'common sense'—he finds it scandalous that anyone should question those certitudes which constitute the academic order which has produced him" (116). But even following the subsequent changes that came to academia in not only France but also the United States, disciplines all too often continue to function, according to Charles Bazerman (2004), as "self-protecting domains of vested interest and social power" (74). The constitutive element for producing and organizing knowledge in the modern university continues to be the discipline, so much so, in fact, that Burton Clark (1983) identifies disciplinarity as the "first principle" of academia (16). Whether as "necessary evils" (Fuller 2014) or, less pejoratively, "silos" (Jacobs 2013), disciplines lay claim to a body of knowledge and organize around the (re)production and extension of that knowledge in the form of ideas, theories, methodologies, and texts. In order for a discipline to constitute its identity and expertise in ways that its worth is recognizable to those outside the discipline, its body of knowledge must have

DOI: 10.7330/9781607326953.c008

relatively stable boundaries that demarcate what it does and why (Abbott 2001; Hyland 2012; Lenoir 1993; Prior 1998). Ideally, for the discipline at least, there is little to no need to justify itself or its work if disciplinarity is done correctly. The work justifies the discipline, and the discipline justifies the work. But this disciplinary recursiveness relies upon a corrupt intellectual tradition that Antonio Gramsci (1996) originally identified as a problematic kind of *esprit de corps*. Although the *Oxford English Dictionary* defines it as "the regard entertained by the members of a body for the honour and interests of the body as a whole, and of each other as belong to it," Gramsci sees in the academic context this body functioning at the expense of productive, even transformative, knowledge generation for the sake of disciplinary continuity and autonomy (200). Because disciplinarity is the source for such fellowship, the perpetuation of the discipline itself is what ultimately serves as the primary, if often tacit, objective of the fellowship, so that, even today, this too often ends up leading to those vices of traditional academic disciplinarity.

In a continuation of those challenges begun in the 1960s, questions have arisen regarding what potentially more worthwhile and beneficial avenues and methods of inquiry are not being pursued because they might challenge or threaten a discipline's and its members' self-interestedness. The call to resist disciplinarity rests in many ways upon a premise that concern for disciplinarity and the status of one's discipline is based upon the vice of magnanimity. Literally translated as "greatness of soul," magnanimity, in the context of Bourdieu's description, is a kind of misplaced pride by which the wrong things are valued for the wrong reasons. The most vocal resistance to disciplinarity has come from Cultural Studies, which rejects what Cary Nelson and Dilip Gaonkar identify as "the McCarthy-era pact guaranteeing silence and irrelevance from the humanities and collaboration from the social sciences, a pact disguised by (and structured in terms of) the proprieties of disciplinarity and its proper boundaries, limits, and conduct" (Nelson and Gaonkar 1996, 2). In our own discipline, Kevin Mahoney and Rachel Riedner further explain that at the heart of this pact are those vices perpetuated by neoliberalism, which they define as "an economic policy of upward redistribution in which public services are privatized, markets are opened up, and weakened government relations are allowing corporations the 'freedom' to pursue capital by extending market relations ever deeper in our social relations" (Mahoney and Riedner 2008, 10). Rather than relations among citizens empowered with the freedom to participate meaningfully in democratic life, neoliberalism constructs individuals through the limited paradigm of producer/

consumer. Central to the success of this paradigm is a pedagogical compulsion by which teachers and students must relate to one another as if engaged in a market transaction. According to Ryan Claycomb and Riedner (2004), disciplinarity is essential to normalizing this transaction as it serves as "a component of neoliberal public pedagogy that focuses on the production of workers and consumers for the newest phase of the capitalist economy." As a result, Randi Kristensen and Claycomb (2010) suggest, "The only inoculation against disciplinarity is anti-disciplinarity" (4). To embrace antidisciplinarity appears to be premised upon humility, a virtue that Harvey Graff (2015) invokes in the move toward the seemingly less insular and boundaried notion of interdisciplinarity (214, 236). In the case of antidisciplinarity, only by rejecting the first principle of the modern university and the neoliberal vices perpetuated, in part, by the disciplines can academics, freed of their sometimes misplaced disciplinary allegiances, come to care about the those things that really do matter and then concentrate on the much-needed interventionist work that can done with scholarship, with teaching, and with the world.

Yet, this characterization of disciplinarity, while it has its merits in some cases, is faulty in the case of our own discipline. In Rhetoric and Composition, we have been enculturated to see ourselves and to accept being seen by others as not worthy of being a discipline, instead better suited to the service of "real" (i.e., traditional) disciplines rather than knowledge creation. Failing to see our worth, we are thus subordinated to such an extent that our claim to be a discipline must be understood as nothing less than transgressive. For our discipline is not rooted in those vices that proliferated through the traditional, boundaried disciplines that constituted the modern university. Nor could it be, as we are and have always been interstitial. Yet, our interstitial nature does not mean that we have no disciplinary expertise, but rather that our expertise necessarily extends across other disciplines and practices. And rather than despair of this fact or shrink in the face of the great challenges this presents, we persist. Consequently, it is not the virtue of humility that we must first and foremost embrace in discussions of disciplinarity, but rather magnanimity, which in contrast to Bourdieu, can be a virtue rather than a vice. In Aristotle's (1984b) conception of ethics, later elaborated upon by Thomas Aquinas (n.d.), the easily misunderstood virtue of magnanimity (*megalopsychia*) exists as the mean between "vanity" in its excess and "undue humility" in its deficiency. Oriented toward doing that which is deemed difficult and good, the virtue of magnanimity, according to Aquinas, "denotes stretching forth of the mind to great things" (Aquinas n.d., 3935). I argue that defining Rhetoric and Composition as a discipline helps us do just this.

## THE VICE OF UNDUE HUMILITY

Although the adoption of humility in light of disciplinarity's destructive shortcomings might appear the most honorable action for us to take in light of traditional disciplinarity's neoliberal servitude, humility is much more complicated in the context of our work. To wit, in a 2014 issue of *JAC*, dedicated to the Watson Conference theme of responsivity, Bruce Horner (2014) examines our grounding in crisis and calls for us to give up our tenuous claim to disciplinarity. Horner (2014) argues that the crisis in the professions generally and our disciplinary profession specifically has increasingly meant the loss of autonomy in the production and circulation of a body of knowledge for which academic disciplines have traditionally been responsible (51). But unlike in other disciplines, our work has never enjoyed the autonomy or garnered the esteem that that those in other disciplines have. We are plagued, according to Horner, by "low academic institutional status" both because of our function as a service provider for undergraduates and because of our failure to persuade others to see that we possess expert knowledge, except possibly in mechanics (52). Arguing that we "can make at best highly suspect claims to the possession of expert knowledge of any recognized value to the public," Horner sees our disciplinary potential as inherently compromised: "But even were we to succeed in persuading others that we possessed such expertise—again, highly unlikely—the knowledge, or rather ability, to write that we claimed to have special knowledge of how to produce continues to be understood as such a simple, mechanical matter that no prestige is earned in claiming expertise in knowing how to produce it, hence the inability to control who might be authorized to teach that ability" (53).

Horner therefore contends that we ought to embrace instead where our true value lies, in our "deep familiarity with the necessity of labor to the ongoing realization of the value of knowledge." In short, we are to help those with expert knowledge produce "use value" from their work and see the value in such labor (58). And how are we to accomplish this? Horner argues that we ought to embrace humility for "there is a use . . . to composition's engagement in the virtue of humility—of knowing, in a root sense, one's 'place,' and what it makes possible and not, and how" (58). For Horner, the fact that we have neither enjoyed the autonomy that other disciplines have nor offered recognized expertise actually gives us an advantage over those in disciplines that have more to lose by admitting that knowledge does not have "inherent value," but instead is dependent upon use in context.

Certainly, it is true that our own disciplinarity and the benefits that can come from it have not been easily achieved, if entirely achieved at all, primarily because of the teaching of composition. Twenty-seven years ago, Robert Connors (1991) noted, "The general perception of composition is that it is a recent and questionable discipline with a shallow and inauspicious past" (18). Born from a need to treat the deficient writing abilities of university students, composition's "pedagogical imperative" has proven a significant challenge to our disciplinary status. In an "abridged version of history" offered by Doug Hesse (2004), it is not difficult to see why: "Since its collegiate birth a century and a quarter ago, composition has led a hard life. Orphaned from rhetoric, a servile Cinderella in the begrudging manor of English-as-literature, composition earnestly began pursuing the research that might win a dance at the academic ball only in the 1960s. But even a closet full of doctoral programs, monographs, professional associations, and journals failed to transform composition's cadre of adjuncts and graduate assistants into a guild of tenure professors. Those who did acquire status achieved it primarily as scholars and administrators rather than as teachers" (ix). The too often myopic emphases on teaching composition and on the research of it signal a clear roadblock to our disciplinarity; and yet, for some, this seems to hold the only path toward disciplinarity. But in his preface to *Rhetoric and Composition as Intellectual Work*, Gary Olson (2002) notes: "While many compositionists insist that all research, all inquiry in the field, should serve the sole purpose of furthering and refining the *teaching* of composition, many of us contend that although we all desire to learn more about the teaching of writing or about our own writing processes, these are not the *only* intellectual concerns we should have as a discipline, that constituting rhetoric and composition as a discipline whose raison d'être is the teaching of writing is dangerously and unacceptably narrow and even, in some people's eyes, as anti-intellectual" (xii).

With the seemingly never-ending questions about our disciplinarity, the discipline, one centered on teaching and researching composition, can hardly be secure in its status, even though what we do as a discipline is essential to a whole range of expertise and practices beyond our own. As Howard Tinberg explains in his 2014 Conference on College Composition and Communication (CCCC) address, "In essence, our discipline, like the humanities generally, aims to provide the means by which to determine who we are and where we belong. These goals have a clear and significant public purpose" (Tinberg

2014, 336). More specifically, Tinberg argues that our disciplinary aim "as teachers of writing" is the facilitation of the "acquisition of literacies" that produce "both individual and collective good" (337). And although much work has been done to facilitate these ends, Tinberg notes, "All of these accomplishments notwithstanding, we clearly have our work cut out for us."

In light of composition's complicated relationship to disciplinarity, Horner's suggestion that what we really need in order to do our work is to learn "our place," meaning a space outside disciplinarity, seems not just pragmatic but essential to our survival because "from a review of current practice, one might reasonably conclude that almost anyone can (and does) teach composition" (53). Lending credence to this argument is the trope of composition's end that sometimes appears in our disciplinary scholarship, an invocation that only works because it falls within the realm of possibility that composition, in its weak case for disciplinarity, might someday meet its final demise. Perhaps the most obvious example is David Smit's (2004) *The End of Composition Studies*. But as Smit is quick to note on the first page of his introduction, his use of "end" is meant to invoke Aristotelian teleology, with its emphasis not on demise, but on outcomes. Likewise, Sid Dobrin (2011) opens *Postcomposition* with this statement: "Don't panic. I am not calling for the end of composition studies or even identifying something as dramatic as the death of composition studies, despite the way that many may read the title of this book" (1). Yet, even if intended as a simply clever play meant to pique the interest of readers, the demise of a discipline centered upon composition, if that discipline does exist, is apparently not so hard to imagine in light of its suspect beginnings and ongoing challenges.

Because of our tenuous, if not, nonexistent disciplinary status, Horner's argument—"There is a use . . . and not just an ethical value, to composition's engagement in the virtue of humility" (58)—may at first appear noble. For, the commonly held view, according to Aquinas (n.d.), is that magnanimity is antithetical to humility because she who is humble does not desire honor that comes from greatness in soul and in deeds (3939). In this way, humility can be understood as moderating a sense of worth both in terms of an appreciation of one's own abilities and of the potential greatness that those abilities can achieve in deeds. Such appreciation is particularly useful in matters where the perception of the magnitude of deeds results from beliefs that are less critical of or reflexive about what really matters in the world than they ought to be, as with Gramsci's *esprit de corps*. We can grasp this point more obviously in discussions of humility in the work of Paulo Freire (1998). In one of his letters to teachers, Freire points to the transformative potential of humility, which he defines as a way of coming to understand that "no one knows it all; no one is ignorant of everything. We all know something; we are all ignorant of something. Without humility, one can hardly listen with respect to those one judges to be too far below one's own level of competence" (39). Humility thus serves to influence choices regarding what constitutes knowledge and challenges the orthodoxy by which the teacher is considered the lone expert upon whom otherwise ignorant students depend upon for literacy acquisition.

But, because our discipline already suffers from low status in comparison to the otherwise established academic disciplines, there is no virtue in giving up that which we barely, if ever, possessed. While embracing humility might certainly be needed among those for whom disciplinarity status has historically been taken for granted, there is no virtue to us doing likewise. In contrast to the intellectual *esprit de corps* described by Bourdieu and Gramsci, our history as a discipline is one of being humbled in the sense that Horner (2014) explicitly states he aims to avoid: "of being subordinate to others" (58). Because of composition's at best questionable grounding for disciplinarity, the suggestion that we embrace humility is problematic in a way similar to charges made against the unreflexive appropriation of Freire's work for the composition classroom: a failure to attend to context differentials between the illiterate poor of Brazil and college students in the United States (see Giroux 1992; Knoblauch 1988; Shor 1996). Freire does not suggest that the illiterate poor of Brazil ought to embrace the virtue of humility in the face of institutional power and disenfranchisement: they had already been humbled in ways that necessitated liberatory pedagogy in the first place. Rather it is to the teacher, in the context of the power dynamics of the teacher-student relationship, to whom Freire primarily makes the case for humility in order to move beyond the conception of student as an empty vessel and teacher as the disseminator of knowledge. Because of the historical and ongoing challenges to the claim that composition is a discipline, the assertion that we are a discipline is an act of transgression that challenges assumptions about our role and the role of composing in knowledge creation, both in the university and beyond. For, the material conditions for teachers and students, especially in what Nancy Welch and Tony Scott (2016) identify as the new normal "age of austerity," is unlikely to improve by embracing humility and grounding ourselves in the "necessity of labor" (Horner 2014, 58), especially because our labor as service is the basis for our questionable, perhaps even nonexistent, disciplinary status now.

Because composition offers questionable grounding for our disciplinarity, the suggestion that we embrace the virtue of humility in the context of disciplinarity reeks of resignation made possible only by failing to attend to our own history and conditions. The result is that what is actually behind calls for a humble rejection of disciplinarity is less virtue than vice. To argue that we are in a discipline institutionally disempowered to such an extent that we may lack disciplinarity entirely smacks of "undue humility," which, in Aristotle's estimation, is worse than vanity. As the deficiency to the mean of magnanimity, the unduly humble "thinks himself worthy of less than he really is . . . whether his deserts be great or moderate, or his deserts be small but his claims yet smaller" (Aristotle 1984b, 1123b10–11). Although we may hardly need a reminder, we can see how undue humility has historically played out in John Trimbur's (1996) description of the relationship of writing to literature: "Writing teachers had cast themselves as a kind of religion of the oppressed, small islands of the saved, where the legitimacy of success seemed to threaten their very identities as the humble and unauthorized professors of a truth our literature counterparts cannot bear: namely, that we care about students precisely because we have invested ourselves, both intellectually and affectively, in their personal growth and well-being instead of a turf warfare over who is qualified to interpret a body of texts" (135–36).

Because of our disposition toward undue humility, to relinquish willingly or to stop working toward disciplinarity is nothing less than a hair shirt meant to testify to a willingness to suffer for the sake of things greater. Although it may seem that by forsaking disciplinarity we are both rejecting the vicious trappings of disciplinarity like autonomy and misplaced pride and committing ourselves toward those truly great challenges that include literacy and empowerment, this is not the case in the context of Rhetoric and Composition. As Brad Hammer (2010) explains, in the corporate university, with its overreliance on contingent faculty, "The reformulation of a first-year curriculum . . . necessitates 'service' over disciplinarity" and affirms "our work as 'labor' and not inquiry" (A1, A3). As a result, it is important that we resist those structures that position us outside of disciplinarity, especially since this positioning necessitates that we misrecognize and encourage others to misrecognize the value of our work. For Bourdieu, "misrecognition," like the etymological roots of humility, creates a "sense of one's place" (Bourdieu 1991, 235). But this sense can be misrecognized or misplaced, much in the same way that the vice of undue humility is based upon a misrecognized sense of one's worth. As Bourdieu explains, misrecognition gives "the sense of what one can or cannot 'allow oneself', implies a tacit acceptance of one's position, a sense of limits ('that's not meant for us') or—what amounts to the same thing—a sense of distances, to be marked and maintained, respected and expected of others." Because disciplinarity has long been considered not for us, the appeal to humility creates a false sense of virtue in how we place ourselves and how we are placed in academia. In truth, the undue humility that actually lies at the heart of such appeals reveals itself for what it is: the vice of pusillanimity. Horner writes, for example:

> Composition's humility, its location on the ground, is, one might say, its saving grace. The perspective that humility, so defined, gives on what the work of responsivity requires—where that work takes place, what it consists of, and why—can keep us from overreaching, from making promises (to ourselves and others) we can't keep. Humility can also enable us to see what that "earth" is capable of, if and when we resign ourselves to it as the site and substance of our work—in short, to the necessity of labor. Responsivity requires first of all a grounding, a knowledge of where and what we are and what we do, and with what, how, so that we can do it better. Composition's lack of professional academic disciplinary status, its failure even to be able to pretend to possess expert knowledge, gives us that. (58–59)

While Horner is correct that the proper measure of humility serves to counterbalance the hubris that can arise when magnanimity turns to vice, locating our worth in a humility that arises out of forced resignation is nothing more than weakness. As Mary Keys (2006) explains in her reading of Aristotle and Aquinas, "Pusillanimity may not be the height of wickedness, but it does reflect a regrettable combination of excessive fear of failure [and] ignorance of one's own worth and capacities . . . Both personal and common goods depend to a significant extent upon spirited and truly magnanimous dispositions" (154–55). Not merely resigning ourselves to this place Horner describes, but actually finding virtue in it most obviously demands that we ignore the large body of expertise that our discipline has generated over the last fifty years (see Adler-Kassner and Wardle 2015). Simply put, what we are asked to embrace in the call for humility in the context of our disciplinarity (or its lack) is nothing less than capitulation.

To claim disciplinarity is not simply an act motivated by vanity, or, in Horner's (2014) words, the fulfillment of a desire to "win from either academic institutions or the public at large the right to exclusive ownership over the production, circulation, or reception of any particular kind of commodified knowledge" (52). A foundational course such as first-year composition has not and will not make us a discipline; it can be argued that it does just the opposite, in fact. But this is the double bind in which a discipline centered on composition finds itself. If the first principle of disciplinarity necessitates some kind of core knowledge production, but composing is something that we acknowledge we do not own in the way that other disciplines claim to own their knowledge, then what is our case for disciplinarity? This may seem the point at which we throw up our hands, rethink the need for disciplinarity, and work to recast antidisciplinarity as the radical opposition to neoliberalism that some argue it to be. But the way out of this bind is not to acquiesce our disciplinarity, for to do so encourages undue humility and welcomes those material conditions that would have us misrecognize this vice as a virtue.

## WHAT'S AT STAKE?

To explain how the conditions in which we find ourselves can render us low and force undue humility upon us, I offer the example of my own department. At a research university with approximately 14,000 students, the Department of English includes 28 core faculty, of whom 13 are tenured or tenure-track; 12 are noncontingent, non-tenure-track faculty (NTTFs); 2 are Professors of the Practice, both of whom are accomplished journalists but do not hold PhDs; and 1 is an Artist in Residence. In addition, there are approximately 15 contingent, part-time faculty. The department has two tracks: Literature and also Communication and Technology (CT), the latter of which would more traditionally be called Rhetoric and Composition. The CT track is staffed primarily by four tenure-line faculty, who completed their PhD studies in the discipline of Rhetoric and Composition, as well as noncontingent NTTFs, whose degrees are in either Creative Writing or Literature. The CT track's vertical curriculum includes two core 300-level courses; four 300-level courses chosen from categories that include Professional/Technical Communication, Rhetoric/Composition, Media Literacies, and Journalism/Nonfiction; and two 400-level courses, one of which must be a seminar. The two core 300-level courses, as well as the 400-level seminar, are taught by the tenure-line PhD's. The four 300-level courses and the remaining 400-level course are taught by a combination of noncontingent NTTFs, the two Professors of the Practice, and the four tenure-line faculty.

But this overview does not reveal another element of the department: The Writing and Rhetoric Division (WARD). From its name, one would expect that this group might include all full-time faculty who teach classes related to the CT track and the Writing Minor. However, this is not the case. Born out of a literature versus composition political brouhaha that predates almost all but a few now in the department, WARD is in many ways a separate entity with its own bylaws, though it is also subject to the general departmental bylaws. The bylaws of WARD explain its responsibilities as follows:

> The Division will have managerial responsibility for the following courses and any new course proposed and approved in any of the categories listed below:
>
> 1. All expository writing courses . . .
> 2. All English-as-a-second language credit courses designed for non-native speakers of English only . . .
> 3. All practical grammar courses: by definition these practical grammar courses are intended as supplemental training for writing and exclude courses that teach theory of English Grammar . . .
> 4. All "peer tutor training" courses: these courses are designed to prepare undergraduates to serve as peer tutors in the Writing Lab or the Writing Center . . .
> 5. All speech courses. (8–9)

Among these courses included in these categories are courses such as ENGL 100: Composition; ENGL 391: Advanced Exposition and Argument; ENGL 393: Technical Communication; and ENGL 395: Writing Internship. But responsibility for these categories and their courses is not limited to a managerial role: "New courses and changes in existing courses in these five areas—will be developed by the Writing and Rhetoric Division and transmitted to the Undergraduate Council through the Director and the Chair of the Department" (9). To qualify for membership in WARD, from which the director, as writing program administrator, is elected, the bylaws state, "Full-time instructors or lecturers in the English Department may be appointed to the Writing and Rhetoric Division. Faculty members, both full-time and adjunct, who teach two or more Writing and Rhetoric courses per year, as defined above, have full voting rights within the Division." Because of the implicit distinction made in the bylaws between WARD courses and those courses taught in the CT track by tenure-line faculty, no tenure-line faculty, meaning those with PhDs in the discipline of Rhetoric and Composition, is eligible for membership in WARD in the course of their regular teaching. In contrast, a contingent NTTF with an MA in Literature who teaches two WARD courses part time is eligible for membership.

A few years ago, I started teaching in the summer two sections of ENGL 393: Technical Communication, a course almost exclusively taught by contingent NTTF. Until that time, none of the four faculty with PhDs in the discipline of Rhetoric and Composition qualified for membership in WARD. However, should I not be granted two 393 summer courses, a prospect that is quite possible due to varying summer enrollment and the dropping of the course as a requirement for some in other majors, it will again be the case that no one with expertise in the discipline enjoys membership in WARD. This is an especially strange phenomenon since the introductory, core course for the CT track—ENGL 300: Texts and Contexts—typically uses either Elizabeth Wardle and Doug Downs' *Writing about Writing* or Bazerman and Paul Prior's *What Writing Does and How It Does It.* Likewise, ENGL 379: Principles and Practices in Technical Communication, a course primarily for English majors, does not qualify as Writing and Rhetoric, at least as envisioned by WARD and the department's bylaws. The same is true for courses such as Principles and Practices of Visual Literacy, Rhetorical Theory, New Media and Digital Literacies, and Web Design and Multimedia Authoring.

Like other tenure-line faculty in CT, I had assumed that I was a part of WARD by nature of my expertise. My initial awakening to things not being as they seemed occurred in my first year on the tenure track. Posted at the entrance to the department was a menu board with faculty names and office numbers. Like the then two other tenure-line faculty in CT, those with PhDs in the discipline of Rhetoric and Composition, I was listed as literature faculty. When I pointed out the error first to the front office staff and then to the department chair, she explained that in the department bylaws all tenure-line faculty were designated "Literature." I politely noted that this was a factual error. And in the name of accuracy, the menu board was corrected, but not by adding "Rhetoric and Composition," but by simply leaving out a discipline designation altogether. And, as the bylaws were amended on this issue at some point, I gave this no other thought.

However, the true extent of the divide between WARD and those with Rhetoric and Composition disciplinary expertise was revealed the following year at a faculty retreat. Having talked briefly in a meeting about the then burgeoning writing-about-writing approach, the department chair asked that I talk about it a bit more at the daylong retreat for full-time faculty that we would be having at the start of the new school year. Having shared with my colleagues the Downs and Wardle (2007) piece "Teaching about Writing, Righting Misconceptions: (Re)Envisioning 'First-Year Composition' as 'Introduction to Writing Studies,'" I talked briefly at the retreat, summarizing its argument and hoping to get a conversation going. The first person to speak was a WARD member who asked me the following question: "What do *you* know about what *we* do?" Shocked at the question to such a degree that I was later told it was written on my face, it took me a moment to answer. And, when I did, I listed my advanced degrees—an MA in English with a concentration in Rhetoric and Composition and a PhD in Rhetoric and Professional Communication—and briefly discussed my then almost decade-long commitment to teaching and researching writing and rhetoric. With that, the discussion of writing at the retreat ended before it began.

The continued institutionalized denial of disciplinary expertise, at least for those from Rhetoric and Composition, affects a whole range of other issues, including first-year composition pedagogy, vertical curriculum scaffolding, Writing Minor participation, GA training, hiring input on NTFF, class size, and even computer classroom assignments, all of which are under the purview of WARD. In fact, the lack of a cohesive, disciplinary rationale for the CT curriculum raises the question as to whether the curriculum is even vertical or just a mishmash of courses that have something to do with topics that are not literature or creative writing. Recently, while talking with a couple of WARD members, I raised the possibility of a tenure-line CT faculty member (i.e., a faculty member with a PhD in the discipline of Rhetoric and Composition) becoming director of WARD at some point, something hardly possible as the director and associate director are elected from the ranks of WARD. I commented, "The Director of WARD should really have expertise in Rhetoric and Composition." The response: "But we have expertise too." According to the Modern Language Association (2014) Issue Brief entitled "The Academic Workforce," "All long-term faculty members need to be fully enfranchised to participate in planning their departments' curricula in the areas in which they teach" (1). Although this brief makes an important call for the increased inclusion and appreciation of the work that long-term NTTF make, this argument, in the context of my own department, actually applies to those disenfranchised tenure-line faculty who have expertise in the discipline of Rhetoric and Composition, yet have little to no say in what constitutes writing/rhetoric in the department or across the university.

Although the circumstances of my department might be unique, they nevertheless illustrate how easily disregard for disciplinary expertise persists, especially once institutionally inscribed. But this dismissal of Rhetoric and Composition's disciplinarity, which lies at the heart of the struggle to assert and have recognized our expertise, is likely familiar to many. In a blog post entitled "Rhetoric and Composition's Dead," Ann Larson (2014), who holds a PhD in Rhetoric and Composition, argues that the emphasis on the teaching and administration of composition is so dependent upon contingent labor that, if the discipline ever did exist, it is surely dead by now: "By giving up our claims to expert knowledge as professional in an unequal system, we can allow ourselves to mourn the loss that really matters: a generation of writing teachers and scholars who have either left the academy or are working in the lower ranks of the education factory that elite members of a moribund discipline hardly acknowledge exists." Although talk of a "moribund discipline" may strike many as strange given the relative health of the job market in comparison to a discipline such as Literature, Larson nevertheless makes quite clear Rhetoric and Composition is in decline, if not dead.

In response to Larson's argument, a poster calling herself "Contingent Cassandra," who identified herself as "a literature Ph.D. who has been teaching primarily composition, as a TA, part-time adjunct, and, for over a decade now, full-time contingent," called for a reimagining of what it meant to be on the tenure track. Rather than privilege research, Cassandra argued, "Putting more teaching-oriented faculty on the tenure-track . . . would signal a respect for actual, in-the-classroom teaching that seems lacking from the structure of Comp and Rhet programs as currently constituted." Acting from what I identify as the virtue of magnanimity, Seth Kahn replies to Cassandra: "I expect you didn't mean this implication, but essentially you've just told people like me, with PhDs in Rhet/Comp in tenure-track/tenured positions who teach a lot of writing and do scholarship *about teaching writing* that our advanced specialization doesn't distinguish us from people who don't have the same advanced specialization." Rather than capitulate to the idea that those who have taught for a long time have the same expertise as those "who teach a lot AND do research in the field," Kahn instead highlights the problem with such thinking, one that stems, in the Aristotelian conception, from vanity. In a similarly motivated response to the same blog post, Steven Krause offers an anecdote about chairing a search for associate director of his department's first-year writing program:

> Someone emailed me and said something kind of like this, "Hey, I've taught part-time in your program off and on for several years and I have an MFA in creative writing, and I think I'd be a really good candidate for this." I emailed back and said something like, "Of course you can apply, but I have to tell you that we are almost certainly going to hire someone with a PhD in composition and rhetoric." This person emailed me back and just was

indignant at this prospect, the idea that someone who didn't have a PhD and who didn't do scholarship in the field. As if that PhD would matter.

Conversely, it is hard not to be indignant when the degree of expertise that the PhD is supposed to attest is so summarily dismissed by so many. The difference in these two instances of indignance, however, lies in the vanity of the applicant who refuses to acknowledge the expertise that comes from earning a PhD in a particular area of study as well as doing ongoing research. As Wardle and Blake Scott (2015) explain, in their discussion of how to help NTTF gain disciplinary knowledge, it can be difficult for some composition teachers, especially those long-time, part-time teachers, to accept that they do not have such expertise already and "that what they had been teaching might be in conflict with disciplinary knowledge about writing and teaching writing" (86). In truth, in Krause's example, the applicant's response raises the question, why even earn a PhD in Rhetoric and Composition? Or, perhaps the better question, in light of differences in pay and tenure (for now at least), is why ought a university invest in hiring PhDs in Rhetoric and Composition to teach writing at all? That such a question can be asked and so often answered in ways that illustrate that a terminal degree in the discipline of Rhetoric and Composition or even a certain familiarity with its disciplinary knowledge is not necessary to teach writing, we might be better off taking the approach of capitulation, even as we might still focus entirely on great deeds such as cultivating the rhetorical literacies of students or fighting the neoliberal agenda that increasingly plagues higher education. But we fall into a trap if we believe that the one is mutually exclusive of the others. Is it not possible, for instance, that the fact that my colleague Jody Shipka and I cannot teach first-year composition as we see fit according to our expertise because of a framework put in place by others who do not have the same kind of disciplinary expertise has material effects not only on students, but also on how we conceptualize the theorizing and practice of composition, as well the work of the university as a whole? To answer "yes" to this question, no matter how tenuous the connection between the one and the others may be, demands a sense of magnanimity.

To act from magnanimity, as Kahn and Krause respectively do in their online posts, might appear to construct the PhD as the singular source for disciplinary magnanimity. Although a PhD in the discipline is the most obvious demonstration of disciplinary expertise in academia, it need not be the only way to gain the kind of necessary expertise that allows an instructor to teach writing in ways consistent with knowledge in the discipline. As the work of so many of the foremother and forefathers who had PhDs in Literature but built the discipline of Rhetoric and Composition evidences, disciplinary knowledge can be cultivated in other ways. But a concerted effort has to be made by those without the PhD credential to engage with disciplinary expertise by other means. For example, in their discussion of how their department helps noncontingent NTTFs, most of whom do not have specialized training in our discipline, teach writing, Wardle and Scott describe the training courses and development program called "Pathways to Expertise." In reading and grappling with conversations in the discipline and interacting with disciplinary experts in order to become enculturated into the discipline, Wardle and Scott (2015) explain, "These instructors become acquainted with some of the knowledge of the field that they could then teach in the first-year courses" as well as in upper-level courses (84). Once some engagement with disciplinary knowledge is undertaken, these instructors often go on to help facilitate an understanding of writing about writing among new instructors. Framed within Harry Collins and Robert Evans's discussion of expertise, Wardle and Scott note, "Although learning 'facts or fact-like relationships' through reading and observation is an important component of expertise, developing the more specialized expertise needed by teachers of a given subject requires 'immersion' in the language and other social practices of domain and its communities" (81). Too often, Collins and Evans (2007) argue, the alternative is simply a matter of the simple application of skills; that is, "expertise is now seen more and more as something practical—something based in what you can do rather than what you can calculate or learn" (23). Thus, if an NTTF with an MA in Literature teaches writing, then immersion in the knowledge of a discipline that cultivates knowledge about writing is, for all intents and purposes, unnecessary.

That instructors from disciplines in Creative Writing and Literature *can* teach writing too often is reason enough for them to do, as if expertise that goes beyond this anemic conception is of little matter. Of course, this does not mean that courses taught by non–Rhetoric and Composition NTTF's cannot be informative and instructive. Many are, and this is in spite of the exploitation of many who teach these courses. But if writing is to be taught from a place of disciplinary expertise, this necessitates the ongoing engagement with disciplinary knowledge that would allow someone not educated in the discipline to become so. This does not mean expertise has to be demonstrated by publishing research, but it does point to a need to recognize and engage with disciplinary knowledge to become what the Committee on Developments in the Science of Learning (2000) describes as "accomplished novices, skilled in many areas and proud of their accomplishments, but" able to "realize that what they know is miniscule compared to all that is potentially knowable" (48). Although this concept may seem to collapse the distinction between novices and experts, Kathleen Yancey, Liane Robertson, and Kara Taczak note that certain distinctions remain clear. What the novice, like the expert, comes to know as the "accomplished novice" is that expertise has "very short shelf life and tentative quality" (Yancey et al. 2014, 40). And this is where the virtue of humility ought to come into play because expertise demands an ongoing engagement with disciplinary knowledge. Only by engaging with disciplinary knowledge in Rhetoric and Composition can non–Rhetoric and Composition NTTFs, as well as tenure-line faculty in Literature and Creative Writing who do writing administration, recognize the need for and engage in opportunities that allow them to "practice expertise" as they come "into expertise" in Rhetoric and Composition (42). In sum, this means "engaging in the social life of the discipline" (Wardle and Scott 2015, 78) and in ways that go beyond simply reading articles from the discipline. But when boundaries are set up to such a degree that they are in my own department, to encourage participation in such opportunities, let alone offer them, can become incredibly difficult, especially since magnanimity on the part of those with disciplinary expertise can too easily come across as a failure to misrecognize one's place as institutionally designated and materialized.

## EMBRACING MAGNANIMITY

What Howard Curzer (1991) describes as a "much maligned" virtue, magnanimity speaks to the belief in an ability to do great and difficult things. Unlike those who claim honor beyond their merit or needlessly think themselves unworthy, one is said to exhibit magnanimity as "proper pride" when she is both "disdainful of what is esteemed great contrary to reason" and "cares about few things only, and those great, and not because someone else thinks them so" (Aristotle 1984a, 1232a38–b6). To this end, the proud individual "is an extreme in respect of the greatness of his claims, but a mean in respect of the rightness of them; for he claims what is in accordance with his merits, while the others go to excess or fall short" (Aristotle 1984b, 1123b13–15). With this description, we might incorrectly understand magnanimity as the vice of misplaced pride that engages that limited and limiting recursiveness that helps to perpetuate everything that is wrong with traditional disciplinarity. (See also Sarch's [2008] reading of *megalopsychia*.) But, as Aquinas (n.d.) explains, "In actions and passions the mean and the extremes depend on various circumstances" (1954). In the case of Rhetoric and Composition, it is the various circumstances of our own history—a history that placed us outside of disciplinarity at the birth of the modern university and for so many years subsequently—that now constitutes us as a unique kind of discipline. More pointedly, our coming into disciplinarity differentiates us from those traditional disciplinary constitutions that have too often been motivated by self-protection, even vanity, and resulted in rigid knowledge boundaries.

Disciplinarity is not something we have been able to take for granted. The reason for this has to do not only with the configuration of our work as service and labor, but also with the fact that we are without the strict boundaries that easily defined, even limited, so many other traditional disciplines, a phenomenon that Yancey (2015) provides in following description: "What is distinctive about the need to inquire further into the study of writing . . . is that such study operates across two important dimensions. Like other academic subjects, it has developed over the last half century to take its place within the academy as a field of study in its own right with established programs operating in colleges and universities across the world. The reach of this discipline goes much further, however, in that the practices and understandings of this particular discipline, composed knowledge, infuse and are intrinsic to successful performance in all other disciplines" (xii).

If the disciplinary core of Rhetoric and Composition is theories and practices of writing, or, in acknowledgment of even greater complexity, composing, then this ought to impede the insularity and autonomy that traditional disciplines once enjoyed and now suffer, especially once we displace the composition classroom as our center. This displacement is necessary because, as Gwendolyn Pough (2011) argues in her CCCC address, "We have often policed our border as a field and been slow to embrace anything that wasn't just about first-year writing or about composition" (306). Although antidisciplinarity, with it lack of boundaries, might seem to promise the ultimate fulfillment of our work, especially in light of writing across the curriculum/writing in the disciplines (WAC/WID), we cannot reject the importance of a certain kind of disciplinary core that provides some center to what we do. The blurring of disciplinary boundaries and knowledges that began in the latter part of the twentieth century (e.g., *interdisciplinarity, multidisciplinarity, transdisciplinarity*, and *postdisciplinarity*) are still very much rooted in disciplinarity and not simply due to borders posed by academic departments or classificatory designations. As unfashionable as it may be to talk of a center in the age of postmodern, posthuman, ambient ecologies, disciplines still rely upon some kind of core that serves the function of both constituting disciplines and differentiating disciplines. According to Julie Klein (1993), "Radical reports on the end of disciplinarity and advent of the postdisciplinary age are naïve, ignoring as they do the power of the prevailing 'first principle'" (207). If we abandon the idea that having a core must automatically lead to marginalization, exclusion, and stagnation—and the struggles within traditional disciplines to define themselves certainly give evidence that this ought to be the case—then disciplinarity can instead be more helpfully understood as an important "discursive strategy" for "positing the existence of a center or core of propositions, procedures, and conclusions, or at the least a shared historical object of theory and practice" (Klein 1993, 206). We can see this approach in Cultural Studies. In spite of being described as antidisciplinarity, Tony Bennett (1998) argues that "culture studies has now acquired all the institutional trappings of a discipline" (528). Yet, from its beginning, Cultural Studies was very much rooted in the transformative possibilities of a radical interdisciplinarity charged with unveiling the complexities of contemporary culture. Reflecting on this beginning, Stuart Hall (1990) summarizes, "What we discovered was that serious interdisciplinary work does not mean that one puts up the interdisciplinary flag and then has a kind of coalition of colleagues from different departments" (16). Instead, "we had to respect and engage with the paradigms and traditions of knowledge and of empirical and concrete work in each of these disciplinary areas in order to construct what we called cultural studies or cultural theory." This approach resulted in both disrupting a discipline by saying "sociology is, is not what it is" and constituting Cultural Studies from the "tradition and paradigms of knowledge" of "disciplinary areas." In many ways, the birth of Cultural Studies, with its original resistance to traditional disciplinarity, is what constitutes it differently in academia, even though it functions in so many ways as a discipline.

Likewise, in the discipline of Rhetoric and Composition, with its inherent interstitiality that is often misrecognized, we similarly are called upon to engage with students, other disciplines, and the world in ways that encourage what Kelly Pender (2011) describes as "opening up" rather than "closing down." Unlike those "mundane" activities that usually occupy textual production that close down what it means to write for the sake of being teachable, opening up, according to Pender, focuses on writing as "productive knowledge" that necessitates innovation and creativity. In recognizing the importance of opening up, "writing both locates us on the threshold between the known and the unknown and intensifies our experience of being there" (141). In this way writing becomes not simply a functional set of skills, but a rhetorical art, in many ways unruly because the conditions and situations in which composing occurs are always changing. And this is where the importance of the virtue of humility comes into play in the context of our disciplinary expertise. Because "magnanimity and humility are not contrary to one another," but "proceed according to different considerations" (Aquinas n.d., 3940), the need for responsivity outlined by Horner does not necessitate that we give up or deny our disciplinarity. But if humility is not to slip into undue humility, this virtue must be practiced in the context of magnanimity. If we were another kind of discipline, one traditional both in its history and its consideration of what constitutes knowledge, then yes, abandoning disciplinarity might be necessary in order to do the kind of dynamic work of opening up that is so needed now. But given our grounding, responsivity calls for us to strengthen our discipline and continue to build "the material social infrastructure necessary to knowledge mobilization" (Horner 2014, 58), not abandon what we have built so far. As Keys (2006) explains in her reading of magnanimity, "External goods . . . find their highest value in assisting their possessor to perform acts of virtue more readily" (147). For us, disciplinarity is such a good because it is not a traditional disciplinarity that closes down. Borrowing from Pough's (2011) discussion of herself as a "sister outside," our disciplinarity, when done right, makes us "distrustful of disciplinary strongholds, rigid definitions, and boundaries that sometimes police the kinds of inquiry and knowledge that academic disciplines both value and make room for" (305). When we foreground our interstitiality and displace the composition classroom as the core of what we do and who we are, this is transgressive in the context of not only academia but also broader politics.

Importantly, policy attacks in the United States on liberal education generally and writing pedagogy specifically illustrate that our disciplinarity might serve as a much-needed source of resistance against the increasing neoliberal emphasis on workforce training and preparedness. As described by Linda Adler-Kassner (2014), Common Core State Standards (CCSS) and competency-based education initiatives such Degree Qualifications Profile (DQP) take an anemic approach to the teaching of writing, and this is often in the best-case scenario. The DQP, for instance, aims to emphasize competencies across five domains that include Applied Learning; Intellectual Skills; Broad, Integrative Knowledge; Specialized Knowledge; and Civic Learning (446). Although offering the potential for writing to learn across these domains, the DQP reinforces "narrow ideas" of writing as the "performance of particular tasks." The educational reforms catalyzed by the CCSS are intended to go a step further in career-preparedness in writing. Analyzing a recent report by a reform organization called Achieve, Adler-Kassner explains that properly implemented CCSS would initially remove the need for "remedial" writing instruction and ultimately "there will be little or no need for first-year writing courses" (427). In order for the DQP and CCSS to construct writing in such ways necessitates that writing be discipline-less, Adler-Kassner writes: "It is likely that the new DQP competencies will reflect the even narrower conception of writing found in the CCSS, building on the effort to alleviate the tension between liberal learning, professional training, and disciplinarity by continuing to merge college and career and to erase disciplinarity in the name of an economically motivated public good" (446–47). Rather than perpetuating the vices encouraged by neoliberalism and undermining the virtues fostered through liberal learning, Rhetoric and Composition's disciplinarity can and must serve as an important bastion for cultivating an empowered citizenry.

Whether stemming from neoliberal education "reform" or, ironically, the radical politics of Cultural Studies, acquiescing or denying our disciplinarity leads to a whole host of potential problems, all with serious material consequences for teachers, students, and civic society, not the least of which is the loss of a means of resistance against those corrupted and corrupting neoliberal values increasingly on display in the twenty-first century university and beyond. Because the virtue of magnanimity encourages great works, even in the face of all kinds of challenges and difficulties, we owe it to ourselves, our colleagues, and our students, in light of the challenges that face not only our discipline, but also the university and the world at large, to acknowledge the worth of Rhetoric and Composition as a unique and important discipline now and for the future. But this means that we must reject the vice of undue humility that has too often plagued us and instead embrace the virtue of magnanimity that compels us to share the knowledge that our discipline has created and continue to expand upon that knowledge without limits or boundaries. And we must do so not because we are simply desirous of that disciplinary status which is too often denied us, but rather because of the good that our work does. In fact, our discipline offers a potent source of resistance to those neoliberal vices that seek to do so much harm in the world. To cast our disciplinary work as anything less is nothing short of vice.

## References

Abbott, Andrew. 2001. *Chaos of Disciplines.* Chicago: University of Chicago Press.
Adler-Kassner, Linda. 2014. "Liberal Learning, Professional Training, and Disciplinarity in the Age of Educational 'Reform': Remodeling General Education." *College Composition and Communication* 76 (5): 436–57.
Adler-Kassner, Linda, and Elizabeth Wardle. 2015. *Naming What We Know: Threshold Concepts in Writing Studies.* Boulder: University Press of Colorado.
Aquinas, Thomas. n.d. *Summa Theologica.* Grand Rapids: Christian Classics Ethereal Library. http://www.ccel.org/ccel/aquinas/summa.html.
Aristotle. 1984a. "Eudemian Ethics." In *The Complete Works of Aristotle*, vol. 2. ed. Jonathan Barnes, 1922–81. Princeton: Princeton University Press.
Aristotle. 1984b. "Nichomachean Ethics." In *The Complete Works of Aristotle*, vol. 2. ed. Jonathan Barnes, 1729–867. Princeton: Princeton University Press.
Bazerman, Charles. 2004. *Constructing Experience.* Carbondale: Southern Illinois University Press.
Bennett, Tony. 1998. "Cultural Studies: A Reluctant Discipline." *Cultural Studies* 12 (4): 528–545. https://doi.org/10.1080/09502386.1998.10383119.
Bourdieu, Pierre. 1984. *Homo Academicus.* Stanford: Stanford University Press.
Bourdieu, Pierre. 1991. *Language and Symbolic Power.* Malden, MA: Polity Press.
Clark, Burton R. 1983. *The Higher Education System: Academic in Cross-National Perspective.* Berkeley: University of California Press.
Claycomb, Ryan, and Rachel Riedner. 2004. "Cultural Studies, Rhetoric Studies, and Composition: Toward an Anti-Disciplinary Nexus." *JAC* 5(2): http://www.enculturation.net/5_2/claycomb-riedner.html.
Collins, Henry, and Robert Evans. 2007. *Rethinking Expertise.* Chicago: University of Chicago Press.
Committee on Developments in the Science of Learning. 2000. *How People Learn: Brain, Mind, Experience, and School.* Washington, DC: National Academy Press.
Connors, Robert J. 1991. "Rhetoric in the Modern University: The Creation of an Underclass." In *The Politics of Writing Instruction: Postsecondary*, ed. Richard Bullock and John Trimbur, 55–84. Portsmouth: Boynton/Cook.
Curzer, Howard J. 1991. "Aristotle's Much Maligned Megalopsychos." *Australasian Journal of Philosophy* 69 (2): 131–51.
Dobrin, Sidney I. 2011. *Postcomposition.* Carbondale: Southern Illinois University Press.
Downs, Douglas, and Elizabeth Wardle. 2007. "Teaching about Writing, Righting Misconceptions: (Re)Envisioning 'First-Year Composition' as 'Introduction to Writing Studies." *College Composition and Communication* 58 (4): 552–84.
Freire, Paulo. 1998. *Teachers as Cultural Workers: Letters to Those Who Dare to Teach.* Boulder: Westview Press.
Fuller, Steve. 2014. *The Knowledge Book: Key Concepts in Philosophy, Science and Culture.* New York: Routledge.
Giroux, Henry A. 1992. "Paulo Freire and the Politics of Postcolonialism." *Journal of Advanced Composition* 12 (1): 15–26.
Graff, Harvey J. 2015. *Undisciplining Knowledge: Interdisciplinarity in the Twentieth Century.* Baltimore: Johns Hopkins University Press.
Gramsci, Antonio. 1996. *Prison Notebooks.* Vol. 2. Ed. and trans. Joseph A. Buttigieg. New York: Columbia University Press.
Hall, Stuart. 1990. "The Emergence of Cultural Studies and the Crisis of the Humanities." *October* 53 (1): 11–23. https://doi.org/10.2307/778912.
Hammer, Brad. 2010. "From the Editor: The Multiple Voices of Compositionist Labor." *Forum: Newsletter for Issues about Part-Time and Contingent Faculty* 13(2): A1–A5. http://www.ncte.org/library/NCTEFiles/Groups/CCCC/Forum/TETYC0373Forum.pdf.

Hesse, Doug. 2004. "Foreword." In *The End of Composition Studies*, by David W. Smit, x. Carbondale: Southern Illinois University Press.
Horner, Bruce. 2014. "Grounding Responsivity." *JAC* 34 (1–2): 49–61.
Hyland, Ken. 2012. *Disciplinary Identities: Individuality and Community in Academic Discourse.* Cambridge: Cambridge University Press.
Jacobs, Jerry A. 2013. *In Defense of Disciplines: Interdisciplinarity and Specialization in the Research University.* Chicago: University of Chicago Press.
Keys, Mary M. 2006. *Aquinas, Aristotle, and the Promise of the Common Good.* Cambridge: Cambridge University Press. https://doi.org/10.1017/CBO9780511498213.
Klein, Julie Thompson. 1993. "Blurring, Cracking, and Crossing: Permeation and the Fracturing of Discipline." In *Knowledges: Historical and Critical Studies in Disciplinarity*, ed. Ellen Messer-Davidow, David R. Shumway, and David J. Sylvan, 185–214. Charlottesville: University Press of Virginia.
Knoblauch, C. H. 1988. "Some Observations on Freire's *Pedagogy of the Oppressed*." *Journal of Advanced Composition* 8:50–54.
Kristensen, Randi Gray, and Ryan Claycomb. 2010. "Introduction: Writing against the Curriculum." In *Writing against the Curriculum: Anti-Disciplinarity in the Writing and Cultural Studies Classroom*, 1–20. Lanham, MD: Lexington Books.
Larson, Ann. 2014. "Rhetoric and Composition's Dead." http://annlarson.org/2014/02/22/rhetoric-and-compositions-dead/.
Lenoir, Timothy. 1993. "The Discipline of Nature and the Nature of Disciplines." In *Knowledges: Historical and Critical Studies in Disciplinarity*, ed. Ellen Messer-Davidow and David R. Shumway, 70–102. Charlottesville: University Press of Virginia.
Mahoney, Kevin, and Rachel Riedner. 2008. *Democracies to Come: Rhetorical Action, Neoliberalism, and Communities of Resistance.* Lanham, MD: Lexington Books.
Modern Language Association. 2014. "MLA Issue Brief: The Academic Workforce." https://apps.mla.org/pdf/awak_issuebrief14.pdf.
Nelson, Cary, and Dilip Parameshwar Gaonkar. 1996. "Cultural Studies and the Politics of Disciplinarity: An Introduction." In *Disciplinarity and Dissent in Cultural Studies*, ed. Cary Nelson and Dilip Parameshwar Gaonkar, 1–22. New York: Routledge.
Olson, Gary A. 2002. "Preface." In *Rhetoric and Composition as Intellectual Work*, ed. Gary Olson, xi–xvi. Carbondale: Southern Illinois University Press. https://doi.org/10.1515/9783110950298.xi.
Pender, Kelly. 2011. *Techne, From Neoclassicism to Postmodernism: Understanding Writing as a Useful, Teachable Art.* Anderson: Parlor Press.
Pough, Gwendolyn D. 2011. "It's Bigger than Comp/Rhett: Contest and Undisciplined." *College Composition and Communication* 63 (2): 301–13.
Prior, Paul A. 1998. *Writing/Disciplinarity: A Sociohistoric Account of Literate Activity in the Academy.* New York: Routledge.
Sarch, Alexander. 2008. "What's Wrong with Megalopsychia?" *Philosophy (London, England)* 83 (324): 231–53.
Shor, Ira. 1996. *When Students Have Power: Negotiating Authority in a Critical Pedagogy.* Chicago: University of Chicago Press.
Smit, David W. 2004. *The End of Composition Studies.* Carbondale: Southern Illinois University Press.
Tinberg, Howard. 2014. "2014 *CCCC* Chair's Address: The Loss of the Public." *College Composition and Communication* 66 (2): 327–41.
Trimbur, John. 1996. "Writing Instruction and the Politics of Professionalization." In *Composition in the Twenty-First Century: Crisis and Change*, ed. Lynn Z. Bloom, Donald A. Daiker, and Edward M. White, 133–45. Carbondale: Southern Illinois University Press.
Wardle, Elizabeth, and J. Blake Scott. 2015. "Defining and Developing Expertise in a Writing and Rhetoric Department." *WPA: Writing Program Administration* 39 (1): 72–93.

Welch, Nancy, and Tony Scott, eds. 2016. *Composition in the Age of Austerity*. Boulder: University Press of Colorado. https://doi.org/10.7330/9781607324454.

Yancey, Kathleen Blake. 2015. "Coming to Terms: Composition/Rhetoric, Threshold Concepts, and a Disciplinary Core." In *Naming What We Know: Threshold Concept of Writing Studies*, ed. Linda Adler-Kassner and Elizabeth Wardle, xvii–xxxi. Boulder: University Press of Colorado. https://doi.org/10.7330/9780874219906.c000a.

Yancey, Kathleen Blake, Laine Robertson, and Kara Taczak. 2014. *Writing across Contexts: Transfer, Composition, and Sites of Writing*. Logan: Utah State University Press.

# 9
# DISCIPLINARITY AND FIRST-YEAR COMPOSITION
## Shifting to a New Paradigm

Liane Robertson and Kara Taczak

As our field considers its disciplinarity, there are complex issues shaping both internal and external perceptions of what we do as scholars and teachers of writing, a perception fraught with tension and potential consequence for our future as a discipline. One such tension is related to the content we teach in our first-year composition (FYC) courses to best benefit student learning. This content dilemma is related to what we want students to learn in FYC and what we see as the role of our first-year courses in the larger picture of academia. Given what's at stake for both our students and our future as a discipline, the question of the content we teach in FYC is complex and somewhat contentious.

In this chapter, we address this tension around content in first-year composition, not because FYC is what our field is all about, or *only* about, but because it is one of the things that most represents us to stakeholders outside of our field. Also, we focus on FYC rather than on advanced composition courses or our majors or graduate programs, where the content is more clearly representative of our field of study. It is in first-year composition where content is loosely defined yet where it impacts students from across the university who will go on to write in multiple disciplines. There is a broad expectation among some, both inside and outside of our field, that FYC courses are preparing students for the writing they will experience beyond FYC, specific contexts outside of our discipline and in nonacademic contexts as well. While this expectation may not be realistic, or is not representative of the entire role of FYC, it nevertheless persists: FYC is often one of a few, or sometimes the only, writing course an institution requires of all students, and the general expectation is that FYC instruction will contribute to their ability as writers in future contexts. Therefore, we focus on content in first-year composition because it (1) ranges so broadly, and sometimes deleteriously so, and (2) represents us to outside stakeholders (whether or not we want it to) and thus impacts how we are and will be perceived as a discipline.

At this moment, we are not a discipline but an "un-discipline." We use the term "un-discipline" to mean that we are a field without a consistent content in the introductory course representing our area of study, without consensus about research-based curricular approaches to FYC, and often without expertise behind the delivery of our FYC courses. To be a discipline, we must have a well-developed paradigm consisting of what we know and why we know it, and of how we investigate to further our knowledge. We must reach a consensus on what constitutes our theory and practice and how we prepare new members of our discipline to enter it. We must represent this paradigm internally and externally so that our theory and practice are commonly understood. If we are to become such a discipline, our attention to the content in FYC, based on the research of our field and delivered using the expertise in our field, must be of primary concern.

However, there are a multitude of reasons why this move to disciplinarity is a challenge: our available labor pool and its wide range of particular expertise and training, and the myriad political and financial issues this involves; the historical role and perception of FYC as a service course within the greater university and how this is perpetuated by practices such as dual enrollment; and conflicting beliefs among those in our field as to the content or curricular design most advantageous for students in FYC courses. This question of content is what we'll focus on most in this chapter, because others in this volume take up the issues of labor and other contributing factors challenging our discipline, and because content is something those of us inside our discipline can change. It is also the area in which we are most familiar, as our research has explored the impact of types of content on how students are able to transfer knowledge about writing out of the FYC classroom and make use of it successfully in other contexts.

## THE QUESTION OF FYC CONTENT

In first-year composition courses across the country there are many types of curricular designs a student might experience as content. As mentioned above, our field can't seem to reach a consensus about content; given the history of our field and its diversity of programs, scholars, teachers, and stakeholder expectations, our broad range of content is understandable. First-year composition, in fact, preceded our field, so its content is inherited from a history of educational revision beginning in the nineteenth century at Harvard and adopted by most other institutions soon afterward (Connors 1995). It has since evolved—or more accurately, perhaps, it has dispersed into a wide variety of pedagogical strategies, implemented according to a range of beliefs and values about the content of FYC. This is, in part, because our field developed from a grassroots level, practitioner-by-practitioner, program-by-program, before its current evolution into the burgeoning discipline it is poised to become. In past years, a wide variety of approaches to teaching FYC has emerged as our field has evolved, and each approach, it might be argued, offers advantages to both teachers and learners of writing (Fulkerson 1979). Maxine Hairston's 1982 article signaled our field had experienced a shift into process-based writing pedagogy, which remains a foundational tenet of our current practices (Hairston 1982); for some, process *is* the content in FYC. For others, as postprocess theory emerged, content took on a greater focus as something about which writing is practiced in a course (Kent 1999). Fulkerson raised issues about the competing content in FYC in his seminal College Composition and Communication (CCC) article in 2005, "Composition at the Turn of the Twenty-First Century," in which he outlined our field's absence of a discernible FYC content (Fulkerson 2005).

As our field has evolved so have our means of delivering FYC courses, and the content around which we focus has been largely unaddressed. We are rich in the pedagogical complexity upon which we routinely draw to benefit our students, and our collective knowledge brings a breadth of unparalleled experience and expertise to our writing classrooms. What we don't know, or perhaps what we don't want to acknowledge, is whether the content matters in FYC beyond the strategies and processes we use to teach it; we assume that any type of content is good for students as long as it engages them in writing. This assumption is no longer acceptable if we are to become a discipline.

To deprioritize the role of content is to discount our field's recent research, which tells us that the type of content matters a great deal. To cite just a few examples over the past several years: Debra Frank Dew recommended over a decade ago that FYC focus on the rhetoric of language as content (Dew 2003); Anne Beaufort's research demonstrated that knowledge domains play a role in students' understanding of writing (Beaufort 2007); Douglas Downs and Elizabeth Wardle (2007) advocated for a Writing about Writing approach to FYC content (Downs and Wardle 2007); Mary Jo Reiff and Anis Bawarshi (2011) have found that students' understanding of written genres and their appropriateness in context requires greater focus if students are to write well outside of FYC (Reiff and Bawarshi 2011); and Kathleen Blake Yancey, Liane Robertson, and Kara Taczak (2014) suggested an explicitly designed Teaching for Transfer model as content that helps students navigate contexts (Yancey et al. 2014).

In this chapter, we will argue for content in first-year composition that represents: (1) what recent research tells us is best for students as they learn to write for the varied contexts of college and beyond, and (2) our unique position as an emerging discipline with additional responsibility for the teaching of writing to first-year students with cross-academic and future needs. When we discuss content, we are referring to the writing knowledge and practices included in a FYC course: any theory, themes, readings, assignments, strategies, processes, techniques, and so on, both at the macro and microlevel; we define content as what the course is about, or focused on, not just what is produced in it, what actions are taken in it, or what its goals are.

## WHY CONTENT MATTERS IN FYC: OUR EMERGING DISCIPLINARITY

Our history as a field is important as it provides a context for understanding that there are many reasons for the wide variety of approaches to teaching FYC content. If we are to move from an "un-discipline" to a discipline, we'll need to further that frame. But within this range of approaches there is no consensus about which ones might be most efficacious. While we have a set of outcomes the field has developed and even recently revised (CWPA 2015), representing the ways in which we want students to develop writing knowledge, those of us teaching FYC might use any number of pedagogical approaches to reach those outcomes, each of us believing our approach to be efficacious. Outcomes are not content. The *WPA Outcomes Statement* might well capture the goals toward which we aim, but we don't all agree on the course content that works at achieving those goals.

Over the years, first-year composition courses have featured content that has varied widely by program across the country (Fulkerson 2005; Tate et al. 2001), resulting in curricular design that often reflects a program's culture or an individual instructor's experience or preference. Our field has experienced a shift from writing about literature, to process as content, to argument writing, to themed courses (Fulkerson 2005). We may follow a pedagogy that is research-based, expressive, critical, rhetorical, or cultural. We may align with genre-based pedagogy or one that is technology-based or founded in the WAC movement. We may also extract bits and pieces from various pedagogies and adapt them (Tate et al. 2001). For some, FYC is a "gatekeeper" (Crowley 1998), and for others it is a chance to expose students to great literature or to engage students in writing for a specific means (community service, for example). As Yancey explains in Section 1 of this volume, our field's historical turns have resulted in various types of content in our teaching. As long as writing is practiced in the course, the content about which students write and read has been deemed by those in the field as relatively inconsequential—in other words, our field's approach has been that any content will do in developing student writing, as long as students are writing, and the more students practice writing about any subject matter the better writers they become. But as Debra Frank Dew (2003), Downs and Wardle (2007), and others have claimed, the specific content of a FYC course is of much greater importance than our field has recognized in the past (Robertson 2011).

## INDIVIDUALITY AND CONTENT

Our wide range of FYC content reflects our field's diversity and interdisciplinarity. Members of our field bring a variety of background and training to their teaching, and faculty outside of Composition studies who often teach our FYC courses bring even greater diversity. As a field, we believe in the individuality of teachers and that every teacher has a way of working with writers to help them improve, just as every writer has the ability to improve. The NCTE (National Council of Teachers of English) features on its website a position statement entitled "Professional Knowledge for the Teaching of Writing," which reflects much of what teachers in our field are doing: assisting students with learning how to engage in the process of writing, to use strategies and techniques; to be aware of audience and purpose; to use writing as a tool for thinking; to understand that writing requires revision and attention to conventions and is composed using various technologies (National Council of Teachers of English 2016). But the statement does not address the field's research about writing that points to the domains of knowledge as necessary for students' transfer of writing knowledge and practices (Beaufort 2007). While it identifies knowledge about writing as important, it does so only within the context of process:

> Knowledge about writing is only complete when writers understand the ensemble of actions in which they engage as they produce texts. Such understanding has two aspects, at least. First is the development, through

extended practice over years, of a repertory of routines, skills, strategies, and practices, for generating, revising, and editing different kinds of texts. Second is the development of reflective abilities and meta-awareness about writing. The procedural knowledge developed through reflective practice helps writers most when they encounter difficulty, or when they are in the middle of creating a piece of writing. How does someone get started? What do they do when they get stuck? How do they plan the overall process, each section of their work, and even the rest of the sentence they are writing right now? Research, theory, and practice in the teaching of writing have produced a rich understanding of what writers do, those who are proficient and professional as well as those who struggle. (NCTE 2016)

The position statement isn't wrong; process is critical and writers do learn by doing more writing, but their knowledge about process isn't enough. Writing happens in context, and each context is different (Bazerman 2015); if students use the writing strategies they learn across each context, they can successfully apply these practices to each writing situation, but in order to write appropriately for that context they need to first understand what the context requires of a writer (Adler-Kassner and Wardle 2015; Reiff and Bawarshi 2011; Wardle 2007; Yancey, Robertson, and Taczak 2014). Crafting a well-written piece is one thing, but understanding what kind of piece is appropriate and how to tailor it to a particular context because of one's conceptual knowledge about writing situations is quite another. Students who write well can fail in a situation in which they apply the same approach to writing they learn in a FYC course to some other context in which that particular approach isn't appropriate (Russell and Yanez 2002; Yancey 2015).[1] In the David R. Russell and Arturo Yanez (2002) case study, the specific disciplinary knowledge required was at odds with the knowledge students took up in general education classes, and in the case of the subject studied, that contradiction led to a failure to see, at least on her own, the connection between writing contexts (Russell and Yanez 2002); students need help making the connections across contexts in order to understand how to write in those contexts. Yancey also documents the need for students to understand both the similarities and differences in writing contexts across disciplines, which relates to their capacity for critical thinking and to seeing the patterns of similarity and difference that experts understand (Bransford et al. 2000; Yancey 2015). These patterns are critical to students' understanding of writing in different contexts, but is this type of content reflected in our FYC courses?

If students are taught only about the writing process in FYC courses, are those courses preparing students to write in the context of other courses or writing situations? When students write in disciplines unlike ours or for nonacademic purposes, our process-based instruction helps them revise and produce writing, but can fail to help them understand what's required of the writer in contexts outside of those they've experienced or to know what is appropriate or strategic in a different situation (Yancey et al. 2014). A well-written personal essay or literary analysis, which students might experience in FYC courses, looks quite different from the writing required of students in lab reports, proposals, or protocols, which they might experience in courses in the sciences or business or social sciences.

An argument could be made that it's not up to FYC programs to teach students to write in such contexts and that FYC instructors are not experts in the expectations of writing found in other disciplines; we expect that professors in biology or history are teaching students about the writing required in those disciplines, and often they are. But then we must ask ourselves what we believe the role of FYC should be, and more important we must ask ourselves if we are best serving our students if we don't help them make those connections, or see those patterns of similarity and difference across contexts. Even though we don't teach the writing of biology or history, our role in FYC should include helping students understand that the writing in biology or history might look different than it does in FYC and that they might rely upon rhetorical concepts to develop the writing they'll need in that context.

## THE IMPORTANCE OF EXTERNAL STAKEHOLDERS: PREVENTING DEVALUATION

Contributing further to our lack of disciplinarity is our field's reluctance to base our FYC curriculum on what newer research is telling us about the outcomes of teaching content other than writing in our first-year courses. Nearly a decade after Downs and Wardle's (2007) Writing about Writing pedagogy suggested more disciplinary content in FYC, results from the growing area of transfer research related to writing and from the teaching of writing indicates that content matters in students' ability to transfer writing knowledge and practice. However, our field continues to resist teaching writing as content in FYC. Perhaps we fear our content must be "sexier" or more exciting to students and to instructors in FYC to be of interest to students, and that if we teach conceptual content about writing it won't be very interesting. And perhaps that fear extends to the stigma of teaching first-year writing; do we prefer to teach something else, that isn't as devalued or perceived as merely a service course, or that is closer to our own interests or backgrounds but possibly less helpful to students? Given the broad range of expertise and backgrounds from which FYC programs draw instructors, and the challenges faced by an often transient and underpaid workforce at no fault of their own, it's understandable that individual FYC courses are delivered according to what an instructor's experience dictates or for which the reality of an instructor's workload allows. This is understandable in the current political and financial situation in higher education, yet its perpetuation continues to affect students who may not be experiencing the type of content in FYC that helps them grow as writers beyond that context. And if FYC doesn't appear to be helping prepare students to write in other college contexts, it stands to reason that those outside of our field won't perceive FYC as contributing to students' overall academic success.

One of the reasons FYC might be devalued by outside stakeholders is our own fault: our field's lack of consistency or divergent sense of content in FYC communicates to outsiders that we don't have a sense of our own discipline; that we are "un-disciplined" in our field of study and consequently our teaching of it. This is perpetuated by the delivery of FYC by nonexperts, and by FYC being delivered more and more in high school settings—it is seen as a course to get out of, to exempt from, to bypass, or as a burden of time and cost if one fails to gain exemption. FYC is perceived by outside stakeholders as unimportant, a course that should be relatively easy, given that students have already learned to write in high school (Jolliffe and Phelan 2006). But our field disagrees: if we didn't believe FYC was so critical to student writing success, we wouldn't have advanced our field through research into its pedagogical practices, theory, assessment, and usage, among other areas. Every year we meet at conferences to discuss its importance to us, among other things. Yet we fail to communicate its worth to those who determine its value to the institutions at which we work, as illustrated by financial and other conditions for contingent faculty and the growing trend toward dual enrollment or other means of exemption of FYC for incoming first-year college students—decisions made often without consulting the expertise of our field (Tinberg and Nadeau 2011). In the current and future economic models of higher education, we can't afford to be absent from the decision making that will affect FYC and our discipline, but that's bound to happen if our value isn't understood. We can't be complacent with the notion of FYC as generating income for the university and assume we will retain the authority to decide its content and how it is delivered; we can't argue expertise and authority for FYC if we can't point to agreement as a discipline and to research on its suggested content. Dual enrollment already eats away at our market share, to borrow a term from the business world, but what else do we expect when we can't point to a college-level curricular approach that is best for students and is consistent across, or even within, institutions. This outside perception of diminished value of FYC will persist until our field commits to a more specific, consistent, research-based content for FYC.

Our field has established some common guidelines for content in FYC,[2] and though many follow these models they are interpreted or enacted in many ways. For example, the *WPA Outcomes Statement* suggests rhetorical concepts that students should understand upon completion of FYC, but including these concepts in the classroom does not necessarily ensure students are learning them. The WPA outcomes represent what our field believes is valuable for students, and we don't argue with that; we argue that there is inconsistency in our field's approach to ensuring those outcomes are met, and we point to recent transfer research that indicates some types of content commonly featured in FYC courses is not efficacious for transfer to new situations, even if using the outcomes as a guideline (Yancey et al. 2014). Although our field might argue that expressly preparing students for specific contexts outside of our discipline is not our role as FYC instructors, if FYC is a course required of all students, there is an expectation (warranted or not, and often unspoken, but expected nevertheless) that what they learn in FYC will have some benefit to them as writers in future contexts. In other disciplines faculty might expect that an introductory course helps students prepare for later work in the discipline—it is reasonable to expect that a course that provides students with an introduction to the field of biology would prepare them in some way for additional courses in that field. But does our field of Rhetoric and Composition see FYC as a parallel? Are we, or should we be approaching FYC as an introduction to our field or to our emerging discipline? In some ways the unfair expectation of those outside (and even inside) our field is that FYC will make students better writers, but our research tells us otherwise: we know writing depends on situation and that each writing situation is different (Bazerman 2015). If we can't prepare students to write in all contexts, or if we feel this is not our role, then what is our role? What is the purpose of FYC, and does it parallel the outcomes of other disciplines? Perhaps our field can do better at communicating the outcomes we aim for in teaching FYC and how it relates to the research about writing and student success.

As a discipline, it would behoove us to respond to the research our field is doing on the content of FYC, and in some ways we are: the recently revised *WPA Outcomes Statement* is one such example but its existence doesn't equate with an increase in disciplinarity if we don't all agree to adopt the outcomes and if we can't point to more evidence of their success and how it is achieved specifically.

Our field shoulders the added responsibility of FYC's perception as delivering a course in how to write to students in all disciplines, an idea we know is impossible and unfair to expect. So we must also communicate more clearly what FYC is and does, and what is more reasonable to expect of students in FYC. But until we can clearly define or explain FYC, and agree upon its content among ourselves within the field, how can it be effectively communicated outside of our field, to those who don't typically understand its function? How are we ensuring outsiders understand what we do and why it's important—or at least why they shouldn't expect FYC to "fix" student writing?

While those in our field may draw upon similar resources, such as the *WPA Outcomes Statement* or the *Framework for Success in Post-Secondary Writing*, and share similar experiences and teaching philosophies (or have assumed we share similar experiences and teaching philosophies) with others at conferences and through LISTSERV discussions, we are far from any consensus on specific content, and this fractured sense of what we teach contributes to the confusion about who we are.[3]

FYC courses may currently reach a large percentage of first-year students across institutions, but those students frequently experience a very different FYC course than other students might, either within the same institution or across different institutions. This inconsistency within cohorts is troublesome; some students have a positive experience with FYC while others don't, but also by allowing this range of experience to be representative of the work of our field (or at least what is most easily perceived as the work of our field) we are externally communicating our lack of consensus, or our "un-disciplinarity" further. We can't very well communicate the value of FYC until we can point to content that represents it more definitively, that students and instructors can recognize as first-year composition content and that all internal and external stakeholders can discern in order to perceive and value it. That value perception will be based on research about FYC's efficacy, the expertise required to develop its content and to teach it, and the positioning of FYC as the space in which students can learn about writing—conceptually as well as procedurally—across a variety of contexts and that will transfer with them as they take on new writing challenges.

## A COMPROMISED DELIVERY MODEL: EXPEDIENCY OVER EXPERTISE

We cannot sustain the current model of delivering first-year composition courses if we remain inconsistent in our content and if we continue to undermine ourselves as a potential discipline. The model, as is, has its drawbacks, not the least of which is that the reliance on contingent faculty or graduate students to represent our field's expertise in many FYC classrooms is not advantageous. The level of preparation of many of those who teach FYC is not as high as tenured or tenure-track faculty, who have the luxury of keeping up with the research in the field but who less frequently teach FYC. We rely on instructors who are less experienced or who are overworked and underpaid to teach FYC, but how else can a WPA staff as many sections each term as an institution requires? There are many other arguments about how faculty are employed to teach FYC, as Kristine Hansen points out in chapter 7 and as many others have argued previously (Applebee and Langer 2009; Hansen and Farris 2010; Kaufer and Young 1993). We raise the issue here because it relates to content: the FYC delivery model continues to compromise expertise for efficiency because we refuse to acknowledge that individualism in the FYC classroom is not serving our students. While it's understandable that we protect contingent faculty wherever possible, and one way to make their lives easier is to allow them flexibility in choosing content that fits their expertise or workload, we perpetuate the misrepresentation of FYC in doing so and we compromise our students' needs as well.

In addition, many of the faculty teaching FYC are not experts in our field; often they bring expertise from a related field such as literature or creative writing and they may be excellent teachers, but they don't have disciplinary expertise in Rhetoric and Composition. Most are not familiar with either the historical approaches of or the latest research in our field, which should inform the teaching of writing. Again, this is understandable, as we rely on a labor pool comprised of expertise in literature, creative writing, or other areas, rather than exclusively in Rhetoric and Composition. Our argument here is not aimed at criticizing contingent faculty or graduate students or faculty without Rhetoric and Composition expertise, but to point out that the model itself is flawed; it perpetuates the delivery of FYC by nonexperts, which means our students don't benefit from our field's research and our disciplinarity is compromised. As Kristine Hansen suggests in chapter 7, the issue is not the status of faculty delivering our FYC courses, but whether or not FYC courses across our country are consistently fostering the knowledge and practices students need to develop as they prepare for their futures;

students should receive a better education in rhetoric and writing not only to allow them to become better writers but also well-informed citizens who understand and engage effectively in our communities, within our overall society, and in our global economy.

As a field, we have always valued the diversity of expertise brought by those within it, and we might continue to draw upon the pedagogical richness of our field's experiences. Our collegiality and our sense of community are important, not only to our identity as a field but also because it models a belief that not just the content of a discipline but the quality and value of its teaching are paramount (Shulman 2004). We want to underscore the importance of retaining this aspect of our field's history. But we argue more imperatively for content to be aligned with our field's research, both to benefit our students and to earn credibility as a discipline, and our research tells us that the type of content in FYC makes a difference in student success. The tail is wagging the dog, currently: the existing model dictates content because we're heavily reliant on faculty without expertise in our field to deliver FYC.

That this model prevails is a different argument than we take up here, and we don't offer a solution to the problems we see the model as perpetuating. Our point in raising the issue of our field's labor reliance is related to the challenge of staffing FYC courses with those trained in composition, with expertise in the kind of writing that we want representing our discipline. When we staff FYC with experts in literature, or even experts in writing who want to teach a particular theme or content that won't help students transfer knowledge and practice about writing beyond the FYC classroom, we are not attending to the long-term needs of students, as Hansen has pointed out in this volume.. If we believe FYC is a course in which students become—or should become—better writers across multiple contexts, this position conflicts with what we're delivering, generally.

## INSTRUCTOR AUTONOMY: MOTIVATION AND BELIEFS

Historically, the delivery of FYC in a number of different ways and in accordance with the particular expertise of the instructor, as the previous section outlines, is in part relevant to the motivations or beliefs about what we should be teaching students held by those who teach it, and these beliefs vary widely. Some believe that in FYC courses we should be teaching students to explore great works of literature, others believe we should prepare students for academic writing (which itself is defined in many different ways), and others believe that to teach self-expression or self-reflection is the best way to foster student writing that will serve them throughout life. Because of our field's history we see a range of program outcomes, and even when program outcomes are provided or the field's outcomes are used as a guideline, instructors still may be motivated to teach or tailor courses to what they believe is best for students. As Elizabeth Wardle outlined, instructors often decide to teach what they think is important for students to know, regardless of program outcomes (Wardle 2003). This mindset isn't found—at least to the same extent—in other disciplines, where an established set of outcomes for an introductory course in a field of study are generally agreed upon with much more consistency.

Despite the fact that the *WPA Outcomes Statement* provides a guideline for organizing FYC according to what our field or emerging discipline suggests is critical for student writing development, the problem remains that a consistent FYC content is thwarted by some of the key factors mentioned above: FYC is not always taught by experts in the field of Rhetoric and Composition, FYC content is often decided upon by individual instructors with varying preferences and beliefs about what students need, FYC is often delivered via a flawed model of contingent faculty who can't develop as professionals in the field with the workload they are forced to take on to make a living wage as Hansen points out in chapter 7.

Related to the content of FYC, this internal struggle to determine what we teach in FYC because we believe we know what students need— that they need to appreciate literature or become self-reflective (Wardle 2003)—is audacious. That students need these things is not the issue; that we should presume it is FYC's role to teach these things, is. As individuals, we are "un-disciplined" in our continued hold on the past while we often ignore or are loathe to change according to the research that tells us what the future should hold for FYC and the students in those courses. There are others—students, parents, those in other disciplines, administrators—counting on us to move forward with what serves students best. As a discipline, supported by our research on how students learn to think and write critically across academia, we can make FYC a more integral and valued part of every student's college experience in a way that our current, dispersed approach to content does not allow.

## FYC CONTENT: MULTIPLE APPROACHES AND OBJECTIVES

Content, at least in first-year composition, to some degree remains ambiguous or ill-defined in part because of the nature of delivery of those courses; the number of sections that must be offered while balancing instructor individualism, program philosophies, and administrators' expectations are all significant challenges for those managing writing programs (Fulkerson 2005; Jolliffe and Phelan 2006). Its ambiguity is also related to our field's values around writing, especially the ideas that writing is a practice, is individual in expression, is learned by doing, and is inclusive. Those in our field see writing as having infinite possibilities for every writer, but that perspective may not be what's best for our students' future writing success, as recent research indicates and which we have discussed above.

In addition to the field's values, there are the perceptions of students to contend with: that writing is something they've already learned in high school (an assumption that is reinforced by content in FYC that mimics that of high school, such as writing about literature), that avoidance by "testing out" of first-year composition courses or enrolling in those courses while in high school is the best option, or that all writing is the same and can be applied similarly in any context (Applebee and Langer 2009, 2011; Fulkerson 2005; Kaufer and Young 1993).

With different types of content, valued for various reasons in our field, how are we meeting the desired outcomes for our students? What do we want them to be able to do with the writing they learn in our FYC classes, both concurrently and once they move beyond it to other writing situations, and are they able to? Which content allows them to use the writing they learn in some other context? We argue that the ultimate, overall goal of FYC should be transfer; our role as teachers of writing should be to prepare students to learn to write in any context by first learning to understand the needs of a context, by then considering what might be used appropriately from their existing (and prior) knowledge in that context, and by repurposing the knowledge they deem appropriate to the new situation in developing writing for that situation. In other words, our role as writing teachers is to help students develop the ability to transfer, appropriately and successfully, writing knowledge and practice to any situation in which they find themselves writing, academically and otherwise. Not just any content will do that (Yancey et al. 2014).

We point to recent research in transfer because it tells us that what students do with what they learn in FYC is often not helpful outside of FYC, unless certain conditions for transfer are designed as part of content. This is the type of research, though there is still much to be done in this area, from which we might draw to communicate the value of FYC to outside stakeholders, to set common objectives for our teaching and outcomes for students that meet their needs as well as the realities of today's educational environment, and as research-based content for teaching writing to first-year students (in college, and not in high school). This is the kind of research-based approach to content that we must take up if we're to be seen as a discipline.

For those of us teaching courses in which students write about literature, or engage in reading and writing assignments about a particular theme, or cultural situation, the research on transfer is troublesome, because it tells us that what we're doing might not be as efficacious as we have assumed, and that we might need to rethink our approach to the content taught in FYC.

The context within which writing occurs influences how and to what extent it is learned (Bransford et al. 2000; Bergmann and Zepernick 2007; Perkins and Salomon 1992; Sommers and Saltz 2004; Wardle 2007) and impacts how to work with prior knowledge and dispositions in ways that won't impede students' ability to use what they've learned in new contexts (Driscoll and Wells 2012; Robertson et al. 2012). Research in the past few years has indicated curricular approaches to transfer are effective in helping students understand and repurpose writing knowledge and practice across various contexts (Downs and Wardle 2007; Nowacek 2011; Wardle 2012; Yancey et al. 2014; etc.). While the research tells us that teaching students to transfer is not only possible, but can be an intentionally and explicitly designed goal of teaching writing, delivery of such content presents a dilemma: how can we expect change from those teaching FYC without expertise in our field, without the support needed to develop expertise, and without the financial support to motivate any change in the way they teach FYC? And how can we expect those in our field who are already experts to adapt their FYC teaching if they don't believe that a transfer-based pedagogy is best for students?

In chapter 7 and as indicated above, Kristine Hansen explains the issue of expertise and teaching in our discipline, or in our future as a discipline. The points she raises about who teaches writing and how it is taught are critical to our argument about the way we look at content in first-year composition. First-year composition content that is rhetorically based, is both conceptual and practical, and FYC content that enables or encourages the development of a framework of writing knowledge and practice, requires a level of expertise that many currently teaching FYC do not possess or have access to, nor are they often afforded the time or compensation for professional development so that such expertise might be gained. Given the challenges of the model of delivery for FYC, if we are to address the issue of content we must also consider that a significant percentage of those teaching FYC have little preparation for the type of content we suggest. Hansen, as Joyce Neff (2006) did previously, outlines options that include a large-class/small-group-breakout model using expertise to develop curriculum, assignments, and teaching material coupled with a paraprofessional model of those with less expertise to help with teaching, grading, working individually with students, and so on. This might be one way to provide content more consistently without compromising the richness of our process-based classroom experience for students, while centralizing writing instruction more by rhetorical need as best represents our (assumed) student learning outcome of successful writing transfer and forward the reputation of our discipline. Hansen also recommends ways to develop faculty education in Composition studies so that writing as content might become more prevalent; this option is less disruptive but perhaps not as efficacious.

As a field, the questions about who teaches in our discipline are central to our future: what do our FYC instructors know about how to teach writing, and is what they teach advantageous to our first-year students?[4] How do we, as a field, add expertise to that model or redesign the model to feature the level of expertise our students deserve? How do compensation for faculty and the bottom line for administrators fit within a revised model? What should our first-year students be experiencing across the board, in FYC courses, even if the level of expertise we desire is not immediately accessible? What responsibility do we have to our students in ensuring FYC is doing all it can for them? What responsibility do we have to those who have taught those courses, with or without expertise in our field yet with other strengths from which our students benefit, who are contingent and unprotected? We need content that is more disciplinary and we need disciplinary expertise in delivering that content, while protecting faculty and providing the best possible experience and preparation for continued writing in college for students.

If we are not teaching writing with students' transfer of knowledge and practice as a course's ultimate, overall goal, we are ignoring the role that FYC plays in helping prepare our students for the writing they will need to do in future. And since FYC courses are filled with students from all majors, we must consider the future writing in which all students will engage—across all disciplines—to be our responsibility, in concert with those who teach the content of and have the expertise in those disciplines. Because of this responsibility to students across the university, and because our discipline must be able to point to FYC as the "ground floor" of writing, FYC content must reflect our responsibility, and reflect the content of our scholarship that has been proven to benefit students.

## THE CONTENT PARADIGM SHIFT

As we move toward disciplinarity, we must consider content that represents us, and that helps us articulate what we do and who we are. We might also consider who we are not, how we are misunderstood, and which types of content—for example, writing about literature—potentially perpetuate this misunderstanding of writing as just something one does, rather than something one also studies (Adler-Kassner and Wardle 2015). Articulating our content as *writing* content helps counter the misinterpretation of us as a service field or as merely teachers of writing about other content, and helps position us as experts within a research-based discipline, a discipline comprised of the same level of expertise and due the respect afforded other disciplines.

Content in FYC that more accurately represents our field, and can more consistently represent what students experience in a first-year composition course, will provide the communication "sound bite" we currently lack. While sound bites can seem superficial, creating a glossed-over simplification of a complex situation, they do provide the anchor of communication that most audiences—especially external audiences, without knowledge of our field—require in order to better understand our point of view, and in order to overcome a prevailing and inaccurate existing perception. We need a more streamlined disciplinary representation of our field. If we don't communicate about our field and our expertise effectively, incorrect assumptions will be made, and we risk not just a continuing misperception but a continued devaluing of what our field provides.

As our field makes its latest turn, as Yancey suggests in Section 1, perhaps it is at this turn that FYC content might be better aligned with our research. The content that we allow to represent us in first-year composition will contribute to how we are defined as a discipline, whether by others or by ourselves. We need a shift toward more defined, discernible content about writing, based on growing scholarship on the efficacy of such content and its capacity for transfer. With research supporting this move toward writing knowledge and practice as content that students can successfully transfer to new contexts, and without research to support themed content or literature as content that can do so, our choice should be clear.

At issue, as Hansen discusses and as we mention above, is faculty expertise at teaching content about writing, and the desire to do so. How can our field even consider a somewhat more centralized content when many of those who teach writing courses are untrained in our discipline and when our current labor models don't allow for individual professional development, much time to redevelop program content, or the type of investment in first-year composition that would be required for such an endeavor? Yet how can we not work toward this end? If we want to legitimize our standing as a discipline, we should begin with FYC content.

However, establishing a greater consistency of content might best work as a gradual process, moving toward writing as content using a systematic approach to course design, in a variation adapted to local context while maintaining coherency across the field. We might create a paradigm shift globally that is enacted locally at a slower pace, allowing for more centralized communication about our discipline at the macrolevel while easing into content at a microlevel that reflects our next historical turn.

Currently, and as suggested above, we are an "un-discipline" with FYC as our public face, made up of writers, teachers of writing, writing researchers, full-timers and part-timers, representing many diverse experiences and areas of scholarly work. But beyond that, to colleagues outside our field, to students, to administrators, to our various publics, FYC is most closely associated with our fledgling discipline. If we are to move forward as a discipline, the content we teach in FYC is vital to and representative of our standing, and so we must agree as a field to revisit the question of FYC's content, and in doing so, consider the following:

- Rhetoric and Composition is a field of pedagogy but also a field of theory, with students who are not only writers but also learners about writing; FYC could better represent that as not only the introduction to *our* discipline but also the cross-disciplinary course that benefits writers for *all* disciplines.
- Our research should be aligned not only with pedagogy but also with inquiry; our theory should support our pedagogy, and our pedagogy should be based on theory.
- The content we teach in FYC should reflect what we know from our most recent research on the efficacy of various curricular models; we should consider that content to be writing—both the knowledge about and practice of writing.
- Since writing is practiced in all disciplines, as both a means of producing and analyzing text, we have an opportunity to continue to be interdisciplinary citizens—to work with faculty across disciplines, to help students navigate the disciplinary expectations of writing to be influencers of how writing is conceived of and taught across the university.

The content of our FYC courses, if discernible and identifiable to all stakeholders, will allow us to evolve into our disciplinarity, to further develop as interdisciplinary faculty, and to better negotiate our expertise and therefore our leadership of the writing we teach and study. Our move toward more specific curricular expectations will enable us to emerge from the "un-discipline" we are to becoming the discipline we want and deserve to be.

## Notes

1. For more information on students' failure to transfer see the examples of "Clay" and "Rick" in Yancey et al. 2014.
2. Both the *WPA Outcomes Statement* and the *Framework for Success in Post-secondary Writing* offer guidelines but interpretation or adaptation of them to course content varies widely—www.wpacouncil.org/positions/outcomes.html or www.wpacouncil.org/framework
3. Reflecting our field's current content paradigm is a recent collection edited by Deborah Coxwell-Teague and Ron Lunsford that features several well-known composition theorists who contributed syllabi for a first-year composition course, along with a rationale explaining the theory on which they based their course development. See Coxwell-Teague and Lunsford 2014.
4. Although advocating for particular content and consideration of corresponding faculty expertise, we realize that a much larger discussion about the treatment of and investment in faculty who deliver FYC than that to which we allude here or that is possible here is necessary and that we merely point to the issue of delivery of FYC as affecting content rather than taking up the larger discussion here.

## References

Adler-Kassner, Linda, and Elizabeth Wardle, eds. 2015. *Naming What We Know: Threshold Concepts in Writing Studies.* Logan: Utah State University Press.
Applebee, Arthur, and Judith Langer. 2009. "What's Happening in the Teaching of Writing?" *English Journal* 98 (5): 18–28.
Applebee, Arthur, and Judith Langer. 2011. "A Snapshot of Writing Instruction in Middle Schools and High Schools." *English Journal* 100 (6): 14–27.
Bazerman, Charles. 2015. "Writing Speaks to Situations through Recognizable Forms." In *Naming What We Know: Threshold Concepts in Writing Studies,* ed. Linda Adler-Kassner and Elizabeth Wardle, 35–36. Logan: Utah State University Press. https://doi.org/10.7330/9780874219906.c002.
Beaufort, Anne. 2007. *College Writing and Beyond: A New Framework for University Writing Instruction.* Logan: Utah State University Press.
Bergmann, Linda S., and Janet S. Zepernick. 2007. "Disciplinarity and Transference: Students' Perceptions of Learning to Write." *WPA: Writing Program Administration* 31 (1/2): 124–49.
Bransford, John D., James W. Pellegrino, and M. Suzanne Donovan, eds. 2000. "How Experts Differ from Novices." In *How People Learn: Brain, Mind, Experience, and School: Expanded Edition,* 31–50. Washington, DC: National Academies Press.
Connors, Robert J. 1995. "The New Abolitionism: Toward a Historical Background." In *Reconceiving Writing, Rethinking Writing Instruction,* ed. Joseph Petraglia, 3–26. Mahway, NJ: Erlbaum.
Council of Writing Program Administrators (CWPA). 2015. "WPA Outcomes Statement for First-Year Composition." http://wpacouncil.org/positions/outcomes.html.

Coxwell-Teague, Deborah, and Ron Lunsford, eds. 2014. *First-Year Composition: From Theory to Practice*. Anderson, SC: Parlor Press.

Crowley, Sharon. 1998. *Composition in the University: Historical and Polemical Essays*. Pittsburgh: University of Pittsburgh Press. https://doi.org/10.2307/j.ctt5hjpc7.

Dew, Debra Frank. 2003. "Language Matters: Rhetoric and Writing I as Content Course." *WPA: Writing Program Administration* 26 (3): 87–104.

Downs, Douglas, and Elizabeth Wardle. 2007. "Teaching about Writing, Righting Misconceptions: (Re)Envisioning 'First-Year Composition' as 'Introduction to Writing Studies.'" *College Composition and Communication* 58 (4): 552–84.

Driscoll, Dana, and Jennifer Wells. 2012. "Beyond Knowledge and Skills: Writing Transfer and the Role of Student Dispositions in and beyond the Writing Classroom." *Composition Forum* 26. http://compositionforum.com/issue/26/beyond-knowledge-skills.php.

Fulkerson, Richard. 1979. "Four Philosophies of Composition." *College Composition and Communication* 30 (4): 343–348. https://doi.org/10.2307/356707.

Fulkerson, Richard. 2005. "Composition at the Turn of the Twenty-First Century." *College Composition and Communication* 56 (4): 654–87.

Hairston, Maxine. 1982. "The Winds of Change: Thomas Kuhn and the Revolution in the Teaching of Writing." *College Composition and Communication* 33 (1): 76–88.

Hansen, Kristine, and Christine R. Farris, eds. 2010. *College Credit for Writing in High School*. Urbana, IL: National Council of Teachers.

Jolliffe, David A., and Bernard Phelan. 2006. "Advanced Placement, Not Advanced Exemption: Challenges for High Schools, Colleges, and Universities." In *Delivering College Composition: The Fifth Canon*, ed. Kathleen Blake Yancey, 89–103. Portsmouth: Boynton/Cook.

Kaufer, David, and Richard Young. 1993. "Writing in the Content Areas: Some Theoretical Complexities." In *Theory and Practice in the Teaching of Writing: Rethinking the Discipline*, ed. Lee Odell, 71–104. Carbondale: Southern Illinois University Press.

Kent, Thomas, ed. 1999. *Post-Process Theory: Beyond the Writing-Process Paradigm*. Carbondale: Southern Illinois University Press.

National Council of Teachers of English (NCTE). 2016. "Professional Knowledge for the Teaching of Writing" Position Statement. http://www2.ncte.org/statement/teaching-writing/.

Neff, Joyce Magnotto. 2006. "Getting Our Money's Worth: Delivering Composition at a Comprehensive State University." In *Delivering College Composition: The Fifth Canon*, ed. Kathleen Blake Yancey, 48–59. Portsmouth: Boynton/Cook.

Nowacek, Rebecca S. 2011. *Agents of Integration: Understanding Transfer as a Rhetorical Act*. Carbondale: Southern Illinois University Press.

Perkins, David N., and Gavriel Salomon. 1992. "Transfer of Learning." In *International Encyclopedia of Education*, 2nd ed., 2–13. Oxford: Pergamon Press.

Reiff, Mary Jo, and Anis Bawarshi. 2011. "Tracing Discursive Resources: How Students Use Prior Genre Knowledge to Negotiate New Writing Contexts in First-Year Composition." *Written Communication* 28 (3): 312–37. https://doi.org/10.1177/0741088311410183.

Robertson, Liane. 2011. "The Significance of Course Content in the Transfer of Writing Knowledge from First-Year Composition to other Academic Writing Contexts." PhD diss., Florida State University, Tallahassee.

Robertson, Liane, Kara Taczak, and Kathleen Blake Yancey. 2012. "Notes toward a Theory of Prior Knowledge and Its Role in College Composers' Transfer of Knowledge and Practice." *Composition Forum* 26, n.p. http://compositionforum.com/issue/26/prior-knowledge-transfer.php.

Russell, David R., and Arturo Yanez. 2002. "Big Picture People Rarely Become Historians: Genre Systems and the Contradictions of General Education." In *Writing Selves/Writing Societies: Research from Activity Perspectives*, ed. Charles Bazerman and David Russell, 331–62. Fort Collins, CO: WAC Clearinghouse.

Shulman, Lee S. 2004. *Teaching as Community Property: Essays on Higher Education*. Ed. Pat Hutchings. San Francisco, CA: Jossey-Bass.
Sommers, Nancy, and Laura Saltz. 2004. "The Novice as Expert: Writing the Freshman Year." *College Composition and Communication* 56 (1): 124–49. https://doi.org/10.2307/4140684.
Tate, Gary, Amy Rupiper, and Kurt Schick. 2001. *A Guide to Composition Pedagogies*. New York: Oxford University Press.
Tinberg, Howard, and Jean-Paul Nadeau. 2011. "Contesting the Space between High School and College in the Era of Dual-Enrollment." *College Composition and Communication* 62 (4): 704–25.
Wardle, Elizabeth. 2003. "Contradiction, Constraint, and Re-mediation: An Activity Analysis of FYC Motives." PhD diss., Iowa State University, Ames.
Wardle, Elizabeth. 2007. "Understanding 'Transfer' from FYC: Preliminary Results of a Longitudinal Study." *WPA: Writing Program Administration* 31 (1–2): 65–85.
Wardle, Elizabeth. 2012. "Introduction: Creative Repurposing for Expansive Learning: Considering 'Problem-Exploring' and 'Answer-Getting' Dispositions in Individuals and Fields." *Composition Forum* 26. http://compositionforum.com/issue/26/creative-repurposing.php.
Yancey, Kathleen Blake. 2015. "Relationships between Writing and Critical Thinking, and Their Significance for Curriculum and Pedagogy." *Double Helix* 3. http://qudoublehelixjournal.org/index.php/dh/article/view/75/252.
Yancey, Kathleen Blake, Liane Robertson, and Kara Taczak. 2014. *Writing across Contexts: Transfer, Composition, and Sites of Writing*. Logan: Utah State University Press.

# 10
## WRITING, ENGLISH, AND A TRANSLINGUAL MODEL FOR COMPOSITION

Christiane Donahue

In a global landscape of expanding contact across societies, groups, institutions, and populations, the ways in which Composition understands the linguistic components of writing ability in higher education are radically evolving.[1] That changing understanding affects our goals in teaching writing and in research about writing. US compositionists are being moved, by both global change and L2 writing scholarship, toward a growing consciousness of the insufficiency of some of our long-standing assumptions about the relationship between language and writing.

Questions about the shape of the future of attention to language in Composition have crystallized currently into a focus on what is being called translingualism: a model that outlines a way of thinking about, framing, studying, and teaching language, in speech or in writing, that focuses on creating and communicating meaning across languages, regardless of the individual languages thus engaged.

In that "trans" model, the relationship between language and writing, between communication and meaning making, between integration or accommodation into dominant language norms and resistance to them, and between theory and practice on the ground, is highlighted. These axes are not new; the translingual model reexamines them and reimagines them as central to the work and the disciplinary contours of Composition as a whole.

A translingual model is intended to support moving beyond binaries about Composition in relation to L2 writing scholarship, multilingual work, or language teaching by shifting the point of departure:[2] in a translingual frame, it isn't English that matters to Composition, but rather an adaptability in *language* that joins the adaptability we already know writers must have across modes and media, genres and contexts.

DOI: 10.7330/9781607326953.c010

Our discipline becomes permanently about composing, about rhetoric, and not about English.

Of course, the case is more nuanced than that. English is the longest-term language in which and through which first-year composition, the ground from which Composition germinated, has done its work in the United States. A translingual model suggests that in the twenty-first century, Composition cannot assume writing to be about "English" alone. Claims made in teaching practice and in some scholarship about the continued, even growing, importance of English today thus bear examination in a translingual model. Moving away from a focus on English at the center toward a translingual model has both conceptual/theoretical and practical consequences for a Composition discipline whose lifespan has been dedicated, predominantly, to work in English. Our very identity is at stake in relation to other disciplines. The question of "language" moves from a subfield or specialized strand to a metafactor.

The heart of Composition's work has been consistently to understand and to support the best possible crafters and communicators of meaning. Writers must *design*—must draw on and control and strategize and flex—which means knowing available resources and when to reuse, adapt, or transform them, in what context, with what influence. The chapter will suggest that a translingual orientation is meant to offer new ways to think about the linguistic resources available to writers and demanded by the expectations of the twenty-first century—resources they must access and appropriate for the successful making and communicating of meaning. Rhetorical flexibility and linguistic adaptability in a writer's ability to construct meaning and design communication are the most important goals (cf. Purdy 2014). They should drive what Composition faculty teach, and why; what we believe is best for our students, and why. The language question is thus an implicit part of the ongoing discussion about our goals and our purposes as scholars and teachers, now and into the future.

This chapter will describe my understanding of that translingual orientation, where I see translingualism coming from and heading, and its potential contributions to Composition's scholarly work and deep commitment to teaching.

## WHAT DOES A TRANSLINGUAL MODEL OFFER TO COMPOSITION IN THE TWENTY-FIRST CENTURY?

A translingual model makes, or can make, specific contributions to Composition. To consider those contributions, I will explore the nature of disciplines and Composition as a discipline; the way a translingual model seems to fit Composition's trajectory; what a translingual model is from my point of view and how it functions; and the way it contributes or could contribute to Composition's scholarly inquiry and teaching.

*What Is a Discipline? What Is Composition as a Discipline?*

In 2008, I delineated the features of the US-specific Composition discipline, in contrast to the disciplines in Europe that study writing and teaching writing in higher education (didactics, linguistics, education sciences, and so on). I argued then that a discipline is a dynamic knowledge-producing community of practice (Wenger 2007) that develops via theoretical exploration, research, pedagogy, and practice. Often defined simply by its modes of official distribution of knowledge (journals, conferences) and its validation processes, it is certainly much more.

Clifford Geertz (1983) has suggested that the deep worldview associated with scholars' choices of disciplines through which they then pursue inquiries is all encompassing:

> The various disciplines (or disciplinary matrices), humanistic, natural science, social scientific alike, that make up the scattered discourse of modern scholarship are more than just intellectual coigns of vantage, but are ways of being in the world, to invoke a Heideggerian formula, forms of life, to use a Wittgensteinian, or varieties of noetic experience, to adapt a Jamesian. . . . It is when we begin to see this, to see that to set out to deconstruct Yeats's imagery, absorb oneself in black holes, or measure the effect of schooling on economic achievement is not just to take up a technical task but to take on a cultural frame that defines a great part of one's life. (155)

This sense of "disciplinarity" for Composition would suggest what many of us feel intuitively—that we have joined a profession that defines our lives—but it also suggests that we are within a framework that defines our parameters as both epistemologically productive and potentially constraining.

A discipline is also recognized by its genres and its routines, which differentiate it from other disciplines. Charles Bazerman (2011) notes, "The modern academy's distinctive disciplines, with different epistemologies, strategies, procedures, and literatures, have created distance from other disciplines' ways of knowing and have reformulated the phenomena they study as disciplinary objects. [They have] not only different theories but their theories address different sets of issues and serve different functional and intellectual roles in each" (10). Those disciplines differentiate themselves but also cluster into broader categories—sciences, social sciences, humanities . . .

Andrew Abbott (2004) suggests that these broad disciplinary divisions are identifiable by their core shared methods. But Composition accepts and endorses multiple methods (ethnography, textual analysis, narrative analysis, big data, quantitative work, quasi-experimental designs, and so on), so method is a complicated way of identifying our disciplinary work. There are perhaps "essences" of methods, again within broader divisions of inquiry, humanistic, social science, science. The "scientific method" might be the extreme example of that essentializing. Divisions, of course, beget trans- and interdivisional work, and interdisciplines are increasingly prominent in the knowledge-production business. If Composition is a discipline, then, what kind are we? Where do we situate ourselves? As humanists? Social scientists? Squarely in the interdiscipline?

Bazerman (2011) notes that we are at heart

> a practical discipline, no matter how far it wanders into arcane corners of history or psychology or sociology. As a field its motive comes from helping people to use written language more effectively, for both production and reception. It is also a discipline closely tied to making and interpreting meaning of written signs within particular socio-historic circumstances, and is thus creative, hermeneutic, and contextual. (15)

In saying this, Bazerman seems to be arguing that we are a discipline with both teaching-oriented and more abstract conceptual aims and works.

Composition is unusually situated for at least one other reason: the role of language in its work. In terms of language, we are both mode and epistemology. Our main way of being is subject (writing, writers) and semiotic, action-production. That is, writing is both subject of study or teaching and mode of constructing knowledge and communicating that knowledge. This makes the discipline of Composition deeply responsive to the question of language.

## So What about That Question of Language?

Of course, the "language question" is not new. It has been answered in the past, for Compositionists, in quite specific, deeply researched and theorized ways by English L2 scholars and teachers. Today, scholars and teachers interested in a particular take on the question, with particular ramifications for Composition, are exploring translingual models of composition. Translingualism has sometimes been misunderstood as an attitude of linguistic laissez-faire, as an "anything goes" attitude for students using languages in heterogeneous ways, and as a rejection of learning languages, including English. In fact, translingualism has the potential to be a theoretically grounded and principled understanding of language for *all* writers in the twenty-first century. In this next section, I will define it as I understand it, drawing on my linguistics and Composition knowledge, and will explore the model's specific relationship to English.

"Translingualism" is a particular orientation to language. Translingual models seek to understand how writing works, in the context of changing world orders, fragmenting norms, and increasing internal-external linguistic diversities. Simply put, the model suggests writers must have the flexible ability, know-how, linguistic knowledge, resources, and in some cases permission or audacity, to choose and use various linguistic features as relevant to the task and the context at hand. In the term itself, I take the "trans" to mean "across," "beyond," and "through," but also "having changed thoroughly" and "transversing" ("situated across"), which suggests that the notion of dynamic change is built in. "Lingual" is, of course, "of or relating to speech or language." The term "translingual" thus suggests seeing language as moving across and through contexts and uses,[3] and in so doing, transforming: seeing language as always in that moving state rather than as a discrete, composed, stable entity. The consequences of a translingual model include the need to study the language aspects of how composers make meaning and communicate and to propose resources for all writers as they design and produce communication using language(s).

A translingual model invokes a set of language attitudes (Canagarajah 2013). It assumes that linguistic negotiation has always been at the heart of the co-construction of meaning (Pratt 1991). In that construction, complex "linguistic repertoires" prime over individual languages as separate bounded entities (Myers-Scotton 1998, 192). Clara Molina (2011) emphasizes Geneviève Zarate's "savoir interprétatif" (interpretive knowledge) that is essential to communication in the multilingual, metrolingual (Otsuji and Pennycook 2014), or cosmopolitan (You 2016) context that translingualists suggest is the new norm (1245). Indeed, for Molina, monolingual students, who might not have that interpretive linguistic mindset, can be at a *dis*advantage in this context (emphasis mine): "multilingual settings are often scenarios in which communication is mediated by a language which is not the L1 of most/some/any of the participants, and so being a native speaker with full linguistic competence in the language chosen for the multilingual exchange may be an obstacle for communication rather than an advantage" (1245).

This sense of fluidity, negotiating, using what's needed when needed to make meaning, suggests competence isn't about "mastery" (or at least isn't only about mastery) but about strategy and rhetorical-linguistic flexibility in composing in a given context.

The emblematic translinguistic activities of code-switching, code-mixing, and code-meshing work creatively across languages to construct meaning in contact situations of the type globalization is driving.[4] They are the moments in which a speaker or writer draws on the resources of more than one "code" in the course of constructing or communicating meaning:[5] moving fluidly, negotiating contexts and meanings, transforming languages and words. But code-switching is not a fluid linguistic free-for-all, any more than a translingual model is. It is a constrained activity that follows systematic rules. Code-switching and code-mixing occur naturally in any bi- or multilingual or -dialectical context; have been identified as meaning-construction tools that can enable creative, resourceful composition interactions; and can be recognized, fostered, or even introduced to writers who don't generally use them, whether multilingual or monolingual. While controversy has swirled around issues of code-switching and code-meshing, I am using the term here as linguists do (Auer 1998; Myers-Scotton 1993; Winford 2003), not as they have been used in some composition and education contexts in recent years, and I wish to thus underscore their role in *design* and as an existing resource in diverse composition contexts.

What a translingual model seems not to have worked out fully yet is a way to account for the reality of individual language, its material reality on the ground; translingual does begin *in* "lingual," after all. Languages—whether spoken or written, as linguists will tell us—tend toward stability and change in constant tension. Any language, longview or even mid-view, is always in flux. But there are still "languages to learn." We might think about languages as we think about genres, always "stabilized-for-now." People who have acquired multiple languages, fully or partially, use them in particular ways that certainly should be recognized and fostered. But people with what appears to be one language also use it in heterogeneous ways, to varying degrees ("languages" here potentially including dialects or registers). And people with English as their only language are still in a heterogeneous world situation of Englishes (see Pennycook 2008), with no hard evidence that one such English leads to better meaning-making, communication, or material success than another (as is the case with people speaking only French are in a context of Frenches; Spanish speakers, in a context of Spanishes . . .).

In terms of writing, all three kinds of language users demand metawork to build competence and rhetorical flexibility: in short, to enable them to develop the ability to *design* what they are composing, at the linguistic level. A translingual model asks writing teachers to add to the choices that must be made and the resources on which writers can draw, and writing scholars to study those choices as made. It's that metawork that translingualism seeks to engage.

*Important Inflections*

As with any development in a discipline, new models rarely appear unprompted. The translingual model has been engendered by changes in the way the world's populations and economies currently interact, and informed by decades of scholarship in allied disciplines. Translingualism makes the most sense in the context of those twenty-first-century literacies, geographic flows, and social contexts. For years now, scholars have been identifying the changing nature of student writers in those contexts. In the United States, Tony Silva and Paul Matsuda (Silva and Matsuda 2001), Matsuda, Michelle Cox, Jay Jordan, and Christina Ortmeier-Hooper (Matsuda et al. 2006), Tardy (2011), Shirley Rose and Irwin Weiser (Rose and Weiser 2015), and many others have been pointing to the increasing diversity of US society and higher education landscapes, including of course US writing programs and classrooms. That diversity has done nothing but increase, to the point where what Steven Vertovec (2007, 2009) and Jan Blommaert (2010, 2013) call "superdiversity" is the broad reality. As C. Donahue (2016a) notes, "such global change cannot *not* affect language and writing. Global interconnectedness affects flows of language, language ability, texts (print and otherwise) and academic participation in multiple pathways" (147).

Translingualism has also grown in parallel to Composition's complicated histories with related disciplines and pedagogies. The areas of focus proposed by translingual scholars, outlined earlier, are "nothing new" (Matsuda 2014, 479), built from decades of work in several disciplines (Matsuda 2013, 128). While L2 writing (with English as the L2) has had the most privileged, well-known relationship with Composition around lingual questions, and by far the most significant impacts on it, there are other disciplines that share some concerns, interests, methods, and goals with Composition's translingual approaches, notably bilingual education, foreign language writing, L2 writing in languages other than English, sociolinguistics (which has long studied language diversity, including the mechanisms of language "death" and language growth and transformation), and Second Language Acquisition, Second Language Writing, and Composition.[6] Translingualism also intersects with lateral literate domains such as translation studies, international research and programmatic work concerning multi- or plurilingualism in writing instruction, and essential, overlapping theories of metrolingualism, heteroglossia, or cosmopolitanism.

*Where Might a Translingual Model Fit in Composition?*
One way to answer this question is to consider the parallels between translingual models and the sweeping change introduced to Composition scholarship and practice by the huge impact of multimodality and new media. Consider Jason Palmeri's (2012) provocative prologue to *Remixing Composition*, which begins, "There once was a time when I knew what it meant to be a compositionist . . . and then everything changed" (i). The instability of his path through new thinking about students, their need to "not compose alphabetic texts alone—that students needed to be able to compose with images, sounds, and words in order to communicate persuasively in the twenty-first century" (ii) and the provisional lack of confidence—and identity—he felt are significant. He reminds us of Cynthia Selfe's warning that composition could become irrelevant, or Kathleen Blake Yancey's picture of literacy in a "tectonic change" as it began to imagine how to work with composition for a digital generation (Yancey 2004, 4–5). Composition has thus seen attention to adaptability in mode (and before that, in genre). Multimodality led the way in helping compositionists see that "writing is not just about 'writing'" and that remediation is essential to understanding meaning making, composing, and design choices. The "re-" activity of remediation is a rhetorical and design decision.

When multimodality surged forward as a defining Composition foundation, we said, "but our history and the formation of our FYC requirement has been about "print text" (though see Palmeri 2012 about the reality of multimodality in earlier decades). That history was no less important to the forward movement of Composition, but multimodal work has convincingly taken its place, not as an add-on interest for Composition but as part of the fundamental cloth of the field. Multimodality reoriented Composition by suggesting there's nothing automatic about the work being in traditional print, just as translingualism suggests there's nothing automatic about the work being about English.

Translingual developments thus provoke similar questions about the purpose(s) of composition itself and the role of language in our work.

This changing, globalizing linguistic context changes our students' needs, just as a digital revolution did. Students in the United States currently need English, though different students need it in different ways, and which "English" they need is not a settled topic. But students *all* need translingual perspectives and resources. Translingualism is pervasive because it applies to every student writer and is a sea change in what Composition needs to teach for twenty-first-century writing ability in a globalized world.

In a similar way, writing might also not be just about English, whether a US student is L1, L2, multilingual, or a different profile. Composition can imagine language activity as a design decision, a "re-" languaging. While Composition's history has been the teaching of academic writing in English, a translingual model suggests it might be more relevant to consider the teaching of academic writing and *language*.

Translingual models in the US may appear to be about English, because English has become such a force in the rapidly globalizing context of the twenty-first century, yet there is no natural reason for that to be so. "Why English?," however, is not a diminishing of the goals and purposes of scholars, teachers, and programs invested in English but a questioning of Composition's *assumptions* about English.[7] The translingual agenda asks, in a changing world context, what is Composition's linguistic purpose? What is successful writing preparation for students: preparation for the US, for the world? And how do we *mean* that success? An ability to "simply" communicate by transmitting information? An ability to co-construct meaning and create new knowledge? And if so, in what language(s)?

The obvious answer might indeed be "in English," given what is spoken and written in most US institutions, most often, though even in the United States, Composition has not always been English-dominant (cf. Peters 2013) Our English history is powerful but there is no evidence US academic English will stay the dominant language as is. Reasons for focusing on teaching writing in English and teaching standard written English include that it is the language of power—of economic success and positioning—and that its rapid growth as a worldwide tool for communication makes it the commonsense language to pursue. Translingual models call both these reasons into question and emphasize instead the value of a critical literacy stance and the findings of internal and cross-linguistic heterogeneity in many studies of language in use. The decisions about standards get made both globally, beyond US reach (though not beyond its influence) and in diverse localities (see Horner and Lu 2007; the Englishes that dominate around the world are not necessarily the one[s] US speakers and writers expect).

The translingual stance implies that compositionists should not seek to bridge students from one language to another in their writing, nor to help them imagine discrete languages they can master in their writing development, nor to think Standard Edited English is the ticket to success they think it is, at least in and of itself. That seems a challenging path to take in the United States in the face of the very long history of writing as naturally "in English" and thus demanding a level of traditional language proficiency that we have striven to provide students from all backgrounds for decades. When we move away from English as the center, toward a translingual model, we are faced with unsettling consequences for our teaching in the United States and our scholarship about that teaching. For example, translingual models might not seek to increase second-language learners' proficiency in standard US English or in standardized conventions of academic English (US or internationally, via, say, EAP/ESP models), but to develop with all writers, a different competence than has been imagined in the past.

*How Does a Translingual Model Contribute to Composition Inquiry?*
In terms of Composition's scholarly work, a translingual model thus opens up avenues of linguistic inquiry about the intricate interrelationship of language—*any* language—and composing. It encourages a fresh look at phenomena such as translation, modern languages teaching, and the construction and communication of meaning via multiple semiotic modes, from street signs in a changing neighborhood (Blommaert 2013) to online self-sponsored English-learning chat rooms in China or multilingual representations in novels (You 2016), or the meaning-making interactions among scholars in multinational, multilingual groups (Fraiberg 2010; Lillis and Curry 2010).

A translingual model offers new interdisciplinary opportunities as well, with the contributions from what Palmeri (2012) called "allied disciplines" in citing the fields that contribute to "disciplinary expertise in multimodal composing" (8), in this case linguistics, sociolinguistics, literary studies, translation studies, modern language writing instruction, and so on mentioned earlier.

*How Does a Translingual Model Contribute to Composition Teaching?*
Composition certainly has drawn on trends that prepared teachers for translingual attitudes, in its focus on multicultural education or the valuing of hybrid literary texts (cf. *Ways of Reading* (Bartholomae and

Petrosky 2014); *ALT DIS* (Bizzell et al. 2002); Matsuda and Silva 1999; Miller-Cochran 2012). Many multilingual and then later translingual proponents have talked about "strategy"—the central importance of enabling students to make strategic choices (cf. Horner and Lu 2007). For different learners the choices might look different, but they are still choices. Every language user, in a translingual model, is involved in language choice and language change; as Bruce Horner and Min-Zhan Lu (2007) point out, it entails "the possibility of promoting interaction between varieties *in ways that change them all*" (Horner and Lu 2007, 147), in a dynamic interaction between institutions and individual learners familiar to Composition.

The translingual perspective is thus particularly important for what it proposes as important to all writers, to better preparing all writers today for the superdiverse, interconnected, shifting world we are in. A translingual model does not suggest that students not learn languages (including English, of course), though it might imply, as have critical literacy models over time, that they take a critical stance as they do.[8] A translingual model could serve to help teachers imagine the learning outcomes it would uphold. For example, Brian Ray (2015) has developed the following outcomes for a first-year composition course. Note in particular that they are appropriate for all writers, and only one involves English.

- Understand language and discourse conventions as organic, fluid, and dynamic—changing over time and in relation to each other.
- Engage in written and oral communication as a process of negotiating multiple codes and (genre) expectations.
- Analyze translingual prose/discourse through a rhetorical lens, focusing on writer-reader relationships.
- Develop and expand a stylistic repertoire drawing on written and spoken varieties of English and other languages.
- Compose writing that exploits/capitalizes on multiple registers and varieties of languages.

We can see that these kinds of outcomes support the development of fluid hybridity, a hybridity that can be celebrated. However, and this is crucial for ongoing work in Composition, there is at this stage little empirical research about the domains in which such celebration is likely and the ones in which it is not. New ways of ensuring "success" in communication and in meaning making have been established in globalized business settings, in international writing teams, in the everyday, certainly in literature, but not yet in educational, high-stakes testing, or other institutional contexts. Certainly there have been powerful arguments for the ways translingual teaching can help to reshape those norms, and powerful arguments for putting our energy into helping multilingual students understand and accommodate those norms. I believe that we need a sharp focus on the gap between the domains in which new hybridities are celebrated and those in which at least to date they are not.

Much more broadly, a translingual model offers at least three major avenues for development of Composition teaching: a new layer for teaching about design, additional material for teaching metacognition, and a potential new component of critical literacy pedagogy.

The additional attention to thinking about design, rhetorical flexibility, and discursive mobility builds on Composition's existing work to teach writers to be flexible across modes, epistemologies, genres, and contexts by adding the expectation that writers should be flexible across languages. This implies that classroom work should take up, for all writers, translingual questions about the role of language, about Englishes, about other languages, about the linguistic choices a writer might make.

The linguistic awareness that might result from this work is directly relevant to other current teaching questions about writing knowledge "transfer" and the role of metacognition. The metawork involved in various translingual activities has the potential to improve students' adaptation of their linguistic knowledge within English, across languages, and in deliberative response to audience and context. Composition might focus more on that particular aspect as part of its long history of purpose. That is, to have writers understand translingual decisions at work and to try them consciously in new contexts develops metalinguistic awareness and rhetorical flexibility, design ability, in ways that should foster and enable knowledge adaptation. I can imagine this work having the same effect that Patricia Dunn (2001) suggests will result from multimodal work, enabling a "metacognitive distance."

And finally, a translingual model seems in direct support of critical literacy pedagogy. First-year composition has of course been promoted in Composition's history as a way to foster critical engagement and empowerment in the face of institutional power structures, rather than acculturation or integration.[9] Critical literacy grounded in Paulo Freire, Ira Shor, Edmund Burke, Michel Foucault, and others has been particularly forceful in Composition's past, during the episode Yancey identifies as a turn to cultural theory (this volume). It emphasizes using literacy to critical ends, "learning to read and write as part of the process of becoming conscious of one's experience as historically constructed within specific power relations" (Anderson and Irvine 1993, 82), examining ourselves and our positions as part of our literate development (Shor 1999, 2).

Critical literacy has sought to empower students to understand and to resist the deep divides, the fundamental inequities in society, including those embedded in education. It supports newcomers to a community of practice in exploring *how* they are becoming a part of that community, with what stakes and gains and losses (Carter 2007).[10]

These emphases lay a foundation for Composition's current attention to a translingual model of language use, both to support and to usefully question it in the way we have usefully questioned critical literacy pedagogies in the past. In the translingual dialogues, scholars call for "more, not less, conscious and critical attention" to every choice a writer makes (Horner et al. 2011, 304); for resisting the dominant ideology of standard writing promoted by textbooks and the media (305); for studying and teaching how all writers can "work with and against, not simply within" dominant monolingual assumptions (305). To adopt these goals implies believing in them.

The approaches recommended by some translingual scholars certainly appear to be in line with the aims of critical literacy. For example, proponents of code-meshing Young and Martínez (2011) call for us to "freely encourage disenfranchised students to engage in practices that involve the meshing of codes at the very same time that they make strategic use of the codes they bring with them to the classroom, along with the ones they learn in class, to gain access to the language of power" (qtd. in Guerra 2012, 34). While it is not clear here how Juan Guerra intends us to recognize "the language of power," I imagine it is not in any case by simply accepting the norms of apparently dominant languages.

The most recent developments in code-meshing support the end of the continuum that seeks to upset the status quo. Guerra (2012), for example, capturing the same tension I mentioned earlier, suggests that "we either accept the world as it is and do our best to self-consciously adapt to it by enacting code-switching in more productive ways than code-segregation would ever allow us to do, or we challenge it by embracing codemeshing and demand that the world adapt to us" (38). Guerra's interest, ultimately, is to "provide our students with what Selfe (2009) calls a full quiver of the cultural, linguistic, and semiotic resources they need" (38). That "full quiver" of resources is exactly the set of resources that enable writers to design their compositions with the most effectiveness and depth.

To conclude this section on possible contributions a translingual model makes to Composition's teaching interests, let me offer a brief list of examples of other types of practices that have been proposed by various scholars and teachers in the past few years, with a note that there are other edited collections and works currently in production with the goal of sharing these kinds of practices:

- A course in first-year composition with a translingual focus that includes readings from translingual composition scholarship; student activities that play with languages, dialects, and registers; and student work on grammatical constructs from several Englishes (Ray 2015).
- A course that asks students to carry out Internet research in languages other than English, using Google Translate, with two identified goals: "to provide students with information or perspectives on their research topics that might not be available on English-language websites [and would] challenge the expectation that all relevant, useful information would always be available in English" and to "engage students in negotiating language difference and uproot the notion that a native-like fluency in another language is needed in order to use it" (Hanson 2013, 209).
- An exercise in a professional writing course that teaches students to analyze writing moves in international texts using a translingual frame, "STEPS" (Structure, Theme[s], Etiquette, Participants and their Purposes, and Style), to understand how the text does its work specifically in a translingual globalized world setting (Pandey 2013, 220–21).

This sampling of concrete teaching activities confronts us with question I have suggested is at the heart of Composition work, always: what do we need to know about writing and how it works, and what do we thus need to teach, in a superdiverse globalized twenty-first-century context? What diverse linguistic resources are most important for a flexible composer designing something meant to construct and communicate meaning? I suspect compositionists do not all agree on the answer, but I believe a translingual model is trying to provide an answer in terms of language.

## CONCLUSIONS

Translingualism may not be more than a stopping place on the river. It has work to do to articulate itself, to study itself empirically, to better represent its relations to L2 scholarship and teaching. But what it is trying to represent can fundamentally rework the underpinnings of Composition.

Translingual scholarship often emphasizes language use, identity, and "play" in first-year composition settings; how might these matter to professional communication or writing-to-learn (say, in the sciences)? These kinds of questions should help Composition to draw from our discipline's broad pool of expertise to provide our students the full set of "cultural, linguistic, and semiotic resources" (Guerra 2012) they need in order to compose appropriately, productively, ethically, critically, and responsively (Kells-Hall 2007) in our superdiverse world, in which meaning making is taking new shapes and monolingual norms and standards are by necessity in question. This will be particularly challenging in writing in the disciplines (WID) and writing across the curriculum (WAC) domains. Translingualism has not attended to WAC-WID scholarship and teaching much yet, and, as with critical literacy pedagogy, translingual attitudes and agendas feel far less at home in WAC-WID, though they are potentially more transformative there. As I mentioned earlier, we are not sure what will in fact enable "success" in every current context—and across disciplines is a good example. There are at least two models potentially in play, one that encourages compliance or integrative accommodation, and the other, resistance or play.

Molina (2011) cites Singh (2010), suggesting that multilingualism is, today, in fact already the linguistically "unmarked" condition. Along a continuum, the "unmarked" linguistic choice is the one that would be predicted by community norms, while the "marked" choice would not be (5). The marked choice indicates intentionality; it is a negotiation and a distinguishing act (6), a set of choices made from a speaker's overall "opportunity set" (7) of language resources: say, using a sentence fragment for emphasis. Unmarked choices are more expected, take less effort, and are less likely to change (4). But the categories are contingent; what is considered unmarked changes over time.

This has profound implications for the translingual perspective; indeed, it might be its very foundation. The purpose of teaching composition and the relationship between writing and language in US composition classrooms would undergo equally profound changes if indeed Composition were to accept that monolingualism, and even more, traditional English monolingualism, is the future's *marked* condition. Linguistic activities such as code-switching or -meshing would thus be unmarked. That transition from code-switching as linguistic phenomenon to code-meshing as promotable phenomenon is an example for understanding the broader question of a translingual model as rhetorical.

Composition must, as a discipline, invest in studying writing from a translingual perspective. Much scholarship to date has focused on choosing and highlighting sample "moments" of translingual activity in the classroom and in the world. I believe a move to a systematic empirical exploration of these new modes of working language in writing, and their reception in various contexts, is an essential next step. If we want to understand writing and writing knowledge in both local and global contexts, we can no longer choose to set aside "the language question" as not central to our scholarship and teaching. It is in fact the metaquestion.

## Notes

1. I'll use "Composition" as the label for the discipline in this chapter, but I am not making an argument for it to be the definitive name for our work.
2. I would argue that the discipline of L2 writing and the translingual model in Composition "don't actually intersect but run parallel; to entwine L2 writing in oppositional translingual discussions or vice versa is to misunderstand the translingual model, which I believe is a rhetorical model important to the work of Composition rather than a model destined to supersede L2 writing (its 'next phase') or to redirect L2 writing instruction." Donahue (2016b), "Writing Programs Administrators in an Internationalizing Future: What's to Know?"
3. While translingualism is the most widespread term currently, other terms seek to represent the same language dynamic. Each offers a slightly different way into the linguistic phenomenon in question. May (2013) reviews several terms developed over the past decade or so, including "flexible bilingualism (Creese et al. 2011); polylingual languaging (Joergensen 2010; Madsen 2011); contemporary urban vernaculars (Rampton 2011); metrolingualism (Otsuji and Pennycook 2011); and "translanguaging" (Creese and Blackledge 2010; Garcia 2009)" (192). But all argue that Composition should build from and move beyond the various scholars focused on "pluri" or "multi" or "trans" or "inter" or "cross." For them, all these prefixes imply an a priori distinct separate set of units (whether language or culture or identity) (see also Horner et al. 2011).

    Matsuda (2013) and others have suggested that "diglossia" might be a stronger linguistic term for side-by-side language uses. Blackledge, Creese, and Takhi (2013) argue forcefully for Bakhtinian-inspired *hetero*glossia (also called polyphony) as the most flexible model for the kind of literate-linguistic action in play.
4. Linguistic contact and its outcomes and consequences have been studied systematically since the 1950s.
5. There is work to be done exploring the use of "code" in "codeswitching" or "codemeshing"; linguistic analyses suggest quite different understandings of the term, antithetical to the fluidity and change translingual models highlight.
6. Much of this work predates translingualism, of course, and sits in complex relationship to Composition via L2 writing, sometimes clearly identified as a separate discipline or a field (Matsuda et al. 2003; Matsuda et al. 2006; Tardy 2011); sometimes identified as a subfield within Composition, similar to basic writing or technical writing for example. Key figures in L2 writing have claimed different fields, though its intellectual heritage certainly involves Composition and SLA (second-language acquisition) work. Silva and Matsuda (2001) describe two "'intellectual formations' that have evolved separately over the past four decades," with different perceptions and expectations, while "with the increasing awareness of the uniqueness of its instructional and research issues, L2 writing came to be recognized as a field of inquiry with its own goals, philosophical orientation, and disciplinary infrastructure" (xiv). Paul Kei Matsuda, A. Suresh Canagarajah, Linda Harklau, Ken Hyland, and Mark Warschauer (Matsuda et al. 2003) note that the "field of 2nd language (L2) writing has come of age" and become an "interdisciplinary field of inquiry with its own disciplinary infrastructure" (151). And Matsuda, Cox, Jordan, and Ortmeier-Hooper (2006) trace the development of L2 writing to status as "an interdisciplinary field situated at the crossroads between 2nd language acquisition and Composition Studies" (7), a field that "seeks to bridge the divide between composition and second-language studies" (9), suggesting indeed separate disciplines. As a discipline, its goals for bi- and multilingual students or emerging bilinguals have been clearly articulated and empirically studied for decades.

7. I am purposefully not evoking "English-only" here, as the important political undertones of scholarship on English-only are not what I'm focused on.
8. In 2002, Suresh Canagarajah noted "the critical approach to L2 writing is arguably one of the most significant recent developments in L2 writing pedagogy," situating himself at first within L2 but with a critical stance (Canagarajah 2002).
9. Critical literacy is a development most often alien to work on higher education writing research in other countries and across the disciplines.
10. Critical literacy pedagogy speaks in ways similar to the UK Academic Literacies domain of scholarly work; a hope for translingual work is that it will open up far more interaction with writing scholars around the world working on questions relevant to their contexts but illuminating to Composition, in part because they help us to resee ourselves.

## References

Abbott, Andrew. 2004. *Methods of Discovery: Heuristics for the Social Sciences*. New York: WW Norton.
Anderson, Gary L., and Patricia Irvine. 1993. "Informing Critical Literacy with Ethnography." In *Critical Literacy: Politics, Praxis, and the Postmodern*, ed. Colin Lankshear and Peter L. McLaren, 81–104. Albany: SUNY Press.
Auer, Peter. 1998. *Code-Switching in Conversation: Language, Interaction and Identity*. London: Routledge.
Bartholomae, David, and Anthony Petrosky. 2014. *Ways of Reading*. Boston: Bedford St. Martins.
Bazerman, Charles. 2011. "Standpoints: The Disciplined Interdisciplinarity of Writing Studies." *Research in the Teaching of English* 46 (1): 8–21. http://mina.education.ucsb.edu/bazerman/articles/documents/Bazerman2011ArtStandpoints.pdf.
Bizzell, Patricia, Chris Schroeder, and Helen Fox. 2002. *ALT DIS*. Portsmouth, NH: Heinemann.
Blackledge, Adrian, Angela Creese, and Jaspreet Takhi. 2013. "Beyond Multilingualism: Heteroglossia in Practice." In *The Multilingual Turn: Implications for SLA, TESOL, and Bilingual Education*, ed. Stephen May, 191–215. New York: Routledge.
Blommaert, Jan. 2010. *The Sociolinguistics of Globalization*. New York: Cambridge University Press. https://doi.org/10.1017/CBO9780511845307.
Blommaert, Jan. 2013. *Ethnography, Superdiversity and Linguistic Landscapes: Chronicles of Complexity*. Bristol: Multilingual Matters.
Canagarajah, Suresh, ed. 2002. *Critical Academic Writing and Multilingual Students*. Ann Arbor: University of Michigan Press. https://doi.org/10.3998/mpub.8793.
Canagarajah, Suresh, ed. 2013. *Translingual Practice: Global Englishes and Cosmopolitan Relations*. New York: Routledge.
Carter, Michael. 2007. "Ways of Knowing, Doing, and Writing in the Disciplines." *CCC* 58 (3): 385–418.
Donahue, C. 2016a. "The 'Trans' in Transnational-Translingual: Rhetorical and Linguistic Flexibility as New Norms." *Composition Studies* 44 (1): 147–50.
Donahue, C. 2016b. "Writing and Global Transfer Narratives: Situating the Knowledge Transformation Conversation." In *Critical Transitions*, ed. Jessie Moore and Chris Anson. Fort Collins: The WAC Clearinghouse.
Dunn, Patricia. 2001. *Talking, Sketching, Moving: Multiple Literacies in the TEACHING of Writing*. Boston: Heinemann.
Fraiberg, Steve. 2010. "Composition 2.0: Toward a Multilingual and Multimodal Framework." *CCC* 62 (1): 100–126.

Geertz, Clifford. 1983. *Local Knowledge.* New York: Basic Books.
Guerra, Juan C. 2012. "From Code-Segregation to Code-Switching to Code-Meshing: Finding Deliverance from Deficit Thinking through Language Awareness and Performance." In *61st Yearbook of the Literacy Research Association,* ed. Pamela J. Dunston, Linda B. Gambrell, Kathy Headley, Susan King Fullerton, and Pamela M. Stecker, 108–18. Old Creek, WI: Literacy Research Association.
Hanson, Joleen. 2013. "Moving Out of the Monolingual Comfort Zones and into the World: An Exercise for the Writing Classroom." In *Literacy as Translingual Practice,* ed. Suresh Canagarajah, 207–14. New York: Routledge.
Horner, Bruce, and Min-Zhan Lu. 2007. "Resisting Monolingualism in 'English': Reading and Writing the Politics of Language." In *Rethinking English in Schools: A New and Constructive Stage,* ed. Viv Ellis, Carol Fox, and Brian Street, 141–57. London: Continuum.
Horner, Bruce, Zhan Lu Min, Jacqueline Jones Royster, and John Trimbur. 2011. "Language Difference in Writing: Toward a Translingual Approach." *College English* 73 (3): 303–21.
Kells-Hall, M. 2007. "Writing across Communities: Deliberation and the Discursive Possibilities of WAC." *Reflections: The SoL Journal* 11 (1): 87–108.
Lillis, Teresa, and Mary Jane Curry. 2010. *Academic Writing in a Global Context: The Politics and Practices of Publishing in English.* London: Routledge.
Matsuda, Paul Kei. 2013. "It's the Wild West Out There: A New Linguistic Frontier in U.S. College Composition." In *Translingual Practice Global Englishes and Cosmopolitan Relations,* ed. Suresh Canagarajah, 128–38. New York: Routledge.
Matsuda, Paul Kei. 2014. "The Lure of Translingual Writing." *PMLA* 129 (3): 478–83. https://doi.org/10.1632/pmla.2014.129.3.478.
Matsuda, Paul Kei, A. Suresh Canagarajah, Linda Harklau, Ken Hyland, and Mark Warschauer. 2003. "Changing Currents in Second Language Writing Research: A Colloquium." *Journal of Second Language Writing* 12 (2): 151–79.
Matsuda, Paul, Michelle Cox, Jay Jordan, and Christina Ortmeier-Hooper, eds. 2006. *Second-Language Writing in the Composition Classroom.* Carbondale, IL: NCTE Press.
Matsuda, Paul, and Tony Silva. 1999. "Cross-Cultural Composition: Mediated Integration of US and International Students." *Composition Studies* 27 (1): 15–30.
May, Stephen. 2013. *The Multilingual Turn: Implications for SLA, TESOL, and Bilingual Education.* New York: Routledge.
Miller-Cochran, Susan. 2012. "Beyond 'ESL Writing': Teaching Cross-Cultural Composition at a Community College." *Teaching English in the Two-Year College* 40 (1): 20–30.
Molina, Clara. 2011. "Curricular Insights into Translingualism as a Communicative Competence." *Journal of Language Teaching and Research* 2 (6): 1244–51. https://doi.org/10.4304/jltr.2.6.1244-1251.
Myers-Scotton, Carol, ed. 1993. *Duelling Languages: Grammatical Structure in Codeswitching.* New York: Clarendon Press.
Myers-Scotton, Carol, ed. 1998. *Codes and Consequences: Choosing Linguistic Varieties.* New York: Oxford University Press.
Otsuji, Emi, and Alastair Pennycook. 2014. "Unremarkable Hybridities and Metrolingual Practices." In *The Global-Local Interface and Hybridity,* ed. Rani Rudby and Lubna Alsagoff, 83–97. Bristol, UK: Multilingual Matters.
Palmeri, Jason. 2012. *Remixing Composition.* Carbondale, IL: NCTE Press.
Pandey, Anita. 2013. "When 'Second' Comes First." In *Literacy as Translingual Practice,* ed. Suresh Canagarajah, 215–27. New York: Routledge.
Pennycook, Alastair. 2008. "English as a Language Always in Translation." *European Journal of English Studies* 12 (1): 33–47. https://doi.org/10.1080/13825570801900521.

Peters, Jason. 2013. "'Speak White': Language Policy, Immigration Discourse, and Tactical Authenticity in a French Enclave in New England." *College English* 75 (6): 563–81.
Pratt, Mary Louise. 1991. "Arts of the Contact Zone." New York: MLA. *Profession* 91:33–40.
Purdy, James. 2014. "What Can Design Thinking Offer Writing Studies?" *CCC* 65 (4): 612–41.
Ray, Brian. 2015. "Translingual Pedagogies and the Promise of Translanguaging the Curriculum." College Conference on Composition and Communication, Tampa, FL, March.
Rose, Shirley, and Irwin Weiser. 2015. *Call for Proposals: The Internationalization of U.S. Writing Programs.*
Shor, Ira. 1999. "What Is Critical Literacy?" *Journal of Pedagogy, Pluralism, and Practice* 1(4) (fall): n.p.
Silva, Tony, and Paul Matsuda, eds. 2001. *Landmark Essays on ESL Writing.* Mahwah, NJ: Lawrence Erlbaum Associates.
Singh, R. 2010. "Multilingualism, Sociolinguistics, and Theories of Linguistic Form: Some Unfinished Reflections." *Language Sciences* 32: 624–37.
Tardy, Christine M. 2011. "Enacting and Transforming Local Language Policies." *College Composition and Communication* 62 (4): 634–61.
Vertovec, Steven. 2007. "Super-Diversity and Its Implications." *Ethnic and Racial Studies* 30 (6): 1024–54. https://doi.org/10.1080/01419870701599465.
Vertovec, Steven. 2009. *Transnationalism.* New York: Routledge.
Wenger, Etienne. 2007. "Communities of Practice. A Brief Introduction." *Communities of Practice.* Accessed July 15, 2015. http://wenger-trayner.com/introduction-to-communities-of-practice/.
Winford, Donald. 2003. *An Introduction to Contact Linguistics.* Malden, MA: Wiley-Blackwell.
Yancey, Kathleen Blake. 2004. "Made Not Only in Word: Composition in a New Key." *CCC* 56 (2): 297–328.
You, Xiaoye. 2016. *Cosmopolitan English and Transliteracy.* Carbondale: Southern Illinois University Press.
Young, Vershawn Ashanti, and A. Martínez. 2011. *Code-Meshing as World English: Pedagogy, Policy and Performance.* Urbana, IL: National Council of Teachers of English.

# 11
## SHARED LANDSCAPES, CONTESTED BORDERS
*Locating Disciplinarity in an MA Program Revision*

Whitney Douglas, Heidi Estrem,
Kelly Myers, and Dawn Shepherd

It is not unusual to consider a discipline spatially as a "*space* defined or touched by a particular characteristic or force" (Wardle and Downs, this collection, emphasis added). This conceptualization makes visible the metaphor at play here: territories are demarcated and differentiated from neighboring environments by borders that can be more or less visible. In this chapter, we use our experience as faculty members invested in a substantive revision of an MA program revision to explore how that process of delineation opens up new questions about disciplinarity. We sought to create a generous curricular space within an MA degree, one that accounted for our own disciplinary expertise, the needs and interests of our students, and the vision of our university. As we did so, we were also constructing a curricular map of what Rhetoric and Composition looks like in the "locus of situated, locally responsive, socially productive, problem-oriented knowledge production" that MA-granting institutions might provide (Vandenberg and Clary-Lemon 2010, 258).[1]

Like critical cartographers, we grew to recognize the rhetorical power of curricular, historical, personal, and pedagogical maps, all of which surfaced as we moved through this process. We realized throughout the revision process that our representations of "the" discipline—the program we wanted to revise, the program we were building, our own educational experiences—were rooted in narratives. Like geographer Denis Wood (2010), we began to understand the connection between mapping and narrative, and we started to envision mapping processes as a form of storytelling.[2] We also grew to realize that our own experiences are always necessarily representational and situated, just as Peter Turchi (2004) asserts that maps cannot be neatly

DOI: 10.7330/9781607326953.c011

classified as reference texts, because they are representations of data. We came to understand that multiple maps could be made from the same data set, allowing us to reorganize information to see knowledge in new ways. That is, "maps suggest explanations; and while explanations reassure us, they also inspire us to ask more questions, consider other possibilities" (11). For us, mapping in newer ways—particularly through threshold concepts—allowed us new insights and raised new questions. And we knew as we worked through this process that any one representation of the discipline in an MA curriculum is necessarily temporary, open to ongoing revision, and only as accurate as we can get it at this moment. Even cartographers allow themselves room for error; The United States National Map Accuracy Standards, for example, allow maps are up to 10 percent inaccurate (US Geological Survey 1947.). Making these pieces visible to one another allowed us to see the perspectives from which we approach the work of the discipline and opened new lines of inquiry into how to revise and create a program identity that is inclusive for the individually situated disciplinary members that comprise it.

In this chapter we examine the larger questions of disciplinarity against the backdrop of our efforts to revise our MA program in Rhetoric and Composition, examining the practical, personal, and theoretical implications of disciplinarity. We begin with an overview of the various invention, revision, and reflection strategies we used in our programmatic revision process—strategies shaped by our disciplinary knowledge. We then transition from the larger revision process to the issue of individual disciplinary situatedness, examining the opportunities and tensions that surface when individual narratives of disciplinarity are made visible. Next, we touch on new lines of inquiry for constructing program identity that emerged during this process. Finally, we offer several implications for considerations of disciplinarity that the curricular revision process has helped illuminate. The ways we worked through our process represent the very values of our discipline: flexibility, generosity, honoring identities, listening, revision, and accepting/living with discomfort in order to sustain an inquiry stance.

## MAPPING THE PROCESS OF OUR MA REVISION

Before describing the specific steps of the process, we want to first provide context for our particular location and the exigence motivating our MA revision. Located in the capital of Idaho, a largely rural state, Boise State University is a public research institution that serves approximately

22,000 students, with almost as many master's (76) as bachelor's (84) degree programs. The majority of our MA students are native Idahoans; many are place bound because of spousal employment and/or other family commitments and historically have applied for part-time adjunct positions in our department after completing their degree. More recently, some have sought positions at the College of Western Idaho, the local community college established in 2009, upon graduation. A portion have pursued doctoral degrees or accepted full-time teaching positions at higher-education institutions elsewhere, and another portion have successfully pursued positions in industry.

In early curricular conversations, it was evident that we still valued aspects of the existing program and so did many of our students. However, some of us were concerned about the program's central commitments to prepare instructors to teach at two-year colleges or to pursue doctoral work. The number of available community college tenure-track or lecturer positions had dwindled severely and continues to do so, and we had concerns about a program heavily focused on preparing writing teachers for jobs that might be limited or nonexistent. In addition, the closest PhD programs in Rhetoric and Composition are in Nevada, Washington, and Utah, a significant impediment for our place-bound students. Therefore, we were unsure about fostering the development of scholars who may not have the option of leaving Idaho to pursue doctoral degrees and eventually secure tenure-track jobs.

Although our program had enjoyed successes during its short existence, we were mindful of Peter Vandenberg and Jennifer Clary-Lemon's admonition that sustained success of MA programs often hinges on the fact that "they fill a distinct need in their region or community, respond to specific job prospects or undergraduate needs, or emerge out of a particular institutional exigence (rather than a discipline-specific one)" (Vandenberg and Clary-Lemon 2010, 268). We speculated aloud about what it might look like to deeply reconsider our program with regional and community needs in mind. Recognizing the importance of our disciplinary knowledge in multiple contexts (business, legal, nonprofit, community), we wondered how we might reframe Rhetoric and Composition theories and pedagogies to make visible their wider implications and applicability. We wanted our MA students, regardless of their professional goals, to have more complex perspectives about the discipline and more ways to conceptualize what the work of the discipline could be and do.

Our MA revision process incorporated mapping strategies and metaphors from the beginning; however, that theme did not emerge until we stepped back to do the reflective work of writing this chapter. Looking back at our conversations, we see a series of strategies aimed at creating both abstract and concrete maps of our larger discipline and our specific MA program. In retrospect, we can also see that the initial conversations unfolded in three main phases. We started with a big-picture mapping phase in which we analyzed the current program and identified our group's core values. Then, in order to translate that mapping into a vision statement and learning outcomes, we worked with threshold concepts. By using threshold concepts as our guide, we were able to blend the larger and more abstract map of our values with the specific language required to establish outcomes. When we transitioned into the development phase, we synthesized our earlier conversations into visual representations that helped us envision how our values and shared vision converge into a curricular path. With these visual maps, we were able to move forward into constructing our proposal for programmatic change.

*Phase One: Big-Picture Mapping*

Under the leadership of our discipline director Bruce Ballenger,[3] we had our first conversation about the MA revision in October 2013, beginning with a SWOT analysis as a way to evaluate the "strengths, weaknesses, opportunities, and threats" in our current program. In this early phase of the discussion, we did big-picture mapping that helped us locate both the assets and the gaps in the MA. Early on we identified a key opportunity: we have diverse backgrounds and interests, but we share a core commitment to students, pedagogy, and learning. With our shared values as the foundation, we started to imagine a new, expanded program that would expose students to a wider range of rhetorical situations on and off campus. We discussed opportunities for more interdisciplinary collaboration, community outreach, and interaction with local political initiatives.

With this emphasis on rhetorical situations, we gravitated toward the term "writing specialist" as a way to create an anchor and identity for our new program. A program that focuses on writing specialists would emphasize flexibility, aiming to cultivate students' rhetorical thinking and provide them with opportunities to write for multiple audiences and purposes. The skills of a writing specialist, as we imagined them, would transfer into a range of professional settings. At the same time, it would provide students who wanted to teach or to pursue doctoral degrees an understanding of Rhetoric and Composition and its position in conversation with other disciplines. Locating and defining the concept of writing specialist were central to moving forward in our MA revision process. Through this concept we could maintain our individual disciplinary identities, unified by the work of training and supporting writing specialists.

However, the SWOT analysis and our movement toward writing specialists revealed what would be underlying tensions throughout the process. First, we wondered whether we should change the program at all. Our MA program was not broken; in fact, there were clear strengths in the original design. Second, several faculty members were, reasonably, deeply connected to the program. They had done the hard work, only six years prior, of navigating significant opposition to get the program approved. Initially considered either unnecessary or threatening to other graduate programs, faculty members in the English Department resisted the proposal to create a separate emphasis in Rhetoric and Composition. In order to create a strong case for the program, faculty focused on two purposes: preparation for doctoral programs and training for two-year college teaching. They consulted with scholars and administrators at two-year colleges to shape curriculum and presented stakeholders with specific data on available jobs in two-year colleges and current trends in doctoral program admissions. Third, when we began the MA revision in fall 2013, there were several new faculty involved. These faculty had not experienced the resistance, conducted the research, or built the case for creating the original program. Some of the newer faculty felt out of place in the current curriculum. With fresh experience from the current higher-education job market, which is challenging enough for candidates with terminal degrees, their understanding reflected a different reality than the MA program had been designed to address just a few short years ago. As a group we value the diversity of our experience and training, but we have also come to realize that these differences can create roadblocks. Like many faculty groups, we had come together to address procedural or administrative issues, but we rarely talked about our values or our professional and scholarly commitments. We each held pieces of a map of Rhetoric and Composition, and we had a sense of those individual pieces, but we could not see how they coalesced into a whole and how we could create a legend that would clearly orient our students as they began graduate-level work in the discipline.

*Phase Two: Articulating Threshold Concepts*

As a way to honor and synthesize our many perspectives, we turned to threshold concepts for our next step. Key ideas or theories that are transformative to understanding, interpreting, and engaging in disciplinary conversations, threshold concepts create openings for learners that result in new dispositions or ways of being (Meyer, Land, and Baillie 2010, ix–x). Once learned, a threshold concept is difficult to unlearn, creating a new stance in learners and a transformed relationship with a discipline, as learners are able to make connections they could not make previously. For our revision process, threshold concepts provided a way for us to balance the larger disciplinary values of Rhetoric and Composition with our specific context and individual commitments.

Early in the conversation, Heidi Estrem shared reading materials and provided theoretical framing to help the group understand threshold concepts.[4] After an initial brainstorming session, we each created an individual list of threshold concepts for Rhetoric and Composition, addressing five key areas: the essential knowledge, skills, and experiences in the discipline; the places where our students struggle the most; what we do instinctively as experts that novices do not; the ways of being in the discipline that are visible to us but invisible to novices; and the first essential thing that Rhetoric and Composition students should understand.

From the individual lists, Bruce compiled a master list of threshold concepts for students in our MA in Rhetoric and Composition program:

- Students both compose and study texts; writing is both an activity and a subject.
- The composition of texts and of their analysis is always rhetorical, undertaken for a range of purposes, in a variety of contexts, and for multiple audiences.
- The study of Rhetoric and Composition involves understanding how purpose, context, and audience influence genres of communication and how these can be used ethically and effectively to explore, inform, persuade, and delight.
- Rhetoric and composition is also a teaching subject, and we have a particular interest in applying new knowledge to sites where teaching takes place: the classroom, writing centers, community literacy projects, and so on.
- Rhetors may use their knowledge for self-expression but also recognize the importance of using what they know to identify and reshape cultural stereotypes that are embedded in certain writing and rhetorical practices.

These threshold concepts provided us another way to describe student learning in our context. We focused less on the threshold concepts that had been written for Linda Adler-Kassner and Elizabeth's Wardle's book and more on what we notice in *our* MA students, on what

> **Vision Statement for the MA Program**
>
> - The program will prepare graduates to be "writing specialists" who can work effectively in settings that demand a flexible writing ability, an understanding of rhetoric and genre, and experience with collaboration.
> - Graduates of the program will be prepared to work as academics, writing instructors in colleges or high schools, specialists in corporate settings, or leaders in non-profit organizations that focus on literacy practices.
> - The program will emphasize *writing and rhetoric in action*, encouraging students to participate in literacy projects in the city and region. In addition to teaching writing, these projects might include internship with a government agency, work with a local non-profit, or participation in a campus initiative that promotes literacy.
> - The program will encourage graduates *to see themselves as writers* as well as people who know how to study writing. Students will experience *composing as a creative activity* in a range of genres and formats, from creative nonfiction to digital texts.

*Figure 11.1.*

we see as critical knowledge for them. Our threshold concepts, then, echo those found in Adler-Kassner and Wardle through their emphasis on social context, rhetorical choice, and ethical means of communication—and yet begin with our understandings of our MA students, not a more abstract student or learner. Clearly this list is an incomplete representation; it does not capture the long conversation we had about MA students' struggles to place themselves in disciplinary conversations, for example, nor does it mention writing *processes*—certainly a value that permeates our program and teaching approaches. However, it took us outside of focusing on students at the *end* of a program and gave us a way to map the messy work of learning and acquiring disciplinary knowledge within a curriculum. Then, Bruce synthesized our lists into a first draft of the vision statement for our new program. Our threshold concepts, and the vision statement that emerged (figure 11.1), formed a temporary map that enabled us to transition into the next phase.

*Phase Three: Creating Visual Maps*

With a strong sense of our values, principles, and ideals, we transitioned into the logistical work of developing and implementing our new program. As a way to move from the idea phase into more concrete

*Figure 11.2.*

planning, we focused on visual rhetoric and design. Building on our work with threshold concepts, we created a draft plan for our new program, beginning with a chart that addressed program graduates' potential characteristics and employment opportunities as well as the program's current and projected audience. Next, we each wrote course descriptions for "dream courses" on notecards and spread them out on a table, moving and sorting the titles into categories to help us envision the new curriculum. Similarly, as figure 11.2 shows, we put our core values and outcomes on sticky notes and organized them into categories on the whiteboard as a way to visualize the alignment of our larger values and the emerging curriculum.

Another significant breakthrough in the overall design and organization of the program came when Dawn Shepherd synthesized themes from our conversations into a revision proposal that included seven visualizations: our current MA structure, current MA course breakdown, a table with four proposed course clusters, a comparison of the requirements for the current and proposed curricula, course offerings for academic years

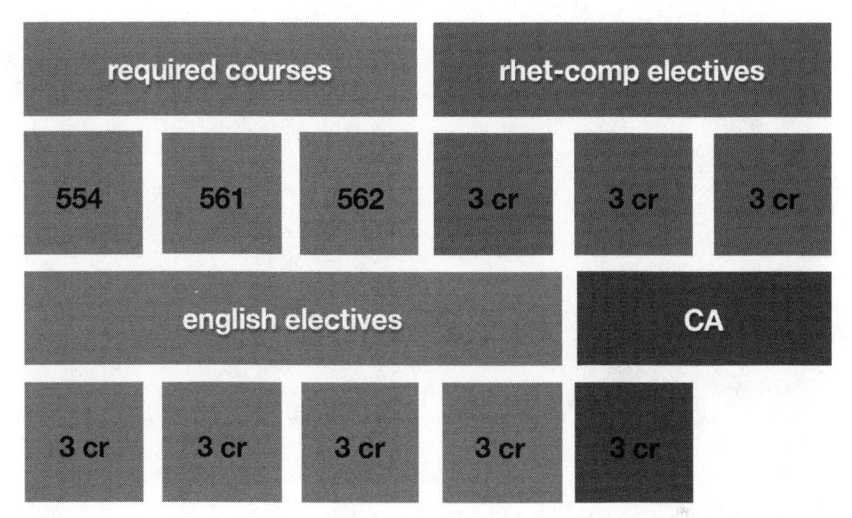

| required courses ||| rhet-comp electives |||
|---|---|---|---|---|---|
| 554 | 561 | 562 | 3 cr | 3 cr | 3 cr |
| english electives |||| CA ||
| 3 cr | 3 cr | 3 cr | 3 cr | 3 cr ||

Figure 11.3.

2013–15, and a proposed two-year sequence of offerings. In these visual representations, she traced our discussions and presented a potential MA curriculum that reflected our shared values and encompassed our year of conversations. In one visualization (figure 11.3), she created broad categories for our current course offerings and color-coded them in order to demonstrate the distribution of program requirements. In another (figure 11.4), she used a table to compare current course requirements to the proposed four-cluster structure. Mapping our current curriculum and then comparing it with the new program allowed us to see more clearly our current location and our eventual destination.

In the four proposed clusters of courses, our existing required research methods, theories of composition, and theories of rhetoric courses were complemented with three new course categories: contemporary issues and institutional contexts in Rhetoric and Composition; issues in writing, teaching, and learning; and writing workshop. We could shape these courses based on our expertise and values, foregrounding for students how a particular course was situated in a larger disciplinary conversation. At the same time that this revised curriculum honored our expertise and values, it remained flexible enough to respond to developments in Rhetoric and Composition as well as higher education more generally. Like any map, our revised curriculum was a representation of data and not a compendium of hard facts.

From big-picture analysis of opportunities and obstacles, to vision statements and multiple paths, to visual organization and presentation

**four clusters of courses**

| cluster | courses | description/information |
|---|---|---|
| foundations | 554<br>561<br>562 | existing theory and methods courses |
| contemporary issues and institutional contexts | 583 | reframed to cover current issues (e.g., contemporary rhetorical or composition studies theory, issues in higher ed, program administration, globalization, digital culture, etc.) from an R/C perspective<br><br>From a former student:<br>• "The theory courses give a good idea of how we got here and where we are, a new course could show us where we're going."<br>• courses on "where writing is in the university" (e.g., FYWP, WID/WAC, WC)<br>• "rhetorical analysis," "theory," "communication" for work outside academia (e.g., developing all-important "soft skills") |
| writing, teaching, and learning | converted current course number (563?)<br>598 or other pedagogy course | a sort of selected topics in teaching and learning, such as some that we already cover in our current structure (basic writing, multilingual writing) but also new topics (teaching writing and technology, gender and writing courses, new approaches to FYW, etc.) and/or courses from other disciplines (English ed) or departments (ed, psych, etc.) |
| writing workshop | 567 (converted to academic writing and publishing)<br>converted current course number (568?)<br>401G | a new required academic writing workshop and new writing workshop with different nonfiction focus (sort of a 401 for grad students) |

*Figure 11.4.*

of information, our various mapping strategies provided ways for us to see/resee our conversations and move forward in new ways. Perhaps the greatest challenge of this process was the tenacity it required. We faced uncomfortable topics, to be sure, and listened to and respected one another. However, as the process continued for more than a year, we did not rush to be done with it. Rather, we tried a range of strategies that got us closer to our destination.

## THE ONGOING PROCESS

During the year of in-depth conversation about our MA program, our personal values and commitments certainly played a role in the conversations (e.g., in identifying threshold concepts), but we did not create an intentional pause to name and discuss our personal interests until we started writing this chapter. We are aware of our individual disciplinary identities, but we rarely talk about them explicitly. We recognize one another's specialties and also know, implicitly, that each has loyalties to certain ideas about what it means to teach writing. To some extent, this loyalty begins with our commitments to our specialties, but the deeper, more emotional part is how we situate ourselves in the face of conflicts that are part of the history of any discipline.

To bring our commitments and individually held core values to the surface, we each wrote a short personal history statement in response to the following question: What are my disciplinary loyalties and why? In this prompt, we deliberately chose the word "loyalties" as a way to move toward the deeper layers of theories, emotions, and motivations that inform our work, and we included the why question as a way to encourage more reflection than we typically include in our bio statements. By writing and discussing these pieces, we illuminated some of the unspoken tensions that had been circumscribing our revision process, setting the stage to better foreground and negotiate our differences as we move forward. In addition, describing our personal histories and disciplinary loyalties helped us to prepare for our upcoming collaborative projects both as a Rhetoric and Composition faculty and with other local colleagues both in our department and across campus.

The narratives revealed locations: the physical locations in which we have worked, our generational and pedagogical locations within the discipline, and the individual and shared locations that we inhabit as a faculty group. When mapping our teaching and research pasts, we saw some overlap in New Hampshire, Arizona, and California, but the range extends from Nevada to Nebraska to Ohio to Michigan to North Carolina to Florida. Beyond the United States, members of the group have held teaching and research positions in Japan, Malaysia, and Spain. We have experience at four-year universities, at two-year colleges, at community organizations, and in the private sector. In these diverse locations, we each explored new theories and pedagogical practices; we found mentors who inspired us to push beyond our comfort zones; and, ultimately, we each shaped a place for ourselves in the world of Rhetoric and Composition. Even those of us who crossed paths at the same institution encountered different terrain, thus crafting our distinct disciplinary commitments. We realized that in collaborative disciplinary work, it is imperative to acknowledge the individual maps, as each collaborator brings a disciplinary history and situatedness that intersects with any conversation about "Rhetoric and Composition"—curricular or otherwise.

Writing the narratives created valuable space for individual reflection, and reading the narratives opened up new understanding and appreciation of our colleagues as specifically situated members of the discipline. The narratives provided insight into the mentors that inspire us, the theoretical frameworks that guide us, and the values that we bring into our teaching and scholarship. Making visible disciplinary histories and situatedness can complicate a line of inquiry, to be certain, but it also allows us to identify new opportunities for collaboration and to better understand where tensions might exist or emerge. For example, in our case, some of us received nearly no rhetorical coursework in our PhDs. Reading the narratives side-by-side revealed core commitments shared by the entire group. For example, we all see ourselves as advocates for students, and we want our students to see themselves as writers and rhetors who can employ diverse literacy practices and navigate varied rhetorical situations. Our commitments to advocacy extend beyond the classroom and into community organizations, political and social movements, and everyday life. We honor what we learned from our mentors and we are all invested in the work of mentorship. As a group, we value writing and the power it holds for us and for others, regardless of our theoretical foundations; pedagogical approaches; or individual values, beliefs, and experiences.

While we can see powerful undercurrents that connect these narratives, we understand that our differences are just as important. For example, Karen Uehling was first to use the word "reading" in her narrative. Many of us focused on "reading" rhetorical situations, but Karen's background in literature brought our attention to text-based literacy practices and both the empowerment and alienation associated with literacy skills. By stepping back and considering larger disciplinary boundaries, Clyde Moneyhun's narrative encouraged us to ask the bigger, harder questions about specialization and identity (e.g., what do we gain and what do we lose in claiming *a* disciplinary identity?). Since the boundaries of disciplinary identity become visible in a MA revision process, Clyde's situatedness directed our attention to those boundaries as a site for inquiry and invention. Gail Shuck's reflections on *all* writing and rhetorical contexts as multilingual pushed us to think of how an ethics of inclusion might shape our approaches to teaching disciplinary subject matter and in developing more culturally aware program graduates.

The narratives also revealed that we differ in the way we label ourselves within the discipline, some of us claiming Rhetoric *and* Composition, with others placing emphasis on one or the other. Some of us refer to "Rhet-Comp," others to "Comp-Rhet," others to "Writing Studies." While this range of labels and associations is quite common, often beginning in graduate school, there are implications when it comes to larger questions of a programmatic revision. How, for example, can individual identities be aligned into a program identity without silencing members of the group? In other words, is it possible to develop a program that has a distinct (and "marketable") identity while still honoring the diverse interests and identities of the faculty? Naming these interests and identities, served as an essential step in addressing the larger questions. When invisible, differing disciplinary identities with their accompanying beliefs, values, and assumptions can become theoretical and emotional roadblocks in collaborative work such as programmatic revision.

Since writing our narratives, additional factors continue to challenge our sense of the discipline in productive ways. Our colleagues in technical communication, for example, recently hired two new faculty members and proposed a substantive MA revision of their own. When we reviewed our proposed programs side by side, the previously clear distinctions between our two programs were no longer quite so distinct. Instead of needing to make an argument about the legitimacy of our discipline—something that our colleagues had to do during the first MA program proposal—we find ourselves currently writing course descriptions that are broad enough to be of interest to students in Rhetoric and Composition, technical communication, and English education. Further, conversations with colleagues in other areas of English Studies point to ongoing change and collaboration, moving us toward the prospect of larger disciplinary connections. These changes are happening as we speak, and our formerly insular programs are coming together in new ways, inviting us to view our discipline through the lens of related disciplines (and vice versa).

Each of us carries our varied graduate experiences at multiple MA- and PhD-granting institutions that have profoundly shaped us, and our disciplinary identities continue to evolve through experiences in institutional contexts after graduate school and in our current shared context at Boise State University. Although our disciplinary identities are not fixed and are always in process, there are certain map pieces each of us holds that remain with us even as our disciplinary identities continue to evolve and even though we may shift the way we position those map pieces. Writing our narratives provided a way to use the central tool of our discipline—writing—to visualize where we are standing as a faculty group. By making visible how we were situated individually, we could see where we are operating in shared spaces; where we are standing near each other but are not connected; and when we are standing in different spaces that do not easily connect. It is in the spaces that are difficult to connect where we may have important stakes as scholars and teachers of Rhetoric and Composition—terrain we cannot ignore if we want to navigate forward.

## NAVIGATING THE BOUNDARIES OF RHETORIC AND COMPOSITION

The process of constructing an MA curriculum reveals insights about the discipline writ large. First, we agree with Wardle and Downs that "embracing disciplinarity does not mean giving up the qualities that make our field unique; it means building on them" (this collection). We also see how the process we have worked through locally echoes what Yancey has identified as occurring within our discipline: that "various scholars have been thinking about our disciplinarity . . . through diverse paths: historical, philosophical, and pedagogical" (this collection). Just as practitioners have explored the histories, philosophies, and pedagogies that make Rhetoric and Composition, then our localized process of committing to contours helps illuminate why curriculum-building matters—and why the work of identifying as a discipline matters, as well.

As we navigated our revision process, it was increasingly clear that a larger disciplinary identity provides cultural capital. Elizabeth Wardle and Doug Downs describe this kind of capital not as power wielded without purpose but as a way to maintain presence in conversations about resource allocation in local contexts (this collection). We work in an institutional culture that offers resources to distinctive, signature programs.[5] Creating a clear, focused MA curriculum ensures that we are visible because it represents a disciplinary currency that is understood on campus. If we abdicate disciplinarity, we run the risk of reverting to providing service to others without a central place for research and inquiry.

Second, just as others in this collection understand disciplinarity not as a static, fixed, modernist representation of knowledge but instead as a process that is dynamic and changeable, we see the more localized act of curriculum mapping as an ongoing process that can in turn shape our individual understandings of what Rhetoric and Composition are. Map making is rife with contradictions; for while critical cartographers understand it as an act that is admittedly "wrapped up in authoring and cementing meanings and visions of the world," it also includes the impulse to "interrogate what counts as a map, and what ways there might be to think about spatial relations or mapping practices 'otherwise' in ways that rewrite power relations and cartographies (Sparke 1995, 1998)" (in Harris 2015). An MA curriculum became the axis of the discipline writ large, our own individual experiences, and our students. Choosing to revise (or create) a graduate program commits us to stabilization while the creation process encourages us to remain restless within that commitment, aware that any existing commitment is just one representation of disciplinarity data.

Third, mapping and remapping our experiences of Rhetoric and Composition using different tools and perspectives can offer new insights to all engaged in conversations about disciplinarity. As we described above, we approached our curriculum revision using a variety of methods as we sought to represent and rerepresent what we valued, what was possible, and what mattered most to us. One especially useful mapping process was that of identifying threshold concepts. Threshold concepts propelled our curricular discussions forward because they focus on describing student learning opportunities, on understanding. They provided a cartographer's eye view, hovering above course objectives to consider what experts know and do. That allowed us to chart the connections between us, tracing our shared values and commitments. Likewise, threshold concepts enabled us to move away from thinking about graduate education in terms of classes we might teach—or experiences we had as graduate students—to what students should learn. We view threshold concepts as Kathleen Blake Yancey does: that they are less canonical and more contingent, an "articulation of shared beliefs providing multiple ways of helping us name what we know and how we can use what we know" (Yancey 2015, xvii). Within Rhetoric and Composition, the effort to describe the threshold concepts (Adler-Kassner and Wardle 2015) are critically important in providing a map of our discipline.

Our MA revision process, as well as the experience of writing this chapter, illuminated even more clearly how similar and yet different our disciplinary maps are. Although we each would map the discipline differently based on our commitments, there are certain identifiable contours on every map that enable productive intersections for collaborative dialogue based on shared values and beliefs and other contours that ask us to slow down and examine what's at stake for us as situated members of the discipline. Our programmatic revision reminds us that welcoming students into Rhetoric and Composition is never solely about their learning; it's about our own as well. As we focused on student learning during programmatic revision, we were also positioned as learners—asking questions; reflecting on beliefs, values, and assumptions; and sponsoring new ways of thinking about writing, rhetoric, and teaching in one another. The learner stance is, perhaps, a hallmark of our discipline, as we aim to consider and reconsider the definition of writing, identify and explore new rhetorical contexts, and reflexively examine our teaching practices to ensure that throughout the process we have engaged in layers of inquiry and reflection: Who are we as individuals? Who are we as a program? Who are we as a discipline?

We are now putting forward a revised curriculum that we still continue to wrestle with in terms of how the curriculum will sponsor a stance of "writing specialist" in our graduates. The dynamic nature of our discipline as it responds to continual changes in writing and writing technologies coupled with our experiences remind us that programmatic revision and disciplinary identity must be viewed as an ongoing process and a living thing.

## Notes

We are indebted to the rest of our colleagues, each of which provided substantive input and feedback on this chapter, and without whom this writing process would have been no fun at all. Bruce Ballenger, Clyde Moneyhun, Michelle Payne, Gail Shuck, and Karen Uehling: you're the best.

1. As a faculty, we use a variety of labels (Composition and Rhetoric, Rhetoric and Composition, Writing Studies, etc.) to name our discipline. Since our MA program uses "Rhetoric and Composition," we have chosen to employ that label throughout this chapter.
2. In *Everything Sings: Maps for a Narrative Atlas*, Denis Wood mapped the Jack-o'-lanterns, wind chimes, streetlights, etc., of his Raleigh, North Carolina, neighborhood. In this "narrative atlas," Woods creates maps that tell multilayered stories, allowing for new and deeper engagement with the place.
3. In our department, there are "discipline directors" with reassigned time to coordinate, for example, program development, curricular revisions, assessment, and student recruitment in that area. Our department's disciplines are Creative Writing, English Education, Linguistics, Literature, Technical Communication, and Rhetoric and Composition.
4. She provided the group with two documents: a handout that she had prepared for a campus-wide discussion about threshold concepts and the table of contents for part 1 of Adler-Kassner and Wardle's (2015) edited collection, *Naming What We Know: Threshold Concepts of Writing Studies*.
5. For example, as we began our curricular revision, Boise State began a process of program prioritization, under which academic programs were evaluated for their alignment with the university's mission and strategic plan. Programs were assessed based on five criteria: relevance, quality, productivity, efficiency, and opportunity analysis.

## References

Adler-Kassner, Linda, and Elizabeth Wardle, eds. 2015. *Naming What We Know: Threshold Concepts of Writing Studies*. Logan: Utah State University Press.

Harris, Leila M. 2015. "Deconstructing the Map after 25 Years: Further Engagements with Social Theory." *Cartographica: The International Journal for Geographic Information and Geovisualization* 50 (1): 50–53. https://doi.org/10.3138/carto.50.1.10.

Meyer, Jan H. F., Ray Land, and Caroline Baillie, eds. 2010. "Editors' Preface: Threshold Concepts and Transformational Learning." *Threshold Concepts and Transformational Learning*. Rotterdam, Netherlands: Sense Publishers.

Turchi, Peter. 2004. *Maps of the Imagination: The Writer as Cartographer*. San Antonio, TX: Trinity University Press.

U.S. Geological Survey. 1947. "United States National Map Accuracy Standards." Last modified June 17. https://nationalmap.gov/standards/pdf/NMAS647.PDF.

Vandenberg, Peter, and Jennifer Clary-Lemon. 2010. "Advancing by Degree: Placing the MA in Writing Studies." *CCC* 62:257–82.

Wood, Denis. 2010. *Everything Sings: Maps for a Narrative Atlas*. Los Angeles: Siglio.

Yancey, Kathleen Blake. 2015. "Coming to Terms: Composition-Rhetoric, Threshold Concepts, and a Disciplinary Core." In *Naming What We Know: Threshold Concepts of Writing Studies*, ed. Linda Adler-Kassner and Elizabeth Wardle, xvii–xxxi. Logan: Utah State University Press. https://doi.org/10.7330/9780874219906.c000a.

# SECTION 4

*Where Are We Going and How Do We Get There?*

# 12
## THE MAJOR IN ~~COMPOSITION~~ WRITING AND RHETORIC
### Tracking Changes in the Evolving Discipline

Sandra Jamieson

As discussions about the nature and status of composition/writing as a discipline continue in our publications and at our conferences, at least 145 institutions have established an undergraduate major in this very discipline. And over the last three decades, thousands of students have graduated with a major in some form of expository writing. As a result, as Greg Giberson (2015) so powerfully observes, the discipline has already been defined for countless students along with their friends, families, employers, and current and future clients, coworkers, and students. Majors, minors, tracks, and concentrations in Writing and Rhetoric energetically identify themselves as representative of a discipline, and thereby shape the expectations graduates bring to doctoral and masters programs and the ways faculty at those institutions understand who we are and what we do. That understanding is frequently in contrast to first-year composition to the extent that though generally embedded in composition theory, almost none of the existing majors include the word "composition" in their names, replacing it with some combination of "writing and rhetoric" and in effect placing their connection to first-year composition under erasure. While many scholars worry about disciplinary exclusion and inclusion on a theoretical level (see Wardle and Downs, this volume), for already existing majors the issue has very real and practical repercussions both in how they present themselves and how they organize their programs of study. If (as Yancey claims in this volume) we can argue we are a discipline because we have a major, it is also the case that we need to study what that major is in order to know what our discipline is becoming, should include, and even, perhaps, what it should be called.

On a basic level, the major in writing fills the void between the first-year course and the doctorate in Composition and Rhetoric.[1] It

DOI: 10.7330/9781607326953.c012

provides a program of study that includes both declarative and procedural knowledge, equipping students for careers in writing-based fields and in any profession that uses writing and communication, and also providing a deeper understanding of writing as a subject. Majors in writing may include courses in journalism, rhetoric, creative writing, literacy theory, professional writing, writing studies, web design, authorship theory, technical writing, editing, business writing, communications, digital studies/rhetoric, argumentation, and writing center theory, to name a few. But the newness of this phenomenon and the evolving understanding of what constitutes Writing Studies have resulted in most majors in writing taking on a very local shape, often developing in the space between institutional need and faculty expertise rather than being modeled on other majors, or being shaped by forces outside the institution or broader disciplinary philosophies. And, given the tenor of many conference papers and articles about the writing major, it is not necessarily the case that if disciplinary structures and outcomes were to be developed, existing majors would revise themselves to conform.

The influence of local context is reflected in the name of the major, along with what courses it includes, how it is structured, where it is located, and what outcomes it works toward. As a consequence, much of the scholarship on writing majors (see for example chapters in edited collections by Giberson and Moriarty 2010b, and by Giberson, Nugent, and Ostergaard 2015) has focused on describing individual programs and tracing their history and local constraints. Other scholarship has traced patterns across existing majors and course offerings, providing classifications (Balzhiser and McLeod 2010; Campbell and Jacobs 2010; Delli Carpini 2007), or proposing ideal form or content for the writing major based on those patterns (Moriarty 2012; Peeples 2012; Shamoon et al. 2000), or on broader "best practices" for majors in other disciplines (Balzhiser and McLeod 2010; McLeod 2010; McLeod et al. 2008; McLeod et al. 2007; Howard 2007; Jamieson 2004). Each article in some way helps us understand how the major has been developing largely outside of disciplinary conversations, and together they give us a sense of the shape the major might take in the future. They also reveal a tension between those who are seeking to define the discipline of Composition and develop majors that reflect that definition, and those who believe the discipline should be defined based on existing majors (Giberson 2015; Carabelli 2011), or that Writing Studies and Composition are two separate entities entirely. As a session description at the Conference on College Composition and Communication (CCCC) 2011 put it, the "dominant narrative about the writing major as a composition studies-oriented content area is often at odds with what is an appropriate curriculum for undergraduates" (Royer et al. 2011). Indeed, practical conversations about what constitutes an "appropriate curriculum for undergraduates" are at the heart of existing writing majors, which in turn shape many people's perception of the discipline in practice; in contrast, discussions about what constitutes the discipline on a theoretical level frequently occur without consideration of what is included in the major that claims to represent it.

So, how might deeper understanding of the evolution and form of the major in writing frame conversations about the discipline of Composition/Writing? One way to start is to focus on three crucial areas:

- The first is one of relationship. This involves efforts to make the major in writing visible and determine what constitutes a writing major, and how (and whether) such majors might be classified and named in relationship to other majors and the broader discipline itself. Included within this conversation is the question of whether majors should (or could) share common structural features or content determined by broader definitions of the discipline. Also included are the relationships between the writing major and the English major and between the writing major and FYC. Finally, there is the question of whether the major in writing is really reflective of one discipline, or whether it is and/or should be an interdisciplinary major drawing on writing courses offered across the curriculum. Understanding these tensions will deepen the dialogue between majors and the evolving discipline.
- The second is one of context. This involves understanding the ways majors have continued to evolve in name and content in response to local needs, alliances, and self-definitions. Understanding this evolution could productively inform discussions of how a more consistently defined discipline might be realized on the ground and potential splits that may occur within the field.
- The third area of consideration might be called narrative, focusing on the way participants have created a coherency within existing majors and developed an explanation of what the major is and what it does. This narrative includes both the content of the majors (the courses and requirements) and the structure and scaffolding provided by the overall design of the major (including its relationship to FYC). Such talk by faculty, students, graduates, administrators, and campus publicity materials has shaped local understanding of the major. It also has a broader voice through publications like those by Giberson et al. (2010b, 2015) and conferences and organizations that address the writing major independently of the FYC, including the first Conference on Rhetoric and Writing Studies Undergraduate Programs in 2016 (sponsored by the Association for Rhetoric and

Writing Studies Undergraduate Programs). Larger conversations about the shape and form of the discipline should reflect these narratives and draw on them to reach a consensus definition of the larger goals of the discipline and its major.

In this chapter I unpack these three areas in order to provide a broader understanding of the state of the writing major and how it relates to the evolving discipline. It is my hope that by tracing aspects shared by existing writing majors, we can both move toward a coherent description—and thereby some agreement—about what the major is and also further the conversation about how it might contribute to our understanding of what constitutes the discipline itself, including what it might be called (Composition or Writing).

## RELATIONSHIPS: MAKING THE MAJOR VISIBLE
*Creating Lists and Thereby Exclusions*
The first step in an understanding of writing majors is to identify what they are, what they include, and how different kinds might be classified. Because writing majors developed locally for two or more decades without a clearly defined discipline, they initially remained invisible to most composition theorists who had no direct connection to one. Because many of the faculty were not involved in FYC or did not see themselves as compositionists, discussions of majors and participation by faculty shaping them also had little presence at academic conferences. The majority of writing majors developed within English departments based on student and faculty interest, available staffing, and the specific local context (see table 12.1). Others evolved within independent writing departments and programs, many of which formed from a breakup of the English department and existed initially as service and general education programs, sometimes with a graduate program in Composition and Rhetoric but generally initially without a major. When a major was formed in those units, it tended to be constrained by interest, available staffing, and local context in much the same way as majors within English departments, though as Blake Scott and Elizabeth Wardle observe, in most cases, as in theirs, the freestanding program has more freedom and flexibility to reshape itself over time (Scott and Wardle 2015).

The descriptions of many of the writing majors featured in Gregory A. Giberson and Thomas A. Moriarty's *What We Are Becoming: Developments in Undergraduate Writing Majors* (Giberson and Moriarty's 2010b) and Giberson, Jim Nugent, and Lori Ostergaard's *Writing Majors: Eighteen Program Profiles* (Giberson, Nugent, and Ostergaard 2015) begin with a

Table 12.1. Words included in the name of the 129 host departments (2015)

|  | Count (n = 129) | Percentage |
|---|---|---|
| English* | 90 | 69.77 |
| Writing | 31 | 24.03 |
| Rhetoric | 17 | 13.18 |
| Communication | 16 | 12.40 |
| Language | 6 | 4.65 |
| Professional | 6 | 4.65 |
| Technical | 5 | 3.87 |
| Literature | 3 | 2.33 |
| Media / emerging media / multimedia | 3 | 2.33 |
| Arts | 3 | 2.33 |
| Foreign languages (and English) | 2 | 1.55 |
| Humanities | 2 | 1.55 |
| Culture | 2 | 1.55 |
| Journalism | 1 | 0.77 |

*See table 12.3 for break-out data on the 93 programs within English departments.*

description of the procedure of creating the major, from initial discussion to program design and implementation. Yet Giberson reports that after editing the first collection, he found what the editors of *Coming of Age: The Advanced Writing Curriculum* (Shamoon et al. 2000) found a decade before: at a certain point in the discussion participants realize the practical need to learn about other writing majors—both as models and as cautionary tales. Such a need first motivated the attempt to create a list of majors to be centrally located and regularly updated. In turn, the construction of a list of writing majors necessitated an attempt at classification, and created a tension about what is and is not included—a tension discussed by several panels and papers at the 2011 CCCC conference following Balzhiser and McLeod's 2010 "The Undergraduate Writing Major: What Is It? What Should It Be?" describing what they define as prototypical majors (see Freeman 2011; Haven 2011; Neely 2011; Royer 2011).

The first list of what its creator, Doug Downs, called "expository" writing majors in the United States was based on responses to a post on the WPA-L LISTSERV in September 2001. Downs described it as "partial and incomplete" and notes at the bottom of the website containing the list that "because the writing major seems to be as much the purview of small liberal arts colleges as of larger universities, and there are so many such institutions, and because programs change relatively quickly, the list of writing majors available at a given time will always be difficult to track." The list he created included twenty-four majors and thirteen more "tracks or concentrations." Following the publication of *Coming of Age* in 2000, I also began compiling a list and added five more concentrations and one major to Downs's list in preparation for a 2002 CCCC preconvention workshop on developing the writing major (Shamoon et al. 2002). These lists raise three essential questions that have shaped much of the conversation around the major since: Who determines that a course of study should be counted as a *major* rather than a track or concentration within another major? Who determines what constitutes a *writing* major? And how does (or should) location, relationship to other majors, and in particular the name adopted by the major shape our consideration of the first two questions?

Downs notes that the programs on his list "are categorized on the basis of *self reporting* by people affiliated with the programs" (emphasis in the original) and therefore, he explains, "one or two programs in the 'Majors' list look very much like concentrations, but if they were reported as majors, that's what I listed them as" (Downs 2001). I initially followed that same practice. With no disciplinary structure to define what is and is not a major, self-reporting appeared to be the only option; yet that also presents a significant challenge because, as Downs suggests, what one institution identifies as a "major" another calls a "concentration," and what some call a writing major others call an English major. For this reason, the creation of a list based on self-reporting alone actually complicates attempts to define the major by suggesting shared characteristics where there may be none. Clearly there was a need to move beyond local definition and approach the question transcontextually based on patterns across those programs.

In 2005 the list of writing majors was expanded again as part of the preliminary report of the CCCC Committee on the Major in Composition and Rhetoric, but this time the forty-four majors and twenty-five tracks or concentrations were listed based on a combination of self-reporting and review of the content and structure of the program. A year before, Yancey's 2004 CCCC Chair's Address "Made Not Only in Words" had called on faculty to develop a major (Yancey 2004b). This was not the first such call (Shumaker made it in 1981 [Shumaker 1981], and Shamoon et al. repeated it in 2000 [Shamoon et al. 2000], building on Sharon Crowley's 1998 challenge); however, Yancey's talk can be seen as a tipping point, speaking to an increasingly energetic conversation in the field. That same year, the CCCC announced the formation of a committee to track the emerging major, which Yancey introduced to CCCC members in her December Chair's report: "The CCCC Committee on the Major in Composition and Rhetoric is intended to review current programs in the majors for Composition and Rhetoric; to identify prototypic majors; and to create a list of resources for faculty, programs, and departments considering creating such a major as well as a structure for networking faculty offering such majors. This committee is being struck this summer; we hope for a preliminary report within a few months" (Yancey 2004a, 366).

Before the committee could "review current programs" the chair, Susan McLeod, and committee members determined that it needed to create a database of majors, and the first step was to create a list of existing majors to explore further.

The process of making a first pass at a list that could ultimately lead to further investigation and identification of "prototypic majors" led the committee to begin to define the major by what committee members determined it is not, though the principle of self-identification was still applied. As a result, the 2006 list (Genova and McLeod 2006) did not include communication studies majors because few identified themselves as having a focus on writing. Creative writing majors were not included, in part because they are already listed by the Association of Writers and Writing Programs (AWP), but also because none were identified that indicated a connection with composition. Most technical writing programs were not included because they, too, are already listed—by the Association of Teachers of Technical Writing (ATTW) and elsewhere—though those that described themselves as writing majors were included even if their focus was clearly technical writing. Criteria beyond self-identification and inclusion on other lists were applied in the case of majors offered as tracks or concentrations in English departments that defined themselves as writing majors in spite of being made up primarily of literature courses. They were not included if more than half of the required courses were literature. Those that were included were counted as majors if the department identified itself as having a writing major (even if the actual name was "English major with a concentration/track in . . ."—see table 12.3).

No attempt at list making is perfect. Some faculty have expressed concern about the impact on professional and technical programs if they are included in a list of general writing majors that also may include the word "composition" (Freeman 2011). Others have observed that the decision not to list literature-centric programs excluded many majors in liberal arts colleges and favored programs that have split from English in addition to more professional and technical programs (Royer et al. 2011). Such tensions bleed over into conversations about the discipline of writing itself (including whether there is such a thing), which majors might be included in it, and which professional organizations can best represent the major.

Meanwhile, as longer-standing majors have evolved and in some cases relocated within the institution, the content has become more balanced between professional and technical writing, creative writing, and writing studies. In addition, such revisions have often been accompanied by name changes. Nonetheless, the same principle has continued to guide the creation of the list of majors: if a program of study names itself a major in a writing-related field, and written communication of some form is the primary content, it is listed. If it identifies as a major but is named as a track or concentration, it is counted as a major but the format is so indicated. Using this principle, the updated list compiled by Gina Genova and Susan McLeod (committee chair) in 2008 included sixty-eight majors in sixty-five different institutions (Balzhiser and McLeod 2010, 416). In late 2015 when the Committee created its final revised list, it stood at 135 majors in 129 departments within U.S. institutions, in addition to one in New Zealand and two in Canada (Jamieson 2015). As was the case with Downs's list, though, the more one works with it, the more one becomes aware of just how "partial and incomplete" the list remains—and of how varied the definition of "writing major" is. Over time, what has also become very apparent is that Downs's concern about what constitutes a writing major and how it can be classified is far from resolved. In the end, the concept of "prototypical majors" may be determined more fully by institutional location than by disciplinary definition or by locally determined outcomes.

*Institutional Location*

The 2015 update of the list of majors incorporates data from the institutions included in the National Census of Writing database (Gladstein and Fralix 2015), and indicates that while the name (see table 12.2) and the content of writing majors have changed in the last two decades, the institutional location of writing majors is less changed, with most remaining in English departments. Interestingly, the names of several departments have changed since 2001, mostly to include more areas and expanded majors, as seen in the change from "Technical Communication and Professional Writing Department" to "Communication, Writing, and

*The Major in ~~Composition~~ Writing and Rhetoric*  251

Table 12.2. Words included in the name of majors (2015)

| All majors, tracks and concentrations | Count (n = 135) | Percentage |
|---|---|---|
| Writing/Written | 131 | 97.03 |
| English | 52 | 38.52 |
| Rhetoric | 41 | 30.37 |
| Professional | 39 | 28.88 |
| Communication | 24 | 17.77 |
| Technical/technology | 17 | 12.59 |
| Media/emerging media/digital media | 6 | 4.44 |
| Science | 3 | 2.22 |
| Culture | 2 | 1.48 |
| Language | 2 | 1.48 |
| Journalism | 2 | 1.48 |
| Linguistics | 1 | 0.74 |
| Discourse | 1 | 0.74 |
| Journalism | 1 | 0.74 |
| Literature | 1 | 0.74 |
| Information | 1 | 0.74 |
| Design | 1 | 0.74 |

the Arts" at Metropolitan State University (Aronson and Hansen 2002). Table 12.1 reflects such expanded departmental names, including all of the words in the names of the 129 departments that house the 135 majors (note that six departments include more than one writing-focused major). In all, 93 of the 135 majors on the 2015 list are located in English departments (69 percent), including many of the 52 (56 percent) that are self-described as majors on websites and in publicity materials, but are also identified institutionally as tracks or concentrations—many of which include some combination of literature and writing in their names (as table 12.1 shows). A total of 42 majors (31 percent) are located in 38 independent writing departments.

In spite of their various names and locations, the majority of these majors include some common areas of content. All include some kind of professional writing; most include courses in creative nonfiction, rhetoric, and media; most include internships; and many include at least a smattering of literature courses and/or literary analysis. As far as I can tell from course titles, most if not all also include courses that call for some degree of theorizing and reflection. What differs is how much of each is included. The name of the major (see table 12.2) still indicates a lot about content, as we might expect. So majors with the word "English" in their name generally include more literature and creative writing electives, while those identified as "Professional" or "Technical" include more preprofessional courses (such as business writing, document design, technical writing, public relations, legal writing, and web advertising), but not completely at the expense of courses that study written communication in some way. In other words, while institutional location has an impact on content as we might expect, the impact is primarily on the quantity of offerings of each type of course and the balance of requirements rather than on the types of courses themselves.

A similar finding is reported by Lee Campbell and Debra Jacobs, who mapped the courses included in forty-three majors on a continuum from liberal to technical and general to specific and found that while courses in different programs clustered in different parts of the map, those parts were all represented in some way in the programs reviewed (Campbell and Jacobs 2010). Freestanding writing majors within or outside of English departments also include a mix of courses that focus on writing as an activity (the practice of writing such as travel writing, journalism, and business writing) and courses that focus on writing as a subject of study (such as rhetoric, authorship studies, and theories of literacy). They seem likely to include an interdisciplinary focus, including courses from programs in communications, journalism, linguistics, and creative writing, and of course English literature. As with embedded majors, this could be a result of local staffing conditions, already-existing courses and specializations, or inter-program negotiations/politics. Whatever the cause, the content of the major becomes part of its narrative of what it is, significantly expanding some understandings of what constitutes the discipline of Writing/Composition as Giberson and others have observed.

## CONTEXTUALIZING THE MAJOR: FROM COMPOSITION TO WRITING

*The Role of Naming*

The challenge of knowing what to identify as a major is reflected in the research on it, which reveals a program of study that takes many forms and names, and one whose forms and names have evolved over time. Early majors and tracks tended to be named "Composition and

Rhetoric," the name of most graduate programs and the classification of graduate and undergraduate programs by the National Research Council (NRC) federal Classification of Instructional Programs (CIP) code (Phelps and Ackerman 2010); however, that is no longer the case. While we may initially overlook the importance of nomenclature, it reflects a larger turn in the evolution of the Writing/Composition major and perhaps the discipline as well.

The initial charge given to the CCCC Committee on the Major was to document the growth of *majors in Composition and Rhetoric*, and its title included those two terms; however, to take that charge literally would be to produce a very short list. Although some scholars propose "Composition and Rhetoric" as the name for our discipline, it is currently not the name selected by the undergraduate majors that represent it (see table 12.2) for reasons many have articulated as they describe their major. No major uses both words in its name, and only 30 percent use "Rhetoric." The most frequent explanations are that few undergraduates understand what rhetoric is when they select a major, and that "Composition" has negative connotations with FYC (Royer et al. 2011). But more important, many designing majors note that they simply did not consider the term "Composition" as part of their name because it fails to capture the many kinds of writing included in writing majors and therefore does not signal to students or to future employers what is represented in their program of study (Carabelli 2011; Foster 2012; Freeman 2011; Neely 2011).

More recently, majors have been named and/or renamed "Writing and Rhetoric," "Writing Studies," or other names that include those words but do not include "Composition" (see table 12.2). So the undergraduate writing major almost universally has a different name than our discipline's graduate degree—even in departments that offer a BA and a PhD in the same discipline.

By 2009, no majors on the CCCC list had the word "Composition" in their title. In its March 2010 request to be reconstituted, the committee asked to be renamed the Committee on the Major in Writing and Rhetoric, a request that was granted. That name echoes the name selected by Thomas Moriarty, Tim Peeples, and Helen Foster, when they formed The Undergraduate Consortium in Rhetoric and Writing in 2008, which met as a special interest group at the annual meeting of the CCCC, and participated in a roundtable discussion with members of the Committee on the Major in Writing and Rhetoric at the CCCC in 2012 (and sponsored its first national conference in 2016). The 2015 list of majors includes six tracks within an English major that include the word

Table 12.3. Words included in the name of majors, concentrations, and tracks within English departments (from table 12.1)

| Words included in the title of the major, concentration, track, emphasis, option, or specialization | Separate writing major (n = 41) | English concentration (n = 28) | English track (n = 6) | English option, emphasis, or specialization (n = 13) | Combined English and Writing (n = 5) | TOTAL (n = 93) |
|---|---|---|---|---|---|---|
| Writing/Written | 39 | 26 | 5 | 11 | 2 | 83 |
| English | 3 | 28 | 6 | 13 | 5 | 55 |
| Rhetoric | 7 | 11 | 2 | 5 | 2 | 27 |
| Professional | 12 | 4 | 2 | 2 | 0 | 20 |
| Communication | 7 | 2 | 1 | 1 | 0 | 11 |
| Composition | 1 | 2 | 0 | 3 | 0 | 6 |
| Media | 1 | 0 | 1 | 1 | 1 | 4 |
| Technical | 1 | 1 | 0 | 1 | 0 | 3 |
| Business | 1 | 1 | 0 | 0 | 0 | 2 |
| Literacy | 0 | 2 | 0 | 0 | 0 | 2 |
| Linguistics | 1 | 0 | 0 | 0 | 0 | 1 |
| Journalism | 1 | 0 | 0 | 0 | 0 | 1 |

"Composition" (see table 12.3), but no freestanding majors that identify themselves purely as Composition or Composition and Rhetoric. While most of the majors include more than one word in their names, 131 of the 135 majors on the list include either "writing" or "written" in their names, sometimes with "rhetoric" (see table 12.2).

This shift reflects a change in how many scholars refer to our work—from Composition to Writing Studies; from first-year composition to first-year writing. But it may be that the terminological change within the field is also being driven more directly—as was the committee's request to the CCCC—by the name and renaming of the major and the broadening of our understanding of the term "writing" that accompanies it (see Conference on College Composition and Communication Committee on the Major in Writing and Rhetoric website, 2006). Name changes also often indicate alliances made between writing-related fields, as was the case at Rowan University. In 2003, creative writing faculty joined the Composition and Rhetoric faculty and to reflect the broadened content the Composition and Rhetoric Department and its major were renamed "Writing Arts." This produced what department members describe as "a more inclusive, but less well-defined, disciplinary department encompassing the values not only of rhetoric / composition but also of creative writing, as well as our electives courses from journalism and communication studies" (Courtney, Martin, and Penrod 2010, 246). This sentiment echoes that used to describe the writing major at Metropolitan State University, which "identified a disciplinary core . . . driven by questions that are familiar to most writing professionals" and whose members understand the work of the department to be "disciplinary in that we are communicating knowledge and a way of knowing that writers across the many divides of genre and profession share" (Aronson and Hansen 2002, 58, 59). This expanded understanding of writing is part of the narrative of many writing majors and the reason given for their name and revisions and additions to it.

While the name of tracks and concentrations within English departments (table 12.3) reflects a slower change, the replacement of the word "Composition" with the word "Writing" by 2009 clearly reflected a significant shift in the major. In 2015, of the 52 majors whose titles were "English major, with a concentration/track/etc. in . . . ," only three included "Rhetoric and Composition" instead of "writing" as part of that title (two others include the word "Composition" but not "Rhetoric"). In addition, of the 41 English department-based writing majors that do not identify themselves explicitly as "English," 39 include the word "Writing" or "Written" in their name, while the remaining two are both identified as "Rhetoric." One includes the word "Composition" in its name (see table 12.3).

As table 12.3 shows, most of the English-plus-writing majors and separate writing majors housed within English departments list more than one field within their name, but more include "rhetoric" than "professional," "technical," or "communication." While the title of the major does not directly reveal the program philosophy or guiding theories or thresholds, it does reveal the public face of the major, serving as PR for the department and program and as professional certification for students who earn the major. The addition of words to the name of the major reveals in important ways how our thinking is evolving as the discipline evolves. Based on the 2015 list, for example (table 12.2 and table 12.3), it would appear that professional writing is being deemphasized, yet we see no significant reduction in the number of professional writing *courses* in majors tracked by Deborah Balzhiser (2009) and discussed by Balzhiser and Susan McLeod (Balzhiser and McLeod 2010), just a deemphasis of the name. (See table 12.4, also.) Instead, the names of majors,

Table 12.4. Response to "What areas of writing can students specialize in as part of your major?"

|  | Count (n = 230) | Percent |
| --- | --- | --- |
| Creative writing | 176 | 76.52 |
| Professional writing | 143 | 62.17 |
| Rhetoric/Composition | 78 | 33.91 |
| Technical writing | 72 | 31.30 |
| Journalism | 15 | 6.52 |
| Digital / new media writing | 11 | 4.78 |
| Other | 4 | 1.74 |

Source: Based on information in the National Census of Writing database (writingcensus.swarthmore.edu).

tracks, and concentrations are growing longer and more inclusive. Adding "writing," "rhetoric" or other kinds of activity (such as "media writing") appears to signal that the major focuses on both the activity of producing different genres of writing and the study of that writing.

It is for this reason that some favor the term "Writing Studies" to describe the major, the term adopted by the Association of Undergraduate Rhetoric and Writing Studies Majors (n.d.), an affiliate of the Master's Degree Consortium of Writing Studies Specialists. The editors of *Coming of Age* likewise referred to both the major and the discipline as "Writing Studies" (Shamoon et al. 2000); today it is increasingly also in use to mark a new kind of first-year writing course focused on writing about writing that is sometimes included as an introductory course for the major. And of course, the term "Writing Studies" evokes staunchly interdisciplinary programs such as gender studies and environmental studies, a model of interdisciplinarity that we also see in many writing majors. When 131 of 135 majors include the word "writing" in their name, frequently marking the kinds of broader mission described at Rowan by including other terms to show the breadth of their offerings, it may be time to reconsider not just the name of the major but also the name of the discipline. The term "Writing Studies" could ultimately serve as an umbrella term to replace the many categories of writing included in the name of most current writing majors in a way that "Composition" or "Composition and Rhetoric" cannot. As the discipline considers its own identity and ways its definition can include the many forms of written communication and rhetoric reflected in our research, the term "Writing Studies" may also be a better way to define the discipline just as it more accurately defines the major.

## NARRATIVE: DEFINING THE MAJOR
*Organization and Content*

The issue of content is at the heart of efforts to define the major, reflected in the name and often shaped by local needs, resources, and constraints. In 2000, *Coming of Age* argued for an intentional content and structure for the major. Rebecca Moore Howard explains that "rather than choosing a selection of courses from a smorgasbord of possibilities, we suggest that faculty develop a structure for the advanced curriculum, and then within that structure, choose courses that match faculty and student interests" (Howard 2000, xvi). In an early version of crowdsourcing, the proposed content was shaped from the very smorgasbord of courses submitted to the collection in addition to an analysis of the issues dominating the CCCC Conference program in the late 1990s: theoretical and historical understanding of writing as a discipline, preparation for careers as writers, and preparation for participation in public and civic affairs through writing. The editors proposed that all advanced writing curricula be developed locally but also include three common dimensions by which the major might be recognized: disciplinary, public, and professional. Helen Foster makes a similar claim for a major that balances local contingencies and national identity, while noting that such a balance will be hard to achieve (Foster 2012). Howard calls for graduates of advanced writing programs to be given "a reflexive sense of themselves as writers; with a historical understanding of the profession of writing; with a sense of the writer's responsibilities to audience, self, and community; and with tools for entering the profession of writing" (xv). Similarly, Moriarty (2012) urged the development of majors that avoid "a purely professional, practical, or academic emphasis," arguing instead for programs organized with civic rhetoric at their hearts and shaping their outcomes, and Tim Peeples (2012) urged majors to find a balance between professional writing and rhetoric to produce well-rounded majors. This focus on what students should understand, rather than what they should know, foreshadows the discussion of threshold concepts described by Scott and Wardle (2015) at Central Florida.

New and revised majors seem to be intentionally or unintentionally striving for this kind of balance, as the examples in *Writing Majors* show, and many long-standing majors have revised their programs in the last half decade (see Brooks, Zhao, and Braniger 2010; Delli Carpini 2007; L'Eplattenier and Jensen 2015; Livesey and Watts 2015; O'Neill and Mallonee 2015; Perron, Rist, and Loewe 2015). Obviously this change reflects larger developments in the field as courses in digital studies and emerging media are added along with writing for the web and courses that study and/or generate text for social media. It also reflects deepening understanding of the employment market for those with degrees in writing and communication. Today it is no longer sufficient to study journalism; one must study images and design and understand how to report information on different platforms. As Matthew Livesey and Julie Watts put it, "careers in our field now routinely involve a host of communication practices far beyond the drafting of a printed user manual . . . today's practitioners repurpose content for emerging media, collaborate across disciplinary lines, and face a never-ending learning curve as new technologies develop" (Livesey and Watts 2015, 87). Whether statistically likely or not, the prevailing claim that graduates will change careers (not jobs) at least six times in their working lives has been picked up by those designing majors in writing, who emphasize the need to prepare students for those changes. In fact, as far back as 1999, Linda Shamoon's (2000) interviews with people who identified their profession as "writer" revealed that even then, the writers reported a series of huge career shifts. As a consequence, those interviewees stressed the need for colleges and universities to provide not just specialty professional and technical writing courses, but also preparation for a range of different writing-related fields, both "a more conscious awareness of the broad-based expertise of the writing professional" and "frames for understanding rhetoric and for participating in various discourse communities" that will also enable them to "anticipate and cope" with developments in the field (50–51).

Whatever the complex interplay of reasons for the changes, to look at the 135 writing majors in 2015 is to see a lot more coherence than difference in terms of the kind and range of courses offered, as noted above. This is reinforced by data from the 2015 National Census of Writing database (Gladstein and Fralix 2015). While the anonymous nature of most of the responses to the survey from which the database was formed allows us to trace patterns but only follow up with those who gave signed permission for researchers to do so, the responses to questions concerning the existence of a writing major and the available emphases is still relevant (see table 12.4). Some of the programs that identify themselves as having a writing major only offer majors, tracks, or concentrations in creative writing, reflected in the fact that 176 of the 230 respondents listed creative writing as a possible emphasis and (probably) in the fact that 79 percent of them identified their institutional home as English, in contrast to 69 percent of those on the 2015 CCCC list. Similarly, only 11 percent identify themselves as being located in a writing department, in contrast to 24 percent of those on the 2015 CCCC list (see table 12.1).

Allowing for the creative writing skew, the list of possible areas of study in the National Census does reveal similar patterns to what we might expect from 2015 program names (table 12.2 and table 12.3). Professional writing is included in about twice as many majors as is technical writing, rhetoric is included in about a third of them, and digital/new media is in about 5 percent. While the term "creative writing" generally includes nonfiction, fiction, and poetry, the survey did not allow respondents to distinguish between them. Many Writing Studies majors include nonfiction, which has some overlaps with journalism, a term that is generally used to indicate news reporting rather than the long-form and magazine articles of nonfiction (travel writing, food writing, nature/environmental writing, profiles and biographies, for example). Overall, the similarities are apparent between these studies, the CCCC list, and the National Census in terms of balance between content areas.

*Finding and Celebrating Difference*

In *What We Are Becoming*, Giberson and Moriarty (2010b) take the opposite position to Balzhiser and McLeod's article published that same year. Balzhiser and McLeod focused on the structural components of model majors and the belief that the writing major should be recognizable to outsiders by its structure and content. In contrast, in their introduction to the edited collection, Giberson and Moriarty celebrate the differences found in the majors they profile, adding that the proposals, curricular decisions, and requirements "become the practical embodiment of the programs we develop and the discipline those programs represent" (2). Giberson (2015) (who began serving on the CCCC Committee on the Major in 2011), repeats that claim with more force in his afterword to *Writing Majors*. Pondering the "unique, locally situated writing majors" described in the collection, he writes that "whether or not all members of the discipline would recognize a specific writing major as a 'real' writing major, the fact that it is identified as such *at that institution* makes it 'real' for the students who graduate with it" (242; my emphasis). This observation allows him to sidestep what he describes as the "macro-level" questions of Balzhiser and McLeod about how the discipline "is or should be reflected in this emerging thing called 'the writing major'" (241) and take the opposite position, that it is the discipline that should reflect the major.

By celebrating the unique aspects of each major and the multiple definitions of the discipline they collectively shape, Giberson appears to be deconstructing the possibility of a coherent disciplinary definition along with his rejection of the idea of a single definition for the major. Both the National Census data and the CCCC list allow us to classify majors based on difference, as did Dominic Delli Carpini (2007) using the categories "professional focus" and "liberal arts focus," which were adapted by Balzhiser and McLeod in 2010 as "professional/ rhetorical" and "liberal arts," mirroring the categories "liberal" and "technical" adopted by Campbell and Jacobs (2010). Yet the program descriptions in *Writing Majors* also point toward increasing coherency, and Campbell and Jacobs found both characteristics to some degree in each major. It may be that the emphasis on differences between majors in these and other studies obscures similarities and thereby the ways the writing major is reshaping itself. Delli Carpini (2007) suggests this trajectory as he describes the changes at York College of Pennsylvania. Under the header "beyond writing in the professions to writing as a discipline" he notes that the major at York was "originally conceived and marketed as a pre-professional program," but only four years into its existence it began to "assert itself as a site of humanistic inquiry as well as a site of career development" (17), and rhetorical and writing theory courses were added. Of course, some programs already included a mix of professional and humanities courses as a consequence of their fraught beginnings (see L'Eplattenier and Jensen's [2015] discussion of the BA in Professional and Technical Writing at the University of Arkansas at Little Rock, 2015; and Smitherman, Mongno, and Payne's [2015] discussion of the Department of Writing at the University of Central Arkansas). However, others have added one or the other to balance the program. Livesey and Watts (2015) describe a program revision of the technical communications major at the University of Wisconsin–Stout in 2010 due to a decline in enrollments, leading to a renamed degree ("Professional Communications and Emerging Media") and the addition of concentrations in applied journalism and digital humanities to the continuing technical communications courses. Overall, these narratives suggest that the move is clearly toward more inclusion and diversity of writing options *within* majors rather than increasing differences between them.

Balzhiser and McLeod note that in 2008, of the twenty-seven writing majors they define as "liberal arts writing majors," twenty-one included required courses in technical, business, or workplace writing, or organizational communication; these courses were required in all of the "professional/rhetorical writing majors," but to find them in 78 percent of the majors classified as *liberal arts* reveals an important overlap. Similarly, they report that 39 percent of the professional majors require courses in "news writing/magazine writing/journalism" while 37 percent of the liberal arts focused majors also require them. While literary criticism and theory, fiction, poetry, and general creative writing dominate the liberal-arts-focused majors studied by Balzhiser and McLeod (2010), they are not absent from the professional majors. Other courses such as document design and new media writing do exist in one category and not the other (421), but a focus on the overlaps between Balzhiser and McLeod's categories allows us to think about what is common to all of the writing majors, while the many published program profiles allow us to track what has been added in the last half decade. A focus on these commonalities may facilitate the articulation of an equally broadly defined discipline within which these evolving majors can find a home.

## CONCLUSION

Despite his celebration of difference, Giberson (2015) ends his "Afterword" to *Writing Majors* with a call for new majors to exhibit a "thoughtful and intentional" approach (242), including consideration of the way program goals and outcomes relate to the discipline and the way "disciplinary values" will be "foregrounded" in the major (244). In 2004 Yancey called for a new curriculum reflected in a major that "has as its goal the creation of thoughtful, informed, technologically adept writing publics" (308), and before her the editors of *Coming of Age* called for a curriculum that produces graduates with "a reflexive sense of themselves as writers; with a historical understanding of the profession of writing; with a sense of the writer's responsibilities to audience, self, and community; and with tools for entering the profession of writing" (Shamoon et al. 2000, xv). This focus on the kinds of writers a Writing Studies major should produce combines with the kinds of writers Yancey called on the full curriculum to produce and indicates the importance of the discussion of threshold concepts and the major begun by Scott and Wardle (2015).

Scott and Wardle propose that discussion of threshold concepts (which they define as "foundational assumptions that inform learning across time," 124) can help faculty as they work to create a major. I'd like to go one step further and suggest that we use them to help us understand existing majors and map their relationship to the broader threshold concepts of the discipline as part of our exploration of disciplinary identity. Threshold concepts are more flexible than outcomes as an organizing principle for a major (Estrem 2015; Douglas et al., this volume), and the discussion of foundational concepts and how to move students through and beyond them is also more generative. It is a small step from the concept of writing and learning as processes to the concept that majors are constructed to facilitate the process of learning about writing, embracing the most primary threshold concept of our discipline, that writing is an activity and a subject of study (Adler-Kassner and Wardle 2015; Yancey, this collection). I believe that this concept is far more evident in the writing major than any other part of the discipline, and closer analysis will give us deeper insight into the ways the discipline is playing out on the ground. Early writing majors may have focused more on the activity of writing, whether creative or professional, but as the experience at York College (Delli Carpini 2007) and other majors show, students quickly move to a desire to understand, recognizing with us this duality of activity and subject of study and pulling the curriculum into balance. Intentionally designed majors or those under revision (see, for example, Estrem 2007; McCormick and Jones 2000) reflect that balance when they recognize that our discipline has "a body of knowledge (including scholarly, pedagogical, and professional knowledge)" and incorporate that into the curriculum as Scott and Wardle (2015, 125) describe.

Whether working toward a balance between genres or thinking through threshold concepts, the evolving major is not trying to teach every aspect of the body of knowledge accumulated in the discipline, and different programs emphasize some genres of writing more than others. If we can discuss the discipline and the major simultaneously and recognize that they both seek to share "what our field knows and . . . [an] understand[ing of] how to use that knowledge" as Linda Adler-Kassner and Elizabeth Wardle put it, it will matter less how many professional or technical writing courses are included in the major, or whether it includes literary criticism or media studies (Adler-Kassner and Wardle 2015, 7). In addition to helping the writing major move beyond debate about structure and content, threshold concepts and other theoretical frameworks included within the discussion of disciplinarity may also help to focus attention on the breadth encompassed in the discipline and the ways we might name it, and thereby clarify the relationship between the discipline and the major that should represent it.

*Note*
1. In this chapter I refer to the major as "the major in writing" because, while terminology is far from consistent across majors (see table 12.2), 97 percent of the majors being tracked include the term "writing" or "written" in their names

## References

Adler-Kassner, Linda, and Elizabeth Wardle. 2015. *Naming What We Know: Threshold Concepts of Writing Studies*. Logan: Utah State University Press.

Aronson, Anne, and Craig Hansen. 2002. "Writing Identity: The Independent Writing Program as a Disciplinary Center." In *A Field of Dreams: Independent Writing Programs and the Future of Composition Studies*, ed. Peggy O'Neill, Angela Crow, and Larry R. Burton, 50–61. Logan: Utah State University Press.

Association of Undergraduate Rhetoric and Writing Studies Majors. n.d. http://www.rhetoricandwritingundergraduatemajor.org. An affiliate of the Master's Degree Consortium Writing Studies Specialists. http://www.mdcwss.com.

Balzhiser, Deborah, and Susan H. McLeod. 2010. "The Undergraduate Writing Major: What Is It? What Should It Be?" *College Composition and Communication* 61 (3): 415–33.

Balzhiser, Deborah. 2009. "Writing Majors at a Glance." January 1, 2009. http://www.ncte.org/library/NCTEFiles/Groups/CCCC/Committees/Writing_Majors_Final.pdf.

Brooks, Randy, Peiling Zhao, and Carmella Braniger. 2010. "Redefining the Undergraduate English Writing Major: An Integrated Approach at a Small Comprehensive University." In *What We Are Becoming: Developments in Undergraduate Writing Majors*, ed. Greg A. Giberson and Thomas A. Moriarty, 32–49. Logan: Utah State University Press. https://doi.org/10.2307/j.ctt4cgppw.6.

Campbell, Lee, and Debra Jacobs. 2010. "Toward a Description of Undergraduate Writing Majors." In *What We Are Becoming: Developments in Undergraduate Writing Majors*, ed. Greg A. Giberson and Thomas A. Moriarty, 277–86. Logan: Utah State University Press. https://doi.org/10.2307/j.ctt4cgppw.19.

Carabelli, Jason. 2011. "Undergraduate Writing Majors: Opening Space for New Voices." Conference on College Composition and Communication, Atlanta, April 8.

Conference on College Composition and Communication Committee on the Major in Writing and Rhetoric. 2016. http://cccc.ncte.org/cccc/committees/majorrhetcomp.

Courtney, Jennifer, Deb Martin, and Diane Penrod. 2010. "The Writing Arts Major: A Work in Process." In *What We Are Becoming: Developments in Undergraduate Writing Majors*, ed. Greg A. Giberson and Thomas A. Moriarty, 243–59. Logan: Utah State University Press. https://doi.org/10.2307/j.ctt4cgppw.17.

Crowley, Sharon. 1998. *Composition in the University: Historical and Polemical Essays*. Pittsburgh: University of Pittsburgh Press. https://doi.org/10.2307/j.ctt5hjpc7.

Downs, Doug. 2001. "Writing Majors (And Tracks): A Starter List." October 29, 2001. Accessed December 1, 2015. Accessed via the Internet Archive at http://web.archive.org/web/20020329080652/http://www.cc.utah.edu/~dd4/writing_majors.html.

Delli Carpini, Dominic. 2007. "Re-Writing the Humanities: The Writing Major's Effect upon Under graduate Studies in English Departments." *Composition Studies* 35 (1): 15–36.

Estrem, Heidi. 2007. "Growing Pains: The Writing Major in Composition and Rhetoric." *Composition Studies* 35 (1).

Estrem, Heidi. 2015. "Threshold Concepts and Student Learning Outcomes." In *Naming What We Know Threshold Concepts of Writing Studies*, ed. Linda Adler-Kassner and Elizabeth Wardle, 89–104. Logan: Utah State University Press; 10.7330/9780874219907.c006.

Freeman, Traci. 2011. "Fraught Relations between Professional-Technical Writing and Writing Writ-Large." Conference on College Composition and Communication, Atlanta, April 7.

Fischer, Ruth Overman, and Christopher J. Thaiss. 2000. "Advancing Writing at GMU: Responding to Community Needs, Encouraging Faculty Interests." In *Coming of Age: The Advanced Writing Curriculum*, ed. Linda K. Shamoon, Rebecca Moore Howard, Sandra Jamieson, and Robert A. Schwegler, 139. Portsmouth, NH: Heinemann Boynton/Cook.

Foster, Helen. 2012. "The Possibility for Compromise: Balancing Local Contingencies with National Identity." Roundtable discussion on Writing Major Outcomes. Conference on College Composition and Communication, St. Louis, March 22.

Genova, Gina L., and Susan McLeod. 2006. "Updated Writing Majors at a Glance." PDF accessed via the Internet Archive at https://web.archive.org/web/20060903150313/http://www.writing.ucsb.edu/faculty/mcleod/documents/Writing_Majors_Final.doc.

Giberson, Gregory A. 2015. "Afterword." In *Writing Majors: Eighteen Program Profiles*, ed. Gregory A. Giberson, Jim Nugent, and Lori Ostergaard, 241–48. Logan: Utah State University Press.

Giberson, Greg A., and Thomas A. Moriarty. 2010a. "Forging Connections among Undergraduate Writing Majors." In *What We Are Becoming: Developments in Undergraduate Writing Majors*, ed. Greg A. Giberson and Thomas A. Moriarty, 1–10. Logan: Utah State University Press. https://doi.org/10.2307/j.ctt4cgppw.4.

Giberson, Greg A., and Thomas A. Moriarty, eds. 2010b. *What We Are Becoming: Developments in Undergraduate Writing Majors*. Logan: Utah State University Press. https://doi.org/10.2307/j.ctt4cgppw.

Giberson, Gregory A., Jim Nugent, and Lori Ostergaard, eds. 2015. *Writing Majors: Eighteen Program Profiles*. Logan: Utah State University Press.

Gladstein, Jill, and Brandon Fralix. 2015. The National Census of Writing Database. http://writingcensus.swarthmore.edu.

Haven, Chris. 2011. "Authors in Depth: Literature for Writing Majors." Conference on College Composition and Communication, Atlanta, April 9.

Howard, Rebecca Moore. 2000. "History, Politics, Pedagogy, and Advanced Writing." In *Coming of Age: The Advanced Writing Curriculum*, ed. Linda K. Shamoon, Rebecca Moore Howard, Sandra Jamieson, and Robert A. Schwegler, xiii–xxii. Portsmouth, NH: Heinemann Boynton/Cook.

Howard, Rebecca Moore. 2007. "Curricular Activism: The Writing Major as Counterdiscourse." *Composition Studies* 35 (1): 41–52.

Jamieson, Sandra. 2015. "Simple List of Writing Majors—CCCC Committee on the Major in Writing and Rhetoric." November.

Jamieson, Sandra. 2004. "The Vertical Writing Curriculum: Theory and Practice." Panel on the Major in Composition and Rhetoric, Annual Convention of the Modern Language Association, Philadelphia, December 29.

L'Eplattenier, Barbara, and George H. Jensen. 2015. "Reshaping the BA in Professional and Technical Writing at the University of Arkansas at Little Rock." In *Writing Majors: Eighteen Program Profiles*, ed. Gregory A. Giberson, Jim Nugent, and Lori Ostergaard, 22–35. Logan: Utah State University Press.

Livesey, Matthew, and Julie Watts. 2015. "Embracing the Humanities: Expanding a Technical Communication Program at the University of Wisconsin–Stout." In *Writing Majors: Eighteen Program Profiles*, ed. Gregory A. Giberson, Jim Nugent, and Lori Ostergaard, 85–97. Logan: Utah State University Press.

McCormick, Kathleen, and Donald C. Jones. 2000. "Developing a Professional and Technical Writing Major That Integrates Composition Theory, Literacy Theory, and Cultural Studies." In *Coming of Age: The Advanced Writing Curriculum*, ed. Linda K. Shamoon, Rebecca Moore Howard, Sandra Jamieson, and Robert A. Schwegler. CD-ROM. Portsmouth, NH: Heinemann Boynton/Cook.

McLeod, Susan M. 2010. "Afterword." In *What We Are Becoming: Developments in Undergraduate Writing Majors*, ed. Greg A. Giberson and Thomas A. Moriarty, 287–89. Logan: Utah State University Press. https://doi.org/10.2307/j.ctt4cgppw.20.

McLeod, Susan, Barbara L'Eplattenier, Barry Maid, Keith Miller, Deborah Balzhiser, and Sandra Jamieson. 2007. "Reviewing, Revamping and Creating Undergraduate Majors: Designing Gateway and Capstone Courses for the Writing Major." Half-day workshop. *Annual Convention of the Council of Writing Program Administrators*. Tempe, AZ, July 15.

McLeod, Susan, Barbara L'Eplattenier, Barry Maid, Keith Miller, Deborah Balzhiser, and Sandra Jamieson. 2008. "Creating the Intentional Writing Major: Models and Recommendations." Half-day preconvention workshop. *Annual Convention of the Conference on College Composition and Communication.* New Orleans, April 2.

Moriarty, Thomas A. 2012. "Recovering Rhetoric and Finding a Focus." Roundtable discussion on Writing Major Outcomes. Conference on College Composition and Communication, St. Louis, March 22.

Neely, Michelle. 2011. "Is There a "There" There? Seeking Relatedness within the Rhetoric and Writing Undergraduate Major." Conference on College Composition and Communication, Atlanta, April 7.

O'Neill, Peggy, and Barbara Mallonee. 2015. "Reforming and Transforming Writing in the Liberal Arts Context: The Writing Department at Loyola University of Maryland." In *Writing Majors: Eighteen Program Profiles*, ed. Gregory A. Giberson, Jim Nugent, and Lori Ostergaard, 47–61. Logan: Utah State University Press. https://doi.org/10.7330/9780874219722.c004.

Peeples, Tim. 2012. "Balancing Professional Writing and Rhetoric in the Major and Its Outcomes." Roundtable discussion on Writing Major Outcomes. Conference on College Composition and Communication, St. Louis, March 22.

Perron, John, Mary Rist, and Drew M. Loewe. 2015. "From 'Emphasis' to Fourth-Largest Major: Learning from the Past, Present, and Future of the Writing Major at St. Edward's University." In *Writing Majors: Eighteen Program Profiles*, ed. Gregory A. Giberson, Jim Nugent, and Lori Ostergaard, 205–217. Logan: Utah State University Press. https://doi.org/10.7330/9780874219722.c016.

Phelps, Louise Wetherbee, and John Ackerman. 2010. "Making the Case for Disciplinarity in Rhetoric, Composition, and Writing Studies: The Visibility Project." *College Composition and Communication* 62 (1): 180–215. https://doi.org/10.2307/27917890.

Royer, Dan. 2011. "The Writing Major as Liberal Arts." Conference on College Composition and Communication, Atlanta, April 9.

Royer, Dan, Ellen Schendel, Chris Haven, and Christopher Toth. 2011. "Beyond Rhetoric and Composition: The Liberal Arts Writing Major." Panel description. Conference on College Composition and Communication, Atlanta, April 9.

Scott, J. Blake, and Elizabeth Wardle. 2015. "Using Threshold Concepts to Inform Writing and Rhetoric Undergraduate Majors The UCF Experiment." In *Naming What We Know: Threshold Concepts of Writing Studies*, ed. Linda Adler-Kassner and Elizabeth Wardle, 122–39. Logan: Utah State University Press. https://doi.org/10.7330/9780874219906.c008.

Shamoon, Linda K. 2000. "The Academic Effacement of a Career: 'Writer." In *Coming of Age: The Advanced Writing Curriculum*, ed. Linda K. Shamoon, Rebecca Moore Howard, Sandra Jamieson, and Robert A. Schwegler, 42–51. Portsmouth, NH: Heinemann Boynton/Cook.

Shamoon, Linda K., Rebecca Moore Howard, Sandra Jamieson, and Robert A. Schwegler, eds. 2000. *Coming of Age: The Advanced Writing Curriculum.* Portsmouth, NH: Heinemann Boynton/Cook.

Shamoon, Linda K., Rebecca Moore Howard, Sandra Jamieson, Robert A. Schwegler, Dianne Comisky, Nancy Nestor, and Kevin Brooks. 2002. "Designing the Vertical Writing Curriculum." Full-day preconvention workshop. *Annual Convention of the Conference on College Composition and Communication.* Chicago, March 20.

Shumaker, Arthur W. 1981. "How Can a Major in Composition Be Established?" *Journal of Advanced Composition* 2 (1–2): 139–46.

Smitherman, Carey E., Lisa Mongno, and Scott Payne. 2015. "Fifteen Years Strong: The Department of Writing at the University of Central Arkansas." In *Writing Majors: Eighteen Program Profiles*, ed. Gregory A. Giberson, Jim Nugent, and Lori Ostergaard, 62–72. Logan: Utah State University Press. https://doi.org/10.7330/9780874219722.c005.

Yancey, Kathleen Blake. 2004a. "CCCC Chair's Letter." *College Composition and Communication* 56 (2): 358–67.
Yancey, Kathleen Blake. 2004b. "Made Not Only in Words: Composition in a New Key." *College Composition and Communication* 56 (2): 297–328. https://doi.org/10.2307/4140651.

# 13
## RHETORIC AND COMPOSITION STUDIES AND LATINXS' LARGEST GROUP: MEXICAN AMERICANS

Jaime Armin Mejía

In this chapter,[1] I claim that the interests of Mexican Americans in the discipline of Rhetoric and Composition Studies have evolved slowly, delaying us from becoming fully incorporated in the discipline. Historical and geopolitical circumstances as well as deeply seated cultural misunderstandings have created and spread stereotypical beliefs about our ethnic identity that have been influential in keeping us from preserving important aspects of our ethnic identity. As I explain below, these circumstances and misunderstandings have created conflicts and tensions associated with Mexican Americans assimilating into mainstream American society. These tensions and conflicts have lingered and restrained many of us from becoming more integrally a part of academia and of our discipline. And because the discipline of Rhetoric and Composition Studies is largely situated at the college level, we as a discipline have not given enough attention to how ethnic groups such as Mexican Americans have become situated in our discipline.

As a Texas Mexican Chicano, I argue that what happens below and at the college level has a direct bearing on how we, as Mexican Americans, have been able to participate in our discipline. The mechanisms which have historically been developed for Mexican Americans assimilating into mainstream American society have primarily been situated in American schools. These schools, including colleges and universities, have had educational policies that have largely been built to keep us out rather than incorporating us as fully fledged members of mainstream American society. As the discipline of Rhetoric and Composition Studies evolved, it too has often walked hand in hand with educational policies and pedagogical approaches that haven't always been welcoming or willing to understand our distinct social, cultural, and historical circumstances. Instead, educational policies and pedagogical approaches have served as a way to discipline us into assimilating while stripping us of our cultural identity.

As assimilation became the coin of the educational realm, we as Mexican Americans, historically made up of and constituted by multiple generational waves of immigration throughout the twentieth and early twenty-first centuries, have been torn about what to do and whom to side with, while also being torn away from what constitutes our complex cultural and linguistic ethnic identity. To explain the place of Mexican Americans in our discipline, I begin by laying out how I entered and then became a member of Rhetoric and Composition Studies. I then delineate, in broad terms, the historical and geopolitical circumstances surrounding Mexican Americans and how these circumstances have had a direct bearing on our participation in Rhetoric and Composition Studies. My hope is that by better understanding these circumstances, our discipline can more deliberately move forward toward integrating us more integrally as an important part of our discipline. In the end, what I'm calling for is for our discipline, as part of its academic mission, to attend more to the rhetorical dimensions Mexican Americans have had to contend with to exist as equal members of our profession. By removing the misunderstandings and stereotypes that have long plagued us, we will see that Mexican Americans have much to contribute to our discipline.

As a Texas Mexican Chicano, I want to begin by saying that the alliances I choose, to the extent that I think I can, work to shape me as an academic, one whose contextual background history is bound up with my ethnic identity. In many respects, I am different from many of my fellow travelers in the discipline of Rhetoric and Composition Studies as well as with other Latinxs around the country and beyond. I believe I share more culturally with Latinxs in the United States than with Anglo-Americans in our profession, but to be an academic in this field, one to some extent has to go with the times and practice and think what others in our profession adopt as common theory and practice. How I have come to be situated in Rhetoric and Composition Studies, though, has changed over time because I certainly situate myself differently today than I did in the past when I was a graduate student.[2] Some of the changes I've undergone are more or less similar to what most folks in the profession have undergone in their careers in recent decades. Like many currently working in our discipline, I was initiated into the profession in graduate school and would undergo more initiation rites as I entered my tenure-track job. Today, many entering the profession of Rhetoric and Composition Studies are becoming professionalized in ways that did not exist over three decades ago when I was first exposed to what existed of our discipline. Even more initiation rites came my way as I gained tenure and then promotion to the status of associate professor, a status that I've held for many years now. But no matter what, with everything that has happened to me or that I've caused to happen, my ethnic identity has inevitably been a part of how I've constructed my academic identity in the discipline of Rhetoric and Composition Studies. I'm not the only one who has had this type of formative experience within our shared profession.

During my early years as a college English professor, I became more active in the Conference of College Composition and Communication (CCCC) than I previously thought I would mainly because a Chicana was hired by my department once I entered the tenure track. Like me, she too was hired to teach Chicanx Literature in the same department, after I'd already been here as an ABD PhD candidate. Since she took over the teaching of Chicanx Literature classes, my fate with respect to my ability to gain tenure by working in this marginalized academic area was cut off, so I in a sense was then forced to turn my attention elsewhere, in my case to Rhetoric and Composition Studies since this academic area was also one of the areas I chose to develop as a graduate student. Over time, I was extremely fortunate to have become active in this profession, particularly with the CCCC, where I've served in various capacities.[3] Much of my good fortune, of course, came from having taken my PhD graduate studies at The Ohio State University.

So as someone who entered graduate school with aspirations to pursue Chicanx literary studies, my professional career thus took a very different turn once I entered my tenure-track job, a job I've now held for twenty-seven years.[4] As a Chicano PhD candidate and then later as a Chicano assistant English professor, no other discipline within academia has drawn my attention more than Rhetoric and Composition Studies, even though I still remain a steady teacher of both American Literature and Chicanx Literature classes in my English Department here at Texas State University. Steady as well has been my interest in combining, in bringing together, Chicanx Studies with Rhetoric and Composition Studies, two academic areas that in no uncertain terms were quite marginalized within English Departments in the 1980s and early '90s. And as the years have rolled by, other Latinxs have shared this interest in bringing together what would otherwise be known as a hybridized merging of ethnic cultural studies and composition studies, with a focus on rhetoric studies entering our shared interests only in recent years. The social turn in Rhetoric and Composition Studies, which John Trimbur is said to have in part initiated, of course coincided with postmodern poststructuralist turns that other disciplines, including other areas in what would become English Studies, were also taking shape at about that same time.

Over time, as many have noted, Rhetoric and Composition Studies became more professionalized as an academic discipline, with more universities creating graduate programs and with many of these programs admitting more Latinx PhD students. With this development, admittedly only a small incremental development, we have seen a shift away from seeing Latinx scholars and graduate students interested in developing composition pedagogies specifically geared toward Latinx college students. Recent years have instead seen more Latinxs in our discipline engaging in rhetorical studies specifically focusing on Latinx cultural and political issues such as the changing definition of citizenship and ill-conceived US immigration policies. Leading us in this area and by some considered the foremost Latinx rhetorician in the United States, Ralph Cintron many years ago announced the death knell to Latinxs' interest in composition studies. What Cintron said, to anyone caring to listen to what he had to say, was that composition studies for Latinxs had run its course and no longer had any credible scholarly interest for us.

Shortly after Cintron made this influential pronouncement, Cristina Kirklighter, Diana Cárdenas, and Susan Wolff Murphy published a landmark coedited volume of essays (Kirklighter et al. 2007). This small volume presented pedagogical offerings to teaching college composition at Hispanic Serving Institutions (HSIs).[5] Its offerings were interesting because some of them included pedagogical approaches to teaching college composition that were rather remarkable and long overdue. For instance, one approach, situated in south Florida, was remarkable because it entertained teaching composition by having almost everything in class delivered in the students' first language, namely, in Spanish.[6] To bridge their students' understanding of how to go about composing essays in English, this approach called for starting with Spanish and gradually transitioning to English. Few if any of the students referenced in this extraordinary bilingual approach, of course, were Mexican Americans.

Another approach in this important coedited volume, this one situated in far west Texas and along the border, would also acknowledge that many of the students situated at that school were in fact ESL/ELL students who required more of a bilingual approach to ease them into academia and college-level writing. This study by Isabel Baca had nothing but Mexican-origin students, but here the question arising for me is just how much of an investment the discipline of Rhetoric and Composition Studies has made in developing theoretical and pedagogical approaches to meet the needs of students like these. Other questions to ask are just how many students like these there are and whether they constitute a significant number. While our discipline created and then sort of backed "The Students' Right to Their Own Language" resolution, the truth is that this resolution has largely been ignored. Except for the rather small number of studies in volumes such as the one where these studies about Latinxs in HSIs come from, no significant inroads have been made in developing theoretical and pedagogical approaches that have caught on and spread across the profession. Except for Isabel Baca's study, I know of no other Latinx scholar who has been sought after for having developed such approaches, though studies of this type are once again beginning to see the light of day.[7]

Another essay from this same collection dealing with HSIs, this one by Beatrice Méndez-Newman, provides a sampling of a Mexican American student's writing that is remarkable because of its skillfully wrought use of code-switching—between English and Spanish. This study is not the first to claim that among some Latinxs, including of course Mexican Americans, code-switching has long existed and should be used, encouraged, and legitimized as a form of academic discourse in college composition classes. It's certainly a shame that such legitimation of code-switching between English and Spanish has yet to happen, even as strands of research interest have taken hold of what's now called code-meshing, a form of code-switching incorporating African American English vernacular, now seen as a completely separate and completely autonomous language instead of as just a dialect of English, standing on the same level with standard English.

Before Kirklighter et al.'s collection of essays came out, several other Latinxs, including me, published different pedagogical takes on teaching Latinxs first-year English college composition. If one were to review issues of *College English* and the *CCC* journal from the 1960s and '70s, one would find a scattering of essays celebrating Mexican American code-switching. It's interesting to think about what must have gone through the minds of editors and reviewers of manuscript submissions of these journals during that countercultural time that they agreed to go to press with studies such as these. Since and before those formative times, there has been an almost absolute and deafening silence about the existence, needs, and scholarly contributions of Latinxs, including, of course, Mexican Americans. While some Latinxs have long been professionally involved within our profession's main organizations (CCCC and NCTE), with the late Mike Anzaldúa from Del Mar College in Corpus Christi, Texas, serving as secretary of the CCCC in the 1980s, our numbers have always been small, even today.

For instance, we can see how deep, or more accurately, how shallow, the professional involvement of Latinxs in our discipline has been by reviewing a recent issue (June 2015) of the *CCC* journal, the leading journal in our discipline. There, one sees a list of all the manuscript reviewers of the previous year, yet by my count, only two Latinxs are listed: Raúl Sánchez, a Cuban American, and me, a Texas Mexican Chicano—in some respects the usual suspects, and with no Latinas nor Latinx LGBT folk. Over the years, I doubt that that number of Latinx manuscript reviewers has at all exceeded in number or diversity what we find in 2015. Our presence as members of the editorial boards of such journals has been tokenizingly small as well. Trying to understand the place of Latinxs in our profession becomes all the more difficult when there are so few of us apparently involved in shaping the path our discipline is to follow in crucial places such as our most important journals. In the history of the CCCC, as Victor Villanueva is always reminding us, there has only been one Latinx Chair of the CCCC—Victor Villanueva himself—as well as only one Latinx recognized and given the CCCC's prestigious Exemplar Award—once again, Victor Villanueva. That the need is great for Latinxs to be participants in our academic discipline should go without saying, but it bears repeating that the need for more of us participate has been stalled by stubborn circumstances that refuse to go away on their own. We see historical reasons for our exclusion in the works of one of our discipline's pioneers, Mina Shaughnessy.

After Mina Shaughnessy (1977) published her monumental *Errors and Expectations* in 1977, many Latinxs such as myself came to believe that we had a duty to follow her professional lead and develop basic writing pedagogical approaches for students from poor backgrounds in need of such approaches. Her work coincided with Open Admissions college programs, which opened up many colleges and universities to formerly excluded, low-income minority students. For some Latinxs, Richard Rodriguez's (1978) essay in *College English* in 1978 also influenced many of us to romanticize our place within academia, as he was one of the first Mexican Americans, a son of immigrants, to talk about our much disputed place in academia.[8] I was one of probably many other Latinxs who was flatly uncritical of Rodriguez's stances against Bilingual Education programs and Affirmative Action policies. The Reagan years would have to pass before I'd gain that critical perspective against Rodriguez, one that came after a slew of Chicanx literary critics, including the late Tomás Rivera, made their views known in various venues.

Since that time and for some decades now, Open Admissions and Affirmative Action policies were implemented, then curtailed, and in some places altogether eliminated. Many college English Departments would take up the challenge of teaching underprepared students, most of them coming from communities where Jim Crow racism resulted in minority students coming from underfunded segregated public schools as well as from segregated neighborhoods. Since the social dynamics in America were often cast in black-and-white terms, opening up our perspective to include brown folk so as to imagine just who can participate and what they can bring to our discipline's table couldn't have been more important at that time in the early 1970s. Because Mexican American communities, too, had long suffered from the toxic effects of Jim Crow racism, many Mexican American students, before Shaughnessy's landmark study, required the attention Shaughnessy later brought to our discipline because they/we also came from Mexican Americans communities where Jim Crow thrived. The Civil Rights Movement created Open Admissions and Affirmative Action policies to help reverse Jim Crow racism and to open up much-needed opportunities for us to obtain higher educations. But as universities began taking on corporatized strategies in the 1980s, in effect creating a tiered system of higher education, top-tier universities and colleges eliminated basic writing classes altogether, relegating them to community colleges, where the grand majority of Latinxs enroll today.[9] The matriculation of Latinxs to four-year colleges and universities and then to graduate and professional schools, predictably enough in this strange democracy, has lagged behind.

Of course, at lower-tier schools, the faculty teaching composition classes, most of them white females, still remain the most undertrained and underpaid in our discipline. Funds for professional development at these schools for the most part remain, back then and even now, limited. Making matters even worse these days is the spread of dual-credit college classes in high schools where the investment in the professional training of composition teachers engaging minority students remains remarkably low. Research into the wisdom of how these dual-credit programs are run is only now beginning to take place, and since there will be so many minorities affected, the need for a push in this area of research to fuel ameliorated action in high school and university policies is needed. For if high school students are being sent into universities and then straight into upper-division college classes, where their skills in academic writing will truly be tested, those with the most at stake in terms of academic success will surely be placed in jeopardy.

The Editorial Board (2015) for the *New York Times*, for instance, recently brought attention to a national problem plaguing our high schools: "Most states still have weak curriculums and graduation requirements that make high school diplomas useless and that leave graduates unprepared for college, the job market or even meeting entry requirements for the Army" (Editorial Board 2015 ["The Counterfeit High School Diploma"]). They further state that "Nationally, graduation rates are rising—yet less than 40 percent of twelfth-graders are ready for math and reading at the college level" ("Counterfeit"). So rather than having our students gain more experience as writers of academic discourse in first-year composition classes, the rise of dual enrollment coupled with the increasingly higher costs of college, among other factors, are undercutting such valuable experience. If our discipline is to influence and change policies surrounding the creation of such reductive dual-credit programs so students are not shortchanged, then surely it will be seen as a force working for the good of all of society and not just the children of the wealthy whose stakes at achieving academic success are much lower than low-income college students.

For many Mexican American college students, certain stereotypes continue to plague us/them because another prevalent assumption operating in many schools has been that second-language (Spanish) interference has incapacitated many of us from gaining proficiency in writing in English at the college level. This perspective, in place for many decades now, is often held by those unfamiliar with the historical and cultural presence of Mexican Americans in the United States. Studies such as the ones discussed above have helped fuel this sinister assumption, even though the actual number of students who fit this kind of profile is considerably fewer than is often assumed. Great interest in ESL and ELL research has nevertheless once again become prevalent in certain college-level segments in our discipline, stemming no doubt from the pedagogical needs of many Mexican immigrant students currently in elementary, middle, and perhaps even high schools.

This strand of research in our discipline is, on the one hand, important, but it is one which amazes me, as I have come to realize that research into teaching writing to ELL college students, while definitely important, in practice might not be engaging as many Mexican American students as one might think. If college-track students are able to get past the college admission requirements at most colleges and universities, such as minimum scores on standardized high-stakes tests such as the SAT and ACT, how likely is it that they will require additional help with English Language Learning?[10] However, a greater pedagogical concern here, seldom acknowledged, much less implemented, is that the presence of Mexican-origin students in our classes is clearly dictating a need for pedagogical approaches that include rhetorical dimensions important to all Mexican Americans, no matter their "generation-since-immigration." One such pedagogical approach, a rhetorical one of course, would be having all FYC students, including Mexican Americans, analyze the question of assimilating mainstream American values at the cost of losing constituent parts of what for many of them is made up by their ethnic cultural values.

Moreover, in their landmark intergenerational and longitudinal study of urban Mexican Americans, prominent Chicanx sociologists Edward Telles and Vilma Ortiz have determined that over the last forty-plus years, Mexican Americans assimilate English by the second generation (Telles and Ortiz 2008). Conducted through interviews, taken twice, a generation apart, with thousands of the same respondents and their children a generation later, their study helps us understand the many reasons Mexican Americans lag behind other groups in terms of their educational success at all levels. What's also important to keep in mind is that when speaking of cohorts of Mexican Americans, a specific generational cohort could be representing people from different generations at the very same time. In other words, if one were to have twenty Mexican American students in the same FYC class, the odds are highly likely that these students could be representing different generations with highly disparate sociological as well as educational characteristics. That is, you could have a highly driven first-generation immigrant student sitting next to a complacent student whose family has resided in the United States for many generations. And of course, these students will be sitting alongside Anglo-American and African American students as well as students from other minority groups, further complicating how composition instructors should be developing Rhetoric and Composition pedagogies for their classes.

While assimilating English by the second generation and attaining proficiency with college-level academic writing are not entirely the same, any student's ability to gain the latter skill is obviously the result of training. This training is exactly what our discipline has spent so much of its energy developing almost since its inception. For if we as a profession already have the pedagogical means to teach students to develop their proficiency in academic writing—in English—then it's curious that, arguably, so many in our country still assume that Mexican

Americans require ESL and ELL approaches at the college level, unless it's not Mexican Americans who are the focus of their forays. Such forays into this kind of research in my view represent and symbolize a greater tension which exists educationally for Mexican Americans as an ethnic group. We, as Mexican Americans, have long been all assumed to be immigrants, but for us as an ethnic group, it's worse than even that—we're now all assumed to be "illegal," all of us, irrespective of how many generations our families have lived and thrived on what's become known through war as American soil. It's not just that we're thought of by the Anglo-American mainstream as unable to assimilate; we're also thought of as people who should not be allowed to assimilate. Why else does our profession continue to disregard the rhetorical dimensions that intersect with the rhetorical dimensions constituting the identity of the dominant group? The central question here for Mexican Americans and Rhetoric and Composition Studies, then, revolves around assimilation. And the key rub that seemingly prohibits our assimilating is too often represented by what some still consider a foreign language, Spanish, despite generational demographic evidence to the contrary.

As members of a prominent American ethnic minority group, Mexican Americans have historically had to assimilate writing and rhetorical skills stemming from the dominant group, skills that apparently can only be expressed in English—and standard English at that. If we as Mexican Americans stubbornly refuse to give up Spanish and the Mexican rhetorical baggage constituting our cultural ethnic identity, we are often disciplined through the standardization of English, a standardization that is all too often expected and enforced in academia. Theoretically, assimilation involves an either/or dynamic. That we, or at least many among us in our discipline, largely refuse to engage and disrupt this either/or rhetorical dynamic that lies at the center of assimilation, of course, is what fundamentally keeps our ability to compromise at bay. If we don't entirely wish to assimilate to this standardization of English, then of course neither does our profession wish to assimilate the values of prominent ethnic groups such as Mexican Americans, a profession that has always sought to represent the values of the dominant Anglo-American group, its democratic yearnings notwithstanding. Democracy for the Anglo-American dominant group has always meant and has almost always intended that "Others" should assimilate Anglo-American values, values expressed almost always exclusively in English and with all the cultural and rhetorical baggage it represents. I say almost exclusively because Latin and classical Greek are and have always been allowed without question.

What's so ironic about this whole rhetorical situation between the dominant group and Mexican Americans, with respect to Mexican Americans within our discipline today, is that recent generations of Mexican Americans are hardly and barely bilingual at all. So, irrespective of what many may say, the dominant group through its educational systems has largely succeeded in converting the most recent generations of Mexican Americans into monolingual English-speaking folk. Many in these generations know no Spanish, nor are they/we literate in Spanish in the same way we wish for them/us to be literate in English. So even if their souls depended on being literate in Spanish, they'd not be saved. Not all Mexican Americans are like this, of course, but more than I would care to think about are, and increasingly so, unless we as a discipline can find a way to value bilingualism, irrespective of what that "other" language is. And many Mexican Americans from these generations are the same students we encounter in our first-year English college composition classes. Most of these students very well know about this erased aspect of their cultural identity and, remarkably enough, will often feel guilty about having arrived at such a monolingual state of being by the time they get to college.[11]

What distinguishes Latinxs, particularly Mexican Americans, and the work we do in this discipline and sets us apart from African Americans and folks from around the world is our own set of historical, social, political, economic, and cultural circumstances, unique to us. In some respects, we hold, in theory and practice, similarities with those working internationally to develop composition and rhetorical approaches that have arisen because of and despite British and American colonialism. But I must emphasize that our circumstances, as Latinxs, are substantially and critically different from those from around the world, for we, as Latinxs and unlike folks from around the world, exist and have long existed within the belly of an imperial beast here on what's become US soil. In fact, we exist and have existed within the bellies of several imperial beasts. And yet despite our circumstances, many of us have indeed resisted, sometimes unsuccessfully, the great demon that has long sought to break and keep us down through the grand Modernist theory of assimilation. Among all Latinxs, though, Mexican Americans make up 65 percent,[12] a demographic fact sometimes lost on many Latinxs speaking on our collective behalf within our discipline. The next-largest group, Puerto Ricans, constitute only 9.2 percent (Motel and Patten 2012).[13]

So when referring to Mexican Americans as constituting the largest of all Latinx groups, the single-most-important factor influencing our collective identity as Mexican Americans is the fact that our history has had wave after wave after wave of immigration throughout the twentieth century and into the twenty-first. This historical fact, unlike other immigrant groups, distinguishes the history of Mexican immigration. Immigrants from Europe in the late nineteenth century and early twentieth never consistently had the large and recurring waves of immigration distinguishing Mexicans who came and settled in the United States, with some arriving in what's now the United States well before Plymouth Rock in 1620. And what these waves of Mexican immigrants brought and continue bringing with them, again and again, is Spanish, Catholicism, and hybridized indigenous cultural roots. Since the only reason these waves of Mexican immigrants were allowed to stay was our ability to supply cheap labor, there was never any intention, on the part of the dominant group in this country, of ever easing our assimilation into mainstream Anglo-American society. And because of the highly racialized reception, many waves of Mexican immigration would suffer, and still suffer, assimilating into mainstream American society wasn't always desired, either.

Why assimilate into a mainstream society wherein you and your culture are treated so despicably? Studies into the history of earlier waves of European immigration show that they completely assimilated into Anglo-American mainstream society by the third generation.[14] Such has never really been the case for Mexican immigrants, something that puzzled sociologists for a long time because they mistakenly based their analysis of Mexican immigrant assimilation on European models of assimilation. While European groups did suffer ethnic discrimination—often due to language, class, and cultural differences—they seldom suffered the racial discrimination they in turn inflicted and continue inflicting on Mexican immigrants and the many generations of their children who have grown up and settled here. And because Mexico has had a longer history of miscegenation than Anglo-America, there are and have long been some Mexicans and Mexican Americans who easily pass as white European Americans. Hybridization among peoples happens in degrees, often painfully so. Just ask African Americans.

Among Mexican Americans throughout the United States, though, significant contextual historical differences exist. While I would like to speak here for all Latinx groups, I can't because I simply don't know enough to be even minimally authoritative about groups other than Mexican Americans. But even then, as I said, differences among Mexican Americans nationally vary, sometimes considerably. For instance, as recently as October 16, 2015, renowned Chicana writer Sandra Cisneros stated something rather remarkable in an interview: she'd read that New Mexicans don't like Mexicans, and that since she's culturally a Mexican, that's why she'd decided not to move there, to Española, in northern New Mexico, after having lived in San Antonio, Texas, for decades. In that same interview in *Pasatiempo*, according to interviewer Jennifer Levin, Cisneros (2015)

> talked at some length about her feelings about being a writer and person of color in the United States. "We never feel welcomed or at home. You never feel like the Statue of Liberty has opened its arms for you. You feel conflicted about the Pledge of Allegiance, because it's not for you. There was one day I felt at home in America, and that was the day the Twin Towers fell. I really felt the pain, and I felt American." She displayed an American flag outside her house for the first time that day, after a lifetime of feeling that the flag represented the superior attitude many Americans take toward other cultures and countries. "In 24 hours, there were signs around San Antonio saying 'God bless America,' and I knew that meant 'God bless us and not you,' so I took the flag down. I got a banner made that said 'God bless everyone.'"

There is no doubt that many Mexican Americans would disagree with Cisneros' (2015) perspective about how much we're welcomed in the United States, a perspective that's not just about New Mexicans' attitudes toward Mexicans, but also about the lack of a positive and welcoming reception people of color feel in America—and in the CCCC. Like with Cisneros, the feeling of being part of the fabric of what constitutes mainstream America can be extended to how many Mexican Americans feel in and with the discipline of Rhetoric and Composition Studies. This sentiment continues to be quite common. In a word, what has long plagued Mexican Americans and perhaps some of the other Latinx groups as well as people of color generally in the United States and in the CCCC is something commonly known as Assimilation.

There is much confusion about just what we have to do to be a part of not just this nation but also this discipline. There are tremendous tensions and sometimes bitter conflicts over how much we as Mexican Americans should assimilate, over how worthwhile it would be for us to do so. There are many reasons, of course, for such conflicts and tensions over how much or whether or not we should completely assimilate, if that's even possible. Our discipline's central mission historically, as I understand it, has been to develop within our students the literacy skills needed for them to navigate their way successfully in academia and in the mainstream of American society. The standardization of English, more often than not, has been at the heart of this intent to develop such important composition and rhetorical skills.

There is no doubt that since the advent of the Chicano movement in the late 1960s, when most Mexican Americans resided in major urban areas in the American Southwest, there has been ardent resistance to assimilating completely. Why? Well, there is a concrete historical record of our being negatively disciplined for maintaining and preserving important aspects of our Mexican cultural identity, an ethnic identity that has long held Spanish as a constitutive part. What assimilating into the Anglo-American mainstream has long meant for most Mexican Americans, then, is losing this most important part of our identity. Ironically, of course, not even Spanish is the native language that constitutively and historically constructed the identity of many Mexicans. Therein lies part of the confusion as well as the cause of much tension as well as of significant conflicts over assimilation. While the Anglo-American mainstream would have us entirely give up this most important part of our ethnic identity to become assimilated, what has nevertheless escaped most educators, for at least a century, is the fact that Mexican Americans make up a highly diverse demographic.

Moreover, since the 1980s, high numbers of Central Americans have also entered the United States due to the wars which have raged in those countries due to covert and the sometimes not-so-covert US involvement in their nations' sovereignty. Even there, the involvement of the United States has been forcing governments in Latin American countries to assimilate ideologically to American mainstream ways. Historically, America's foreign policy has advanced notions of America's Manifest Destiny and its Good Neighbor foreign policy to lead Latin America out of its "primitive" and Communist ways. More recently, of course, NAFTA has wreaked havoc on Mexico's economy and incited further waves of immigration, not just from Mexico, but from Central American and Caribbean countries as well as from South American countries that were not left unaffected. As a consequence, what Americans need to gain is a perspective that sees how the United States has been responsible for causing the many waves of Mexican and Central American immigration into the United States throughout the twentieth century, and continuing into the twenty-first. It's these waves that have created the diversity in our circumstances as Latinx American citizens. And once situated in this country, with a desire to enter academia as members of the discipline of Rhetoric and Composition Studies, our ethnic identity must undergo many negotiated adjustments, accommodations, if we are to be a part of our profession, of our discipline.

Imagine, if you will, a Mexican American son or daughter of New Mexico or of Texas or California as a graduate student in a leading PhD program in Rhetoric and Composition Studies. It could be anywhere, at Syracuse University, Purdue University, the University of Pittsburgh, The Ohio State University in Columbus, Arizona State University at Tempe, or the University of Texas at Austin. Even as recently as within a decade ago, just how many Rhetoric and Composition Studies tenured full professors would such a graduate student find, professors whose major research interest focused on the dynamics of Mexican American rhetorics? Or on innovative composition pedagogies specifically focusing on Mexican Americans residing in major urban areas in the American Southwest? What kind of curriculum, do you think, would such graduate students find? More specifically, what if these Mexican American graduate students identified as Chicanxs, folk whose political consciousness had long been raised before arriving at any of these leading PhD programs in our profession? To incite your imagination further, just think about the possibilities some African American graduate students have if they were to go and study with leading lights in African American Rhetoric and Composition Studies? With well-known scholars such as Geneva Smitherman or Keith Gilyard or Jackie Jones Royster or Shirley Logan, all of whom are leading lights in African American Rhetoric and Composition Studies?

If the discipline of Rhetoric and Composition Studies is to welcome and more fully advance the place of Mexican Americans into its midst, it's therefore important for us to keep in mind that since 1848, Mexican Americans were legally created into and granted de facto US citizenship by a momentous treaty—the Treaty of Guadalupe-Hidalgo. A little over half a century later, starting in 1910, the Mexican Revolution would initiate the first of many major waves of Mexican immigration into the United States. Those early twentieth-century waves of immigrants, as well as those which followed them, would find themselves received by prior waves of Mexicans as well as by those who were in what became the United States prior to 1848. Interestingly enough, the new territory and what much later became the state of New Mexico in 1912 would have the largest demographic of Mexicans in 1848. Turned into (Mexican) Americans by fiat, in the newly ceded Mexican territories the United States acquired through the auspices of the Mexican American War, their fate quickly turned dark for most of them. The acquisition of these territories through this war in part sought to expand the number of slave-holding states, with Texas being a principal prize for southern states, after its joining the Union in 1845. In the background of this major historical transition for Mexicans in the American Southwest, of course, we can't forget the major Native American tribes, who had inhabited these lands for millennia.

That New Mexicans don't like Mexicans today, as Cisneros has suggested, goes back to at least the eventual arrival of the Anglo after it was acquired as a territory, but that there has been wave after wave of Mexican immigrants in the twentieth century should also not be overlooked. As time has gone by, largely through the convenient neglect and absence of an intelligent US immigration policy, there are now significant concentrations of Mexican immigrants in most urban centers in the Southwest as well as in many other major cities throughout the entire United States. Regions such as the Northwest, the Midwest, and the South, and now even cities such as Atlanta and New York City, have for decades experienced a population growth that has long been fed by these waves of Mexican immigration that arrive, indeed are invited, to feed America's need for cheap exploitable labor. And over these previous decades, generation after generation of Mexican Americans, many descended from former Mexican immigrants, established themselves as US citizens, despite the incredible racism that has been categorically lodged against them, against us, throughout the United States. The 1930s saw the amazing deportation of hundreds of thousands of Mexicans, and the true racialized crime was that [Mexican] American citizens were also included in great numbers in this forced expulsion. But many of these deported were then invited back through the federally backed Bracero program that began in 1942 and lasted through 1964.

What this historical overview suggests is that any snapshot of an urban demographic of Mexican Americans will show a cohort comprised of Mexican Americans originating from many different "generations-since-immigration." The mixed cultural and mainstream experiences of Mexican Americans will likely always differ widely, from one Mexican American to the next. As Mexican Americans, we all come from succeeding waves of immigrants that have each carried different rhetorical baggage, depending on which generation-since-immigration we originate from. Scholars in Rhetoric and Composition Studies directing their attention to developing pedagogical approaches and culturally based rhetorical theories with Mexican Americans in mind, then, have tasks that call for understanding the highly complex rhetorical dynamism existing within this kind of highly diverse ethnic cohort. So when this diverse cohort enrolls in classes predominantly attended by mainstream Anglo-Americans, then the dynamism becomes considerably more complex. And being mixed in with students from the other Latin@ groups will complicate this highly charged rhetorical dynamics all the more.

The educational systems in most American public schools have by now largely succeeded in stripping a great deal of the ethnic cultural baggage of Mexican Americans, ethnic cultural baggage that has been instilled in us at home, as Richard Rodriguez once noted in his autobiographical work, *Hunger of Memory*. For if there's anything American public schools and universities have been good at, it's been succeeding in facilitating the demise, as I've previously noted, of an important ethnic group's center of identity. In the chapter from *Generations of Exclusion* devoted entirely to the education of Mexican Americans, sociologists Telles and Ortiz end their chapter by stating the following: "The low status we find among Mexican Americans of later generations occurs at the same time that they also experience diminishing attachment to Mexican culture, Spanish, and Catholicism. . . The cultural protections these may provide seem to wear off for most Mexican Americans by the third or fourth generation. Unlike European Americans, education gets worse as culture wears off—a potentially explosive combination" (134).

If Rhetoric and Composition Studies is to lead academia as a fully mature and humane discipline, in my view it should do more to open itself up to reversing the ill effects an either/or theory of assimilation has long had on Latinx groups and on the biggest of these Latinx ethnic groups—Mexican Americans.

Our discipline should also be aware that many Latinxs like me, a Texas Mexican Chicano, have clearly been affected and are still continuing to be adversely affected by the forces of assimilation that are pervasive in academia and in our discipline. For when an ethnic person has to exist and work in an academic environment where standard English and the rhetorical cultural baggage it carries are the coins of the realm, our discipline should recognize the tremendous willpower it takes to fight off those forces and sustain an ethnic identity that one has every right to own. In this country and in the discipline of Rhetoric and Composition Studies, such willpower should be celebrated. In the future, I trust that such acknowledgment and celebration will be a constituent part of what's at the heart of our discipline.

## Notes

1. There's a new nuanced way of spelling a term of self-identification for folks, who until recently, were previously known as Latinos or Latinas or Latin@s. The *x* in this new nuanced term is intended to cast aside the fixed gender suffix endings of an *a* or an *o*, which indicate female or male, respectively. Since folks' identification with gender is more fluid, the *x* is intended to signify folks who claim neither male nor female as terms of gender self-identification. Where this nuanced change originated, I don't know, but it's a recent change or nuance.

2. The change in how I've situated myself within the profession of Rhetoric and Composition Studies hasn't exactly paralleled how I've changed from a fanatic to a fan of the Dallas Cowboys, but it would be interesting to look more deeply into these changes. More about that later.
3. I served a term as well as an additional year on the CCCC Executive Committee, terms on the editorial boards of NCTE Publications as well as *College Composition and Communication*. I would also serve on different committees, sometimes more than once (Best Book of the Year Committee, twice; the Braddock Award Committee for choosing the best essay published in the CCC journal during that given year; and the Exemplar Award Committee, twice; and as well as a task force to settle on multicultural curricular principles, which never materialized after the task force was disbanded), all within the CCCC. I've also served for many years as a Stage I and II reviewer (the latter about ten times) of conference proposals for the CCCC as well as a reviewer of Rhetoric Society of America (RSA) conference proposals. I've been invited to write book reviews for *College English* and the *CCC* journal, and have reviewed many essay manuscripts for possible publication in these two journals. I have also been fortunate enough to review book-length manuscript projects, both single-authored and collections of essays by different authors, for different presses, most of these university presses.
4. I'd be willing to bet the ranch that less than a handful of Latinx English professors in Rhetoric and Composition Studies have held a college teaching job longer than twenty-five years.
5. The Hispanic Serving Institution is a federal designation that gives such institutions access to federal grants for conducting research associated with Latinxs.
6. Just imagine a research strand today in Rhetoric and Composition Studies that transitioned French or German students into English, and you can begin to see how remarkable this approach is.
7. Todd Ruecker's (2015) *Transiciones: Pathways of Latinas and Latinos Writing in High School and College*, is just one example of a recent study that explores pedagogy for Latinx. Another recent volume that enters this type of arena, a reader offering a broader, more nuanced approach to the rhetorical dynamics of multilingualism in academia by people of color through collected readings is *A Language and Power Reader: Representations of Race in a "Post-Racist" Era*, 2014, edited by Robert Eddy and Victor Villanueva (Eddy and Villanueva 2014).
8. Rodriguez would not be the first Mexican American to publish in *College English* or in the *CCC* journal, but no other Latinx, except for Victor Villanueva, has received as much attention as Rodriguez.
9. See Mary Soliday's (2002, 20) *The Politics of Remediation*, to get a better understanding of just how this elimination and marginalization of basic writing worked.
10. Of course, the place of these standardized tests, their value in predicting anything other than family income, is finally beginning to be questioned. That they're racially biased should go without saying, but I shall not be pursuing this question here; it's something better left for another time.
11. One must certainly acknowledge other strands of scholarship in our discipline that have arisen during the last decade and had a direct bearing on where Latinxs, especially Mexican Americans, stand in our discipline. These other strands of course include code-meshing or code-switching, as led by leading African American scholars such as Vershawn Young and Elaine Richardson, whose work follows the groundbreaking path that Geneva Smitherman began long ago. The inimitable Suresh Canagarajah, with his important introduction to the pluralization of English through what he's come to call world Englishes, has also been groundbreaking in recent years. Also included among these strands are significant technological

developments in multimodal composition with its important and diverse rhetorical dimensions. The development of these strands in recent years has impacted and has been impacted by the work of Latinx scholars within the discipline of Rhetoric and Composition Studies. Victor Villanueva, Raúl Sánchez, Damián Baca, René de los Santos, Adela Licona, Aja Martinez, Steven Alvarez, and Cruz Medina, among others, have published innovative rhetorical analyses of Mexican American as well as Mexican, Mesoamerican, and Latin American cultural dimensions that intersect with mainstream society, academia, and American popular culture. In addition to these scholars, there are also other scholars making important inroads into Latinx rhetorical dimensions. Several notable Latinx graduate students and newly minted PhDs from programs around the country will soon be making an impact of their own within Rhetoric and Composition Studies. Among these are Ana Milena Ribero, José Cortez, Sonia Arellano, James Chase Sanchez, Romeo García, and, notably, Gabriela Raquel Ríos.

12. Sociologists Motel and Patten, in their cited study, inform us that "Among the 50.7 million Hispanics in the United States, nearly two-thirds (65%), or 33 million, self-identify as being of Mexican origin, according to tabulations of the 2010 American Community Survey (ACS) by the Pew Hispanic Center, a project of the Pew Research Center. No other Hispanic subgroup rivals the size of the Mexican-origin population. Puerto Ricans, the nation's second-largest Hispanic origin group, make up just 9 percent of the total Hispanic population in the fifty states and the District of Columbia."

13. Seth Motel and Eileen Patten's study shows that the demographic numbers indicating nearly 34 million Mexican Americans, compared to the next-largest group, Puerto Ricans with 4.6 million, a difference of nearly 30 million.

14. *Generations of Exclusion: Mexican Americans, Assimilation, and Race* by Edward Telles and Vilma Ortiz (Telles and Ortiz 2008) represents the single-most-important sociological study of Mexican Americans because of its longitudinal and intergenerational coverage of Mexican Americans, covering more than forty years, from 1965 to 2005 in San Antonio and Los Angeles. As the authors inform us, by 1965, the majority of Mexican Americans lived in urban areas like LA and SA.

## References

Cisneros, Sandra. 2015. "Interview by Jennifer Levin." *Pasatiempo: The New Mexican's Weekly Magazine of Arts, Entertainment and Culture. Santa Fe New Mexican,* October 16.

Eddy, Robert, and Victor Villanueva, eds. 2014. *A Language and Power Reader: Representations of Race in a "Post-Racist" Era.* Logan: Utah State University Press.

Editorial Board. 2015. "The Counterfeit High School Diploma." *New York Times,* December 31.

Kirklighter, Cristina, Diana Cárdenas, and Susan Wolff Murphy, eds. 2007. *Teaching Writing with Latino/a Students: Lessons Learned at Hispanic-Serving Institutions.* Albany: SUNY Press.

Motel, Seth, and Eileen Patten. 2012. "The 10 Largest Hispanic Origin Groups: Characteristics, Rankings, and Top Counties." Pew Research Center: Hispanic Trends, April 27.

Rodriguez, Richard. 1978. "The Achievement of Desire: Personal Reflections on Learning 'Basics.'" *College English* 40 (3): 239–54. https://doi.org/10.2307/375783.

Ruecker, Todd. 2015. *Transiciones: Pathways of Latinas and Latinos Writing in High School and College.* Logan: Utah State University Press.

Shaughnessy, Mina. 1977. *Errors and Expectations: A Guide for the Teacher of Basic Writing.* Oxford: Oxford University Press.
Soliday, Mary. 2002. *The Politics of Remediation: Institutional and Student Needs in Higher Education.* Pittsburgh: University of Pittsburgh Press.
Telles, Edward E., and Vilma Ortiz. 2008. *Generations of Exclusion: Mexican Americans, Assimilation, and Race.* New York: Russell Sage Foundation.

# 14
## REDEFINING DISCIPLINARITY IN THE CURRENT CONTEXT OF HIGHER EDUCATION

Doug Hesse

In her famous 1984 Conference on College Composition and Communication (CCCC) Chair's Address, Maxine Hairston argued that composition needed to cleave itself from English departments, which too long had devalued teaching writing and the expertise that undergirded it. Hairston's argument was partly grounded in material circumstances. She joined the long and true litany of grievances—regarding salaries, teaching loads, professional support, and hiring practices/working conditions—that writing teachers faced in comparison with their literature masters, the mandarins, as she called them (Hairston 1985, 273).

However, Hairston's main argument for writing exerting its separate agency was fueled less by equity than by psychology: Composition needed to remove itself emotionally and intellectually from English studies. While one might leave a bad marriage for all sorts of reasons, including material ones, perhaps the best is because a dominant partner suppresses agency and authority. Hairston (1985) states, "For us, I think the issue is survival. We must cut our psychological dependence in order to mature" (274).

I bring up Hairston to analyze the motivations for reasserting the disciplinary status of Composition studies now, in the second decade of the twenty-first century. Is it because we perceive disciplinarity as the path to resources, with a certain status enabling certain material conditions? Or is it because we want to be taken seriously—that we want our work to "count" in a way we perceive it hasn't previously, that we want our scholarship recognized as real scholarship, that we want recognition for professional practices (and approbation for unprofessional ones)? Both these motivations underlay the work of the CCCC Visibility Committee, part of whose accomplishment was changing how Rhetoric and Composition studies appear in Department of Education data (Phelps and Ackerman 2010). Of course, recognition and reward are entwined—or at least perceived to be. However, my argument in this chapter is that some presumptions about the value of disciplinary status may be based on an ideal that no longer holds. In the American university prior to the 1980s—the pre-neoliberal university of relatively sound funding and prospects—being counted a discipline generally brought assurances about faculty lines and status, and about scholarly, curricular, and physical space. Since then, the conditions of higher education generally in American society have shifted dramatically, with clear consequences for both resources and intellectual value.

Suppose that some all-powerful wizard bestowed on Composition studies full recognition as a discipline in the hearts and minds of all possible stakeholders, rendered it the disciplinary peer of history, philosophy, psychology. Some things would change—most notably, the qualifications deemed necessary to till our professional field. But many things would not; the mantle of discipline doesn't mean what it once (or perhaps ever) did. Fortunately, Composition studies is poised to assert its value as a discipline in the current university, though the terms of its disciplinarity may strike some apologists as insufficient.

### DISCIPLINES AND STATUS IN THE CHANGING ACADEMY

In May 2014, I was invited to a one-day meeting hosted by the American Association of Colleges and Universities (AAC&U) at its offices in Washington, DC. The purpose was to generate ideas for a "new faculty model," and among the fifteen or so invited were a few senior administrators, a few executive directors of education associations, and a couple professors of higher-ed administration. As the only faculty member from a traditional academic department, I was invited because writing programs were perceived to have a particular stake in this effort, because I'd served on the MLA contingent labor committee, and because I'd previously participated in a larger Delphi Project meeting, dedicated to addressing contingent and adjunct labor issues. Convening both meetings was Adrianna Kezar, from the University of Southern California, who has produced numerous studies of staffing, work conditions, and their effects.

We started with two assumptions. First, the number of adjunct and contingent faculty is vast and growing, and their teaching conditions are mostly inequitable and deleterious to student learning and to higher education. (Note the word "mostly"; medical schools, for example, have a strong percentage of contingent faculty who share nearly none of the concerns facing first-year writing colleagues.) Second, these problems are not going to be solved by a wholesale return to traditionally construed tenure-track positions. For reasons both economical and philosophical, there will be no second coming of traditional tenure, so pining for vast conversions of adjunct lines to tenure is delusional. Worse, it could lead to inaction; the absence of intentional decisions and planning by higher-educational faculty and administrators will fairly well ensure chaotic ad hoc solutions. After a day of intense debate, we'd filled several flip charts with ideas, some of which filtered into a report Kezar published a year later.

Before characterizing those conclusions, let me address a quite reasonable question: What do faculty roles have to do with disciplinarity? Generally, disciplinary status is marked by three features: existence of a body of knowledge and generally agreed-upon epistemologies, a curriculum and pedagogy for transmitting that knowledge, and recognition and funding within institutional spaces. The important and potentially vexed borderline is between "discipline" and "department" or "program." One could imagine history, for example, existing as a discipline without there existing any history departments or, perhaps, any history courses. But, in fact, the existence of institutional structures actually confers disciplinary status—or at the very least, makes it worth worrying about. Furthermore, there has been a close line between a discipline's status on a campus, and the status of its faculty. "Full" disciplines, with clearly marked research agendas, expect faculty research and reassign time for doing it, rewarding its production highly with status—especially when it generates external funding. Historically, venerable "pure" disciplines such as physics or philosophy have enjoyed higher status on campuses—at least in the abstract—than have "hybrid" or "opportunistic" disciplines such as accounting or engineering; the insistence by many on rhetoric as the ancient root of Composition studies wells largely from the pursuit of pure status.

However, that historical calculus has changed, with a unit's disciplinary lineage meaning less than other factors for material conditions such as salaries and teaching loads. At a time of declining support for public education and shaky academic funding, an academic unit's ability to attract funding plays a larger role, whether through grant making or attracting tuition-paying students. Students, parents, and even the secretary of education tend substantially to weigh attraction in terms of economic return on investment. Intrinsic intellectual value less determines a discipline-enacted-as-department's material worth than does its exchange value in the neoliberal academy.

In *College Unbound: The Future of Higher Education and What It Means for Students*, Jeffrey Selingo, a *Chronicle of Higher Education* reporter, lays out the case explicitly. Selingo cites five factors he believes mandate a radical change in higher education, "a perfect storm of financial, political, demographic, and technological forces" (Selingo 2013, 58). Three are most salient:

- "The well of full-paying students is running dry." (64)
- "The unbundled alternatives are improving," primarily through technological delivery systems but also through credentialing mechanisms other than degrees (67).
- A "growing value gap" makes students, parents, and stakeholders increasingly suspicious of the return on investment as tuitions skyrocket (70).

As a result, colleges cannot rely on traditional identities as knowledge makers that invite students to dwell with them for a few years. Instead, they have to see themselves concerned first with student learning—including the kinds of learning that students perceive as having exchange value. Now, many of us will bristle at this consumerist mentality (I surely do), but the cost of higher education in competitive global market makes "life of the mind" arguments awfully difficult. Reclaiming a "learning-for-learning's-sake—and-trust-us-to-determine-that" mentality would be possible only if student costs are dramatically reduced or gainful employment is strongly assured. Selingo isn't calling exclusively for vocational departments and majors, isn't echoing pronouncements by recent Florida and North Carolina governors, for example. Citing employer interests more in skills than in specific majors, Selingo asserts, "Subjects don't matter; cognitive abilities do" (148). He reacts positively to calls for abolishing traditional academic department structures, imagining, for example, "a broad range of topics around which . . . zones of inquiry could be organized" (149).

The point is that he sees the best hope of higher education as increasing its focus on undergraduate learning. Selingo is hardly alone. In his magisterial *Higher Education in America*, Derek Bok sees only two urgent problems needing improvement. (There are others, but to him they aren't urgent.) One is "to raise the percentage of young Americans who earn a college degree," and the second is "to improve the quality of education that undergraduates receive and halt the erosion that has apparently occurred in the effort they devote to their college studies" (Bok 2013, 408).

In a certain profound respect, then, Composition studies may seem to be poised to have status (if not traditional disciplinarity) thrust upon us—if we only claim it. After all, teaching undergraduates has been at the heart of composition's identity for decades, which explains why so many of us have yawned at—perhaps even resented—calls for teaching improvements in colleges. Active learning? Flipped classrooms? Project based? We've done that through decades of peer review, workshops, drafting, writing studios, writing across the curriculum, and so on.

Yet, for an awful lot of folks in the field, if those are the conditions for status, even the grounds for disciplinarity, then no thank you. For understandable reasons, we've long resented our work being cast only as teaching, our teaching being cast only as service (most centrally through first-year composition), and our service being treated—most dramatically in terms of staffing and compensation—as the equivalent of pot scrubbing or corn detasseling. Greg Colomb aptly notes, "As a label for what we do, service does not serve us well." He explains: "When we use service to frame our thinking about who we are and our planning for what we do, we mislead both ourselves and others about our accomplishments and our possibilities. The outcome is not better when, to escape the burden of the service frame, we try to understand what we do as the contrary of service, identifying our practices with the most theoretical, least practical of our academic colleagues" (Colomb 2010, 11–12).

Colomb goes on to argue for embracing our service mission but under different terms, those of "franchise," a role publicly granted to perform a public good, in this case, teaching writing. No doubt, many in Composition studies would and do embrace that identity, even consider it a worthy basis for a disciplinary identity. However, just as many or more would insist on disciplinarity less in terms of teaching than of research or other intellectual work. One argument (only one) of the new "abolitionist" movement was that doing away with required composition would unshackle Composition studies from its service identity and create room for a scholarly one, whereby scholars in the field could hold roles similar to their literature or history or psychology colleagues. One hears echoes of this in Gary Olson's pointed response to Wendy Bishop's call for increased attention to teaching, which he cast as "the potential death of composition as an intellectual discipline" (Olson 2000, 4).

Now, obviously, this is not an either/or, teaching/research question. Few people imagine purely one pole or the other. And clearly even the "teaching" side looks different when it manifests as a few required courses, predominantly first year, versus as full-flowered majors and graduate programs. I've gone into this seeming digression to make that point that if the material advantages of disciplinarity are conceived too exclusively in terms of faculty as researchers, especially researchers oriented "away" from teaching, those proponents may be disappointed. The larger context of higher education is poised to reward teaching (yes, I know, it hasn't so far!) and certain kinds of research, most notably "practical" research that solves "real-world" problems or creates goods and services.

## FACULTY STATUS AND DISCIPLINARY STATUS

In 2015, Adrianna Kezar and her colleague Daniel Maxey issued a report that synthesized their explorations of new faculty models, including the input of the May 2014 meeting I described earlier. *Adapting by Design* summarizes familiar economic and other challenges to higher education that have led to approximately 70 percent of current instructional faculty in nonprofit institutions being non-tenure-track, with two-thirds of this number being part-time (6). Beyond the issues of equity and professionalism, Kezar and Maxey (2015) point out that "numerous studies have found that growing reliance on adjunct faculty has a negative impact of student retention rates, successful transfers from two- to four-year institutions, student grade point averages, and graduation or completion rates" (6). They summarize nine problems with overly relying on adjunct faculty.

1. Inequities in composition, access to benefits, working conditions, and involvement in the life of the department and campus.
2. Adverse effect on student success outcomes.
3. A lack of professional development opportunities for adjunct faculty members limits their access to and practice of effective pedagogies, high-impact practices, and innovative strategies to promote student learning, as well as current knowledge in their disciplines.
4. Little, if any, constructive evaluation of their work to assess their effectiveness.
5. [The lack of] important information about academic policies and practices, programs available to students, the curriculum, or overall learning goals for their departments and institutions.
6. Higher rates of turnover [create] a lack of stability for academic programs and their students.
7. The adjunct faculty model encourages institutions to view faculty members merely as tools for facilitating content delivery, downplaying the important contributions of educators to student learning—to the detriment of both the faculty and the students whose learning they support.
8. The adjunct model distances faculty from their disciplinary (or inter-, cross-, and multi-disciplinary) roots and content knowledge.

9. Dependence on the adjunct model makes it more difficult for institutions to meet their broader goals related to service, community engagement, leadership, and larger public good. (22–25)

However, tenure-track positions also come under critique:

1. A disproportionate emphasis on conducting research and publishing has essentially downplayed the importance of teaching—the core part of the mission of most institutions.
2. Institutions face a lack of flexibility to hire in new fields.
3. The tenure model limits emphasis on teaching and learning and incentives to improve and innovate teaching.
4. The tenure structure pays little attention to important other roles faculty can play in service, civic engagement, and local leadership.
5. Some alternative models suggest that academic freedom can be protected without tenure, at least as it is conceived of today.
6. Faculty who are not yet tenured, but are on the tenure track . . . often feel constrained in their focus. (26–28)

While both lists occlude exceptions at whole swathes of types of institutions (especially tenure as construed at many two-year and small colleges), they combine with the financial straits and prospects facing higher education to necessitate intentional new faculty models. Kezar and Maxey outline processes for enacting those models, which might effectively take different forms at different campus as long as they satisfy "five key components": "promoting equity among academic appointments," "vigorously protecting academic freedom," "ensuring flexibility in appointments," "fostering professional growth," and "promoting collegiality" (37).

Several models are already available. One is a full-time non-tenure-track one, focused primarily on teaching (62). A second is creativity contracts, whereby faculty define and negotiate professional goals over a specified period (often three to five years), so that at some periods they may focus on teaching, in others on scholarship—including the scholarship of teaching and learning (65). A third model is differential staffing, what Kezar and Maxey label the "medical school model," in recognition of the fact that medical schools increasingly hire faculty in one of three tracks: research, education, and clinical, with some of those appointed in tenure lines but others in long-term non-tenure track (63).

The differential staffing model has had a long and contested history within higher education. A 2015 book by Michael Bérubé and Jennifer Ruth argues how differential staffing should look within English departments. In a nutshell, they propose that "many full-time faculty lines off the tenure track be converted to teaching-intensive tenured positions. The tenure process for such faculty would involve rigorous peer review, conduction by their tenured colleagues at the same institution, but would carry no expectations for research or creative activity" (Bérubé and Ruth 2015, 19).

In making a plain call for a two-track faculty, they cite equity issues, of course, but they also perceive in the tenure process the kind of disciplinary rigor they (and others like Kezar) find lacking in the current adjunct or contingent systems. I find their motivations occasionally a little questionable, as preserving doctoral programs in English is a primary concern; they see "the structural cause of the crisis in graduate education" as the fact that thousands of positions are held by teachers without doctorates (20). I also have doubts that hierarchies can be avoided. Even if salaries are absolutely equal between research lines and teaching lines, can we avoid perceiving the former as more important or desirable, given our long-standing history? I actually have to be optimistic that this is possible with time and through using much richer means of describing and evaluating teaching than our common impoverished student evaluations, syllabus review, and occasional classroom observation.

My biggest concern with Bérubé and Ruth, however, is their reassurance that teaching lines "would carry no expectations for research or creative activity" (19). I understand the impetus for this condition, even the recognition of the time it takes to teach well, especially as I'm sure that part of these appointments is a larger teaching load than their researcher counterparts. Still, part of the identity of college professor—an important identity—is as knowledge maker. In the case of faculty in Composition studies, it's vital that they are writers themselves, as well as scholars of writing. To imagine that a dissertation might be the last scholarly or creative work one might produce bodes ill well for the quality of teaching and the advancement of the discipline. Of course, one component of evaluating teaching might well include evidence of professional development and currency. Still, I suggest that members of a teaching community and a teaching profession ought to be contributing to them, however modestly, even if locally and occasionally. There's a long range of possible expectations between doing no scholarship or creative work whatsoever and publishing a couple of peer reviewed articles every year or a book every five. Kezar and Maxey observe that the kind of activity that Ernest Boyer described a quarter century ago in *Scholarship Reconsidered* might finally get its recognition in new faculty models.

My point in this section is that higher education is closer now to a tipping point than it perhaps ever has been, at least in terms of faculty roles. The numbers of adjunct faculty are unprecedented at a time when tuition costs are skyrocketing and external stakeholders are more skeptical than ever about the values of a education. It's always fashionable to sound the crisis trumpet, but Kezar and Maxey are right, I think, that the time has come either for academic institutions to be intentional about creating new faculty models and academic structures that can address current conditions or for those institutions to continue being pushed by storm winds into haphazard coves they haven't sought and hardly desire.

My point, further, is that these new models converge on either teaching or research as central, the two roles increasingly becoming separated. Research, further, is increasingly valued—even defined—in terms of external funding. Composition studies, as a field and as enacted on individual campuses, might wish to pursue the research identity. But it may be require embracing some kinds of research over others, most notably kinds that attract grants and generates indirect costs. Going all in as a teaching field that provides value to students—in ways they and the larger culture defines—is another prospect. Many of us in Composition studies have resisted identity as a teaching enterprise—and for good historical reason. Universities in particular have little valued teaching, especially lower-division teaching, especially general education, especially first-year writing, which they've often perceived as remedial and even more frequently regarded as commonsensical, the kind of teaching anyone could do. As Hairston and other have outlined, even our seemingly most obvious allies in English departments frequently have held that position. It may seem simply unfair that the historical moment when the plenitude of our publications and doctoral programs asserts our disciplinary and often departmental status is the moment when undergraduate teaching is being pushed as the activity most central to higher education's future health and vitality. Other departments and disciplines may be pressed to claim teaching in a way that we've done for decades, but they've had their time in the research sun. Where's ours?

Now, no one is calling for historians to stop writing history and start writing only lesson plans or chemists to quit their labs, and surely no one should be calling for Composition scholars to stop doing "basic" research: archival, critical, or empirical in ways not apparently tied to teaching. But unless we're able to reembrace the teaching of writing as a central—even as the most central—core of our disciplinary identity, we're going to find that identity doesn't get us nearly as much as we'd like in the emerging university.

At the same time—and this is crucial—we need broadly to expand the identity of teaching beyond something done only with students for credit in classrooms. I'm invoking a definition of teaching as developing knowledge and abilities in a wide range of settings—not only classrooms but also in faculty seminars, workshops, and offices; in libraries, museums, and community centers; not through lectures or discussions but also through materials produced for teaching—and for wide audiences—not only tuition-paying undergraduates and graduates but also for faculty colleagues and publics beyond the academy.

## A NEW BASIS FOR DISCIPLINARITY

A growing number of schools have adopted new kinds of full-time faculty roles, models somewhere sideways of the traditional tenure track, distinguished from the latter by heavier teaching loads, scant research expectations, term appointments, different advancement paths (or, sometimes none), and so on. Examples that come quickly to mind are those at Albany, Stanford, Colorado, UC Santa Barbara, and Wake Forest. Often configured as lecturer, "teaching professor," or "professor of the practice" lines, these positions have potential for reimagining the basis of disciplinarity in Composition studies. In saying this, I'm surely not advocating that Composition should unilaterally abandon the pursuit of tenure-line positions. Rather, I'm saying that addressing a practical problem—how to teach writing more equitably and professionally—also happens to create a pretext for thinking about how we might now construe disciplinary status.

As backdrop for this claim, let me use the context of the Writing Program at the University of Denver, a 150-year-old, medium-size (5,000 undergraduates, 6,000 graduate students) private university with a modest endowment (certainly for schools in its category) of $480 million and, thus, heavily dependent on tuition. In 2006, DU created a new program that reported directly to the provost, with faculty, program offices, writing center, and seminar space housed in the library. National searches initially hired twenty lecturers (and eventually twenty-six), most with terminal degrees on lines that are fully benefited and indefinitely renewable. These faculty have a teaching load, on a quarter system, of six courses per year, distributed in a 0/3/3 fashion, in sections capped at fifteen students. Instead of teaching during the fall quarter, faculty participate in weekly professional development activities and perform an annual program/campus professional service project. Funding for travel and professional development equals that for tenured faculty in

Arts, Humanities, and Social Sciences; writing faculty are eligible for all internal grants and awards, and have won many. A budget for assessment, research, and outreach allows the program to pay research subjects, supports program projects, supports writing across the curriculum (WAC), and maintains community outreach projects including at shelters in downtown Denver and at neighboring schools.

A significant change occurred in 2015, when lecturer ranks across campus were upgraded into a new series: Teaching Assistant Professor, Teaching Associate Professor, and Teaching Professor. There are specific criteria and process for annual merit raises, and periodic reviews for reappointment and promotion lead to appointments lengthening to seven years. In DU's case, the obvious material difference between the Teaching Professor series and the "Traditional" Professor series is a higher teaching load (one or two courses per year), a salary difference of 10–15 percent, and a considerably reduced publication expectation. Reduced but not absent. From 2010 to 2015, twenty-six writing faculty published six books and eighty-one articles/chapters, and made 133 conference presentations.

Underpinning all of this, an annual programmatic review process weights teaching 60 percent (with annual teaching portfolios at the center), professional service 30 percent, and scholarly/other productivity 10 percent. The professional service and scholarship components reinforce collegiality both within the program and beyond it, demonstrating that holding a position in the program means more than leading a succession of courses. In that respect, the Denver program addresses a shortcoming I described above with Bérubé and Ruth's call for exclusively teaching positions.

Or, rather, while teaching is at the center of the DU program, it is teaching understood and practiced well beyond classrooms and credit. For example, an ongoing professional service effort is the "Writing in the Majors Project" (affectionately acronymed as WIMP), in which two writing faculty team with two faculty from a department (economics, chemistry, theater, and anthropology are among the dozen so far) and two undergraduates selected by the department. The team researches the department's teaching and writing practices, using a combination of assignment analyses, interviews, and text analysis to write a report on for that department's faculty and students. This is knowledge making and research—but it is also teaching, action research serving curricula and pedagogy. Or, to cite another example, working through the writing center, faculty consult with over one hundred faculty members per year about writing issues in their courses, individual thirty- to sixty-minute consultations. These happen in addition to traditional faculty development workshops and seminars, some extending several days. Annual institutes bring together twenty-five to thirty faculty from across campus for writing projects that have resulted in miniconferences and the publication of three essay collections. The program organizes events in which faculty from various disciplines talk to students about their own writing, as do professionals from the community. We offer workshops on designing research posters and print them for free, workshops on writing applications and proposals, too. We organize two student events around writing and publish an annual magazine. A longitudinal research project followed fifty-nine undergraduates throughout their time at Denver, reporting findings to the campus.

In short, in pursuing its mission of "creating a robust culture for writing" on campus, the DU writing program does substantially more than offer classes and occasional activities led by a few administrative faculty with reassigned time for that purpose. Instead all faculty have "reassigned" time for projects that blur lines between teaching, professional service (in fact, more or less defines professional service as teaching), and research. Teaching is evaluated not only in terms of how well faculty develop content and skills with students enrolled for credit but also for how well they do so for colleagues. Professional service is defined not merely as "committee work" but as building a knowledgeable teaching and learning community, in multiple levels, an enterprise that's fundamentally one of teaching writ large. Research is valued not only in terms of how it circulates through prescribed journals and presses but also in terms of how it circulates on campus, inflecting practice.

The superstructure of all this activity is teaching, but teaching imagined expansively. Such teaching requires faculty deeply steeped in—and contributing to—a body of knowledge and practices. However, and this is the crucial redefinition, it is a form of disciplinarity that, instead of finding its measure nationally as knowledge production for expert insiders, derives it "locally" by addressing the institutional interests of students, colleagues, and communities. The effort includes shaping those interests, resisting too-restricted understandings of writing, its origins, consequences, practices, ends, and development.

My position seems to make a virtue of necessity, I know. If new faculty roles discourage discipline-as-research, then just redefine discipline as a particular teaching formation, especially because such a redefinition fits extant higher education aims and interests. I'll cite two points against charges of crass opportunism. Composition has long prized teaching, with other disciplines coming lately and often reluctantly to the mission;

it's in our heritage. And Composition historically has viewed teaching as an intellectual, knowledge-making activity. We might just press further.

## WHAT KIND OF DISCIPLINARITY GETS US WHAT?

I'm hardly the first to embrace the centrality of teaching. Discussing how Composition studies might address the ongoing challenge of teaching writing on a mass scale, Joe Harris finds shortcomings with two ideas to advance composition's disciplinary status and address persistent issues with academic labor and teaching expertise. One action, abolishing the universal requirement in favor of a major and offering only as many writing courses as there are qualified faculty to teach them, he faults for "giv[ing] up our main source of influence in the curriculum and the lives of students in order to claim academic status for ourselves" (Harris 2012, 158). A second option, teaching required composition as writing about writing, as an introductory course in a discipline, Harris faults because he sees countless possible subject matters for "intellectual engagement" in a first-year course. Harris suggests a third approach, a "programmatic" rather than a disciplinary ethos focuses on changing "local, material conditions rather than overhauling the intellectual superstructure of our field" (159).

Now, these orientations aren't mutually exclusive. Clearly, there are best practices in teaching courses umbrella'ed under Composition studies, and "discipline" is a reasonable construct for that umbrella. Disciplinary authority is a useful bulwark against people whose "common sense" about the nature of writing and its teaching is useful. My personal preference is for the broadest possible definition of discipline; I'd carry Janice Lauer's (1984) "dappled" characterization to its piebald extreme.

Where I differ from Harris is calling for a larger view of teaching, one that includes typical elements of service and research, one that fosters multiple audiences and spheres of performance distinguished toward the ends not of contributing to knowledge for national fellowship of experts but, rather of expanding local expertise. Adamantly, I'm not saying we should abjure "basic" research. Rather, I'm asserting that even full recognition of Composition studies' status as a research discipline cannot garner what many hope it might in the new higher educational climate. Now isn't the time nostalgically to hope for status enjoyed by academic departments of a golden yesteryear.

In a perceptive analysis of current attempts to constitute Creative Writing Studies as a discipline, Mary Hedengren quotes Tony Becher and Paul Trowler from *Academic Tribes and Territories: Intellectual Enquiry and the Culture of Disciplines*: "'Boundaries [between disciplines] do not exist merely as lines on a map: they denote territorial possessions that can be *encroached on, colonized* and *reallocated*' and 'when patriotic feelings within a discipline run high, deviations from the common cultural norms will be penalized'" (my emphasis 59) (Hedengren 2015, 2–3).

Hedengren observes that "the metaphor of territory that can be contested in bitter and raging wars highlights the real stakes, both material and philosophical, at risk with the advent or growth of a new discipline" (3). She's right that any new academic unit competes with other units, both for resources and curricular space. But, I suggest, success depends less on disciplinary purity than on what the unit can offer, either by attracting students, accruing funding, or meeting a curricular need defined as vital. When my own university, for example, founded its Center for the Study of Aging, there was no time spent debating whether "aging studies" was a discipline. There was endowment money available, grant money to be pursued, and students to be recruited with the promise of future employment opportunities with a graying population. Decision done.

Now, Composition studies can be a destination, as it is at schools with successful technical and applied writing majors and programs: through teaching. Too, it can attract funding—though probably less for a new edition of Hugh Blair's Lectures on *Rhetoric and Belles Lettres* or an archival study of writing in one-room schoolhouses than for empirical studies of machine scoring versus human. Historically, mounting the kinds of research that generate significant grants with attractive indirect costs has been a part—but not the core part—of composition's identity, which just as often has depended on historical, theoretical, interpretive, or reflective scholarship. In pursuit of resources, how far might we be willing to limit our research agenda? If "not very," then celebrating our "service" or Colomb's "franchise" role would probably be a better strategy. Kairos matters.

Which brings me back to Adrianna Kezar and the realpolitik of higher education in the 2010s. My argument risks the scorn of seeming complicit with a status quo easily read as wrong, open to the charge that it forfeits historical faculty models as irrecoverable, collaborating with neoliberal calls for educational "reform." A recent book by Sandra Featherman represents the tenor: *Higher Education at Risk: Strategies to Improve Outcomes, Reduce Tuition, and Stay Competitive in a Disruptive Environment*. Featherman's "prescriptions for higher education" include advice to "focus on outcomes," "strengthen customer service," "develop and market a brand," "phase out tenure," and "use technology to enhance academic programs" (Featherman 2014, 208–12). Technology's role is reflexively celebrated—and just as often critiqued. Les Perelman labeled Jeff Selingo's book, characterized earlier, "a love letter to ed-tech companies" (qtd. in Losh 2014, 59). Critics like Henry Giroux fret, "There is a sustained effort to dismantle education from the discourse of democracy, public values, critical thought, social responsibility, and civic courage" (Giroux 2014, 31). While I generally agree with him, I suggest that considerable suspicion of higher education derives, rightly or wrongly, from the sense that professors are mostly oriented toward disciplinary formations that seem little to foster the discourses that Giroux mourns, except through critique. Teaching practiced and promoted fully and well counters that suspicion.

Composition studies has historically focused on teaching even when teaching was undervalued, has been interested in technologies for their affordances of production and circulation, has embraced sophisticated ideas of assessment well before more simplistic notions gained sway, has supported faculty development both within writing programs and beyond them. Given that these orientations have historically gone unrewarded, it's made sense to privilege the scholarly dimension of our work. We should keep doing so. But we should simultaneously foreground those aspects of our collective self that prize teaching in the broadest sense—to students, to colleagues and campuses, to publics. The time to press that case has come. It's ironic or, rather, perverse that being historically so far ahead of today's call to embrace teaching—so far ahead that we were dismissed as "behind"—now puts Composition studies at potential advantage. Some new faculty models offer pretexts for thinking how we might constitute a discipline that is significantly (though most assuredly not exclusively) identified as teaching, but teaching practiced as a wide set of activities necessarily including knowledge making, activities shaped in and shaping local communities. Such an orientation offers the best current path to the material institutional status and independence for which the field, thirty years after Hairston, still longs.

*References*

Bérubé, Michael, and Jennifer Ruth. 2015. *The Humanities, Higher Education, and Academic Freedom: Three Necessary Arguments*. New York: Palgrave Macmillan. https://doi.org/10.1057/9781137506122.

Bishop, Wendy. 1999. "Places to Stand: The Reflective Writer-Teacher-Writer in Composition." *CCC* 51 (1): 9–31.

Bok, Derek. 2013. *Higher Education in America*. Princeton: Princeton University Press.

Colomb, Gregory G. 2010. "Franchising the Future." *CCC* 62 (1): 11–30.

Featherman, Sandra. 2014. *Higher Education at Risk: Strategies to Improve Outcomes, Reduce Tuition, and Stay Competitive in a Disruptive Environment.* Sterling, VA: Stylus Publishing.

Giroux, Henry A. 2014. *Neoliberalism's War on Higher Education.* Toronto: Between the Lines.

Hairston, Maxine. 1985. "Breaking Our Bonds and Reaffirming Our Connections." *CCC* 36 (3): 272–82.

Harris, Joseph. 2012. *A Teaching Subject: Composition Since 1966.* Logan: Utah State University Press.

Hedengren, Mary. 2015. "Disciplining the Muse: Evaluating Creative Writing Studies' Effort to Establish Itself as an Academic Discipline." Dissertation, University of Texas, Austin.

Kezar, Adrianna, and Daniel Maxey. 2015. *Adapting by Design: Creating Faculty Roles and Defining Faculty Work to Ensure an Intentional Future for Colleges and Universities.* Los Angeles: Delphi Project on the Changing Faculty and Student Success and the University of Southern California Earl and Pauline Pulias Center for Higher Education.

Lauer, Janice. 1984. "Composition Studies: Dappled Discipline." *Rhetoric Review* 3 (1): 20–29. https://doi.org/10.1080/07350198409359074.

Losh, Elizabeth. 2014. *The War on Learning: Gaining Ground in the Digital University.* Cambridge, MA: MIT.

Olson, Gary A. 2000. "The Death of Composition as an Intellectual Discipline." *Composition Studies* 28 (2): 33–41.

Phelps, Louise Wetherbee, and John M. Ackerman. 2010. "Making the Case for Disciplinarity in Rhetoric, Composition, and Writing Studies: The Visibility Project." *CCC* 62 (1): 180–215.

Selingo, Jeffrey J. 2013. *College (Un)Bound: The Future of Higher Education and What It Means for Students.* Boston: New Harvest/Houghton Mifflin.

# 15
## LOOKING OUTWARD
*Disciplinarity and Dialogue in Landscapes of Practice*

Linda Adler-Kassner

By now, the news that writing is implicated in a number of recent policy debates is not new. In what seems like an increasingly distant past, Brian Huot (2007) and Angela Green (2009), among others, examined the construction of education and writing education in *A Test of Leadership*, the report from the Spellings Commission on Higher Education. Doug Hesse (2012) described the problematic development of the Common Core Standards, examining inattention by developers to input from professional organizations. Arthur Applebee (2013) has discussed the construction of writing and reading in the Common Core Standards, which have implications for college writing courses as well.

These analyses illustrate the ways in which many policy actors believe that writing is their business. In this belief they are joined by countless others: business leaders, politicians, officials of all types, and—of course!—writing faculty. None are entirely wrong, either. Writing is an activity through which individuals and groups both develop and represent their understandings of important ideas; for this reason it is of great concern to many.

At the same time, what goes into an individual's ability *to* develop and represent understanding of important ideas is enormously complex. While many refer to what they consider to be ideas about good writing as common sense, "common sense is only commonsensical because it is sense held in common" (Wenger 1999, 47). Developing what seem to be "commonsensical" ideas of good writing doesn't happen by just hanging around and watching people write or reading what they produce or through osmosis; commonsense ideas are also not value neutral. In fact, as writing teachers well know, understanding qualities of good writing— in fact, understanding that particular qualities are associated with "good writing" at all—requires a way of seeing writing as a subject of study, not just an activity (Adler-Kassner and Wardle 2015). Absent this focus on

DOI: 10.7330/9781607326953.c015

writing as a subject of study *and* an activity, the ways that writing is used in policy and in the practices that stem from policy are not only potentially problematic, but they are also potentially unjust because they take into account only part of what writing is and does. Historically, evidence of the ways in which ideas about writing have wronged writers, especially in school, are everywhere, from students forced to reject their home registers in favor of standardized American English to be considered "successful" to efforts to valorize particular kinds of literacy experiences as better than others.

I summarize this situation to adapt and reinforce a point: while many speak for writing, not all understand writing in the same ways (Hesse 2012). We spend our work lives teaching and studying questions associated with the subject of our discipline, composed knowledge (*CCC*). We ask, for instance: How is "good writing" defined in different contexts—in school, in workplaces, in sites within the community? Who are identified as "good writers," who are not, and what are the consequences of these labels? How is writing assessed? How is it taught, by whom, and in what conditions? What are the consequences—for learners and teachers—with material conditions associated with writing and literacy development? These questions lead us to deeper understandings of writing and writers, and sometimes to strongly held positions about the implications and consequences of decisions related to both. At the same time, we ignore others' understandings of these questions and interests in writing at our own peril. In the same way, when we ask questions about what "disciplinarity" means in Writing Studies, we must take these broader situations and conversations into account.

In this chapter, I make an argument for reconceptualizing disciplinarity in order to genuinely engage with the reality that, to some extent, writing *is* everybody's business and that discussions about (and policy actions related to) writing will likely continue to take place well beyond the confines of postsecondary writing classrooms. The concept of knowledgeability, an idea developed by Etienne and Beverly Wenger-Trayner's continuing work on social learning theory, provides a framework for this reconceptualization. To explain this framework requires a brief review of three ideas developed throughout this body of scholarship: communities of practice, regimes of competence, and landscapes of practice.

Communities of practice, first, are groups sharing understandings, ways of doing, and strategies for learning how to do. In his 1998 book, Wenger explained that this concept of "practice" included both "explicit and tacit"—"language, tools, documents" and so on, and also "implicit relations, tactic conventions, social cues . . ." (Wenger 1999, 47). The boundaries of these communities, Wenger later explained, are constituted by participation in "regimes of competence[,] . . . criteria and expectations by which [communities] recognize membership" (Wenger 2010, 180). Competence gives rise to shared perception: "understanding what matters, what the enterprise of the community is, and how it gives rise to a perspective on the world," among other features (180). The concept of "regimes of competence," then, contributed to a theory that could distinguish how boundaries between communities of practice were constituted.

As Wenger continued to explore communities and their regimes, though, he realized that while their activities could be circumscribed by the boundaries of the community, these communities also existed within larger terrains populated by other communities invested or involved in shared concerns or activities. He labeled these terrains "landscapes of practice," areas containing many communities with common interests (Wenger 2010; Wenger-Trayner et al. 2015). Knowledgeability is an enactment within these landscapes of practice. It occurs when participants in the regimes of competence of individual communities of practice within a common landscape are able to meaningfully engage with one another and the regimes of the one or more other communities in order to produce new ideas, ways of seeing, and/or actions that would not exist without the synergistic connections and activities that occur as a result of genuine engagement. "The ability to do this," write Etienne and Beverly Wenger-Trayner, "depends on the depth of one's competence in . . . core practice(s), which ground the experience of the landscape in specific locations" and on understanding of "other practices and [community of practice] boundaries within the landscape" (Wenger-Trayner and Wenger-Trayner 2015, 23). Knowledgeability occurs when individuals "broker" (Wenger 2010) between communities in ways that result in benefit to the competence of both communities. It is my contention that within Writing Studies, knowledgeability can (and perhaps must) become a frame for understanding and enacting disciplinarity as an outward-facing, dialogic activity, helping to operationalize and make concrete what Gwendolynne Reid and Carolyn Miller (this volume) conceive of as an "open, evolving, networked category."

## WRITING DISCIPLINARITY

This idea of disciplinarity as outward- rather than inward-facing in many ways runs counter to the historical development of disciplinarity.

Researchers in the sociology of knowledge who have studied disciplinarity, for instance, have primarily focused on attempts to identify the elements that constitute the whole of "disciplinarity" especially as disciplines are contrasted to *other* disciplinary contexts. This interest in identifying the boundaries (hard or soft, permeable or more substantial) stems in part from the value that distinctive disciplinary identities hold within academic institutions. A number of researchers (e.g., Oleson and Voss 1979; Bender 1997; Carey 1989; Kreber 2009a) contend that throughout the nineteenth and twentieth centuries, the university increasingly valued specialization and disciplinary distinction. John Higham (1979) traces the connections between the academic movement to specialization and the nation's movement into a more uniformly industrialized culture, noting that "by 1920 . . . America had embraced the specialist and sanctified the expert with an enthusiasm unmatched elsewhere" (5). While American education during the first part of the twentieth century reflected a tension between broad learning and specialization, by the 1950s, the emphasis on specialization had prevailed, leaving "liberal learning" as the domain of often ill-defined general education programs and a few distinctive colleges (e.g., St. John's). From this perspective, then, identifying the distinct boundaries of disciplines mattered because that naming and those boundaries were linked to status within institutions.

Researchers have also attempted to name the elements that contribute to disciplinary formation, as Elizabeth Wardle and Doug Downs and Reid and Miller also note in their chapters in this volume. The literature on the sociology of knowledge, for instance, has examined how disciplines are defined and constructed or has examined their central concerns or orientations. In a meta-analysis of the literature on disciplinarity, for instance, Armin Krishnan (2009) notes that definitions of disciplines have been developed through investigation of what objects or questions are researched, what knowledge has been developed, how the knowledge is organized, what methods are used to gather knowledge and what theories used to interpret it, and what terminology is used to convey that knowledge. Janet Donald (2002), who studies knowledge practices within and among disciplines, examines what methods are used to arrive at knowledge, how that knowledge is validated, and what "truth criteria [are] employed in that process" (Kreber 2009b, 23). Based on his research, Ian Winchester contends that "disciplines are based on an organized body of facts and theories which are treated as true, . . . characteristic subject matter, [and] definite methods of control" (qtd. in Kreber 2009b, 23). Other researchers have developed taxonomies to describe perspectives that span disciplines, such as Biglan's oft-cited distinctions between "hard" and "soft" paradigms, "pure" versus "applied" knowledge, and "life" versus "non-life" subjects of study. Tony Becher and Paul Trowler, examining the distinctions between academic "tribes" and "territories," examined the distinction between "convergent" and "tightly knit" disciplines and more "loosely knit" ones (Becher and Trowler 2001, 59, 64).

This literature demonstrates that degrees of consensus around objects of study, methods of research, theories of interpretation, language, and truth criteria have long been fundamental to the literature about the constitution of disciplines. It is with these characteristics, says higher education scholar Burton Clark (1983), that academics "identify." A discipline, he says, is "comprehensive in that it . . . pulls together a craftlike community of interest" that reaches across different sites such as academic institutions (29). Bound by their commitments to these characteristics, disciplines have shared beliefs, cultures, values, rituals, terminology, and approaches to learning. In this regard, a discipline can in many ways be understood as a broadly constituted community of practice as defined by Jean Lave and Etienne Wenger, a group sharing common values, rituals, language, and strategies for learning how to learn (see Wenger 1999; see also Land, Vivian, and Rattray 2014, 5).

## WRITING AND DISCIPLINARITY

Within Writing Studies, researchers also have attempted to identify moments of disciplinary identification, discussion, or turns as a way of outlining—or, in some cases, rejecting—disciplinary boundaries. Kathleen Blake Yancey, for instance, points to several such moments: John Gerber's introduction to the first issue of *College Composition and Communication*, which pointed to the integral connection between teaching and the discipline itself; Richard's Fulkerson's attempts to "trace the field's coherence" (in 1979, 1990, and 2005); Janice Lauer's efforts to "[map] the field"; Collin Brooke's and Derek Mueller's use of databases to analyze the field's scholarship to outline its shape(s) (Yancey 2015, xv–xvi, xxvii). Reid and Miller's chapter in this volume reviews some of this literature as part of their argument for an "open and networked" idea of disciplinarity.

There is also a body of literature within the field that raises concerns about the idea of Writing Studies as a discipline. Some within the movement question or reject the so-called pedagogical imperative, the intimate connection between research and teaching that is associated with the position of composition courses (especially first-year writing) as "service." Karen Kopelson (2008), drawing on Stephen North, Jan Swearingen, and Sid Dobrin, argues that while we should not reject the praxis-oriented elements of the field's work, the focus on teaching "is actually symptomatic, not necessarily of a *demand* for application, but of a continual, overarching separation of use, service, intervention, and action." (765). What is needed instead, she contends, is a sharper focus on theorizing and theory making specific to the field and not necessarily connected to teaching in addition to scholarship that turns away from our discipline's "unrivaled . . . proclivity for self-examination" (775). Dobrin's (2011) more recent work expands on Kopelson's call to look to theory as a site of focus for the field. He calls for "postcomposition," a focus "away from student writers to the act of writing in general, and more specifically to the phenomena of writing itself" (193), a "constant nascent state of becoming beyond" (196) by engaging in "the untested potential for theorizing writing" (199).

Turning away from theory, Bruce Horner (2014) builds a practice-based argument against disciplinarity. He argues that Composition lacks "the material social infrastructure necessary to knowledge mobilization on anything like a mass scale"; it also can only make "at best highly suspect claims to possession of expert knowledge of any recognized value to the public" (57–58). The field is also marginalized within the academy because of its foci: on "knowledge of writing as an ongoing activity and ability" and on the "concrete labor of writers and readers" (57), both of which remind others that such labor is necessary and that knowledge is not produced simply through "individual brilliance and merit alone" (57). As a result, disciplinary efforts to do "something 'more'—to 'matter' in ways recognized as mattering much at all to anyone—are unlikely to succeed." At the same time, Horner contends that the same characteristics that position writing instruction as a service are its strengths. While it "[lacks] claims to an expert knowledge to dispense," he says, "[Composition] possesses a deep familiarity with the necessity of labor to the ongoing realization of the value of knowledge [and thus] is actually better positioned to accomplish more in that ongoing work of producing use value from knowledge than those working in disciplines whose claims to (commodified) expert knowledge invest them in denying the necessity of such labor" (57–58). As a result, Horner argues that Composition should embrace the virtue of humility, remembering its roots on the ground, engaged with students and with writing. The field's "lack of professional academic disciplinary status, its failure even to be able to pretend to possess expert knowledge, gives us that" (59).

Each of these arguments associated with and, sometimes, against disciplinarity points to important aspects of our discipline's focus—study of and practice with composed knowledge—that are integral for the idea of reconceptualizing disciplinarity as I am proposing in this chapter. Kopelson suggests that the constant search for a solid definition of the discipline's boundaries is solipsistic; Dobrin contends the discipline should extend beyond student writing (and the teaching of student writing); Horner argues that the field's disciplinary identity should not emulate the other identities of other disciplines and rest on claims to expert knowledge. At the same time, a number of recent texts, including *Naming What We Know: Threshold Concepts of Writing Studies* (Adler-Kassner and Wardle 2015), which I coedited, outline elements that are part of what could be considered the "regime of competence" of Writing Studies (see Yancey, Robertson, and Taczak [2014]; Heilker and Vandenberg [2015]; and Ruiz and Sánchez [2016] for other recent texts that also outline elements of this regime of competence). This more recent literature asserts that we do possess expert knowledge based on sixty-plus years of teaching and research into writing and writers and drawing on extensive research into literacy development from aligned disciplines. In addition, this work makes the case that we must draw on this research as we engage in discussions about writing and writers in our programs, with our colleagues, in our institutions, and with stakeholders who also have stated or implied interests in writing development (see, for instance, Adler-Kassner 2012; Adler-Kassner and Wardle 2015; Downs and Wardle 2007; Hesse 2012).

But. While some researchers in our discipline have argued that we must and should draw on this research in order engage in discussions with stakeholders, our attempts to do so have not always been met with success, as Hesse has discussed. Other examples abound, as well. For instance, many of our colleagues, prevented from revealing details by the nondisclosure agreements they have had to sign to get in the door, have discussed in broad-brush strokes the frustrations of participating in test development or score-setting activities with the companies developing tests for the Partnership for Readiness in College and Career (PARCC) and Smarter Balanced. Still other colleagues describe attempts to talk with state legislators about policy related to "remedial" education, or testing practices, or outcomes development. The wpa-l LISTSERV continues to include messages from faculty members seeking advice on how to respond to challenges to their ideas about writing that come in the form of requests for assessments or other activities.

Examples like these, which chronicle a litany of frustrations, suggest that new strategies for engaging in discussions with others who believe that they can "speak for writing" might useful. For these purposes, we must draw on the regime of competence in which we participate. This competence is rooted in the "criteria and expectations" of the community, which necessarily lead to a shared "understanding [of] what matters, what the enterprise of the community is, and . . . a shared perspective." From this understanding and perspective, competence also involves "using appropriately the repertoire of resources that the community has accumulated through its history of learning" (Wenger 2010, 180). But we also must extend *from* that competency to others' competencies, adopting a receptive stance engaging with others and their understandings of the focal point of our competence, the study of composed knowledge.[1]

### KNOWLEDGEABILITY AND/IN LANDSCAPES OF PRACTICE

The strategies I am starting to describe here extend from knowledgeability. This practice, again, emerges within a landscape of practice, that conceptual territory "consisting of a complex system of communities of practice and the boundaries between them" (Wenger-Trayner and Wenger-Trayner 2015, 13). Because writing is perceived to be the business of so many, the landscapes of practice in which writing is involved are many and diverse. Within a postsecondary institution, for instance, a landscape associated with "writing competence" might be populated by the following:

- communities constituted by different academic disciplines (each of which, extending from their own regimes of competence, have ideas about the roles that writing as a form of representation plays within their community);
- administrators, who must describe to multiple audiences (including but not limited to parents, employers, and accreditors) how students develop as writers as a result of their experiences within the institution);
- policy makers, who must develop or articulate expectations and standards for writing that the institution must consider or demonstrate in some way(s).

And then, of course, there are the actual writing faculty within the institution who express affinity with or allegiance to the field—people like readers of this book—who have research- and practice-based expertise that mark us as emerging or existing experts within the regime of practice within our own community.

While the expert knowledge of other disciplines is sometimes seen as contested terrain (see, for instance, revision, debate over, and subsequent second revision of the AP History standards in 2014 and 2015 [see Lerner 2015]), writing is unique in that so many feel that their experiences lead them to expertise in both what constitutes the "content" of writing knowledge ("good grammar," "clear and concise writing," "accurate punctuation," and so on) and a vision of how that content should be conveyed (strict standards, assessments focusing on < x, y, and z > , and so on). The landscapes of practice of which writing is a part, then, are case studies for additional characteristics of the terrain defined by the Wenger-Trayners: they are dynamic, shaping and shaped by practices within, and they are "political," containing "competing voices and competing claims to knowledge" (15–16). The landscapes and communities within them are sometimes complementary and sometimes overlapping; hence, the boundaries of the communities are more or less permeable.

Knowledgeability, as described earlier, is enacted within these sometimes clamorous landscapes. Knowledgeability involves drawing on expertise within one community of practice and its regime of competence, then attempting to listen to and understand, as thoroughly as possible, the elements of competence that exist within one or more other communities within shared landscapes. "In this sense," the Wenger-Trayners explain, "*knowledgeability is not defined with respect . . . to a single community, but within a broader landscape* that includes a set of practices beyond a person's ability to claim competence in all" (23; emphasis added). Through the lens of knowledgeability it is possible to contend that focusing on the identification of boundaries—as the literature on disciplinarity reviewed earlier has done and as researchers in our field like Kopelson, Dobrin, and Horner have asserted, sometimes has taken place within our discipline—misses the ways that competence (including knowledge and ideas) travel through enactment and potential embodiment within a landscape of practice (Wenger 2010).

*Enacting Knowledgeability*

This idea of knowledgeability might provide outlines of a structure through which to enact Reid and Miller's idea of open, networked disciplines or what Chris Gallagher called "participatory professional practices, shared knowledge-making with partners inside and outside the academy" (Gallagher 2005, 88). This enactment is rooted in participation in the regime of competence of a community plus the core knowledge, values, and ideas within the community with which they are most associated. With reference to academic communities, one way to label this participation is to say that the individual must participate in a community's threshold concepts, ideas critical for epistemological participation (Meyer and Land 2006, 9). As Kathleen Blake Yancey (2015) notes, "threshold concepts . . . are specific to a discipline and a community of practice; they often function as a kind of boundary object in dialogue with local situations and/or other frameworks" (xxviii). Participating in threshold concepts of a community of practice is certainly more possible when those concepts are made explicit so that individuals can understand what they are. Within our discipline efforts such as the one that resulted in *Naming What We Know*, a mini-crowdsourced effort to which thirty-one Writing Studies teachers and researchers generated ideas that led to articulation of some of the field's threshold concepts, can be seen as one effort to make these concepts explicit. Heilker and Vandenberg's (2015) *Keywords in Composition Studies* is another such attempt. These texts represent, in part, efforts to make threshold concepts (in the case of *Naming What We Know*) or key concepts ("Keywords"; "Decolonizing") more explicit for those entering or already within the community of practice. Naming, interrogating, and continuing to explore key or threshold concepts that are central to expertise within a community of practice have, historically and conventionally, been key activities associated with disciplinarity.

When disciplinarity is reconceived through the idea of knowledgeability, though, this naming and interrogating are steps in an ongoing dialogic process. Another involves learning more about the key or threshold concepts, values, ideas, language, and practices of others within the landscapes of practice that we inhabit, and then considering how and whether we (as individuals within a landscape and as a discipline whose very subject is included in many landscapes) might genuinely engage in discussion with them. In the case of our discipline and its two-sided foci on composed knowledge and knowledge of composing, aka written or produced text and the array of practices and process contributing to production, this means genuinely attempting to engage in discussion with others who also believe that they "speak for writing" and, importantly, shifting our perspective slightly, believing not only that working from our discipline's expert knowledge might have some influence on their ideas, but being open to having their ideas influence our own.

In some landscapes—say, conversations within a landscape of practice among faculty from different disciplines (communities of practice) and faculty members from a writing program about what "good writing" looks like and how it might be taught—the prospect of facilitating connections that are meaningful for both communities (or, to use the language of knowledgeability, to seek for points of identity alignment within a landscape of practice) is not so difficult. In others, though—say, a discussion among officials who are policy makers and members of that same writing program—it becomes more daunting. It requires an identity shift that may be uncomfortable or, in the language of threshold concepts, "troublesome." Sometimes, members of our discipline have worked from the principle that we need to "fight" to ensure the knowledge- and practice-based threshold concepts at the core of our (disciplinary) identities to make sure that they are recognized and taken up by others. Instead, genuinely enacting knowledgeability means that we work from the stance that while we *have* core values and knowledge represented—for instance, in keywords or threshold concepts—others have ideas and concepts that are valuable within their own communities and may also be useful for ours. These ideas and concepts may lead to a reconsideration of some of our own ideas—their definitions or the actions that we take extending from them, or even the ideas themselves (an experience I speak to in "Enactment 1" later in this chapter).

To be sure, then, this is an optimistic vision. It proceeds from the presumption that fundamentally, people are interested in doing good, and that if we dig deep enough, we will find connections within this common goal from which to proceed, an idea analogous to the philosophy embraced by community organizer Saul Alinsky that fundamentally, individuals' self-interest would contribute to the public good (see Alinsky 1946). A hopeful caution is useful here, too. As Beverly and Etienne Wenger-Trayner explain, seeking alignment between communities "does not displace people's agendas; on the contrary it embraces these agendas to make them more ambitious, more connected, and in the end more likely to be effective" (109). NCTE Communications Coordinator Jenna Fournel describes this kind of discomfort, but also discusses the benefits that can accrue from genuine engagement when she talks about making connections with others—community members, policy makers, legislators—who care about literacy learning, for instance. To do so, she says, we need to practice "learning to listen and observe and be a careful student of the context and the people that you're around. It's a learning curve to arrive at that understanding," though, she concedes. "When I'm passionate about an issue I want to go in there asserting everything that I know and how smart and knowledgeable I am about this thing and why you're wrong and I'm right and I need to tell you why to think differently" (Fournel 2015). Reconceptualizing Writing Studies' disciplinarity through this idea of knowledgeability, then, requires *identifying* the expert knowledge within our community of practice (an inward-facing activity), but also seeing that knowledge as outward-facing, putting it into dialogue with the ideas of other communities that coinhabit landscapes of practice, possibly adjusting the knowledge and/or boundaries of our discipline/community of practice in response to others in a recursive way. As Fournel notes, this requires a stance that isn't always familiar or even comfortable—but it is necessary.

For some writing instructors or program directors, this concept of knowledgeability might seem to be a new name assigned to an old practice: drawing on "appropriate rhetoric" or participating in "rhetorically motivated efforts" to make connections within a program or between a program and others. For others, this idea of knowledgeability might seem entirely new. In either case—that is, whether knowledgeability is perceived as a new way to think about an existing practice or a new practice entirely—it offers a more precise language for this idea, as well as characteristics that can be used to both engage in it and assess the fruits of that engagement. These are qualities associated with what Etienne Wenger-Trayner refers to as "the creation of a technical language," language that has a "formal role in . . . theory" (Wenger-Trayner 2013, 107). Such language, he writes, has four characteristics. It is "generative," opening new questions or insights; "evocative," providing new ways to expand perspective and "stimulate imagination [to] encourage us to see things in new ways"; "recogni[z]able . . . resonat[ing] with our experience in ways that make it easy to appropriate . . . "; and "systematic," contributing to a "systematic whole, which results in a coherent perspective" (Wenger-Trayner 2013, 107–8).

While terms like "rhetorically motivated efforts" may (or may not) be associated with an individual's or a program's efforts to engage in connection making, the conceptualization of that term is left to the individual or program. It might be carefully conceptualized and defined; it also might not be. A benefit of the concept and the *term* "knowledgeability," then, is that it is initially "technizised" through the Wenger-Trayners' work. For some, it might provide a way to describe practices already within the regime of competence. For others, it might be a new way of thinking about something that is useful for that regime. In either case, the practice of introducing language and ways of thinking about practice are a central part of blending theory and action. "Good social theory," Wenger-Trayner argues, "produce[s] knowledge not by telling people things they do not know, but by providing tools to make sense of what they already know through personal experience and hence know it anew," understanding that experience from a different and potentially more generative perspective (Wenger-Trayner 2013, 106). The concept of knowledgeability might thus provide a more precise way to think about an old practice for some, or introduce a way to conceive of a new practice for others. If it is taken up within our discipline, Writing Studies researchers and teachers can build on this foundation, ultimately perhaps coming to an understanding of the idea as we have understandings of other ideas that have become part of the regime of competence—the knowledge and practice base—of the discipline.

## ENACTING DISCIPLINARITY AS KNOWLEDGEABILITY

At this point, it would be conventional for me to provide an illustration of the ways in which I or others have enacted this reconceptualized idea of disciplinarity in order to ground a somewhat theoretical discussion in concrete practices. However, I'm not sure that I've arrived at a fully developed enactment of this idea. There are two reasons for this. First, the "meaningful discussion" portion of knowledgeability as I think about some audiences (say, some policy makers) is still troublesome to me. Second and perhaps more important, though, I'm only beginning to articulate these ideas (in this chapter and elsewhere). To represent any illustrations as at-the-time conscious applications of the ideas here, then, would be inaccurate. With these caveats, however, I will discuss three efforts with which I have been associated that I believe can begin to demonstrate aspects of this reconceptualized idea of disciplinarity as enactment of knowledgeability; in fact, the first two of these illustrations has led me to the idea of disciplinarity-as-knowledgeability as I am outlining it here. I also will discuss a third illustration I am in the midst of designing that will do so more consciously. These examples telescope out: the first is the most focused application of this idea (designing a class); the second broadens to focus on writing within a program and, ultimately, the institution; the third to undergraduate education within the institution. Each, then, is located within different institutional landscapes of practice. For the purposes of illustration, I focus on the institutional level for two reasons. First, we are more likely to be able to enact knowledgeability at that level—just as we are able to affect change more profoundly at the local level. Second and related, it is easier to see the idea of disciplinarity-as-knowledgeability (which is complex enough on its own) focusing at the level of the local/institutional. Beyond that level, the landscape becomes ever more complex, as do the communities of practice and regimes of competence within the landscape. I will close by discussing how the principles inherent in each also would apply to an application of the idea if disciplinarity-as-knowledgeability in a landscape outside of the institution, such as one populated by communities whose members believed that they "speak for writing."

***Enactment 1: Designing and Teaching a "Linked" First-Year Writing Course***
As I was interviewing for the position as director of the UC Santa Barbara Writing Program in 2007, a number of administrators outside of the Writing Program emphasized to me what they perceived to the value of "linked" first-year writing courses offered by the program. In these courses students simultaneously enrolled in large lecture courses and a second of Writing 2, UCSB's required lower division general education course. These sections of Writing 2, it was explained to me, helped students write more effectively in the large lecture course. As someone who has long chafed at the idea of first-year composition as a "service" course, I found the idea of these courses troubling. My perception was that these courses were positioned as "in service" to the large lecture courses with which they were linked; this contradicted principles and elements of the regime of competence that I believed to be associated with Writing Studies.

After I was hired into the position as director, I spent the first summer I was in residence meeting with any and all faculty members outside of the Writing Program that I could. I started by contacting chairs of departments in the same academic division within the College of Letters and Science as the Writing Program, Humanities and Fine Arts, and especially with department chairs whose graduate students taught Writing 2 (since most Writing Program TAs come from other HFA departments). Among the first of these discussions was one with the then-chair of the History Department, John Majewski. We discussed his department and then moved to his research focus, economic history just after the US Civil War. He asked me about my research; I explained that some of it focused on learning about how "good writing" was defined and advocating for ideas associated with "good writing" in policy. I pointed to the debate in the early 1990s over standards for American history as somewhat analogous to my research.

As our discussion unfolded along these points of shared interest, John asked me: "Do you know anything about assessment?" I conceded that yes, I did. He then said, "I'm really interested in what makes students good historical thinkers." I then suggested that this was a subject in which I also was deeply interested,[2] and I asked if he would like to continue talking about it, perhaps thinking about how he was defining "good historical thinking." At some point early in these discussions, I quickly realized that there would be great possibilities for our shared development if I taught a Writing 2 that was "linked" to a large lecture course that John taught. Committing to the course required me to confront the beliefs that I describe earlier—which stem directly from my competence as a participant in a disciplinary community of practice—and to put aside objections related to my participation in a regime of competence.

The "linked" Writing 2 course that I designed in collaboration with John was like no course I had ever designed or taught before. To invoke the language of knowledgeability, I had began to step outside of the traditional boundaries of my identity as a participant in a disciplinary community of practice—an identity, again, linked to my own participation in a regime of competence—since taking on the course itself was in some ways anathema to what I perceived to be the values and practices of the discipline. At the same time, I also considered what core knowledge, values, and practices I would need to include in the "linked" Writing 2 course that *were* associated with that competence. For me (and at that point, in fall 2010 / winter 2011), these were ideas associated with the importance of genre study; studying genres and recognizing the ways in which genres were situated in context and that genre conventions emerged in relation to context were critical. Assignments in the first iteration of the course thus immersed students in study of genres and "literacy practices" (Barton and Hamilton 2003) in a specific context familiar to them (assignment one); John's history course broadly and an assignment that they had written for that course (assignment two); the relevance of literacy practices and genres in the study of history (assignment three); and a portfolio that included revisions of two of these assignments.

Each of these assignments extended from what I considered to be key elements associated with the regime of competence of the discipline. Drawing on some of the threshold concepts of the discipline (that were not yet articulated at the time), for instance, the first assignment reflected the idea that "writing is a social and rhetorical activity" (Roozen 2015) and a number of subconcepts related to that broader one; the second "writing speaks to situations and contexts through recognizable forms" (Bazerman 2015) and subconcepts related to it; and the third that "writing enacts identities and ideologies" (Scott 2015) and subconcepts related to it and the previous two broad concepts, as well. The portfolio, finally, reflected concepts related to writers' development, such as "text is an object outside of one's self that can be improved and developed" (Bazerman and Tinberg 2015), "revision is central to developing writing" (Downs 2015), and "reflection is critical for writers' development" (Taczak 2015).

The process of designing and teaching the course and the process of ongoing discussions about and research into the course with John represented "claims to knowledgeability . . . negotiated within the politics of knowledge" from our specific communities of practice, but within our shared landscape of practice—in this case, the general education program and our disciplines on our campus. These moments of knowledgeability, I would contend, constituted significant contributions for both of us and, ultimately, to the institutional landscape of practice that we shared. Individually, our thinking about both courses contributed enormously to both of our approaches to thinking about our courses, teaching, and disciplines. From this collaboration we both began to think about core concepts for epistemological participation in our disciplines; once we stumbled across threshold concepts, we quickly began to use that idea as we thought about our courses, a process that we described in our first collaborative publication (Adler-Kassner et al. 2012). We began interviewing faculty in different departments about threshold concepts in their disciplines; as a result of that work, I began thinking about these ideas within and across general education courses (Adler-Kassner 2014). With other participants in a three-year research seminar in which I was participating, I also began to think about the value of articulating threshold concepts of a discipline and the value of doing so for discussions about writing in and beyond the classroom, thinking that ultimately led to the collaboration with Elizabeth Wardle and twenty-seven other authors on *Naming What We Know*.

Meanwhile, at UCSB, John "transformed" his large GE history course, a process that contributed to the experience of students in the course (Adler-Kassner and Majewski 2015) and the experience of TAs working with John (McGowan). I also began to think about how using John's history course as a subject of study for Writing 2 could serve as a model for working with graduate students learning to teach Writing 2 (students who, remember, are primarily from other HFA departments such as history, English, music, religious studies, and so on) in the Writing Program's TA practicum, and how positioning the study of writing in different sites (i.e., courses) *as* a sort of boundary subject could make study and teaching of writing more meaningful for those graduate students. These enactments of knowledgeability would not have occurred within a more conventional idea of "disciplinarity," as they were spurred initially by a collaboration (i.e., teaching the Writing 2 "linked" class) that, to me, ran counter to key disciplinary precepts as I interpreted them at the time. This example, then, illustrates the idea of knowledgeability as it extended from discussions about teaching into a writing course.

### Enactment 2: Writing Development via Institutional Assessment

The second example of knowledgeability I will describe here concerns the development and reach of a writing program within an institution. It focuses on the UCSB Writing Program—which, to the best of my knowledge and that of my colleagues, is the oldest independent writing program in the country. Established as an independent unit in 1991, the program will celebrate its twenty-fifth anniversary in 2017.

The Writing Program was created when three existing units were brought together under a common administrative roof: the Freshman English Program, a two-course, literature-based, lower-division writing sequence; the Program in Intensive English, which offered lower-division writing courses specifically for low-income and (at that time) designated minority students through the university's Educational Opportunity Program; and the Interdisciplinary Writing Program, which offered technical writing and upper-division adjunct "writing for" courses—that is, courses intended to be taken concurrently with academic courses in a variety of disciplines. These "writing for" courses, especially, were seen as crucial for the program's continued survival, especially in the midst a budget crisis in the early 1990s. General education requirements stated that students needed two writing courses—one at the lower division and one at the upper. If students were required by other majors to enroll in "writing for" courses at the upper-division level, those courses would always be in demand and the non-Senate faculty who taught them (and whose salaries came from soft money) would always be needed.

As I note in Enactment 1, I interviewed for the position of director of the Writing Program in 2007, sixteen years after the program's founding and in the midst of yet another budget crisis. At the time, I perceived the idea of "writing for" courses to be anathema to the principles and perspective I associated with the discipline of Writing Studies. I believed they positioned writing instructors as people who taught the things that other people didn't want to teach and writing as something that got done in other places but had no substance or content of its own. After I was hired as the program's director, I spent the 2009–10 academic year traveling between my former institution and UCSB. During this time, I held two rounds of one-to-one discussions with all thirty-four or so faculty members in the program to hear about what they liked about the program and their jobs, what they wanted to change, and what they brought to the program from their experiences.[3] Across the range of these discussions, faculty said that they wanted the university to have greater respect for their knowledge as teachers of writing. Coming into these discussions I believed that the program's "writing for" courses not only did not contribute to the respect that my new colleagues sought, but detracted from it. At the same time, my colleagues enjoyed teaching the courses; they also represented ties to other disciplines (e.g., economics) and types of writing (e.g., business writing) that colleagues agreed were valuable and important.

Working with my colleagues and their desires and beliefs to reposition the Writing Program in the institutional landscape required me to confront beliefs about how writing was represented in a program that not only relied on "writing for" courses, but also embraced them. Rather than try to persuade colleagues that the courses were part of the issue (though I believed they were), I put this position aside. Instead, together colleagues and I worked through a series of iterative workshops in which we articulated the values and ideals at the core of our teaching, then thought about what these would look like within and across our large and vertically integrated program. This process led to a revised mission statement that identified the program's three areas of foci: writing for academic, civic, and professional life. Over the next two or so years and through workshops and other professional development activities, it also led to a definition of what students in the program *did* in relation to writing in these sites: they *studied* and *practiced with*. "Study of and practice with writing in specific contexts," especially academic, civic, and professional life, became central to all of our work—from designing courses to reviewing curriculum guides, to looking at connections across programs to conducting assessments of those courses.

Ultimately, "study of and practice with writing" also led us to represent the work of the Writing Program very differently within the context of the university, as well. When I arrived, our courses were referred to as "service." We began to reframe this idea. We agreed that engaging with the expertise of our discipline, the study of composed knowledge was indeed a "service," since the ability to study and practice with writing in academic, civic, and professional contexts—an ability that students would learn in no other discipline but ours—would serve them well across the remainder of their academic and professional careers. We also suggested that since studying composed knowledge and helping others to practice with that knowledge was at the core of our disciplinary expertise, this "service" might be useful to others on campus, building on work that my predecessor Sue McLeod and colleague Karen Lunsford had done with other faculty and departments on campus.

Two years into the Writing Program's active reframing, an ongoing activity that I argue illustrates one enactment of knowledgeability, we had the opportunity to engage in another through UCSB's institutional accreditation activities. In addition to the "Area A" requirement that required students to take a lower- and upper-division writing course (all but one of which were and still are offered only in the Writing Program), the general education program includes an additional six course "writing requirement" referred to as WR. Writing requirement courses are offered by almost every department in the College of Letters and Science.[4] In 2011–12, Writing Program faculty were centrally involved in the design and execution of the assessment of newly developed WR outcomes. These revolved around a central precept associated with the regime of competence of Writing Studies: the idea that qualities of good writing are context specific (or, to use the language of two threshold concepts, "writing speaks to situations and contexts through recognizable forms" [Bazerman 2015] and "writing is a way of enacting disciplinarity" [Lerner 2015]).[5]

Working with Lorna Gonzalez, a graduate researcher, and Laurel Wilder, associate director of UCSB's Office of Institutional Research as well as program faculty, we designed a multistep process for this assessment. Here, I focus on the first part: a workshop bringing together twenty-two faculty members from eighteen disciplines. Its purposes were to first, have faculty define key focal points of each outcome—rhetorical conventions, roles of writing, roles of evidence, use of evidence, and conventions—as reflected in writing in their discipline; and to describe what different levels of demonstration of these outcomes would look like in student writing in their general education course(s). In the workshop, participants began by working with faculty in "like" disciplines to define the outcomes in their disciplines.[6] Next, to further define and describe these characteristics, faculty worked with colleagues from disciplines as "unlike" theirs as possible (e.g., feminist studies and earth science; English and engineering). This process of discussion also led them to clarify the characteristics identified in the first stage because the contrasts were so pronounced. Finally, they drew on student work to identify what these characteristics looked like in student writing, identification that would contribute to the development of scoring guides that would eventually enable raters to see how these ideas were operationalized. This workshop, like the WR outcomes, reflected principles associated with the regime of competence of Writing Studies, such as the threshold concepts described earlier about genre, context, and disciplinarity. It also reflected principles associated with the role that Writing Studies professionals and the knowledge of our discipline can play for others and in situations not directly associated with our discipline, such as a discussion about writing in the WR courses.

Applying the idea that knowledgeability often requires an identity shift as members work from competence in one community of practice (for instance, my interpretation of principles associated with ideas about writing and context) and attempt to understand and remain receptive to principles of other communities, the WR workshop in many ways was an embodiment of this concept for faculty participants. Two, for instance, described what I would (in retrospect) identify as enacting knowledgeability in interviews that Lorna and I conducted with participants shortly after the workshops (Adler-Kassner and Gonzalez 2016). A faculty member from an ethnic studies discipline, for instance, said that she realized following participation in the workshop that the guidelines she had previously written for students with regard to their papers were both generic and rigid; "after going through the workshop," she "was appalled that [she] had said that," adding that "[the thesis] is different for every discipline."

A faculty member in environmental, ecology, and marine biology (EEMB) similarly reported that the workshop helped him realize his insistence that "clear writing" was all that was required to achieve the WR outcomes was overly broad. Especially in his general education courses (including those fulfilling the WR), he realized that "these are students who should come to communicate *about* biology. And, the worst thing we can do for those students is to teach them to write in what people perceive as very drab, dull, dry, scientific style . . . We'd actually rather they not do that." Both of these faculty members, then, enacted knowledgeability as they drew on principles of one community (principles associated with Writing Studies), experienced challenges to identities within their own communities, and came to realizations that they also translated into pedagogical activities, "meaningful moment[s] of service" (Wenger-Trayner et al. 2015, [23]) within the landscape of practice associated both with general education, and with faculty members who "speak for writing" in their disciplines.

At the same time, the WR workshops and the process of developing the WR assessment contributed to the Writing Program's ongoing efforts to build connections with others who are invested in writing across the campus. Writing Program faculty were actively involved in the workshop itself and in the analysis of the data; the experience of hearing from faculty in a wide range of disciplines about the expectations for writing in their disciplines has contributed to everything from conceptual framing of course (e.g., an enhanced focus on metacognitive practices that enable students to recognize the contexts in which they are working in a range of Writing Program courses, from first-year writing to Writing for Business and Administration; to specific assignments intended to engage students in that conceptual thinking. The WR workshop and subsequent assessment, then, represents one moment in a long journey of knowledgeability in which the Writing Program has been and remains engaged as it positions its work as outward facing and dialogic within the university's landscape of practice. It also illustrates the ways in which participation in discussions *about* what "labor" is associated with knowledge and the value of knowledge (to use the language of Horner's concerns)—that is, what efforts associated with composing are considered good, useful, less good, inappropriate, and so on—becomes a significant contribution that Writing Studies' disciplinarity, as knowledgeability, can provide to an institution. Put more directly: If we understand our roles as being involved with facilitating, sometimes even enabling, discussions about "good writing" (or "good composed knowledge"), and we bring to these genuine commitments to openness and a stance that welcomes (or at least is respective to) identity challenge, these roles *are* enactments of our expertise and knowledge.

### Enactment 3: Understanding Undergraduate Education

Where the previous two examples are ones where I have applied the lens of knowledgeability over past processes, the third illustration represents an effort designed through this lens, but which has not yet taken place. This is from the broadest perspective, undergraduate education within an institution.

The value of undergraduate education at the University of California is a subject of considerable public discussion within the state right now. Governor Jerry Brown, whose artful political work resulted in voter approval of a desperately needed initiative to increase funding to K–12 and postsecondary education in 2012, has taken an active role in discussions about higher education. Most recently, following extensive budget negotiations (and resultant discussions) with Brown, UC President Janet Napolitano has asked UC campuses to engage with a number of challenges associated with undergraduate education, including exploring the possibility of three-year undergraduate degrees and expanding the number of cross-campus online classes. At the same time, my own campus has hired a number of new administrators, the most senior of whom is undertaking strategic conversations about academic planning.

With these discussions and challenges as a backdrop (and from the perspective of my own new administrative position), I am in the midst of designing a series of discussions about the value of undergraduate education at UCSB. While the landscape of practice for these discussions, "undergraduate education at UC Santa Barbara," might seem to extend beyond the boundaries of Writing Studies as a discipline, the effort is shaped from the idea of knowledgeability-as-disciplinarity within Writing Studies and from my own "competence" within this community of practice. In this sense, then, it is like the assessment that I describe in enactment 2, which extended disciplinary principles (and threshold concepts) beyond the discipline. At the same time, as I've suggested, as Chris Gallagher has asserted, and perhaps as Bruce Horner would suggest, this extension is necessarily part of Writing Studies' disciplinarity-as-knowledgeability as I am outlining it here.

To conduct these mapping conversations, I will adapt a strategy outlined by Mark Coenders, Robert Brood, and the Wenger-Trayners (Coenders et al. 2015) that parallels ones used by community organizers (see Adler-Kassner 2008). This begins with identification of a problem or a question—here, "What is the value of undergraduate education?" The first goal of the discussions is to identify boundaries between definitions of "value" as outlined by specific communities that can produce new forms of knowledgeability, new "meaningful moments of service" that emerge when "practices and boundaries" come into synergistic contact (Wenger-Trayner and Wenger-Trayner 2015, 23). For instance, it may be possible to articulate shared ideas about value more clearly to a variety of interested parties, locate areas where existing initiatives can enhance areas of shared value, create new initiatives, and so on. The second goal is to identify boundaries where these definitions of "value" may be quite disparate and to consider the implications of those disparate definitions.

To reach these goals, the "Mapping the Value of Undergraduate Education" discussions will bring together stakeholders from communities on and off campus interested in the value of an undergraduate education: students who are part of the formally constituted student-governing body (Associated Students); faculty who are part of the formally constituted faculty governing body (Faculty Senate); administrators and staff who are part of different aspects of student affairs; administrators and faculty who are part of academic affairs; parents; donors to undergraduate education efforts; development officers, employers working with undergraduate interns; and so on. However, not everyone in those groups is part of these discussions; they will involve "enterprising group[s] of people whose circumstances and priorities enable them to take risks and responsibility in dealing with the problems in new ways" (Coenders et al. 2015, 126). Neither coming to vent nor to "take" are acceptable. Instead, all participants "must be ready to interweave their practices, perspectives, and competencies to explore possibilities and take action as a group. This entails a responsibility to engage seriously across boundaries without knowing future outcomes beforehand and to build on each other's practices to develop new practices as a group. It requires a sense of accountability to a new configuration of actors involved in (re-) thinking the solution" (Coenders et al. 2015, 126–27).

In the first stage of these discussions, representatives constituting the "enterprising groups" will come together to articulate responses to the questions about the value of undergraduate education within their communities. Next, representatives from each community will come together in cross-group sessions to discuss shared responses and identify points of agreement and divergence, moments where they see value (as defined within the different communities) being enacted, possibilities for new initiatives, and areas that need attention. Participants will then explicitly consider how the cross-group responses contribute to existing and potential efforts related to statements about the value of undergraduate education that speak with, and perhaps to, others invested with questions about this value, such as Brown and Napolitano.

Drawing on the experiences of enactments 1 and 2, the "Mapping the Value of Undergraduate Education" discussions will be another step in the manifestation of Writing Studies' reconceptualized disciplinarity I am outlining here. That is: these discussions will be rooted in principles of our discipline, such the idea that "disciplinary and professional identities are constructed through writing" (Estrem 2015); they will then build from those principles. While these may not always directly revolve around writing, writing will doubtless be involved in the discussions—because as I've said above, it always is. Writing *is* everybody's business (in some ways), and everybody believes that they can and sometimes should "speak for writing." Placing ourselves in positions where we enable and participate in these discussions, then, is at the core of each of these enactments. They require us to identify the principles, values, language, strategies for learning how to learn, and so on that are associated with the community of practice constituted by and within our discipline. But rather than do so in order to draw boundaries around the discipline for the purposes of institutional status, professional identity, or other separating activities, knowledgeability compels us to then begin identifying moments where encounters between these boundaries and others can lead to new ideas, initiatives, even knowledge practices.

To be sure, there are issues of power (and power imbalance) here. Examples like the ones I cited in the opening of this chapter—the

Spellings Commission, the Common Core discussion, even those about institutional assessment—attest to the fact that other voices (such as those of policy makers, politicians, and grant makers) have been far more powerful than our own in recent experience. The illustrations I've drawn on in this concluding portion of the chapter also point to another reality: the more contained the landscape of practice, the more conceivable it is to enact disciplinarity-as-knowledgeability. The landscape across two courses (enactment1), while complicated, essentially involved two faculty members and twelve TAs; the landscape across twenty-two disciplines within a general education program was larger but still within an institution; the landscape across an institution and those invested in it, even extending to stakeholders outside, is still linked to the institution. But there are far larger landscapes involving writing, such as statewide policies or even national standards or assessments (e.g., the Common Core standards and their assessments), where we hope that our competence plays a role. As we consider how to enact disciplinarity-as-knowledgeability within these landscapes, we must also consider what *effective* engagement between our disciplinary regime of competence and other regimes might look like—in other words, what it might mean to be *successful* in this process. For instance, if language from a document that we feel reflects principles associated with our regime of competence such as *The Framework for Success in Postsecondary Writing* is taken up in a state's policies with regard to writing, and then the statewide assessment contains items that test students' abilities with the habits of mind outlined there, does that represent knowledgeability in action? Anecdotally, I have heard colleagues in the discipline complain bitterly about such examples—but their concerns lead me to wonder what a "win" might look like.

As this example attests, enacting disciplinarity-as-knowledgeability, an outward-focused and dialogic activity, raises complex questions that can be identity challenging and (to use language associated with threshold concepts) troublesome. But as we encounter a landscape of practice where politicians, policy makers, foundation officers, parents, employers, administrators, faculty colleagues, and so many others make assertions about what writing is or should be, and when their voices are both more powerful than ours (often buoyed by significant funding from foundations and others), reconceptualizing disciplinarity through knowledgeability, as this kind of outward-facing activity that involves opening may provide possibilities for reimagining this landscape that we have yet to consider.

## Notes

1. It is extremely important to emphasize that I am using the term "competency" here as Wenger and Wenger-Trayner do, as expert practices that are included in "regimes of competency" circulating within and developed by members of communities of practice. This is quite distinct from the usage of the term "competency" invoked by advocates of competency-based education. In that context, "competencies" refer to particular goals, often described in terms of performance, that learners are expected to achieve which can then be measured or otherwise made evident in particular types of assessments.
2. I am a former history teacher, and much of my earlier research was historical; my dissertation research lay at an intersection between literacy studies, historiography, American studies, and communication.
3. Most of these were (and remain) non-Senate faculty; by the time I arrived, all held full-time appointments. A system for stable employment and regular review had also been established by the time I arrived (through the efforts of the UC-AFT union and the university). Faculty received multiyear contracts, had regular review, and worked toward "continuing" status, which was granted after a review of teaching, professional development, and service in the fifth year. Once achieved, continuing lecturers receive rolling, three-year contracts with no end date. Many of the faculty in the Writing Program had by then been there since before the program became independent.
4. Currently, more than 200 courses carry WR credit.
5. The outcomes were developed the previous academic year through a process involving faculty members teaching courses in all GE area, including WR. The revised outcomes state that students will (1) produce writing that uses rhetorical conventions appropriate to different disciplines and, if appropriate, languages; (2) identify the roles that types of writing play in the production and circulation of knowledge within specific disciplines; (3) identify the role of evidence in writing within specific disciplines; (4) locate, interpret, and use discipline-specific evidence appropriately; and (5) use conventions of organization, style, coherence, structure, syntax, and mechanics appropriate to specific disciplines.
6. These included groupings such as history and classics, environmental and ecological biology and earth science, English and comparative literature. To construct these groups, we collected and analyzed a sample of 100 papers from WR courses.

## References

Adler-Kassner, Linda. 2008. *The Activist WPA: Changing Stories about Writing and Writers.* Logan: Utah State University Press. https://doi.org/10.2307/j.ctt4cgqss.

Adler-Kassner, Linda. 2012. "The Companies We Keep *Or* the Companies We Would Like to Try to Keep: Strategies and Tactics in Challenging Times." *WPA: Writing Program Administration* 36 (1): 119–40.

Adler-Kassner, Linda. 2014. "Liberal Learning, Professional Training, and Disciplinarity in the Age of Educational 'Reform': Remodeling General Education." *College English* 76 (5): 436–57.

Adler-Kassner, Linda, and Lorna Gonzalez. 2016. "Everybody Writes: Accreditation and Assessment at UC Santa Barbara." In *Reclaiming Accountability: Improving Programs through Accreditation and Large-Scale Assessment,* ed. Wendy Sharer, Tracy Morse, Michelle Eble, and William F. Banks, 242–62. Utah State University Press. https://doi.org/10.7330/9781607324355.c012.

Adler-Kassner, Linda, and John Majewski. 2015. "Extending the Invitation: Threshold Concepts, Professional Development, and Outreach." In *Naming What We Know: Threshold Concepts of Writing Studies*, ed. Linda Adler-Kassner and Elizabeth Wardle, 186–202. Logan: Utah State University Press. https://doi.org/10.7330/9780874 219906.c0012.

Adler-Kassner, Linda, John Majewski, and Damian Koshnick. 2012. "The Value of Troublesome Knowledge: Transfer and Threshold Concepts in Writing and History." *Composition Forum* 26. http://compositionforum.com/issue/26/troublesome-knowl edge-threshold.php.

Adler-Kassner, Linda, and Elizabeth Wardle, eds. 2015. *Naming What We Know: Threshold Concepts of Writing Studies*. Logan: Utah State University Press.

Alinsky, Saul. 1946. *Reveille for Radicals*. New York: Random House.

Applebee, Arthur. 2013. "Common Core State Standards: The Promise and the Peril in a National Palimpsest." *English Journal* 103 (1): 25–33.

Barton, David, and Mary Hamilton. 2003. *Local Literacies: Reading and Writing in One Community*. London: Routledge.

Bazerman, Charles. 2015. "Writing Speaks to Situations through Recognizable Forms." In *Naming What We Know: Threshold Concepts of Writing Studies*, ed. Linda Adler-Kassner and Elizabeth Wardle, 35–37. Logan: Utah State University Press.

Bazerman, Charles, and Howard Tinberg. 2015. "Text Is an Object Outside of One's Self that Can Be Improved and Developed." In *Naming What We Know: Threshold Concepts of Writing Studies*, ed. Linda Adler-Kassner and Elizabeth Wardle, 61–62. Logan: Utah State University Press.

Becher, Tony, and Paul R. Trowler. 2001. *Academic Tribes and Territories*. 2nd ed. Buckingham: Society for Research into Higher Education and Open University Press.

Bender, Thomas. 1997. *Intellect and Public Life: Essays on the Social History of Academic Intellectuals in the United States*. Baltimore: Johns Hopkins University Press.

Carey, James. 1989. *Communication as Culture: Essays on Media and Society*. Boston: Unwin and Hyman.

Clark, Burton. 1983. *The Higher Education System: Academic Organization in Cross-National Perspective*. Berkeley: University of California Press.

Coenders, Marc, Robert Bood, Beverly Wenger-Trayner, and Etienne Wenger-Trayner. 2015. "Habiforum: Convening Stakeholders to Reinvent Spatial Planning." In *Learning in Landscapes of Practice*, ed. Etienne Wenger-Trayner, Mark Fenton-O'Creevy, Steven Hutchinson, Chris Kubiak, and Beverly Wenger-Trayner, 119–31. London: Routledge.

Dobrin, Sidney. 2011. *Postcomposition*. Carbondale: Southern Illinois University Press.

Donald, Janet. 2002. *Learning to Think: Disciplinary Perspectives*. San Francisco: Jossey-Bass.

Downs, Doug. 2015. "Revision Is Central to Developing Writing." In *Naming What We Know: Threshold Concepts of Writing Studies*, ed. Linda Adler-Kassner and Elizabeth Wardle, 66–67. Logan: Utah State University Press.

Downs, Doug, and Elizabeth Wardle. 2007. "Teaching about Writing, Righting Misconceptions: (Re)Envisioning 'First-Year Composition' as 'Introduction to Writing Studies.'" *CCC* 58 (4): 552–85.

Estrem, Heidi. 2015. "Disciplinary and Professional Identities Are Constructed through Writing." In *Naming What We Know: Threshold Concepts of Writing Studies*, ed. Linda Adler-Kassner and Elizabeth Wardle, 55–56. Logan: Utah State University Press.

Fournel, Jenna. 2015. "Introduction to the Taking Action Workshop Facilitators: Jenna Fournel." YouTube. https://www.youtube.com/watch?v=Ykiv-sGFq-A.

Gallagher, Chris. 2005. "We Compositionists: Toward Engaged Professionalism." *JAC* 25 (1): 75–99.

Green, Angela. 2009. "The Politics of Literacy: Countering the Rhetoric of Accountability in the Spellings Report and Beyond." *College Composition and Communication* 61 (1): W367–84.

Heilker, Paul, and Peter Vandenberg. 2015. *Keywords in Writing Studies*. Logan: Utah State University Press.
Hesse, Doug. 2012. "Who Speaks for Writing? Expertise, Ownership, and Stewardship." In *Who Speaks for Writing: Stewardship for Writing Studies in the 21st Century*, ed. Jennifer Rich and Ethna D. Lay, 9–22. New York: Peter Lang.
Higham, John. 1979. "The Matrix of Specialization." In *The Organization of Knowledge in Modern America, 1860–1920*, ed. Alexandra Oleson and John Voss, 3–18. Baltimore: Johns Hopkins University Press.
Horner, Bruce. 2014. "Grounding Responsivity." *JAC* 34 (1–2): 49–61.
Huot, Brian. 2007. "Consistently Inconsistent: Business and the Spellings Commission Report on Higher Education." *College English* 69 (5): 512–25.
Kopelson, Karen. 2008. "Sp(l)itting Images; or, Back to the Future of (Rhetoric and?) Composition." *College Composition and Communication* 59 (4): 750–80.
Kreber, Carolin. 2009a. "Supporting Student Learning in the Context of Diversity, Complexity, and Uncertainty." In *The University and Its Disciplines: Teaching and Learning within and beyond Disciplinary Boundaries*, ed. Carolin Kreber, 3–18. New York: Routledge.
Kreber, Carolin, ed. 2009b. *The University and Its Disciplines: Teaching and Learning within and beyond Disciplinary Boundaries*. New York: Routledge.
Krishnan, Armin. 2009. "What Are Academic Disciplines?: Some Observations on the Disciplinarity vs. Interdisciplinarity Debate." Southampton: University of Southampton National Centre for Research Methods. http://eprints.ncrm.ac.uk/783/1/what_are_academic_disciplines.pdf.
Land, Ray, Peter Vivian, and Julie Rattray. 2014. "A Closer Look at Liminality: Incorrigibles and Threshold Capital." In *Threshold Concepts: From Personal Practice to Communities of Practice*, 1–12. Proceedings of the National Academy's Sixth Annual Conference and the Fourth Biennial Threshold Concepts Conference. January 2014. Cork, Ireland: NAIRTL.
Lerner, Adam. 2015. "AP U.S. History Controversy Becomes a Debate on America." *Politico (Pavia, Italy)*, February 15, 2015. https://www.politico.com/story/2015/02/ap-us-history-controversy-becomes-a-debate-on-america-115381.html.
Meyer, Jan H. F., and Ray Land, eds. 2006. *Overcoming Barriers to Student Learning*. London: Routledge.
Oleson, Alexandra, and John Voss, eds. 1979. *The Organization of Knowledge in Modern America, 1860–1920*. Baltimore: Johns Hopkins University Press.
Roozen, Kevin. 2015. "Writing Is a Social and Rhetorical Activity." In *Naming What We Know: Threshold Concepts of Writing Studies*, ed. Linda Adler-Kassner and Elizabeth Wardle, 17–19. Logan: Utah State University Press.
Ruiz, Iris, and Raúl Sánchez, eds. 2016. *Decolonizing Rhetoric and Composition Studies: New Latinx Keywords for Theory and Pedagogy*. New York: Palgrave Macmillan. https://doi.org/10.1057/978-1-137-52724-0.
Scott, Tony. 2015. "Writing Enacts and Creates Identities and Ideologies." In *Naming What We Know: Threshold Concepts of Writing Studies*, ed. Linda Adler-Kassner and Elizabeth Wardle, 48–50. Logan: Utah State University Press.
Taczak, Kara. 2015. "Reflection Is Critical for Writers' Development." In *Naming What We Know: Threshold Concepts of Writing Studies*, ed. Linda Adler-Kassner and Elizabeth Wardle, 78–79. Logan: Utah State University Press.
Wenger, Etienne. 1999. *Communities of Practice*. New York: Cambridge University Press.
Wenger, Etienne. 2010. "Communities of Practice and Social Learning Systems: The Career of a Concept." In *Social Learning Systems and Communities of Practice*, ed. Chris Blackmore, 179–98. London: Springer. https://doi.org/10.1007/978-1-84996-133-2_11.
Wenger-Trayner, Etienne. 2013. "The Practice of Theory: Confessions of a Social Learning Theorist." In *Reframing Educational Research: Resisting the 'What Works' Agenda*, ed. Valerie Farnsworth and Yvette Solomon, 106–18. London: Routledge.

Wenger-Trayner, Etienne, Mark Fenton-O'Creevy, Steven Hutchinson, Chris Kubiak, and Beverly Wenger-Trayner. 2015. *Learning in Landscapes of Practice: Boundaries, Identity, and Knowledgeability in Practice-Based Learning*. London: Routledge.

Wenger-Trayner, Etienne, and Beverly Wenger-Trayner. 2015. "Learning in a Landscape of Practice: A Framework." In *Learning in Landscapes of Practice: Boundaries, Identity, and Knowledgeability in Practice-Based Learning*, ed. Etienne Wenger-Trayner, Mark Fenton-O'Creevy, Steven Hutchinson, Chris Kubiak, and Beverly Wenger-Trayner, 13–29. London: Routledge.

Yancey, Kathleen, Liane Robertson, and Kara Taczak. 2014. *Writing across Contexts: Transfer, Composition, and Sites of Writing*. Logan: Utah State University Press.

Yancey, Kathleen Blake. 2015. "Coming to Terms: Composition/Rhetoric, Threshold Concepts, and a Disciplinary Core." In *Naming What We Know: Threshold Concepts of Writing Studies*, ed. Linda Adler-Kassner and Elizabeth Wardle, xvii–xxxi. Logan: Utah State University Press. https://doi.org/10.7330/9780874219906.c000a.

# EDITORS' CONCLUSION
## Where Are We Going and How Do We Get There?

Rita Malenczyk, Susan Miller-Cochran,
Elizabeth Wardle, and Kathleen Blake Yancey

This collection has taken up a number of thorny and complicated questions about the status of Rhetoric and Composition as a discipline. While it has not, of course, provided definitive answers, the chapters have explored those questions carefully in an attempt to move forward the conversation about what, in fact, Rhetoric and Composition is. It has asked what it means to be a discipline; whether Rhetoric and Composition is one and, if so, what kind of discipline we are and want to be; what it means to have "expertise" in Rhetoric and Composition; what our scholarship tells us; and how to communicate what we know to a broader audience, enacting what we know about writing generally as well as in classrooms and programs at all levels and in public policy.

### WHAT IS A DISCIPLINE?

Underlying the entire collection is the question of what it actually means to be a discipline. In their contribution to this volume, Gwendolynne Reid and Carolyn R. Miller note that many people in our field see disciplines as "hegemonic, modernist structures of power," rightly observing that such structures are antithetical to what writing teachers and scholars value. Rhetoric and Composition scholars have offered all sorts of alternative terms so as not to call Rhetoric and Composition a discipline, in part to avoid the power structures the term seems to entail, in part to express how many in the field perceive its complex work, especially as captured in a range of associated terms: multidiscipline, interdiscipline, post-discipline, anti-discipline, meta-discipline. In this collection, Reid and Miller and Elizabeth Wardle and Doug Downs argue that this avoidance of disciplinarity stems from a misunderstanding of what disciplines are—or can be. Disciplines

DOI: 10.7330/9781607326953.c016

are not necessarily closed categories, but can be open ones: Reid and Miller and Downs and Wardle draw on Wittgenstein and Lakoff to claim that disciplinarity is actually a set of "continually emergent intellectual categories of networked interests, goals, and practices" (Reid and Miller). If we can, as Wardle and Downs argue, avoid "confus[ing] the shortcomings of a *given discipline* with the nature of *disciplinarity itself*" (italics in original), then we can move to consider what it means for Rhetoric and Composition to be a discipline. As editors, we, too, see disciplines—particularly our discipline—as (potentially, at least) open and dynamic. Concerns over the nature of disciplinarity certainly have merit, as Jennifer Helene Maher points out in her chapter. But our discipline can embody the best of its elements, rather than the worst— and in doing so, can provide important benefits to students, teachers, schooling, workplaces, and sites of civic engagement.

Has the book made a case that we are, in fact, a discipline—albeit, a discipline that is, to borrow from Catherine Schryer (1993), only ever stabilized-for-now? As Kathleen Blake Yancey points out, much has been accomplished as we have moved toward this turn to disciplinarity—among such accomplishments the acquisition of a Classification of Instructional Programs (CIP) code identifying our programs and documenting our expertise, which in turn informs hiring at all levels; the increased numbers of rhetoric and writing departments; the continuing proliferation of majors; and the increased emphasis on and support for research from our major organizations and journals. At a growing number of schools, the days of first-year composition (FYC) or graduate coursework with nothing in between are in the past, as Sandra Jamieson points out in her chapter on writing majors. At those institutions, coursework in Rhetoric and Composition now more closely resembles coursework for any other discipline—with beginning, intermediate, and advanced undergraduate offerings, perhaps in addition to graduate offerings.

But at many other schools, first-year composition or graduate courses in Rhetoric and Composition remain the only options. In such cases, it may be even more important to claim both disciplinarity and expertise given the potential of both to provide legitimacy for curricular and labor issues, as Barry Maid demonstrates. Likewise, as Kristine Hansen argues in this collection, the continued practice of staffing writing classes with teachers who do not have expertise in Rhetoric and Composition not only means that writing classes are taught by teachers without current, relevant knowledge about writing and the teaching of writing, but also results in a discredited argument for disciplinarity.

The range of undergraduate and graduate course offerings in many growing Rhetoric and Composition programs underscores the discipline's commitment to the teaching of writing, although Rhetoric and Composition is not exclusively about the teaching of writing. Our work in first-year composition is an important part of what we do, however, and the knowledge the discipline has amassed about writing and the teaching of writing can and should inform practices in writing programs. These practices include labor; addressing labor issues is an important disciplinary responsibility itself for several reasons, among them to assure the best curriculum and instruction, to assure the best working conditions for colleagues, and to assure that FYC and other writing programs accurately enact the discipline's body of knowledge.

### WHAT DOES IT MEAN TO BE A MEMBER OF THIS DISCIPLINE?

The labor issue is one that brings up, again, concerns about disciplinarity as exclusionary and hegemonic. Who is a member of the discipline of Rhetoric and Composition, even if that discipline is seen as an open category? As Wardle and Downs explain in their chapter in this collection, we are a discipline that values inclusion and access, so any attempt to define who is in and who is out sets off alarm bells, and it's an attempt that Rhetoric and Composition has resisted. Many people active in Rhetoric and Composition, teaching writing and directing writing programs, have degrees in other disciplines; others may not have the PhD. They are members of the discipline, however, by virtue of participation: they pay attention to disciplinary conversations, reading the journals and attending conferences, demonstrating what Harry Collins and Robert Evans would call interactional expertise (Collins and Evans 2007, 32–33), if not contributory expertise (14). Still others do have contributory expertise, writing for journals and presenting at conferences, both participating in and shaping disciplinary conversations. Yet many of these contributions are overlooked in disciplinary conversations, as Rochelle Rodrigo and Susan Miller-Cochran argue, especially those from faculty at community colleges. Still others have both degrees and contributory expertise, but their work does not inform the direction of the field and is often discounted, as Jaime Armin Mejía explains.

At the center of this issue is what constitutes expertise in Rhetoric and Composition. Thus, who is included in in disciplinary conversations— and who brings expertise to them—manifests not only in hiring decisions in writing programs and departments but also in decision making about the shape of curricula in Rhetoric and Composition. As Whitney Douglas et al. illustrate in their chapter, the process of determining what a graduate curriculum in Rhetoric and Composition should include can be a challenging enterprise, involving the mapping of multiple disciplinary backgrounds of the faculty involved, even within Rhetoric and Composition, as they look for "productive intersections for collaborative dialogue based on shared values and beliefs."

Not everyone who teaches writing, however, wants to be "in" the discipline—or even acknowledges that a distinct discipline with a body of knowledge, especially including knowledge and practices that all writing teachers and scholars should know, exists. This is the concern that Hansen takes up at length in this collection. Given that our discipline has generated knowledge that can positively impact learners and writers, how do we ensure that writing teachers at all levels have not only familiarity with that knowledge, but also some level of facility with drawing upon it effectively in a writing classroom? If we don't do so, then not only is our teaching more likely to be ineffective, but also much of the knowledge claimed by the discipline is untapped and thus futile. Moreover, if we conduct research that can enhance the teaching of writing and yet daily practices in writing classrooms do not reflect such knowledge, even in programs directed by those in Rhetoric and Composition, any claim we make to disciplinarity is lessened, as Liane Robertson and Kara Taczak point out. If we do set minimal standards for what writing teachers should know and enact based on our disciplinary knowledge—as articulated, for example, in the *CCCC Statement on Preparing Teachers of College Writing* and the *TYCA Guidelines for Preparing Teachers of English in the Two-Year College* (CCCC 2015; TYCA 2016)—how do we implement those standards in hiring and rehiring processes? Likewise, how do we also provide writing teachers without significant graduate training in Rhetoric and Composition necessary ongoing opportunities to support their engagement as members of the discipline through other means? One argument made repeatedly in this collection, especially by Robertson and Taczak, is that our teaching practices and course content must reflect our research and our understanding of what writing is and does—which is only possible if those employed to teach writing courses are familiar with and draw upon that research. These tangled questions about knowledge, practice, and expertise are some of the most challenging asked in this collection, but they are questions that must be answered in practical and effective ways that are appropriate at the wide range of institutions where writing is taught.

## SCHOLARSHIP AND RHETORIC AND COMPOSITION

Of course, teaching and its associated labor issues constitute only one dimension, albeit an important one, of what our discipline is, does, and values. As we suggested in the introduction, scholars such as Charles Bazerman have pointed out that we still have much to learn about writing, especially writing taking place beyond the walls of the academy. Such research continues to be taken up by scholars in Rhetoric and Composition, extending far beyond scholastic curriculum, pedagogy and administration, even though these areas of research often intersect and inform each other in important ways. Within the discipline of Rhetoric and Composition, scholars conduct research in rhetoric, rhetorical theory, historiography, cultural rhetorics, genre studies, digital rhetorics, race studies, second-language writing, translingualism, multimodal composing, material rhetorics, visual and spatial rhetorics, everyday writing, and writing research methods. While this list is certainly not exhaustive, it gives a sense of the range of research interests within Rhetoric and Composition. Furthermore, these various scholarly areas intersect with other disciplines such as cultural studies, applied linguistics, and media studies. These intersections are productive, yet they have also sometimes made it challenging to clarify disciplinary boundaries for Rhetoric and Composition, reinforcing the importance and the value of understanding the discipline as open and dynamic, rather than as a closed system.

## RESPONSIBILITIES AND CONSEQUENCES

Why does it matter whether or not Rhetoric and Composition is a discipline? Some suggest that the bid to be understood as a discipline is a desire for resources, power, and status simply for their own sake. Doug Hesse suggests another reason: that we want to be a discipline because we "want to be taken seriously." We agree that our disciplinary expertise warrants being taken seriously; our intent in creating this collection of essays asking explicitly about disciplinarity is also to raise questions about the relationship of material consequences, impact, and responsibility to disciplinarity. We want to pursue this line of thinking in two ways: first, about taking responsibility for our own discipline, our behaviors, attitudes, and material conditions; and second, about engaging an outward focus in order to have an impact far beyond ourselves.

### Disciplinary Responsibilities—Inward Facing

If we are not a discipline, we are not responsible for the problems Hansen or Mejía raise in this collection. If we aren't articulated as an entity, even a fluid and networked entity, we then have very little means for addressing these matters. We can bemoan labor issues and working conditions and lack of expertise; we can accuse one another and our institutions of not being sensitive or inclusive, of not getting educated about historical and cultural injustices and their continuing consequences. If there is no disciplinary "we," then all of these concerns are someone else's problem.

But if we are, in fact, a discipline—with the knowledge, resources, recognition, and collective identity that disciplinarity entails—then we must also assume the responsibilities of that designation. If we are a discipline, then we are, to paraphrase Barack Obama, the ones we have been waiting for, the ones who have to leverage what we know and do, the ones who need to create and enact solutions to the problems that have plagued us. We must set up more institutes, seminars, and other opportunities for sharing and gaining expertise and for helping us all better inform ourselves about issues we cannot and should not ignore. Because we have disciplinary knowledge that can uniquely contribute to better practices in teaching writing, we have to make arguments for expert labor, and use what we understand about the system, and what we have gained from the system (such as CIP codes), to insist on expert labor—and to ensure that expert labor is compensated fairly. We can no longer justify an identity of powerless supplicant, blaming everyone else for problems and asking everyone else to fix them. We are not the sad women in the basement, but full members of the academy, sitting at the table with resources, expertise, and information that enable us to remedy problems.

Our disciplinary knowledge also compels us to pay attention to questions of inclusion and diversity and obliges us to educate ourselves and others about issues of race, ethnicity, histories, and the consequences of privilege of all kinds—especially as these issues relate to writing and literacy practices. Because we are often perceived as being in the position of language gatekeepers in the academy through the requirement of first-year composition, we must use our disciplinary knowledge to communicate the complexity of language use and language learning. Christiane Donahue's chapter in this collection highlights one of the lenses through which Rhetoric and Composition can question assumptions about language and writing acquisition and what the enterprise of writing instruction means and does.

*Disciplinary Responsibilities—Outward Facing*

That's one side of the coin; if we are a discipline, we have the resources and responsibility to handle our own business and solve our own problems. The other side of the coin is outward facing, as Linda Adler-Kassner, in this collection, puts it. The literate lives of everyday people in myriad circumstances are impacted by how writing is understood and taught and assessed from kindergarten on. Both historically and currently, misunderstandings about what writing is and how it works negatively impact people's sense of themselves as readers and writers, their ability to succeed in school and out, their ability to use writing as a means of making knowledge, and their ability to critically engage with the writing and thinking of others. Misunderstandings of how writing works have serious and negative material consequences for individuals and for society. If we are a discipline, we have both a right and a responsibility to change popular understandings of and practices regarding writing.

If we are a discipline, then arguments that we don't have any content expertise don't hold. We can see all around us instances where literacy practices could be radically improved if we were able to bring our expertise to bear. For example, how writing is assessed at all levels across the United States is problematic for many reasons: it is often neither valid nor reliable, and it very often discriminates against students who do not come from white, middle-class backgrounds. We know these practices are problematic because members of our discipline have expertise in the subject. But we don't just know there is a problem: we also know how to solve it, and we know what can be done differently. Practices such as directed self-placement and electronic portfolios, for example, which resulted from and are used as a result of our research and theory, radically improve the lives of students and teachers. In other words, as the contributors to Linda Adler-Kassner and Elizabeth Wardle's *Naming What We Know* project demonstrated, Rhetoric and Composition scholars know quite a lot about writing and how it works as a result of our many years of scholarship about writing (Adler-Kassner and Wardle 2015). But much of that knowledge is not widely understood and, as a result, many of the practices not widely enacted. And the consequences—for everyday people; for employers; for problems that need solving—are real. The contexts in which our disciplinary knowledge has relevance and potential impact are numerous, and they extend far beyond postsecondary education.

As one example, we know that legislators and policy makers intervene in assessment, curricular requirements, and reward systems with negative consequences for students, teachers, and the broader society.

Legislators in Florida, for instance, made sweeping changes to general education requirements, reducing the number of hours required and determining what general education should look like across all institutions, and penalizing what they called "excess hour credits," essentially requiring students to pay extra tuition if they take more than the minimal number of hours required for their degree and thus potentially reducing the number of writing courses students could take. Had we been included in the discussions about these changes—to explain the time and experiences needed to educate successful writers—we would have had the opportunity, at least, to explain why additional hours for courses like writing might be well spent and thus to exert positive and innovative impact on how general education is understood and designed in that state, and elsewhere.

Another example of educational change requiring our engagement involves the increasing use of big data in "predictive analytics" platforms to tell students, advisors, and teachers what academic choices to make and paths to pursue. For-profit companies such as EAB and Brightspace are currently making major inroads selling their predictive and learning analytics platforms to colleges and universities, mining data using proprietary software, and making recommendations regarding particular classes and majors to pursue and avoid—thus potentially impacting, as only one example, students' willingness or even freedom to take difficult writing courses where failure might be seen as an important part of learning, but where such a view is at odds with the formulas for "success" that analytics produce. Such companies must be communicated with— or communicated *about*—to stakeholders such as parents and students. Our expertise enables us to "talk back" regarding matters such as how learning happens, especially when it involves writing.

A third example involves the role we play in educating critical citizens who can analyze political arguments and understand the important role of evidence, ethics, and credibility—especially in the recurringly charged political atmospheres characteristic of the United States. Rhetoric plays a fundamental role in conversations about what it means to engage in healthy and informed debate and thus has a fundamental role to play in order for democracy to thrive.

We could go on, but the point seems clear. We have knowledge that can, should, and needs to extend far beyond ourselves.

What, then, is required for us to become "outward facing"—to influence policy and practice, to inform public dialogue, and to ensure that literate learners and writers of all kinds are positively impacted and supported? That sort of impact requires resources, capital, structure, and influence. Having departmental status at the postsecondary level, as Barry Maid argues, is one way to gain this kind of impact locally. While not all institutions function this way—community colleges or small liberal arts institutions, for instance, where multiple disciplines are often housed together, and generalists are valued and needed more than specialists—those institutions that can support independent departments of Rhetoric and Composition provide important opportunities for action. In a department, resources can be devoted to proactive (rather than reactive) efforts to create courses and structures that best teach and support writing; professional development can be offered and required; CIP codes can be enforced and linked to accreditation and assessment efforts; FYC can be taught as a content course. Thus, students within a particular institution can be positively impacted as a result of the kinds of resources and capital that come with departmental status.

We also need to do more to be public intellectuals, blogging and engaging in public forums that reach more than academics. Colleagues such as Mike Rose, whose books on learning and literacy circulate widely in popular as well as academic circles; Dennis Baron, whose blog on the Web of Language reaches far beyond his own university; Rebecca Moore Howard, whose knowledge has enriched public discussions of plagiarism; and Les Perelman, who has fought an ongoing battle in the popular press against high-stakes machine scoring of student writing, provide models we can all learn from and emulate.

We continue to argue with one another over whether or not we are a discipline, whether disciplinarity is bad or good, whether we actually know anything, or whether setting minimal standards for teachers might exclude someone. In the meantime, all around us and in our own classrooms and departments, people continue to be negatively impacted by the fact that we are not involved in the activities governing our efforts: conversations, policy-making endeavors, test-creation, public discussions of writing, rhetorical engagement in public forums on issues as varied as immigration, health care, social justice, and so on. As Robertson and Taczak put it in this volume, "To be a discipline, we must have a well-developed paradigm consisting of what we know and why we know it, and of how we investigate to further our knowledge." There is a difference between rigorous questions regarding methods and the meaning of results and continued arguments over what our name should be and whether we actually know anything—when there is clear evidence that we do, and that we should be putting that knowledge to work, whatever we decide to call ourselves, so that stakeholders can recognize us when they are interacting with us. As we continue to argue with one another over whether we exist, legislators and for-profit companies, big publishers, and well-meaning but uninformed high-level administrators continue to act out of misconceptions and misunderstandings about writing, and politicians and journalists engage in the worst kinds of specious, hate-filled, and unsupported arguments while many citizens know little about how to analyze such claims for logic and evidence. If we turn our attention toward action based on our disciplinary knowledge, they may continue to do these things anyway, of course. But we can more effectively work to make change and get into (or help create) rigorous debate if we can agree that we know something about writing and that what we know has value beyond our individual classrooms and institutions.

We understand that what we are asking for related to education is doubly hard because of the massive upheaval occurring today in the US education system, particularly in higher education. There is a great deal of disruption—planned and otherwise—as leaders consider, for example, dismantling the "Carnegie unit" (Fain 2012), expanding college credit for work experience, widening competency-based learning (US Department of Education n.d.), authorizing Massive Open Online Courses (MOOCs) for college credit, and, of course, relying more frequently on predictive analytics. Many of these changes sound antithetical to the view of teaching and learning that we value (Welch and Scott 2016). Thus, although we may not agree on all the issues and their implications, our research and teaching practices mean we have a lot to offer to these conversations. We are, in other words, well poised to make integral contributions if what higher education in the twenty-first century needs to accomplish is what the Association of American Colleges and Universities claims: educating students who "become responsible citizens and help[ing] them navigate their way through a challenging world," a goal facilitated through significant "writing, research, and project-based learning activities" (AAC&U 2013) that are integrated and reflected upon across time. And no discipline, as Rita Malenczyk, Neal Lerner, and Elizabeth H. Boquet point out in their chapter, is better equipped to support this aim, given that as a discipline, we have always put active student-centered research, teaching, and learning at the forefront of what we do. Such a practice is exactly what seems to be called for at this current time. But offering something to the conversation means we have to find ways to be *in* the conversation. If we—our discipline, majors, courses, research findings—are visible and identifiable *as disciplinary activities*, that can make being in the conversation more likely.

In sum, as the chapters here suggest, Rhetoric and Composition qualifies as an open, networked discipline. It's a discipline with both inward and outward responsibilities and with several tasks at hand, among them providing for more inclusion, addressing labor practices, expanding research-based curricula and pedagogy, participating in the public sphere, and documenting wider writing practices. In other words, we have much to contribute as recognized disciplinarity experts and engaged public intellectuals. Our hope is that this volume supports us in all these efforts.

*References*

AAC&U. 2013. "Success after College: What Students, Parents, and Educators Need to Know and Do." *Association of American Colleges and Universities* 99 (2). https://www.aacu.org/publications-research/periodicals/success-after-college-what-students-parents-and-educators-need.

Adler-Kassner, Linda, and Elizabeth Wardle, eds. 2015. *Naming What We Know: Threshold Concepts of Writing Studies.* Logan: Utah State University Press.

CCCC. 2015. "CCCC Statement on Preparing Teachers of College Writing." *Conference on College Composition and Communication.* cccc.ncte.org/cccc/resources/positions/statementonprep.

Collins, Harry, and Robert Evans. 2007. *Rethinking Expertise.* Chicago: University of Chicago Press. https://doi.org/10.7208/chicago/9780226113623.001.0001.

Fain, Paul. 2012. "More Cracks in the Credit Hour." *Inside Higher Ed.* https://www.insidehighered.com/news/2012/12/05/carnegie-foundation-considers-redesign-credit-hour.

Schryer, Catherine. 1993. "Records as Genre." *Written Communication* 10 (2): 200–234. https://doi.org/10.1177/0741088393010002003.

TYCA. 2016. "TYCA Guidelines for Preparing Teachers of English in the Two-Year College." *Two-Year College English Association.* www.ncte.org/library/NCTEFiles/Groups/TYCA/GuidelinesPrep2YCEngFac_REVISED.pdf.

US Department of Education. n.d. "Competency-Based Learning or Personalized Learning." https://www.ed.gov/oii-news/competency-based-learning-or-personalized-learning.

Welch, Nancy, and Tony Scott, eds. 2016. "Introduction." In *Composition in the Age of Austerity,* ed. Nancy Welch and Tony Scott, 3–17. Logan: Utah State University Press, 3–17. https://doi.org/10.7330/9781607324454.c000.

# CONTRIBUTORS

**LINDA ADLER-KASSNER** is Professor of Writing Studies and Interim Co-Dean of Undergraduate Education at University of California, Santa Barbara, where she works to make connections from the principles of Writing Studies within and across the institution. She is author, coauthor, or coeditor of nine books, including *Naming What We Know: Threshold Concepts of Writing Studies* (with Elizabeth Wardle and many other contributors) and *The Activist WPA: Changing Stories about Writing and Writers*. She also has published many articles and book chapters. Her research focuses broadly on how literacy is defined and by whom, and how it is assessed and with what consequences. She engages these questions with students in classes ranging from first-year writing to graduate courses in Composition, and with faculty colleagues on her campus and others in workshops focusing on subjects ranging from threshold concepts to assessment practices. She is currently Chair of the Conference on College Composition and Communication (CCCC) and is a past president of the Council of Writing Program Administrators (CWPA).

**ELIZABETH H. BOQUET** is Professor of English and Director of the Writing Center at Fairfield University in Fairfield, Connecticut. She is the author of *Nowhere Near the Line* and *Noise from the Writing Center* and coauthor of *The Everyday Writing Center: A Community of Practice*, all published by Utah State University Press. Her scholarship has appeared in *College English*, *College Composition and Communication*, and the *Writing Center Journal*, among others.

**CHRISTIANE DONAHUE** is Associate Professor of Linguistics, Director of the Institute for Writing and Rhetoric at Dartmouth, and member of the Théodile-CIREL research laboratory at l'Université de Lille, France. She teaches writing and works cross-culturally and cross-disciplinarily with research groups in the United States and Europe on questions including university student writing across cultures, international research and cross-disciplinary influence, accuracy in accountings of the spread of English, studies of the losses and gains entailed in globalization of research and writing, research methods that work across humanistic and social science modes, traditional corpus linguistic analyses and their contribution to current big data and digital humanities questions, and studies of writing knowledge adaptation across modes and contexts.

**WHITNEY DOUGLAS** is Assistant Professor of English at Boise State University, where she teaches classes on feminist and disability rhetorics, community literacy, and writing theory and pedagogy. Her current research interest centers on creating a pedagogy of equitability.

**DOUG DOWNS** is Associate Professor of Writing Studies and Director of Composition in the Department of English at Montana State University. He researches conceptions and practices of writing, reading, and research among college students, focusing on writing-about-writing pedagogies, undergraduate research, and students' screen-reading habits. Downs is coauthor of *Writing about Writing* (3rd ed., 2017) and numerous chapters and articles on WAW instruction, and currently serves as Editor of *Young Scholars in Writing*, the national peer-reviewed journal of undergraduate scholarship in writing and rhetoric studies.

**HEIDI ESTREM** is Professor of English and director of the first-year writing (FYW) program at Boise State University. Her research interests in FYW pedagogy, writing program administration, assessment, and instructor development and support have led to publications in *Writing Program Administration, Rhetoric Review, Composition Studies*, and several edited collections. She is the coeditor (with Todd Ruecker, Dawn Shepherd, and Beth Brunk-Chavez) of the recent edited collection *Retention and Persistence in Writing Programs*. She regularly teaches a graduate course for new teaching assistants, undergraduate writing courses, and FYW courses.

KRISTINE HANSEN is Professor of English at Brigham Young University, where she teaches undergraduate courses in advanced writing, rhetorical style, and the history of rhetoric, and graduate courses on rhetorical theory and research methods. She has directed the English Department's Composition program and served as Associate Dean of Undergraduate Education, directing the Writing Across the Curriculum (WAC) program. Her recent research has focused on granting precollege credit for writing to high school students. In 2012, her coedited book (with Christine Farris), *College Credit for Writing in High School: The "Taking Care of" Business* won the Best Book Award from the Council of Writing Program Administrators.

DOUG HESSE is Executive Director of Writing and Professor of English at the University of Denver, where he was named University Distinguished Scholar. He is past President of the National Council of Teachers of English, former Chair of the Conference on College Composition and Communication, and past President of the Council of Writing Program Administrators. He's published some sixty essays and cowritten four books, mainly on creative nonfiction and professional issues in Composition and English studies. Previously, Hesse taught at Illinois State University, where he directed the Center for the Advancement of Teaching and the Honors Program. His PhD is from Iowa.

SANDRA JAMIESON is Professor of English and Director of Writing Across the Curriculum at Drew University, where she teaches in the Writing and Communication Studies track of the English Major and the Two-Year College Teaching Concentration in the Caspersen School of Graduate Studies. She chaired the Conference on College Composition and Communication (CCCC) Committee on the Major in Writing and Rhetoric (2007–15) and is a Citation Project Principal Researcher. Her books include *Coming of Age: The Advanced Writing Curriculum*; *Information Literacy: Research and Collaboration across Disciplines*; and *Points of Departure: Rethinking Student Source Use and Writing Studies Research Methods*.

NEAL LERNER is Associate Professor of English and Writing Program Director at Northeastern University in Boston. He is the author of *The Idea of a Writing Laboratory*, which won the 2011 NCTE David H. Russell Award for Distinguished Research in the Teaching of English, and coauthor of *The Longman Guide to Peer Tutoring*, 2nd ed., and *Learning to Communicate in Science and Engineering: Case Studies from MIT*, winner of the 2012 Conference on College Composition and Communication (CCCC) Advancement of Knowledge Award. More recently, he is the coauthor of *The Meaningful Writing Project: Learning, Teaching and Writing in Higher Education*.

JENNIFER HELENE MAHER is an associate professor of English in the Communication and Technology track at the University of Maryland, Baltimore County. Her research interests include rhetorical constructions of goodness, the city of Baltimore, technical communication, and software studies. Maher's book *Software Evangelism and the Rhetoric of Morality* examines rhetorics of freedom in software development; her forthcoming work addresses topics such as feminist hacking practices in open source and locally driven public health campaigns aimed at addressing racial disparities in health care.

BARRY MAID is Professor and Founding Head of the Technical Communication Program at Arizona State University. Previously, he was Chair of English at the University of Arkansas at Little Rock, where he helped lead the creation of the Department of Rhetoric and Writing. He is the author of numerous articles and chapters primarily focusing on technology, information literacy, independent writing programs, and program administration including assessment. In addition, he is a coauthor of *The McGraw-Hill Guide: Writing for College, Writing for Life*. Most recently he is coeditor of *Information Literacy: Research and Collaboration across Disciplines*.

**RITA MALENCZYK** is Professor of English and Director of the Writing Program and Writing Center at Eastern Connecticut State University. Her work has appeared in numerous edited collections, most recently *Retention, Persistence and Writing Programs* (2017), and journals including *WPA: Writing Program Administration, Writing Center Journal,* and *College Composition and Communication*. Her own edited collection *A Rhetoric for Writing Program Administrators* is now in its second edition (2016). She is a past president of the Council of Writing Program Administrators.

**JAIME ARMIN MEJÍA** is Associate Professor at Texas State University. He has long researched and written about Rhetoric and Composition Studies and Chicanx Studies, attempting and sometimes succeeding in bringing these two fields together. Originally and proudly from south Texas, from the lower Rio Grande Valley, he has taught in central Texas for over twenty-seven years and is looking to retire at some point hopefully in the not too distant future, though he has no plans at present for doing so. He has published reviews and invited essays in various collections as well as in *College English, College Composition and Communication,* and *JAC*. Often swept along by the currents of contemporary popular topics, he often tries going against the grain, difficult as that may sometimes be, in order to capture nuances in the profession of Rhetoric and Composition Studies that may have been overlooked by others in the profession.

**CAROLYN R. MILLER** is SAS Institute Distinguished Professor of Rhetoric and Technical Communication, Emerita, at North Carolina State University, where she taught from 1973 to 2015. She received her PhD in Communication and Rhetoric from Rensselaer Polytechnic Institute in 1980. Her research interests include genre studies, digital rhetoric, rhetorical theory, and rhetoric of science and technology. Recently, she coedited *Emerging Genres in New Media Environments* with Ashley R. Kelly (Mehlenbacher). Her professional service includes terms as president of the Rhetoric Society of America and editor of its journal, *Rhetoric Society Quarterly*. She was named a Fellow of the Rhetoric Society of America in 2010 and Fellow of the Association of Teachers of Technical Writing in 1995.

**SUSAN MILLER-COCHRAN** is Professor of English and Director of the Writing Program at the University of Arizona, where her research focuses on the intersections of technology, multilingual writing, and writing program administration. Her work has appeared in *College Composition and Communication, Composition Studies, Computers and Composition, Enculturation,* and *Teaching English in the Two-Year College,* and she is also an editor of *Rhetorically Rethinking Usability* (Hampton Press, 2009) and *Strategies for Teaching First-Year Composition* (NCTE, 2002). In addition, she is a coauthor of *An Insider's Guide to Academic Writing* (2017), *The Cengage Guide to Research* (Cengage, 2017) and *Keys for Writers* (Cengage, 2016). Before joining the faculty at the University of Arizona, she was Director of First-Year Writing at North Carolina State University (2007-15) and also a faculty member at Mesa Community College (AZ). She currently serves as past President of the Council of Writing Program Administrators.

**KELLY MYERS** teaches courses in argument, nonfiction and creative nonfiction, and rhetorical theory. After completing her PhD at the University of Arizona, she taught in the Program in Writing and Rhetoric and served as a Resident Fellow at Stanford University. Now at Boise State University, she is the cofounder and faculty mentor for the Ethos Project, a student-run organization that focuses on research-based advocacy projects. Her research explores the concepts of kairos and metanoia (opportunity/missed opportunity). In recent articles, she has applied the kairos and metanoia partnership to rhetorical theory and writing processes.

## CONTRIBUTORS

**GWENDOLYNNE REID** is Assistant Professor of English and Director of the Writing Program at Oxford College of Emory University. Her qualitative research examines digital and multimodal composing practices in the disciplines. Her research interests include writing across the curriculum, genre studies, information literacy, and writing program administration. Her writing can be found in *Across the Disciplines*, WPA-CompPile Research Bibliographies, *Scientific Communication: Principles, Practices, and Methods, Twenty Writing Assignments in Context,* and *Contingent Faculty Publishing in Community*.

**LIANE ROBERTSON** is Associate Professor of English and Director of the Writing across the Curriculum program at William Paterson University of New Jersey. She is coauthor of *Writing Across Contexts: Transfer, Composition, and Sites of Writing* (2014), winner of the Conference on College Composition and Communication (CCCC) 2015 Research Impact Award and the Council of Writing Program Administrators' 2014 Best Book Award. Her most recent research on knowledge transfer in writing has appeared in *Understanding Writing Transfer: Implications for Transformative Student Learning in Higher Education* (2017), *Critical Transitions: Writing and the Question of Transfer* (2016), *A Rhetoric of Reflection* (2016), and *Naming What We Know: Threshold Concepts of Writing Studies* (2015).

**ROCHELLE (SHELLEY) RODRIGO** is Assistant Professor, Director of Online Initiatives, and Associate Director of Online Writing in the Department of English at the University of Arizona. She researches how "newer" technologies better facilitate communicative interactions, specifically teaching and learning. As well as coauthoring three editions of *The Wadsworth/Cengage Guide to Research*, Shelley also coedited *Rhetorically Rethinking Usability* (Hampton Press). Her scholarly work has appeared in *Computers and Composition, C&C Online, Teaching English in the Two-Year College, EDUCAUSE Quarterly, Journal of Interactive Technology & Pedagogy*, and *Enculturation*, as well as in various edited collections. In 2014 she was awarded Old Dominion University's annual Teaching with Technology Award and in 2012 the Digital Humanities High Powered Computing Fellowship.

**DAWN SHEPHERD** is Associate Professor of English and Associate Director of the First-Year Writing (FYW) Program at Boise State University. She is the author of *Building Relationships: Online Dating and the New Logics of Algorithmic Culture* and coeditor of *Retention, Persistence, and Writing Programs*. Her work has been published in edited collections as well as in *Computers and Composition* and *WPA: Writing Program Administration*; two chapters on genre and weblog, coauthored with Carolyn R. Miller, have been translated into Portuguese. She teaches undergraduate courses in rhetoric, writing, and media and graduate seminars on research methods and digital rhetoric.

**KARA TACZAK** is Teaching Associate Professor at the University of Denver. Her research centers on the transfer of knowledge and practices. Her current project, the Writing Passport Project, examines the efficacy of the Teaching for Transfer curriculum in multiple courses across multiple institutional sites. This research is the third phase of the study described in her coauthored book *Writing Across Contexts*, which received the 2015 Conference on College Composition and Communication Research Impact award and the 2016 Council of Writing Program Administrators Book Award. Taczak's other publications have appeared in *Composition Forum, Teaching English in a Two-Year College*, and *Across the Disciplines*.

**ELIZABETH WARDLE** is Director of the Roger & Joyce Howe Center for Writing Excellence and Howe Professor of English at Miami University. She previously directed writing programs at the University of Central Florida (UCF) and University of Dayton. The Writing Program at UCF won a Conference on College Composition and Communication (CCCC) Certificate of Excellence under her direction. With Linda Adler-Kassner she is the coeditor of *Naming What We Know: Threshold Concepts of Writing Studies*, winner of the CWPA Award for Outstanding Contribution to the Discipline (2015). With Doug Downs, she is the coauthor and coeditor of *Writing about Writing*, a textbook currently in its third edition. She has published in *CCC*, *Composition Forum*, *Technical Communication Quarterly*, and *Enculturation*, among other venues, on her scholarly interests include writing transfer, genre theory, pedagogy, WPA work, and composition as disciplinary content. With Donna Kain, she won the NCTE Best Article of the Year Award in Teaching of Scientific and Technical Communication (2006).

**KATHLEEN BLAKE YANCEY**, Kellogg W. Hunt Professor of English and Distinguished Research Professor at Florida State University, has served as President of the National Council of Teachers of English; as Chair of the Conference on College Composition and Communication (CCCC); and as President of the Council of Writing Program Administrators. Cofounder of the journal *Assessing Writing*, she is also immediate past Editor of *College Composition and Communication*; she also cofounded and codirects the Inter/National Coalition for Electronic Portfolio Research. Author, editor, or coeditor of fourteen scholarly books—among them *Reflection in the Writing Classroom*; *Writing across Contexts: Transfer, Composition, and Sites of Writing*; *A Rhetoric of Reflection;* and *Assembling Composition*—she has authored co/authored over 100 articles and book chapters. She is the recipient of several awards, including the CCCC Research Impact Award, two best book awards from the Council of Writing Program Administrators, the FSU Graduate Teaching Award, the Purdue Distinguished Woman Scholar Award, and the Donald Murray Prize.

# INDEX

AAC&U (American Association of Colleges and Universities), 288, 340
AAUP (American Association of University Professors), 145
Abbott, Andrew, 114, 141, 142, 209
academic degrees, 172–76
academic freedom, 111
access, 123–24
Ackerman, John M., 27, 47, 87, 91
adaptability, 206, 217
adjunct faculty. *See* contingent faculty
Adler-Kassner, Linda, 11, 26, 231, 262, 303, 312, 343
Affirmative Action, 272–73
African-American scholars, 284–85(n11)
Alexander, Jonathan, 99
Andelora, Jeffrey, 58
Anderson, Chuck, 44
Anson, Chris, 23, 24
Anzaldúa, Mike, 272
apocalyptic turn, 15
Applebee, Arthur, 303
Aquinas, Thomas, 163–64, 166
archival turn, 15
Aristotle, 163, 177
Arizona State University: Interdisciplinary Humanities and Communication, 45; Technical Communication program, 36, 45–46
assessment, 316–23
assimilation, 268, 275–79
Atkinson, Dwight, 20
ATTW (Association of Teachers of Technical Writing), 249
audience (composition), 39
autonomy, 61–62

Baca, Isabel, 270
Ballenger, Bruce, 228, 231
Balzhiser, Deborah, 255, 259, 261
Banks, Adam, 123
Bar, Libby, 65(n8)
Baron, Dennis, 339
Bawarshi, Anis, 187
Bazerman, Charles, 5–6, 21–22, 30, 97–101, 120, 161, 209
Beaufort, Anne, 187
Becher, Tony, 299–300

Béubé, Michael, 293–94
bilingual education, 272
bilingualism, 270
Bishop, Wendy, 124, 291
Bizzell, Patricia, 19
Blommaert, Jan, 212
Boise State University, 226–27, 240(n3), 240(n5)
Bok, Derek, 290
Boland, Mary, 111
Boquet, Elizabeth H., 9, 70, 340, 343
Bourdieu, Pierre, 112, 161, 162, 163, 168–69
Bousquet, Marc, 142–43, 144
Bowker, Geoffrey C., 90
Boyer, Ernst, 56, 63, 294
Brightspace, 338
Brood, Robert, 324
Brooke, Collin, 307
Brooklyn College, 72, 74–82; Brooklyn College Writing Center, 77; Brooklyn Plan, 77; Summer Institute, 73
Brown, John Seely, 78
Bruffee, Kenneth, 70–84; administrator at Brooklyn College, 74–82; collaboration, 75; social class and, 71–72; WCRP interview, 74
Burke, Kenneth, 95, 130–31(n2)
Burton, Larry, 29–30

Campbell, Lee, 252, 260
Canagarajah, Sureah, 284(n11)
Cárdenas, Diana, 270
Carlton, Susan Brown, 112, 116, 122
category theory, 89, 93–95, 113; family resemblance, 89, 94, 97, 107(n9). *See also* classification
CCCC (Conference on College Composition and Communication), 11, 28–29, 32(n2), 60, 78, 120, 130, 137, 269; 1985 address "Breaking Our Bonds" (Hairston), 36, 40–46, 287; 2004 address "Made Not Only in Words" (Yancey), 248–49; 2014 address (Tinberg), 165; Chairs, 53, 248–49; Hispanic participation, 272; key concepts, 33(n10); position papers, 146–50; Research Initiative, 23, 25; *Second*

*Language Writing and Writers*, 148–49; *Statement of Principles*, 145; *Statement on Preparing Teachers of College Writing*, 334; Task Force, 93; Visibility Committee, 47–48, 91, 287; writing majors, 244–45, 247, 248, 253, 259; Wyoming Resolution, 144–45
CCSS (Common Core State Standards), 180–81, 303, 326
centering *vs.* privileging, 125–26
Cheetham, Graham, 140
Chicano Movement, 280
Chivers, Geoff, 140
Choseed, Malkiel, 152
Cintron, Ralph, 270
CIP (Classification of Instructional Programs), 47, 91, 95, 96, 253, 332, 339
Cisneros, Sandra, 278–79
Civil Rights Movement, 273
Clark, Burton, 161, 307
Clary-Lemon, Jennifer, 227
classification, 87–110, 113; family resemblance, 89, 94, 97, 107n9. *See also* category theory
Claycomb, Ryan M., 122, 163
cluster hiring, 103
code switching, 211, 218, 220, 221n5, 271, 284(n11)
Coenders, Mark, 324
collaboration, 70–84 *passim*, 75, 118
*College Composition and Communication*, 26, 28, 271, 272
*College English*, 271
*College Unbound: The Future of Higher Education and What It Means for Students* (Selingo), 289–90
Collins, Harry, 176, 333
Colomb, Greg, 291, 300
Columbia College Chicago, 25
*Coming of Age: The Advanced Writing Curriculum* (Shamoon et al.), 27–28, 32(n4), 247, 248
common sense, 303
communication movement, 106(n7)
communities of practice, 27
community, 61–62
community college, 155–56(n1); issues, 64n4; nomenclature, 64(n2)
community college scholarship, 53–65; acknowledging scholarship, 58–61; categories of scholarship, 56, 61–62; contributions, 56–58; definitions, 53–56; digital technologies, 65(n7); publications focused on teaching, 61, 63; range of scholarship, 62–64; topics of scholarship, 58, 64(n4)

*Composition, Rhetoric, and Disciplinarity* (Malenczyk et al): content, 8–11; structure, 8–11
composition studies. *See* Rhetoric and Composition
*Composition Studies*, 28
composition theory, 152
CompPile, 23
Connors, Robert J., 15, 21, 32(n4), 87, 165
contingent faculty, 88, 134–36, 144–45, 155–56(n1), 170, 195, 288; problems with relying on, 292–93
Corder, Jim, 27
creative writing, 259
creativity contracts, 293
Crisp, Sally, 40, 41
cultural studies, 20
CUNY (City University of New York), 71, 72
Curzer, Howard, 177
CWPA (Council of Writing Program Administrators), 60, 65(n10), 120, 127–28, 188; network for media action, 130; *WPA Outcomes Statement*, 127

*Dangling Modifier, The*, 79
Daniell, Beth, 20
Dartmouth Seminar, 23, 24
Darwin, Charles, 89
Delli Carpini, Dominic, 260, 262
departmentalization, 101–5, 119–20; case study of department, 170–77; departments *vs.* programs, 45–48; usefulness of department, 104
departments *vs.* programs, 45–48
Derrida, Jacques, 125
Dew, Debra Frank, 187, 189
Digital Studies, 120
disciplinarity: benefits of, 6–8, 161–81; boundary work, 7, 140, 300, 306, 309; budgetary control, 48; canonizing nature of a discipline, 114; category theory, 93–95; classification issues, 87–110; current analysis, 7, 15–34, 303–27; curricular control, 48; definitions, 89, 111–16, 137–40, 208–9, 237–40, 287–301, 307, 331–33; diffuse disciplines, 7, 87–110, 178; funding issues and, 300; historical analysis, 15–34, 305–6; intentionality, 7; knowledgeability and, 315–26 (*see also* knowledge); lack of consensus, 87, 303; locating, 225–40; membership of discipline, 333–34; multi *vs.* inter *vs.* trans *vs.*, post, 107(n12), 115–16, 178, 215–16; networked discipline, 96–101, 311; new models of, 296–301, 303–27; pedagogy

and, 7; permeation as part of character, 113–14; personal account, 36–52; personnel control, 48; postdisciplinarity, 114; programs *vs.* departments *vs.* field *vs.* discipline *vs.* profession, 3–4, 45–48, 134–58, 289; resistance to, 161–63; responsibilities, 335–41; specialization, 114–15, 130–31(n2), 306; status and, 288–96, 291–96; subdisciplines, 32(n1); turn to, 15–34, 70, 307–10; values and, 121–31. *See also* research (Rhetoric and Composition); writing major
disciplinary turn, 15–34, 70, 307–10
Dobrin, Sid, 5, 166
Donahue, Christiane, 206, 212, 343
Donald, Janet, 306
Dong, Yu Ren, 57
Douglas, Whitney, 10, 225, 333, 343
Downs, Doug, 9, 49, 111, 152, 187, 191, 237–38, 247, 248, 331–32, 343
DQP (Degree Qualifications Profile), 180–81
dual-credit classes, 273
Dubson, Michael, 59
Duguid, Paul, 78
Dunn, Patricia, 217

EAB, 338
economics of value, 138–39
Elbow, Peter, 126
Elon Institute, 23, 25
empowerment, 128–29, 218
*Enculturation*, 4
*End of Composition Studies, The* (Smit), 166
English departments, 5, 101–5
English language: Englishes, 211, 214, 284–85(n11); English only, 222n7; language question, 209–12; standard English, 215; translingual model and, 207
epistemology, 77
Ericsson, K. Anders, 146
*Errors and Expectations* (Shaughnessy), 57, 272
Estrem, Heidi, 10, 225, 343–44
evaluation (composition), 39
Evans, Robert, 176, 333
expediency, 195–96
expertise, 61–62, 130–31(n2), 143–50, 170–77, 180, 313–14; *vs.* expediency, 195–96; *vs.* solidarity, 5

faculty: creativity contracts, 293; differentiated tracking, 293–94; full-time non tenure track, 293; hiring practices, 52(n3), 102, 103, 292–301, 327(n3); New Faculty Model, 288; new models of disciplinarity, 296–301; roles and disciplinarity, 289; salary, 289; status, 292–96; teaching loads, 289; teaching professor, 296–301; tenure-track, 289, 293. *See also* contingent faculty; writing teacher
Faigley, Lester, 20
family resemblance (category theory), 89, 94, 97, 107(n9)
Featherman, Sandra, 300–301
*Field of Dreams*, 29–30
fields, 3–4, 16, 113. *See also* disciplinarity
Fitzgerald, Lauren, 79
Foster, Helen, 257
Fournel, Jenna, 313–14
Fox, Tom, 153, 156(n3)
*Framework for Success in Post-Secondary Writing*, 194, 203(n2)
Freire, Paulo, 166–67
Fulkerson, Richard, 20, 307
FYC (first-year composition), 24–25, 40–41, 332, 339; content, 186–91, 192–93, 197–203; as gatekeeper, 189; linked, 316–18; Mexican-Americans and, 275; paradigm shift, 201–3
FYW. *See* FYC (first-year composition)

galaxy, concept of, 115
Gaonkar, Dilip, 162
Gardner, Clint, 61
Garrison, Roger, 126
Gebhardt, Richard, 62
Geertz, Clifford, 208
*Generations of Exclusion: Mexican Americans, Assimilation, and Race* (Telles and Ortiz), 285(n14)
Genova, Gina, 250
Gentile, James M., 59
Gerber, John, 307
Gere, Anne, 32n6, 112
Giberson, Gregory A., 246, 247, 252, 259
Giordano, Joanne Baird, 54–55, 58
Gitterman, Alex, 77
Gladwell, Malcolm, 26
globalization, 213–14
global turn, 15
Gonzalez, Laura, 321
Googin, Maureen Daly, 59, 87
graduate students (Rhetoric and Composition), 60–61, 91, 120, 147–48, 156(n2), 195, 225–40; socialization, 60–61, 63; TAs, 128, 134–36, 147–48. *See also* MA programs
Graff, Harvey, 163

Gramsci, Antonio, 162, 166
Graves, Donald, 126
Green, Angela, 303
Green, Ann, 88

Hacker, Diana, 53
Hairston, Maxine, 18, 36, 40–46, 124, 287
Hall, Stuart, 179
Hammer, Brad, 168
Hansen, Kristine, 9, 16, 21, 135, 138, 195–96, 199, 344
Harris, Joseph, 6, 88, 96, 156(n3), 299
Hassel, Holly, 31, 54–55, 58
Haswell, Rich, 23–24, 31
Hawkes, Peter, 73
Hayes, Carol, 33(n9)
Hedengren, Mary, 299–300
Heilker, Paul, 4, 312
Hesse, Doug, 10, 165, 287, 303, 344
heterogeneous networks, 97
Higham, John, 306
higher education: changes in status of, 289–91, 337–38; new models of disciplinarity, 296–301; undergraduate, 323–26. *See also* faculty
*Higher Education in America* (Bok), 290
Horner, Bruce, 5, 163–64, 166, 169, 216, 308, 324
Howard, Rebecca Moore, 257, 339
HSIs (Hispanic Serving Institutions), 270, 271, 284(n5)
humility, 164–70, 180
Huot, Brian, 303
hybridity, 216

immigration, 281–82
inclusion, 123–24
individuality, 189–91
Inman, James, 61
intentionality, 7
IWCA (International Writing Centers Association), 78

*JAC*, 164
Jacobs, Debra, 252, 260
Jamieson, Sandra, 10, 344
Jaxon, Kim, 153, 156(n3)
Jim Crow racism, 273
*Journal of Basic Writing*, 57
*Journal of Second Language Writing*, 20
jumbo courses, 153, 156(n3)

Kahn, Seth, 174, 175
Kail, Harvey, 71
Kent State University Seminar, 24

*Keywords in Writing Studies* (Heilker and Vandenberg), 4, 312
Kezar, Adrianna, 292, 294, 300
Kirklighter, Cristina, 270, 271
Klein, Julie, 112, 115, 121, 179
knowledge, 118–19, 138, 155–56(n1), 189–90, 308; closed questions, 118–19; composed knowledge, 304, 309; as created by community, 78; disciplines and, 161–62; interpretive, 210; knowledge-ability, 304, 310–26; knowledge areas, 149; knowledge consolidation, 17, 25–27; knowledge making, 23, 54, 56, 61, 70–82, 297, 299, 301, 311; practice and, 310–15; social class and, 71–72; social construction of, 70; sociology of, 306; in writing administration, 70–84; writing knowledge, 201–3
Kopelson, Karen, 308, 309
Krause, Steven, 174, 175
Kristensen, Randi Gray, 122, 163
Kuhn, Thomas, 114

L2 writing, 221(n2), 221(n6). *See also* translingual model
Lakoff, George, 93, 113, 332
*Language and Power Reader: Representations of Race in a "Post-Racist" Era* (Eddy and Villanueva), 284(n7)
language question, 209–12
Larson, Ann, 174
Larson, Magali Sarfatti, 141
Latinxs, 267–85. *See also* Mexican Americans
Latour, Bruno, 97
Lauer, Janice, 47, 99, 299, 307
Lave, Jean, 27, 124, 307
learning: incidental learning, 78; as social process, 78
legislation, 337–38
Lerner, Neal, 9, 70, 340, 344
Levin, Jennifer, 279
Lewiecki-Wilson, Cynthia, 57
literacy, 20; critical literacy, 218, 222(n9), 222(n10); literacy pedagogy, 217; theory, 20; visual literacy, 22–23
Livesey, Matthew, 258
localism, 127–28
location, 225–40, 250–52
Lu, Min Zhan, 216
Lunsford, Andrea, 123, 130
Lynch, Paul, 15–16

machine reading of student writing, 120
Macrorie, Ken, 126

magnanimity, 163, 177–81
Maher, Jennifer Helene, 10, 161, 332, 344
Mahon, Deirdre, 88
Mahoney, Kevin, 162
Maid, Barry, 8–9, 339, 344–45
Majewski, John, 316
Malenczyk, Rita, 9, 70, 331, 340, 345
mapping processes, 225–40, 240(n2); creating visual maps, 231–34
MA programs, 225–40, 281, 285(n11); narratives, 225, 234–37; vision statement, 231. *See also* graduate students (Rhetoric and Composition); mapping processes
Maxey, Daniel, 292, 294
McDonald, James, 144
McLeod, Susan, 29–30, 249, 250, 255, 259, 261
McQuade, Don, 76
Mejía, Jaime Armin, 10, 267, 333, 345
Messer-Davidow, Ellen, 137–40, 141
methodology, 96, 118
Mexican Americans, 267–85; assimilation, 268, 275–79; attitudes toward, 278–80; immigration, 281–82; statistics, 285(n12), 285(n13); stereotypes, 274
Mexican Revolution, 281
Miller, Carolyn, 9, 49, 87, 89, 331–32, 345
Miller, Susan, 32(n6), 117, 129
Miller-Cochran, Susan, 9, 53, 331, 333, 345
Millward, Jody, 57
MLA (Modern Language Association), 78; categories at conventions, 90–91
Molina, Clara, 210, 220
Moneyhun, Clyde, 122
Moriarty, Thomas A., 246, 257, 259
Mueller, Derek, 307
multi-modal approach to writing, 25, 213
Murphy, Michael, 151–52
Murphy, Susan Wolff, 270
Murray, Donald, 126
Myers, Kelly, 10, 225, 345

NAFTA, 280
*Naming What We Know: Concepts of Writing Studies* (Adler-Kassner and Wardle), 26, 309, 312
National Census of Writing database, 250–52, 258, 260
National Endowment for the Humanities (NEH) summer institutes, 37
National Science Foundation, 101
National Writing Project, 120, 128
NCES (National Center for Education Statistics), 89, 95, 107(n10)

NCTE (National Council of Teachers of English), 59, 78, 120; *NCTE Beliefs about the Teaching of Writing*, 189; *Students' Right to Their Own Language*, 127, 271
Neff, Joyce, 200
Nelson, Cary, 144, 162
networked disciplines, 96–101, 311; heterogeneous networks, 97
New Media, 93, 100, 105, 120, 213
New Mexico, 279, 282
*New York Times*, Editorial Board, 274
North, Stephen M., 56, 61, 75, 96
NRC (National Research Council), 47, 91, 107(n10), 117–18, 253; revisions, 95
NTTF (non-tenure-track faculty), 170–77
Nugent, Jim, 246
NWA (National Writers Association), 128
NWCA (National Writing Centers Association), 78

Odell, Lee, 36, 37–40
Ohio State University, 269
Ohmann, Richard, 142
Olson, Gary, 124, 165, 291
Onondaga Community College, 151–52
Open Admissions, 73, 75, 272–73; student exigency, 71
Ortiz, Vilma, 275, 285(n14)
Ostergaard, Lori, 246
Other, the, 276
outcomes, 166, 188, 193, 197–98, 216, 228, 250, 327(n5); for writing requirement courses, 315, 321, 322, 325, 327(n5)
*Oxford Guide for Writing Tutors, The*, 79

paraprofessionals, 154–55
PARCC (Partnership for Assessment of Readiness for College and Careers), 120, 309
Parisi, Hope, 57
Parker, William Riley, 101–5, 107(n16)
*Pasatiempo*, 279
Paulson, Eric J., 58
pedagogy, 5–6, 30, 284(n7); disciplinarity and, 7; research and, 6
Peeples, Tim, 257
peer mentorship, 153–54
*Peer Review, The*, 79
peer tutoring, 76
Pender, Kelly, 179
Penrose, Ann M., 61
Perelman, Les, 120, 339
Phelps, Louise Wetherbee, 27, 47, 87, 91, 117
Pickett, Nell Ann, 53

Index    353

*Postcomposition* (Dobrin), 166
post-process writing, 20
Pough, Gwendolyn, 178
Powers-Stubbs, Karen, 55
practice and practitioner, 138; communities of practice, 304–7; knowledge and, 310–15; outcomes, 166, 188, 193, 197–98, 216, 228, 250, 315, 321, 322, 325, 327(n5); "practitioner inquiry," 75; "practitioner lore," 56, 61
predictive analytics, 338
Preparing Future Faculty (PFF) initiative, 63
Prior, Paul, 97–101
privileging *vs.* centering, 125–26
process, composing, 17, 39, 118
professionalism, 65(n10), 156(n4), 292; definitions, 140–43; markers of, 61–62; professional development, 273; profession *vs.* discipline, 134–58
progress, ideas of, 139
public turn, 15
purpose (composition), 39

queer turn, 15

racial issues, 73–74
radial category, 107(n9), 113, 115, 125
Ray, Brian, 216
regimes of competence, 305, 309; nomenclature, 327(n1)
Reid, Gwendolynne, 9, 87, 136, 307, 333–34, 346
Reiff, Mary Jo, 187
remediation, 6, 309
research (Rhetoric and Composition), 118, 335; categories of scholarship, 56, 61–62; community college scholarship, 53–65; current scholarship, 5–6; disciplinarity, 7, 17, 23–25; disciplinarity status and, 289, 291–92; ELL, 274, 276; ESL, 274, 276; funding for, 24; L2 scholarship, 206–22; new models of disciplinarity, 296–301; pedagogy and, 6; qualitative, 64n3; RAD research, 24, 130; range of scholarship, 62–64; self reporting, 248; theory and, 6, 63; translingual model, 206–22
Research EX project, 23
Resnick, Paul, 58
revisions, 95
Reynolds, Mark, 56
Rhetoric and Composition: classification, 90; closed *vs.* open approach, 96–101, 118–19, 311; community college, 53–65; content of, 22–23, 25, 186–91, 192–93, 197–203; exigences, 3–5; external credibility, 120–21; field vs. discipline, 3–4, 16, 116–21 (*see also* disciplinarity); future visions, 5–6, 29–301; hiring practices, 52(n3), 102, 103, 292–301; historical legacy, 5–6; as knowledge-producing discipline, 70–84; majoring in, 17, 27–29, 119–20, 243–62 (*see also* writing major); Mexican American participation, 267–85 *passim*; as networked discipline, 96–101, 311; nomenclature, 4, 11(n1), 52(n1), 64(n1), 88, 117–18, 130(n1), 240(n1), 252–56; placement within academia, 17, 29–30, 41, 48–49, 296–301; range of scholarship, 62–64; status of, 167–70, 191–94, 288–96; as subject of study and activity, 303–27 (*see also* research [Rhetoric and Composition]); timeline of development, 37; translingual model, 206–22; values and, 121–31; writing development, 319–23. *See also specific topics*
*Rhetoric Review*, 112
Rhetoric Society of America, 5, 23, 24
Rhodes, Jacqueline, 99
Riedner, Rachel, 162–63
Robertson, Liane, 10, 25, 177, 185, 188, 346
Rodrigo, Rochelle, 9, 53, 333
Rodriguez, Richard, 272, 284(n8)
Rogers, Will, 135
Rosch, Eleanor, 94–95
Rose, Mike, 339
Ruecker, Todd, 284(n7)
Russell, David R, 190
Ruth, Jennifer, 293–94

Sánchez, Deborah M., 58
Sánchez, Raul, 272
Schell, Eileen, 144
scholarship. *See* community college scholarship; research (Rhetoric and Composition)
Schryer, Catherine, 102, 115, 332
Schwalm, David, 45
Scott, Blake, 175, 176, 261
second language training, 148–49
SEEK (Search for Excellence, Elevation, and Knowledge), 74
Selfe, Cynthia, 213
Selingo, Jeffrey, 289–90
service mission, 291, 299, 308, 316
Severin, Laura, 103

Shaughnessy, Mina, 53, 57, 75, 76, 126, 272
Shepherd, Dawn, 10, 225, 232, 346
Shumway, David R., 137–40, 141
Singh, R., 220
Sledd, James, 116, 122
Smit, David, 142, 166
socialization: expansion of, 63; four stages of, 60–61
*Social Life of Information, The* (Brown and Duguid), 78
social turn, 15–16, 18–20, 32(n3); social vs. individual, 18
solidarity, 5
Sommers, Jeff, 55, 57
*Sorting Things Out* (Bowker and Star), 90
Spanish language, 270, 276
specialization, 114–15, 130–31(n2), 306
Spellings Commission on Higher Education, 303, 326
standardized tests, 284(n10)
Star, Susan Leigh, 90
STEPS (Structure, Themes, Etiquette, Participants and their Purposes, and Style), 219
Strasma, Kip, 58
Stratton, John, 41
*Structure of Scientific Revolutions, The* (Kuhn), 114
students: as consumers, 71; full-paying, 290; as knowledge producers, 70, 71; as members of discipline, 71, 79–80; monolingual, 210; student publishing, 79
"study of and practice with writing" courses, 319–23
Sullivan, Patrick, 57, 59
SUNY Council on Writing (1980), 36, 37–40; attendees, 50–51; keynote address, 37–40
SWOT (strengths, weaknesses, opportunities, and threats) analysis, 228–29
Sylvan, David, 137–40

Taczak, Kara, 10, 25, 177, 185, 188, 346
Tade, George, 27
Tate, Gary, 27
taxonomy, 47, 87–110
teacher-scholars, 5
*Teaching English in the Two-Year College (TETYC)*, 59, 63; 64–65(n5)
team-based work, 103
technical writing, 36, 45–46, 170, 172, 221(n6), 237, 244, 249, 250, 252, 260, 268, 249

technology, 33, 56, 170, 251, 300–301
Telles, Edward, 275, 285(n14)
tenure, 289, 293
Texas State University, 269
textual production, 129
TFT (teaching for transfer), 25
themed approach to writing, 25, 33(n9)
theory, 6, 63; category theory, 89, 93–95; composition theory, 152; critical theory, 116; ideological commitment, 19; literacy, 20
threshold concepts (TC), 26–27, 32(n5), 62, 119, 229–31, 261, 312
Tinberg, Howard, 53, 57, 59, 165–66
Toth, Christie, 65(n10)
Toulmin, Stephen, 88, 105
transfer concepts, 25, 62, 188, 191, 198–200, 203(n1), 217
*Transiciones: Pathways of Latinas and Latinos Writing in High School and College* (Ruecker), 284(n7)
translingual model, 206–22; definitions, 210; developing composition, 217, 221(n6), 222(n8); hybridity, 216; language question, 209–12; marked vs. unmarked choices, 220; nomenclature, 221(n3); practices, 219
Treaty of Guadalupe-Hidalgo, 281
Trimbur, John, 5, 15–16, 18–20, 22, 74, 75, 112, 122, 168, 270
Trowler, Paul, 299–300
Troyka, Lynn, 53
Turchi, Peter, 225
"turn," metaphor of, 15; apocalyptic turn, 15; archival turn, 15; disciplinary turn, 15–34, 70, 307–10; global turn, 15; public turn, 15; queer turn, 15; social turn, 15–16, 18–20, 32n3; "x turn," 15
tutoring-training program, 76
TYCA (Two-Year College English Association), 56–57, 58; guidelines, 334

UALR (University of Arkansas–Little Rock), 40–44, 260
UC Santa Barbara, 316–26
University of Denver, 296–98

values, 121–31; access, 123–24; Anglo-American, 276; difference, 125–26; empowerment, 128–29; inclusion, 123–24; interaction, 126; localism, 127–28; textual production, 129
Vandenberg, Peter, 4, 227, 312
Vertovec, Steven, 212
Villanueva, Victor, 272

Visibility Project, 47–48, 91, 287
visual literacy, 22–23

WAC (writing across the curriculum), 220
Wardle, Elizabeth, 9, 26, 49, 111, 152–53, 175, 176, 187, 191, 197, 231, 237–38, 261, 262, 312, 331–32, 346–47
Watson Conference, 21, 32(n4), 163
Watts, Julie, 258
WAW (writing about writing), 25, 33(n8), 152–53, 191
Weidman, John, 60
Wenger, Etienne, 27, 124, 307
Wenger-Trayner, Beverly, 304–5, 307, 324
Wenger-Trayner, Etienne, 304–5, 307, 324
*What Is College Writing?* (Sullivan and Tinberg), 57, 59
*What We Are Becoming* (Giberson and Moriarty), 259
WID (writing in the disciplines), 220
Wiener, Harvey, 76
Winchester, Ian, 306
Wittgenstein, Ludwig, 89, 94, 97, 99, 113, 228, 332
*Women, Fire, and Dangerous Things* (Lakoff), 113
Wood, Denis, 225
workplace writing, 45
WOVE (written, oral, visual, and electronic communications), 100–101
WPA (writing program administrator), 40–41, 70–84 *passim*, 126, 143, 155–56(n1); listserve, 31, 194; nomenclature, 82(n1)
*WPA: Writing Program Administration*, 79
WPA Outcomes Statement, 127, 193–94, 197, 203(n2)
WR (writing requirement) courses, 321–23; outcomes, 315, 321, 322, 325, 327(n5)

writer's voice, 128
Writing and Rhetoric, 11(n1). *See also* Rhetoric and Composition
*Writing Center Journal*, 79
writing centers, 70–84 *passim*
Writing Centers Research Project (WCRP), 71
writing contexts, 190, 198. *See also* transfer concepts
"writing for" courses, 319–23
*Writing Lab Newsletter*, 79, 82(n2)
writing major, 17, 27–29, 119–20, 243–60; contextualizing, 252–55; descriptions of programs, 246–50, 257–61; differences found in majors, 259–61; framework, 245–46; institutional location, 250–52; nomenclature, 251, 252–56
writing program administration, 70. *See also* WPA (writing program administrator)
Writing Studies, 4, 11(n1), 52(n1). *See also* Rhetoric and Composition
writing teacher: autonomy, 196–97; beliefs, 196–97; without degree in rhetoric, 150–55; individuality of, 189–91; teaching professor, 296–301; as underclass, 144
Wyoming Resolution, 144–45

"x turn," 15

Yancey, Kathleen Blake, 6, 8, 15, 70, 128, 177, 188, 213, 248, 307, 331, 332, 347
Yanez, Arturo, 190
York College, 260, 262
*Young Scholars in Writing*, 28

Zarate, Geneviève, 210

*The Major in ~~Composition~~ Writing and Rhetoric*